OSF/1 System and Network Administrator's Reference

Revision 1.0

Open Software Foundation

Prentice Hall, Englewood Cliffs, New Jersey 07632

Cover design
and cover illustration: **Beth Fagan**

This book was formatted with troff

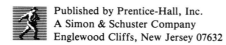
Published by Prentice-Hall, Inc.
A Simon & Schuster Company
Englewood Cliffs, New Jersey 07632

Printed in the United States of America
10 9 8 7 6 5 4 3 2

ISBN   0-13-643602-1

Prentice-Hall International (UK) Limited, *London*
Prentice-Hall of Australia Pty. Limited, *Sydney*
Prentice-Hall Canada Inc., *Toronto*
Prentice-Hall Hispanoamericana, S.A., *Mexico*
Prentice-Hall of India Private Limited, *New Delhi*
Prentice-Hall of Japan, Inc., *Tokyo*
Simon & Schuster Asia Pte. Ltd., *Singapore*
Editora Prentice-Hall do Brasil, Ltda., *Rio de Janeiro*

Contents

Preface vii

  1.1 Audience vii

  1.2 Applicability viii

  1.3 Purpose viii

  1.4 Document Usage viii

  1.5 Reference Page Format ix

  1.6 Related Documents x

  1.7 Typographic and Keying Conventions xi

  1.8 Problem Reporting xii

Permuted Index xiii

Chapter 1 Commands 1-1

         ac 1-2

         acct 1-4

         acctcms 1-12

         acctcom 1-15

         acctcon 1-22

         acctcon1 1-27

         acctcon2 1-28

         acctdisk 1-29

         acctdusg 1-32

         acctmerg 1-33

         accton 1-38

         acctprc 1-39

         acctprc1 1-42

         acctprc2 1-43

         acctwtmp 1-44

         adduser 1-45

         arp 1-47

         cfgmgr 1-50

         chargefee 1-52

chroot 1-53
ckpacct 1-55
clri 1-56
comsat 1-57
config 1-58
cron 1-60
df 1-62
diskusg 1-63
dodisk 1-66
dump 1-67
dumpfs 1-73
edquota 1-74
fastboot 1-77
fasthalt 1-78
fingerd 1-79
fsck 1-81
fsdb 1-89
ftpd 1-98
fwtmp 1-102
gated 1-106
getty 1-110
grpck 1-111
halt 1-112
icheck 1-114
ifconfig 1-116
inetd 1-120
init 1-122
killall 1-124
kloadsrv 1-126
last 1-128
lastcomm 1-130
lastlogin 1-132
lib_admin 1-133
lpc 1-135
lpd 1-138
lptest 1-142
lvchange 1-143
lvcreate 1-145
lvdisplay 1-148
lvextend 1-151
lvreduce 1-153
lvremove 1-155
lvsync 1-156
mailstats 1-157
mklost+found 1-159
mknod 1-160
mkpasswd 1-162

mkproto 1-164
monacct 1-166
mount 1-167
mountd 1-172
named 1-173
ncheck 1-178
newfs 1-180
nfsd 1-186
nfsiod 1-188
nfsstat 1-189
nslookup 1-190
nulladm 1-197
pac 1-198
ping 1-201
portmap 1-205
prctmp 1-206
prdaily 1-207
printpw 1-208
prtacct 1-210
pvchange 1-211
pvcreate 1-213
pvdisplay 1-216
pvmove 1-219
pwck 1-221
quot 1-222
quotacheck 1-223
quotaoff 1-225
quotaon 1-226
rc0 1-228
rc2 1-230
rc3 1-232
rdump 1-234
reboot 1-235
remove 1-237
renice 1-238
repquota 1-240
restore 1-242
rexecd 1-250
rlogind 1-252
rmt 1-254
route 1-257
routed 1-260
rrestore 1-264
rshd 1-265
runacct 1-268
rwhod 1-273
sa 1-275

savecore 1-281
sendmail 1-283
showmount 1-292
shutacct 1-293
shutdown 1-294
slattach 1-296
startup 1-298
strace 1-299
swapon 1-302
sync 1-304
sysconfig 1-305
sysconfigdb 1-307
syslogd 1-309
talkd 1-312
telnetd 1-314
tftpd 1-316
timed 1-317
timedc 1-319
trpt 1-321
tunefs 1-323
turnacct 1-325
umount 1-326
update 1-327
uucheck 1-328
uucico 1-330
uucleanup 1-334
uucpd 1-338
uusched 1-339
vgchange 1-341
vgcreate 1-343
vgdisplay 1-346
vgextend 1-349
vgreduce 1-351
vgremove 1-352
vgsync 1-353
vipw 1-354
wtmpfix 1-356

Chapter 2 File Formats 2-1
.Admin 2-2
Command(C.*) 2-3
.Corrupt 2-7
Data(D.*) 2-8
Dialcodes 2-10
Dialers 2-12
Directories 2-18
Execute(X.*) 2-19
Foreign 2-23

.Log 2-24
.Old 2-26
.Status 2-27
Temporary(TM.*) 2-28
.Workspace 2-29
.Xqtdir 2-30
acct.h 2-31
aliases 2-35
audit 2-36
errors 2-37
exports 2-39
fstab 2-41
ftpusers 2-44
gated.conf 2-45
gateways 2-62
hosts 2-65
hosts.equiv 2-66
inetd.conf 2-68
inittab 2-70
mqueue 2-73
named.boot 2-74
named.* 2-77
networks 2-82
printcap 2-83
protocols 2-87
remote.unknown 2-89
resolv.conf 2-90
sendmail.cf 2-92
services 2-109
stanza 2-111
sysconfigtab 2-113
xferstats 2-114

Preface

The *OSF/1 System and Network Administrator's Reference* contains reference pages for OSF/1™ system administration and network management commands and related file formats.

1.1 Audience

The *OSF/1 System and Network Administrator's Reference* is written for OSF/1 system administrators and network managers.

1.2 Applicability

This book applies to Release 1.0 of the OSF/1 operating system.

1.3 Purpose

The purpose of the *OSF/1 System and Network Administrator's Reference* is to provide a complete description of system administration and network management commands and file formats.

1.4 Document Usage

This document is organized as follows:

- *Permuted Index*. The permuted index is created from the descriptions in the **Purpose** section of each reference page. Use the permuted index to find the reference page you want by searching for any term that might appear in a brief description of a command's purpose.

- *Chapter 1* is a reference to system administration and network management commands in OSF/1. These Section 8 reference pages are organized alphabetically (U.S. English).

- *Chapter 2* is a reference to system administration and network management file formats in OSF/1. These Section 4 reference pages are organized alphabetically (U.S. English).

- As an additional aid for locating information, the *OSF/1 System and Network Administrator's Reference* also contains an *Index*.

1.5 Reference Page Format

Each reference page in the *OSF/1 System and Network Administrator's Reference* is organized into sections. The sections always appear in the same order, but some appear in all reference pages and some are optional. In the following list, section titles that appear in all reference pages are shown in **bold** type, while optional sections are not in bold type.

Purpose
Provides a brief description of its purpose. (If the reference page describes more than one command, all the commands are listed.)

Synopsis
Includes a diagram that summarizes the use of the command and a brief synopsis its use and function.

Flags
Lists and describes the command's required or optional flags, if any.

Description
Describes the command more fully than the **Purpose** and **Synopsis** sections.

Subcommands
Describes in detail the command's subcommands, if any.

Cautions
Cautions users about circumstances to be avoided when using the command, or about loss of data that may result if the command is used incorrectly.

Notes
Provides additional information about the command that is not of general interest.

Examples
Provides examples of ways in which the command is typically used.

Exit Values
Lists and describes exit values returned by the command.

Files
Lists any OSF/1 system files that are read, employed, referred to, or written to by the command, or that are otherwise relevent to its use.

Diagnostics   Provides information useful for diagnosing errors
                          that may result when the command is used.

Related Information

                          Lists OSF/1 commands, functions, file formats,
                          and special files that are employed by the
                          command, that have a purpose related to that of
                          the command, or that are otherwise of interest
                          within the context of the command. Also lists
                          related OSF/1 documents and other related
                          documents, and miscellaneous information
                          related to the command.

1.6 Related Documents

The following documents are also included with the OSF/1 documentation
set.

- *OSF/1 Command Reference*
- *OSF/1 Programmer's Reference*
- *OSF/1 System Programmer's Reference Volume 1*
- *OSF/1 System Programmer's Reference Volume 2*
- *OSF/1 User's Guide*
- *OSF/1 System Administrator's Guide*
- *OSF/1 Network and Communications Administrator's Guide*
- *OSF/1 Applications Programmer's Guide*
- *OSF/1 System Extension Guide*
- *OSF/1 Network Applications Programmer's Guide*
- *OSF/1 System Porting Guide*
- *OSF/1 Security Features User's Guide*
- *OSF/1 Security Features Programmer's Guide*
- *OSF/1 Security Features Administrator's Guide*

- *Application Environment Specification - Operating System/Programming Interfaces Volume*
- *Design of the OSF/1 Operating System*
- *OSF/1 POSIX Conformance Document*

1.7 Typographic and Keying Conventions

This document uses the following typographic conventions:

Bold   **Bold** words or characters represent system elements that you must use literally, such as commands, flags, and pathnames. **Bold** words also indicate the first use of a term included in the glossary.

Italic   *Italic* words or characters represent variable values that you must supply.

`Constant width`   Examples and information that the system displays appear in `constant width` typeface.

[ ]   Brackets enclose optional items in format and syntax descriptions.

{ }   Braces enclose a list from which you must choose an item in format and syntax descriptions.

| A vertical bar separates items in a list of choices.

< >   Angle brackets enclose the name of a key on the keyboard.

...   Horizontal ellipsis points indicate that you can repeat the preceding item one or more times. Vertical ellipsis points indicate that you can repeat the preceding item one or more times.

This document uses the following keying conventions:

<Ctrl-*x*> or ^*x*   The notation **<Ctrl-*x*>** or ^*x* followed by the name of a key, indicates a control character sequence. For example, **<Ctrl-c>** means that you hold down the control key while pressing **<c>**.

<Return>   The notation **<Return>** refers to the key on your terminal or workstation that is labeled with the word Return or Enter, or with a left arrow.

Entering commands   When instructed to *enter* a command, type the command name and then press **<Return>**. For example, the instruction "Enter the **ls** command" means that you type the **ls** command and then press **<Return>** (enter = type command + press **<Return>**).

1.8 Problem Reporting

If you have any problems with the software or documentation, please contact your software vendor's customer service department.

Permuted Index

Address Resolution Protocol	(ARP) tables /and controls	arp(8)
name/ /uses to initialize the BIND	(Berkeley Internet Name Domain)	named.*(4)
directions for the/ Command	(C.*): Contains file transfer	Command(C.*)(4)
to remote systems Data	(D.*): Contains data to be sent	Data(D.*)(4)
/the number of disk blocks	(including indirect blocks)/	acctdusg(8)
/inthe File parameter, gives read	(r) and write (w) permissionsto/	nulladm(8)
/file owner and group, and read	(r) permission to otherusersSee/	nulladm(8)
transfers to remote/ Temporary	(TM.*): Stores data files during	Temporary(TM.*)(4)
and/ /gives read (r) and write	(w) permissionsto the file owner	nulladm(8)
running commands that/ Execute	(X.*): Contains instructions for	Execute(X.*)(4)
and writes to/ grpck: Scansthe	/etc/group file or the named file	grpck(8)
vipw: Edits the	/etc/passwd file	vipw(8)
log file and temporary files/	/usr/spool/mqueue : Contains the	mqueue(4)
administrative files used by the/	/usr/spool/uucp/.Admin: Contains	&.Admin(4)
Contains copies of files that/	/usr/spool/uucp/.Corrupt :	&.Corrupt(4)
the uucp program log files	/usr/spool/uucp/.Log : Contains	&.Log(4)
the combined uucp program log/	/usr/spool/uucp/.Old : Contains	&.Old(4)
Contains information about the/	/usr/spool/uucp/.Status :	&.Status(4)
temporary files used internally/	/usr/spool/uucp/.Workspace: Holds	&.Workspace(4)
temporary files used by the/	/usr/spool/uucp/.Xqtdir: Contains	&.Xqtdir(4)
ee/ /into summary files in the	/var/adm/acct/fiscalsubdirectoryS	monacct(8)
//var/adm/acct/sum/pacct*, and	/var/adm/acct/nite/lock* files as/	remove(8)
to show/ lastlogin: Updatesthe	/var/adm/acct/sum/loginlog file	lastlogin(8)

/ofthe /var/adm/acct/sum/wtmp*, /var/adm/acct/sum/pacct*, and/ .... remove(8)
remove: Deletes all ofthe /var/adm/acct/sum/wtmp*,/ .... remove(8)
/on or off, or to create a new /var/adm/pacctn process/ .... turnacct(8)
the activeprocess accounting file /var/adm/pacctSee acct(8) /of .... ckpacct(8)
daemon errors errors : Contains a record of uucico .... errors(4)
could/ /usr/spool/uucp/.Corrupt : Contains copies of files that .... &.Corrupt(4)
status/ /usr/spool/uucp/.Status : Contains information about the .... &.Status(4)
program log/ /usr/spool/uucp/.Old : Contains the combined uucp .... &.Old(4)
temporary/ /usr/spool/mqueue : Contains the log file and .... mqueue(4)
files /usr/spool/uucp/.Log : Contains the uucp program log .... &.Log(4)
previous logins last : Displays information about .... last(8)
traffic mailstats : Displays statistics about mail .... mailstats(8)
accounting data of/ prdaily : Formats an ASCII file of the .... prdaily(8)
by user ID diskusg : Generates disk accounting data .... diskusg(8)
into an intermediary/ acctmerg : Merges total accounting files .... acctmerg(8)
named.boot : named configuration file .... named.boot(4)
last commands executed lastcomm : Outputs information about the .... lastcomm(8)
accounting record/ acctcom : Outputs selected process .... acctcom(8)
password database printpw : Outputs the contents of the .... printpw(8)
acctdisk, acctdusg : Perform disk-usage accounting .... acctdisk(8)
summaries from/ acctcms : Produces command usage .... acctcms(8)
for shell scripts acct/* : Provides accounting commands .... acct(8)
interactively nslookup : Queries Internet name servers .... nslookup(8)
runacct : Runs daily accounting .... runacct(8)
transport program uusched : Schedules work for the file .... uusched(8)
to network hosts ping : Sends ICMP ECHO_REQUEST packets .... ping(8)
sa : Summarizes accounting records .... sa(8)
gated : The gateway routing daemon .... gated(8)
trpt : Transliterates protocol trace .... trpt(8)
records ac: Outputs connect-session .... ac(8)
systems remote.unknown: Logs access attempts by unknown remote .... remote.unknown(4)
rmt: Allows remote access to magnetic tape devices .... rmt(8)
/acctprc1 and summarizes them according to user ID and nameSee/ .... acctprc2(8)
acct.h: Account include files .... acct.h(4)
acctprc(8) accton: Turns account processing on and offSee .... accton(8)
dodisk: Initiates disk-usage accounting by callingthe diskusg/ .... dodisk(8)
scripts acct/* : Provides accounting commands for shell .... acct(8)
diskusg : Generates disk accounting data by user ID .... diskusg(8)
/: Formats an ASCII file of the accounting data of theprevious/ .... prdaily(8)
/the size of the activeprocess accounting file /var/adm/pacctSee/ .... ckpacct(8)
an intermediary file or a daily accounting file /files into .... acctmerg(8)
/a new /var/adm/pacctn process accounting file.See acct(8) .... turnacct(8)
acctmerg : Merges total accounting files into an/ .... acctmerg(8)
startup: Turns on the accounting functionsSee acct(8) .... startup(8)
pac: Outputs printer/plotter accounting information .... pac(8)
shutacct: Turns process accounting offSee acct(8) .... shutacct(8)
/accton command to turn process accounting on or off, or to/ .... turnacct(8)
acctprc2, accton: Perform process accounting procedures acctprc1, ... acctprc(8)
/: Outputs selected process accounting record summaries .... acctcom(8)
/wtmpfix: Modify connect time accounting records to change/ .... fwtmp(8)
sa : Summarizes accounting records .... sa(8)

command usage summaries from	accounting records /: Produces	acctcms(8)
/command intoconnect time total	accounting records.See acctcon(8)	acctcon2(8)
acctcon2: Outputs connect-time	accounting summaries acctcon1,	acctcon(8)
runacct : Runs daily	accounting	runacct(8)
acctdusg : Perform disk-usage	accounting acctdisk,	acctdisk(8)
/Formats and displays any total	accountingfile specified by the/	prtacct(8)
/Collects daily or other periodic	accountingrecords into summary/	monacct(8)
are in a format defined by the	acct structure in/ /inputthat	acctprc1(8)
process accounting file.See	acct(8) /a new /var/adm/pacctn	turnacct(8)
by the File parameterSee	acct(8) /accountingfile specified	prtacct(8)
(r) permission to otherusersSee	acct(8) /and group, and read	nulladm(8)
called by the runacct commandSee	acct(8) /daily cleanup procedure	remove(8)
and the acctdisk commandSee	acct(8) /diskusg command	dodisk(8)
data of theprevious daySee	acct(8) /file of the accounting	prdaily(8)
last date each userlogged inSee	acct(8) /file to show the	lastlogin(8)
accounting file /var/adm/pacctSee	acct(8) /of the activeprocess	ckpacct(8)
created by theacctcon1 commandSee	acct(8) /specified by File and	prctmp(8)
/var/adm/acct/fiscalsubdirectorySee	acct(8) /summary files in the	monacct(8)
by the User parameterSee	acct(8) /the login name specified	chargefee(8)
Turns process accounting offSee	acct(8) shutacct:	shutacct(8)
on the accounting functionsSee	acct(8) startup: Turns	startup(8)
	acct.h: Account include files	acct.h(4)
commands for shell scripts	acct/* : Provides accounting	acct(8)
summaries from accounting/	acctcms : Produces command usage	acctcms(8)
process accounting record/	acctcom : Outputs selected	acctcom(8)
time total accounting records.See	acctcon(8) /command intoconnect	acctcon2(8)
of login and logout recordsSee	acctcon(8) /to write asequence	acctcon1(8)
/session records produced by the	acctcon1 command intoconnect/	acctcon2(8)
connect-time accounting/	acctcon1, acctcon2: Outputs	acctcon(8)
normally called bythe runacct/	acctcon1: This command is	acctcon1(8)
accounting summaries acctcon1,	acctcon2: Outputs connect-time	acctcon(8)
called bythe runacct shell/	acctcon2: This command is usually	acctcon2(8)
/diskusg command and the	acctdisk commandSee acct(8)	dodisk(8)
each user to standard output.See	acctdisk(8) /record for	acctdusg(8)
disk-usage accounting	acctdisk, acctdusg : Perform	acctdisk(8)
accounting acctdisk,	acctdusg : Perform disk-usage	acctdisk(8)
from standardinput and computes/	acctdusg: Reads a list of files	acctdusg(8)
accounting files into an/	acctmerg : Merges total	acctmerg(8)
/Provides an interface tothe	accton command to turn process/	turnacct(8)
on and offSee acctprc(8)	accton: Turns account processing	accton(8)
accounting/ acctprc1, acctprc2,	accton: Perform process	acctprc(8)
/header file.See	acctprc(8)	acctprc1(8)
according to user ID and nameSee	acctprc(8) /and summarizes them	acctprc2(8)
account processing on and offSee	acctprc(8) accton: Turns	accton(8)
/input, the records writtenby	acctprc1 and summarizes them/	acctprc2(8)
Perform process accounting/	acctprc1, acctprc2, accton:	acctprc(8)
standard inputthat are in a/	acctprc1: Reads records from	acctprc1(8)
accounting procedures acctprc1,	acctprc2, accton: Perform process	acctprc(8)
input, the records writtenby/	acctprc2: Reads, from standard	acctprc2(8)
time accounting records/ fwtmp,	acctwtmp, wtmpfix: Modify connect	fwtmp(8)
record to standard output See/	acctwtmp: Writesa utmp formatted	acctwtmp(8)

ckpacct: Checks the size of the activeprocess accounting file/ .... ckpacct(8)

/Extend a volume group by adding physical volumes to it .... vgextend(8)

swapping swapon: Specifies additional device for paging and .... swapon(8)

arp: Displays and controls Address Resolution Protocol (ARP)/ .... arp(8)

adduser: Adds a new user interactively .... adduser(8)

interactively adduser: Adds a new user .... adduser(8)

lib_admin: Administers shared libraries .... lib_admin(8)

/usr/spool/uucp/.Admin: Contains administrative files used by the/ .... &.Admin(4)

sendmail/ aliases: Contains alias definitions for the .... aliases(4)

definitions for the sendmail/ aliases: Contains alias .... aliases(4)

one physical/ pvmove: Moves allocated physical extentsfrom .... pvmove(8)

/the numberof physical extents allocated to a logical volume .... lvextend(8)

/the numberof physical extents allocated to a logical volume .... lvreduce(8)

the/ /(including indirect blocks) allocated to each file divided by .... acctdusg(8)

tape devices rmt: Allows remote access to magnetic .... rmt(8)

process renice: Alters the priority of a running .... renice(8)

Address Resolution Protocol/ arp: Displays and controls .... arp(8)

of/ prdaily : Formats an ASCII file of the accounting data .... prdaily(8)

/the log file and temporary files associated with the messages in/ .... mqueue(4)

nfsiod: The local NFS compatible asynchronous I/O server .... nfsiod(8)

network interface slattach: Attaches a serial line to a .... slattach(8)

remote.unknown: Logs access attempts by unknown remote/ .... remote.unknown(4)

Foreign: Logs contact attempts from unknown systems .... Foreign(4)

from the uucico daemon audit: Contains debug messages .... audit(4)

yes or no vgchange: Sets the availability of a volume group to .... vgchange(8)

hosts: The host name data base .... hosts(4)

printcap: printer capability data base .... printcap(4)

Subsystem definition data base sysconfigtab: .... sysconfigtab(4)

/Creates a version of the basic user database organized for/ .... mkpasswd(8)

comsat: The biff server .... comsat(8)

/daemon uses to initialize the BIND (Berkeley Internet Name/ .... named.*(4)

/and computes the number of disk blocks (including indirect/ .... acctdusg(8)

/disk blocks (including indirect blocks) allocated to each file/ .... acctdusg(8)

/the inode table and writes buffered files to the disk .... sync(8)

config: Builds system configuration files .... config(8)

/the number of units specified bythe Number parameter to the/ .... chargefee(8)

/This command is usually called bythe runacct shell procedure and/ .... acctcon2(8)

/This command is normally called bythe runacct shell procedure to/ .... acctcon1(8)

/of the daily cleanup procedure called by the runacct commandSee/ .... remove(8)

/This command is normally called bythe runacct shell/ .... acctcon1(8)

acctcon2: This command is usually called bythe runacct shell/ .... acctcon2(8)

started by the user, except the calling process /all processes .... killall(8)

the/ /disk-usage accounting by callingthe diskusg command and .... dodisk(8)

printcap: printer capability data base .... printcap(4)

/device all files changed after a certain date in the specified/ .... rdump(8)

daemon cfgmgr: Configuration manager .... cfgmgr(8)

/time accounting records to change formats and to make/ .... fwtmp(8)

the/ /storage device all files changed after a certain date in .... rdump(8)

logical volume lvchange: Changes the characteristics of a .... lvchange(8)

physical volume in a/ pvchange: Changes the characteristics of a .... pvchange(8)

command chroot: Changes the root directory of a .... chroot(8) volume lvchange: Changes the characteristics of a logical .... lvchange(8)

volume in/ pvchange: Changes the characteristics of a physical .... pvchange(8)

units specified bythe Number/ chargefee: Charges the number of .... chargefee(8)

specified bythe/ chargefee: Charges the number of units .... chargefee(8)

Provides file system consistency check and interactive repair /: .... fsck(8)

required by uucp uucheck: Check for files and directories .... uucheck(8)

File system storage consistency check icheck: .... icheck(8)

Reboots the system without checking file systems fastboot: .... fastboot(8)

consistency quotacheck: Checks filesystem quota .... quotacheck(8)

files for/ pwck, grpck: Checks the password and group .... pwck(8)

activeprocess/ ckpacct: Checks the size of the .... ckpacct(8)

directory of a command chroot: Changes the root .... chroot(8)

activeprocess accounting file/ ckpacct: Checks the size of the .... ckpacct(8)

/files as part of the daily cleanup procedure called by the/ .... remove(8)

clri: Clears i-nodes .... clri(8)

cron: The system clock daemon .... cron(8)

clri: Clears i-nodes .... clri(8)

accountingrecords into/ monacct: Collects daily or other periodic .... monacct(8)

/: Contains the combined uucp program log files .... &.Old(4)

transfer directions for the/ Command (C.*): Contains file .... Command(C.*)(4)

/accounting by callingthe diskusg command and the acctdisk/ .... dodisk(8)

/requests for file transfers and command executions on remote/ .... Directories(4)

runacct shell/ acctcon1: This command is normally called bythe .... acctcon1(8)

runacct shell/ acctcon2: This command is usually called bythe .... acctcon2(8)

uuxqt daemon to execute remote command requests /used by the .... &.Xqtdir(4)

stopping the system rc0: Run command script executed when .... rc0(8)

entering a multiuser/ rc2: Run command script executed when .... rc2(8)

entering a multiuser/ rc3: Run command script executed when .... rc3(8)

an interface tothe accton command to turn process/ /Provides .... turnacct(8)

accounting/ acctcms : Produces command usage summaries from .... acctcms(8)

/records produced by the acctcon1 command intoconnect time total/ .... acctcon2(8)

Changes the root directory of a command chroot: .... chroot(8)

to remote/ uucico: Transfers uucp command, data, and executefiles .... uucico(8)

written with the dump or rdump command, respectively /from tapes .... restore(8)

information about the last commands executed /: Outputs .... lastcomm(8)

acct/* : Provides accounting commands for shell scripts .... acct(8)

/and users that can execute commands on the local system .... hosts.equiv(4)

Contains instructions for running commands that require the/ /(X.*): .... Execute(X.*)(4)

diskusg command and the acctdisk commandSee acct(8) /by callingthe .... dodisk(8)

procedure called by the runacct commandSee acct(8) /daily cleanup .... remove(8)

File and created by theacctcon1 commandSee acct(8) /specified by .... prctmp(8)

uucpprogram and/ uucpd: Manages communications between the .... uucpd(8)

Lists modems used for uucp remote communications links Dialers: .... Dialers(4)

talk(1)command talkd: The remote communications server for the .... talkd(8)

server nfsiod: The local NFS compatible asynchronous I/O .... nfsiod(8)

mountd: Services remote NFS compatible mount requests .... mountd(8)

showmount: Shows remote NFS compatible mounts on a host .... showmount(8)

nfsd: The remote NFS compatible server .... nfsd(8)

of files from standardinput and computes the number of disk/ /list .... acctdusg(8)

comsat: The biff server .... comsat(8)

configuration files config: Builds system .... config(8) sysconfigdb: Maintains the system configuration database .... sysconfigdb(8)

/Contains the sendmail configuration file data .... sendmail.cf(4)

daemon inetd.conf: The default configuration file for the inetd .... inetd.conf(4)

named.boot : named configuration file .... named.boot(4)

resolv.conf: resolver configuration file .... resolv.conf(4)

config: Builds system configuration files .... config(8)

gated/ gated.conf: Contains configuration information for the .... gated.conf(4)

cfgmgr: Configuration manager daemon .... cfgmgr(8)

sysconfig: Modifies the system configuration .... sysconfig(8)

interface parameters ifconfig: Configures or displays network .... ifconfig(8)

fwtmp, acctwtmp, wtmpfix: Modify connect time accounting records/ .... fwtmp(8)

ac: Outputs connect-session records .... ac(8)

acctcon1, acctcon2: Outputs connect-time accounting summaries .... acctcon(8)

/numbers used to establish remote connections over a telephone line .... Dialcodes(4)

fsck : Provides file system consistency check and interactive/ .... fsck(8)

icheck: File system storage consistency check .... icheck(8)

Checks filesystem quota consistency quotacheck: .... quotacheck(8)

newfs: Constructs a new file system .... newfs(8)

system mkproto: Constructs a prototype file .... mkproto(8)

systems Foreign: Logs contact attempts from unknown .... Foreign(4)

/the status of the uucp program contacts with remote systems .... &.Status(4)

systems and/ hosts.equiv: A file containing the names of remote .... hosts.equiv(4)

daemon errors errors : Contains a record of uucico .... errors(4)

used by/ /usr/spool/uucp/.Admin: Contains administrative files .... &.Admin(4)

the sendmail program aliases: Contains alias definitions for .... aliases(4)

information for the/ gated.conf: Contains configuration .... gated.conf(4)

could/ /usr/spool/uucp/.Corrupt : Contains copies of files that .... &.Corrupt(4)

remote systems Data (D.*): Contains data to be sent to .... Data(D.*)(4)

uucico daemon audit: Contains debug messages from the .... audit(4)

for the uucico/ Command (C.*): Contains file transfer directions .... Command(C.*)(4)

status/ /usr/spool/uucp/.Status : Contains information about the .... &.Status(4)

status of file/ xferstats: Contains information about the .... xferstats(4)

commands that/ Execute (X.*): Contains instructions for running .... Execute(X.*)(4)

transfers and/ Directories: Contains queued requests for file .... Directories(4)

the/ /usr/spool/uucp/.Xqtdir: Contains temporary files used by .... &.Xqtdir(4)

program/ /usr/spool/uucp/.Old : Contains the combined uucp .... &.Old(4)

telephone numbers/ Dialcodes: Contains the initial digits of .... Dialcodes(4)

temporary/ /usr/spool/mqueue : Contains the log file and .... mqueue(4)

networks: Contains the network name file .... networks(4)

configuration file/ sendmail.cf: Contains the sendmail .... sendmail.cf(4)

files /usr/spool/uucp/.Log : Contains the uucp program log .... &.Log(4)

printpw : Outputs the contents of the password database .... printpw(8)

init: Process control initialization .... init(8)

lpc: Line printer control program .... lpc(8)

Protocol (ARP)/ arp: Displays and controls Address Resolution .... arp(8)

process inittab: Controls the initialization .... inittab(4)

at system startup timed: Controls the time server daemon .... timed(8)

timedc: Controls the timed daemon .... timedc(8)

/bythe runacct shell procedure and converts asequence of login/ .... acctcon2(8)

processed /: Contains copies of files that could not be .... &.Corrupt(4)

device all files changed/ rdump: Copies tothe dump_file storage .... rdump(8)

savecore: Saves a core dump of the operating system .... savecore(8)
/to change formats and to make corrections in the records .... fwtmp(8)
/records in the wtmp format for corrupted date and timestamp/ .... wtmpfix(8)
/accounting on or off, or to create a new /var/adm/pacctn/ .... turnacct(8)
/record file specified by File and created by theacctcon1 commandSee/ .... prctmp(8)
volume group lvcreate: Creates a logical volume in a .... lvcreate(8)
can be used as part of/ pvcreate: Creates a physical volume that .... pvcreate(8)
mknod: Creates a special file .... mknod(8)
user database/ mkpasswd: Creates a version of the basic .... mkpasswd(8)
vgcreate: Creates a volume group .... vgcreate(8)
File parameter, gives/ nulladm: Creates the file specified inthe .... nulladm(8)
cron: The system clock daemon .... cron(8)
timed: Controls the time server daemon at system startup .... timed(8)
: Contains a record of uucico daemon errors errors .... errors(4)
/temporary files used by the uuxqt daemon to execute remote command/ .... &.Xqtdir(4)
/Defines the data that the named daemon uses to initialize the/ .... named.*(4)
cfgmgr: Configuration manager daemon .... cfgmgr(8)
cron: The system clock daemon .... cron(8)
gated : The gateway routing daemon .... gated(8)
lpd: line printer daemon .... lpd(8)
timedc: Controls the timed daemon .... timedc(8)
information for the gated daemon /Contains configuration .... gated.conf(4)
directions for the uucico daemon /Contains file transfer .... Command(C.*)(4)
routing information to the routed daemon /Specifies Internet .... gateways(4)
debug messages from the uucico daemon audit: Contains .... audit(4)
configuration file for the inetd daemon inetd.conf: The default .... inetd.conf(4)
into an intermediary file or a daily accounting file /files .... acctmerg(8)
runacct : Runs daily accounting .... runacct(8)
the runacct/ /files as part of the daily cleanup procedure called by .... remove(8)
monacct: Collects daily or other periodic/ .... monacct(8)
Protocol server ftpd: The DARPA Internet File Transfer .... ftpd(8)
mapper portmap: The DARPA port to RPC program number .... portmap(8)
telnetd: The DARPA TELNET protocol server .... telnetd(8)
Protocol server tftpd: The DARPA Trivial File Transfer .... tftpd(8)
sent to remote systems Data (D.*): Contains data to be .... Data(D.*)(4)
hosts: The host name data base .... hosts(4)
printcap: printer capability data base .... printcap(4)
Subsystem definition data base sysconfigtab: .... sysconfigtab(4)
: Generates disk accounting data by user ID diskusg .... diskusg(8)
remote/ Temporary (TM.*): Stores data files during transfers to .... Temporary(TM.*)(4)
/an ASCII file of the accounting data of theprevious daySee/ .... prdaily(8)
to/ named.*: Defines the data that the named daemon uses .... named.*(4)
Data (D.*): Contains data to be sent to remote systems .... Data(D.*)(4)
the sendmail configuration file data sendmail.cf: Contains .... sendmail.cf(4)
uucico: Transfers uucp command, data, and executefiles to remote/ .... uucico(8)
/a version of the basic user database organized for efficient/ .... mkpasswd(8)
the contents of the password database printpw : Outputs .... printpw(8)
the system configuration database sysconfigdb: Maintains .... sysconfigdb(8)
/the wtmp format for corrupted date and timestamp entries.See/ .... wtmpfix(8)
acct(8) /file to show the last date each userlogged inSee .... lastlogin(8)
all files changed after a certain date in the specified/ /device .... rdump(8)

accounting data of theprevious daySee acct(8) /ASCII file of the .... prdaily(8)

daemon audit: Contains debug messages from the uucico .... audit(4)

fsdb: File system debugger .... fsdb(8)

extents allocated to a/ lvreduce: Decreases the numberof physical .... lvreduce(8)

the inetd daemon inetd.conf: The default configuration file for .... inetd.conf(4)

/inputthat are in a format defined by the acct structure in/ .... acctprc1(8)

NFS mount requests exports: Defines remote mount points for .... exports(4)

daemon uses to/ named.*: Defines the data that the named .... named.*(4)

used on the local/ protocols: Defines the Internet protocols .... protocols(4)

used for Internet/ services: Defines the sockets and protocols .... services(4)

sysconfigtab: Subsystem definition data base .... sysconfigtab(4)

groups/ vgremove: Removes the definition of one or more volume .... vgremove(8)

program aliases: Contains alias definitions for the sendmail .... aliases(4)

/var/adm/acct/sum/wtmp*,/ remove: Deletes all ofthe .... remove(8)

the uucp spool/ uucleanup: Deletes selected old files from .... uucleanup(8)

/Copies tothe dump_file storage device all files changed after a/ .... rdump(8)

swapon: Specifies additional device for paging and swapping .... swapon(8)

tape orother specified storage device.See restore(8) /magnetic .... rrestore(8)

remote access to magnetic tape devices rmt: Allows .... rmt(8)

disk space df: Displays statistics on free .... df(8)

digits of telephone numbers used/ Dialcodes: Contains the initial .... Dialcodes(4)

uucp remote communications links Dialers: Lists modems used for .... Dialers(4)

Dialcodes: Contains the initial digits of telephone numbers used/ .... Dialcodes(4)

/(C.*): Contains file transfer directions for the uucico daemon .... Command(C.*)(4)

uucheck: Check for files and directories required by uucp .... uucheck(8)

requests for file transfers and/ Directories: Contains queued .... Directories(4)

Makesa lost+found directory for fsck mklost+found: .... mklost+found(8)

chroot: Changes the root directory of a command .... chroot(8)

old files from the uucp spool directory /Deletes selected .... uucleanup(8)

type, modes, speed, and line discipline /Sets the terminal .... getty(8)

diskusg : Generates disk accounting data by user ID .... diskusg(8)

/and computes the number of disk blocks (including indirect/ .... acctdusg(8)

df: Displays statistics on free disk space .... df(8)

and writes buffered files to the disk /Updates the inode table .... sync(8)

callingthe/ dodisk: Initiates disk-usage accounting by .... dodisk(8)

acctdisk, acctdusg : Perform disk-usage accounting .... acctdisk(8)

accounting data by user ID diskusg : Generates disk .... diskusg(8)

/accounting by callingthe diskusg command and the acctdisk/ .... dodisk(8)

mount, umount: Mounts and dismounts file systems .... mount(8)

Resolution Protocol (ARP)/ arp: Displays and controls Address .... arp(8)

specified/ prtacct: Formats and displays any total accountingfile .... prtacct(8)

more physical volumes/ pvdisplay: Displays information about one or .... pvdisplay(8)

groups vgdisplay: Displays information about volume .... vgdisplay(8)

previous logins last : Displays information about .... last(8)

logical volumes lvdisplay: Displays information about .... lvdisplay(8)

ifconfig: Configures or displays network interface/ .... ifconfig(8)

traffic mailstats : Displays statistics about mail .... mailstats(8)

space df: Displays statistics on free disk .... df(8)

messages strace: Displays STREAMS event trace .... strace(8)

/blocks) allocated to each file divided by the number of hard/ .... acctdusg(8)

accounting by callingthe diskusg/ dodisk: Initiates disk-usage .... dodisk(8)

named: Internet domain name server .... named(8)

/the BIND (Berkeley Internet Name Domain) name server file .... named.*(4)

savecore: Saves a core dump of the operating system .... savecore(8)

files from tapes written with the dump or rdump command,/ /Restores .... restore(8)

dumpfs: Dump UFS file system information .... dumpfs(8)

in the specified filesystem.See dump(8) /after a certain date .... rdump(8)

file system dumps dump, rdump: Performs incremental .... dump(8)

information dumpfs: Dump UFS file system .... dumpfs(8)

Performs incremental file system dumps dump, rdump: .... dump(8)

files/ rdump: Copies tothe dump_file storage device all .... rdump(8)

/(TM.*): Stores data files during transfers to remote/ .... Temporary(TM.*)(4)

hosts ping : Sends ICMP ECHO_REQUEST packets to network .... ping(8)

vipw: Edits the /etc/passwd file .... vipw(8)

edquota: Edits user quotas .... edquota(8)

edquota: Edits user quotas .... edquota(8)

basic user database organized for efficient searches /of the .... mkpasswd(8)

shutdown: Ends system operation .... shutdown(8)

/Run command script executed when entering a multiuser run level .... rc2(8)

/Run command script executed when entering a multiuser run level .... rc3(8)

for corrupted date and timestamp entries.See fwtmp(8) /format .... wtmpfix(8)

uucico daemon errors errors : Contains a record of .... errors(4)

a record of uucico daemon errors errors : Contains .... errors(4)

a/ /of telephone numbers used to establish remote connections over .... Dialcodes(4)

strace: Displays STREAMS event trace messages .... strace(8)

records in the wtmp/ wtmpfix: Examines standard inputor File .... wtmpfix(8)

processes started by the user, except the calling process /all .... killall(8)

instructions for running/ Execute (X.*): Contains .... Execute(X.*)(4)

remote systems and users that can execute commands on the local/ /of .... hosts.equiv(4)

/files used by the uuxqt daemon to execute remote command requests .... &.Xqtdir(4)

rc2: Run command script executed when entering a/ .... rc2(8)

rc3: Run command script executed when entering a/ .... rc3(8)

rc0: Run command script executed when stopping the system .... rc0(8)

about the last commands executed /: Outputs information .... lastcomm(8)

/Transfers uucp command, data, and executefiles to remote systems .... uucico(8)

rexecd: The remote execution server .... rexecd(8)

/for file transfers and command executions on remote systems .... Directories(4)

tunefs: Tune up an existing UFS file system .... tunefs(8)

points for NFS mount requests exports: Defines remote mount .... exports(4)

physical volumes to it vgextend: Extend a volume group by adding .... vgextend(8)

/Increases the numberof physical extents allocated to a logical/ .... lvextend(8)

/Decreases the numberof physical extents allocated to a logical/ .... lvreduce(8)

pvmove: Moves allocated physical extentsfrom one physical volume/ .... pvmove(8)

without checking file systems fastboot: Reboots the system .... fastboot(8)

fasthalt: Halts the system .... fasthalt(8)

/of the activeprocess accounting file /var/adm/pacctSee acct(8) .... ckpacct(8)

/session record file specified by File and created by theacctcon1/ .... prctmp(8)

associated/ /: Contains the log file and temporary files .... mqueue(4)

//etc/group file or the named file and writes to standard/ .... grpck(8)

remote systems/ hosts.equiv: A file containing the names of .... hosts.equiv(4)

the sendmail configuration file data sendmail.cf: Contains .... sendmail.cf(4)

hard/ /blocks) allocated to each file divided by the number of .... acctdusg(8)

/The default configuration file for the inetd daemon .... inetd.conf(4)

stanza: Stanza file format .... stanza(4)

prdaily : Formats an ASCII file of the accounting data of/ .... prdaily(8)

/files into an intermediary file or a daily accounting file .... acctmerg(8)

to/ grpck: Scansthe /etc/group file or the named file and writes .... grpck(8)

/and write (w) permissionsto the file owner and group, and read/ .... nulladm(8)

/Creates the file specified inthe File parameter, gives read (r)/ .... nulladm(8)

accountingfile specified by the File parameterSee acct(8) /total .... prtacct(8)

prctmp: Outputsthe session record file specified by File and/ .... prctmp(8)

parameter,/ nulladm: Creates the file specified inthe File .... nulladm(8)

interactive/ fsck : Provides file system consistency check and .... fsck(8)

fsdb: File system debugger .... fsdb(8)

dump, rdump: Performs incremental file system dumps .... dump(8)

dumpfs: Dump UFS file system information .... dumpfs(8)

quot: Summarizes file system ownership .... quot(8)

quotaon(8) quotaoff: Turns file system quotas offSee .... quotaoff(8)

check icheck: File system storage consistency .... icheck(8)

mkproto: Constructs a prototype file system .... mkproto(8)

newfs: Constructs a new file system .... newfs(8)

tunefs: Tune up an existing UFS file system .... tunefs(8)

the system without checking file systems fastboot: Reboots .... fastboot(8)

umount: Mounts and dismounts file systems mount, ... mount(8)

umount: Unmounts file systemsSee mount(8) .... umount(8)

//var/adm/acct/sum/loginlog file to show the last date each/ .... lastlogin(8)

uucico/ Command (C.*): Contains file transfer directions for the .... Command(C.*)(4)

ftpd: The DARPA Internet File Transfer Protocol server .... ftpd(8)

tftpd: The DARPA Trivial File Transfer Protocol server .... tftpd(8)

information about the status of file transfer requests /Contains .... xferstats(4)

/Contains queued requests for file transfers and command/ .... Directories(4)

uusched : Schedules work for the file transport program .... uusched(8)

/files used internally by file transport programs .... &.Workspace(4)

ftpusers: The ftpd security file .... ftpusers(4)

mknod: Creates a special file .... mknod(8)

named.boot : named configuration file .... named.boot(4)

vipw: Edits the /etc/passwd file .... vipw(8)

file or a daily accounting file /files into an intermediary .... acctmerg(8)

Internet Name Domain) name server file /the BIND (Berkeley .... named.*(4)

Contains the network name file networks: .... networks(4)

resolver configuration file resolv.conf: .... resolv.conf(4)

process accounting file.See acct(8) //var/adm/pacctn .... turnacct(8)

the/usr/include/sys/acct.h header file.See acctprc(8) /structure in .... acctprc1(8)

uucp uucheck: Check for files and directories required by .... uucheck(8)

/and /var/adm/acct/nite/lock* files as part of the daily/ .... remove(8)

/the log file and temporary files associated with the/ .... mqueue(4)

/dump_file storage device all files changed after a certain/ .... rdump(8)

Temporary (TM.*): Stores data files during transfers to remote/ .... Temporary(TM.*)(4)

Checks the password and group files for inconsistencies /grpck: .... pwck(8)

orother/ rrestore: Reads files from a remote magnetic tape .... rrestore(8)

acctdusg: Reads a list of files from standardinput and/ .... acctdusg(8)

dump/ restore, rrestore: Restores files from tapes written with the .... restore(8)

uucleanup: Deletes selected old files from the uucp spool/ .... uucleanup(8)

accountingrecords into summary files in the/ /or other periodic .... monacct(8)

or a/ /: Merges total accounting files into an intermediary file .... acctmerg(8)

/: Contains copies of files that could not be processed .... &.Corrupt(4)

inode table and writes buffered files to the disk /Updates the .... sync(8)

/Contains administrative files used by the uucp program .... &.Admin(4)

execute/ /Contains temporary files used by the uuxqt daemon to .... &.Xqtdir(4)

transport/ /Holds temporary files used internally by file .... &.Workspace(4)

acct.h: Account include files .... acct.h(4)

the combined uucp program log files /: Contains .... &.Old(4)

: Contains the uucp program log files /usr/spool/uucp/.Log .... &.Log(4)

Builds system configuration files config: .... config(8)

quotacheck: Checks filesystem quota consistency .... quotacheck(8)

quotaon, quotaoff: Turns filesystem quotas on or off .... quotaon(8)

repquota: Summarizes filesystem quotas .... repquota(8)

a certain date in the specified filesystem.See dump(8) /after .... rdump(8)

fstab: Static information about filesystems .... fstab(4)

server for networks fingerd: The user information .... fingerd(8)

from unknown systems Foreign: Logs contact attempts .... Foreign(4)

/from standard inputthat are in a format defined by the acct/ .... acctprc1(8)

/File records in the wtmp format for corrupted date and/ .... wtmpfix(8)

stanza: Stanza file format .... stanza(4)

accounting data of/ prdaily : Formats an ASCII file of the .... prdaily(8)

accountingfile/ prtacct: Formats and displays any total .... prtacct(8)

/time accounting records to change formats and to make corrections/ .... fwtmp(8)

output/ acctwtmp: Writesa utmp formatted record to standard .... acctwtmp(8)

df: Displays statistics on free disk space .... df(8)

consistency check and/ fsck : Provides file system .... fsck(8)

lost+found directory for fsck mklost+found: Makesa .... mklost+found(8)

fsdb: File system debugger .... fsdb(8)

filesystems fstab: Static information about .... fstab(4)

ftpusers: The ftpd security file .... ftpusers(4)

Transfer Protocol server ftpd: The DARPA Internet File .... ftpd(8)

ftpusers: The ftpd security file .... ftpusers(4)

startup: Turns on the accounting functionsSee acct(8) .... startup(8)

date and timestamp entries.See fwtmp(8) /format for corrupted .... wtmpfix(8)

record to standard output See fwtmp(8) /Writesa utmp formatted .... acctwtmp(8)

connect time accounting records/ fwtmp, acctwtmp, wtmpfix: Modify .... fwtmp(8)

daemon gated : The gateway routing .... gated(8)

configuration information for the gated daemon /Contains .... gated.conf(4)

configuration information for/ gated.conf: Contains .... gated.conf(4)

gated : The gateway routing daemon .... gated(8)

routing information to the/ gateways: Specifies Internet .... gateways(4)

ncheck: generate names from i-numbers .... ncheck(8)

user ID diskusg : Generates disk accounting data by .... diskusg(8)

test pattern lptest: Generates the line printer ripple .... lptest(8)

modes, speed, and line/ getty: Sets the terminal type, ... getty(8)

/specified inthe File parameter, gives read (r) and write (w)/ .... nulladm(8)

to it vgextend: Extend a volume group by adding physical volumes .... vgextend(8)

vgreduce: Reduce a volume group by removing one or more/ .... vgreduce(8)

/grpck: Checks the password and group files for inconsistencies .... pwck(8)

Sets the availability of a volume group to yes or no vgchange: .... vgchange(8) vgcreate: Creates a volume group .... vgcreate(8)

can be used as part of a volume group /a physical volume that .... pvcreate(8)

physical volumes within a volume group /about one or more .... pvdisplay(8)

logical volumes from a volume group /Removes one or more .... lvremove(8)

of a physical volume in a volume group /the characteristics .... pvchange(8)

a logical volume in a volume group lvcreate: Creates .... lvcreate(8)

/permissionsto the file owner and group, and read (r) permission to/ .... nulladm(8)

definition of one or more volume groups from the system /the .... vgremove(8)

are stale in one or morevolume groups /volume mirrors that .... vgsync(8)

Displays information about volume groups vgdisplay: .... vgdisplay(8)

group files for/ pwck, grpck: Checks the password and .... pwck(8)

or the named file and writes to/ grpck: Scansthe /etc/group file .... grpck(8)

halt: Stops the processor .... halt(8)

fasthalt: Halts the system .... fasthalt(8)

file divided by the number of hard links then writes an/ /each .... acctdusg(8)

/in the/usr/include/sys/acct.h header file.See acctprc(8) .... acctprc1(8)

/usr/spool/uucp/.Workspace: Holds temporary files used/ .... &.Workspace(4)

hosts: The host name data base .... hosts(4)

protocols used on the local host /Defines the Internet .... protocols(4)

remote NFS compatible mounts on a host showmount: Shows .... showmount(8)

ECHO_REQUEST packets to network hosts ping : Sends ICMP .... ping(8)

the names of remote systems and/ hosts.equiv: A file containing .... hosts.equiv(4)

hosts: The host name data base .... hosts(4)

clri: Clears i-nodes .... clri(8)

ncheck: generate names from i-numbers .... ncheck(8)

local NFS compatible asynchronous I/O server nfsiod: The .... nfsiod(8)

consistency check icheck: File system storage .... icheck(8)

network hosts ping : Sends ICMP ECHO_REQUEST packets to .... ping(8)

summarizes them according to user ID and nameSee acctprc(8) /and .... acctprc2(8)

disk accounting data by user ID diskusg : Generates .... diskusg(8)

network interface parameters ifconfig: Configures or displays .... ifconfig(8)

acct.h: Account include files .... acct.h(4)

the password and group files for inconsistencies /grpck: Checks .... pwck(8)

and writes to standard output any inconsistencies.See pwck(8) /file .... grpck(8)

extents allocated to a/ lvextend: Increases the numberof physical .... lvextend(8)

dump, rdump: Performs incremental file system dumps .... dump(8)

/number of disk blocks (including indirect blocks) allocated to/ .... acctdusg(8)

to/ /of hard links then writes an individual record for each user .... acctdusg(8)

configuration file for the inetd daemon /The default .... inetd.conf(4)

configuration file for the inetd/ inetd.conf: The default .... inetd.conf(4)

inetd: The internet super-server .... inetd(8)

fstab: Static information about filesystems .... fstab(4)

lvdisplay: Displays information about logical volumes .... lvdisplay(8)

physical/ pvdisplay: Displays information about one or more .... pvdisplay(8)

last : Displays information about previous logins .... last(8)

commands/ lastcomm : Outputs information about the last .... lastcomm(8)

the uucp program/ /: Contains information about the status of .... &.Status(4)

file/ xferstats: Contains information about the status of .... xferstats(4)

vgdisplay: Displays information about volume groups .... vgdisplay(8)

/Contains configuration information for the gated daemon .... gated.conf(4)

fingerd: The user information server for networks .... fingerd(8)

/Specifies Internet routing   information to the routed daemon .... gateways(4)

dumpfs: Dump UFS file system   information .... dumpfs(8)

printer/plotter accounting   information pac: Outputs .... pac(8)

initialization   init: Process control .... init(8)

numbers/ Dialcodes: Contains the   initial digits of telephone .... Dialcodes(4)

inittab: Controls the   initialization process .... inittab(4)

init: Process control   initialization .... init(8)

/that the named daemon uses to   initialize the BIND (Berkeley/ .... named.*(4)

by callingthe diskusg/ dodisk: Initiates disk-usage accounting .... dodisk(8)

initialization process   inittab: Controls the .... inittab(4)

files to the/ sync: Updates the   inode table and writes buffered .... sync(8)

acctprc2: Reads, from standard   input, the records writtenby/ .... acctprc2(8)

wtmpfix: Examines standard   inputor File records in the/ .... wtmpfix(8)

by/ /Reads records from standard   inputthat are in a format defined .... acctprc1(8)

the last date each userlogged   inSee acct(8) /file to show .... lastlogin(8)

that/ Execute (X.*): Contains   instructions for running commands .... Execute(X.*)(4)

file system consistency check and   interactive repair /: Provides .... fsck(8)

adduser: Adds a new user   interactively .... adduser(8)

: Queries Internet name servers   interactively nslookup .... nslookup(8)

Configures or displays network   interface parameters ifconfig: .... ifconfig(8)

turn/ turnacct: Provides an   interface tothe accton command to .... turnacct(8)

a serial line to a network   interface slattach: Attaches .... slattach(8)

/total accounting files into an   intermediary file or a daily/ .... acctmerg(8)

/Holds temporary files used   internally by file transport/ .... &.Workspace(4)

named: Internet domain name server .... named(8)

server ftpd: The DARPA   Internet File Transfer Protocol .... ftpd(8)

/to initialize the BIND (Berkeley   Internet Name Domain) name server/ .... named.*(4)

interactively nslookup : Queries   Internet name servers .... nslookup(8)

local/ protocols: Defines the   Internet protocols used on the .... protocols(4)

the routed/ gateways: Specifies   Internet routing information to .... gateways(4)

sockets and protocols used for   Internet services /Defines the .... services(4)

inetd: The   internet super-server .... inetd(8)

sendmail: Sends mail over the   Internet .... sendmail(8)

(r)/ /Creates the file specified   inthe File parameter, gives read .... nulladm(8)

kloadsrv: Loads   kernel modules into the kernel .... kloadsrv(8)

Loads kernel modules into the   kernel kloadsrv: .... kloadsrv(8)

started by the user, except the/   killall: Terminates all processes .... killall(8)

into the kernel   kloadsrv: Loads kernel modules .... kloadsrv(8)

about the last commands executed   lastcomm : Outputs information .... lastcomm(8)

/var/adm/acct/sum/loginlog file/   lastlogin: Updatesthe .... lastlogin(8)

when entering a multiuser run   level /command script executed .... rc2(8)

when entering a multiuser run   level /command script executed .... rc3(8)

lib_admin: Administers shared   libraries .... lib_admin(8)

libraries   lib_admin: Administers shared .... lib_admin(8)

terminal type, modes, speed, and   line discipline getty: Sets the .... getty(8)

lpc: Line printer control program .... lpc(8)

lpd: line printer daemon .... lpd(8)

lptest: Generates the   line printer ripple test pattern .... lptest(8)

slattach: Attaches a serial   line to a network interface .... slattach(8)

connections over a telephone   line /used to establish remote .... Dialcodes(4)

/divided by the number of hard   links then writes an individual/ .... acctdusg(8) for uucp remote communications links Dialers: Lists modems used .... Dialers(4)

and computes/ acctdusg: Reads a list of files from standardinput .... acctdusg(8)

communications links Dialers: Lists modems used for uucp remote .... Dialers(4)

kernel kloadsrv: Loads kernel modules into the .... kloadsrv(8)

Internet protocols used on the local host /Defines the .... protocols(4)

I/O server nfsiod: The local NFS compatible asynchronous .... nfsiod(8)

that can execute commands on the local system /systems and users .... hosts.equiv(4)

/usr/spool/mqueue : Contains the log file and temporary files/ .... mqueue(4)

the combined uucp program log files /: Contains .... &.Old(4)

: Contains the uucp program log files /usr/spool/uucp/.Log .... &.Log(4)

lvcreate: Creates a logical volume in a volume group .... lvcreate(8)

stale in/ lvsync: Synchronizes logical volume mirrors that are .... lvsync(8)

stale in/ vgsync: Synchronizes logical volume mirrors that are .... vgsync(8)

physical extents allocated to a logical volume /the numberof .... lvextend(8)

physical extents allocated to a logical volume /the numberof .... lvreduce(8)

that are stale in one ormore logical volume /volume mirrors .... lvsync(8)

Changes the characteristics of a logical volume lvchange: .... lvchange(8)

lvremove: Removes one or more logical volumes from a volume/ .... lvremove(8)

Displays information about logical volumes lvdisplay: .... lvdisplay(8)

/procedure to write asequence of login and logout recordsSee/ .... acctcon1(8)

/bythe Number parameter to the login name specified by the User/ .... chargefee(8)

rlogind: The remote login server .... rlogind(8)

the/ /and converts asequence of login session records produced by .... acctcon2(8)

information about previous logins last : Displays .... last(8)

/to write asequence of login and logout recordsSee acctcon(8) .... acctcon1(8)

remote systems remote.unknown: Logs access attempts by unknown .... remote.unknown(4)

unknown systems Foreign: Logs contact attempts from .... Foreign(4)

syslogd: Logs system messages .... syslogd(8)

mklost+found: Makesa lost+found directory for fsck .... mklost+found(8)

lpc: Line printer control program .... lpc(8)

lpd: line printer daemon .... lpd(8)

printer ripple test pattern lptest: Generates the line .... lptest(8)

characteristics of a logical/ lvchange: Changes the .... lvchange(8)

volume in a volume group lvcreate: Creates a logical .... lvcreate(8)

about logical volumes lvdisplay: Displays information .... lvdisplay(8)

physical extents allocated to a/ lvextend: Increases the numberof .... lvextend(8)

physical extents allocated to a/ lvreduce: Decreases the numberof .... lvreduce(8)

logical volumes from a volume/ lvremove: Removes one or more .... lvremove(8)

volume mirrors that are stale in/ lvsync: Synchronizes logical .... lvsync(8)

reboot: Restarts the machine .... reboot(8)

rmt: Allows remote access to magnetic tape devices .... rmt(8)

/Reads files from a remote magnetic tape orother specified/ .... rrestore(8)

sendmail: Sends mail over the Internet .... sendmail(8)

with the messages in the mail queue /files associated .... mqueue(4)

: Displays statistics about mail traffic mailstats .... mailstats(8)

about mail traffic mailstats : Displays statistics .... mailstats(8)

configuration/ sysconfigdb: Maintains the system .... sysconfigdb(8)

for fsck mklost+found: Makesa lost+found directory .... mklost+found(8)

cfgmgr: Configuration manager daemon .... cfgmgr(8)

the uucpprogram and/ uucpd: Manages communications between .... uucpd(8)

routed: Manages network routing tables .... routed(8) route: Manually manipulates the routing tables .... route(8)

tables route: Manually manipulates the routing .... route(8)

DARPA port to RPC program number mapper portmap: The .... portmap(8)

into an intermediary/ acctmerg : Merges total accounting files .... acctmerg(8)

audit: Contains debug messages from the uucico daemon .... audit(4)

/files associated with the messages in the mail queue .... mqueue(4)

syslogd: Logs system messages .... syslogd(8)

Displays STREAMS event trace messages strace: .... strace(8)

/Synchronizes logical volume mirrors that are stale in one or/ .... vgsync(8)

/Synchronizes logical volume mirrors that are stale in one/ .... lvsync(8)

lost+found directory for fsck mklost+found: Makesa .... mklost+found(8)

mknod: Creates a special file .... mknod(8)

the basic user database/ mkpasswd: Creates a version of .... mkpasswd(8)

file system mkproto: Constructs a prototype .... mkproto(8)

communications/ Dialers: Lists modems used for uucp remote .... Dialers(4)

getty: Sets the terminal type, modes, speed, and line discipline .... getty(8)

sysconfig: Modifies the system configuration .... sysconfig(8)

fwtmp, acctwtmp, wtmpfix: Modify connect time accounting/ .... fwtmp(8)

kloadsrv: Loads kernel modules into the kernel .... kloadsrv(8)

periodic accountingrecords into/ monacct: Collects daily or other .... monacct(8)

mirrors that are stale in one or morevolume groups /logical volume .... vgsync(8)

requests exports: Defines remote mount points for NFS mount .... exports(4)

remote mount points for NFS mount requests exports: Defines .... exports(4)

Services remote NFS compatible mount requests mountd: .... mountd(8)

umount: Unmounts file systemsSee mount(8) .... umount(8)

dismounts file systems mount, umount: Mounts and .... mount(8)

compatible mount requests mountd: Services remote NFS .... mountd(8)

mount, umount: Mounts and dismounts file systems .... mount(8)

Shows remote NFS compatible mounts on a host showmount: .... showmount(8)

extentsfrom one physical/ pvmove: Moves allocated physical .... pvmove(8)

script executed when entering a multiuser run level /Run command .... rc2(8)

script executed when entering a multiuser run level /Run command .... rc3(8)

hosts: The host name data base .... hosts(4)

/the BIND (Berkeley Internet Name Domain) name server file .... named.*(4)

networks: Contains the network name file .... networks(4)

(Berkeley Internet Name Domain) name server file /the BIND .... named.*(4)

named: Internet domain name server .... named(8)

nslookup : Queries Internet name servers interactively .... nslookup(8)

Number parameter to the login name specified by the User/ /bythe .... chargefee(8)

named.boot : named configuration file .... chargefee(8)

the/ /Defines the data that the named daemon uses to initialize .... named.*(4)

/Scansthe /etc/group file or the named file and writes to standard/ .... grpck(8)

the named daemon uses to/ named.*: Defines the data that .... named.*(4)

file named.boot : named configuration .... named.boot(4)

server named: Internet domain name .... named(8)

ncheck: generate names from i-numbers .... ncheck(8)

that can/ /A file containing the names of remote systems and users .... hosts.equiv(4)

them according to user ID and nameSee acctprc(8) /summarizes .... acctprc2(8)

i-numbers ncheck: generate names from .... ncheck(8)

ICMP ECHO_REQUEST packets to network hosts ping : Sends .... ping(8)

ifconfig: Configures or displays network interface parameters .... ifconfig(8)

Attaches a serial line to a network interface slattach: .... slattach(8)

networks: Contains the network name file .... networks(4)

routed: Manages network routing tables .... routed(8)

The user information server for networks fingerd: .... fingerd(8)

name file networks: Contains the network .... networks(4)

system newfs: Constructs a new file .... newfs(8)

server nfsiod: The local NFS compatible asynchronous I/O .... nfsiod(8)

mountd: Services remote NFS compatible mount requests .... mountd(8)

showmount: Shows remote NFS compatible mounts on a host .... showmount(8)

nfsd: The remote NFS compatible server .... nfsd(8)

Defines remote mount points for NFS mount requests exports: .... exports(4)

nfsstat: Reports NFS statistics .... nfsstat(8)

server nfsd: The remote NFS compatible .... nfsd(8)

asynchronous I/O server nfsiod: The local NFS compatible .... nfsiod(8)

nfsstat: Reports NFS statistics .... nfsstat(8)

shell/ acctcon1: This command is normally called bythe runacct .... acctcon1(8)

servers interactively nslookup : Queries Internet name .... nslookup(8)

specified inthe File parameter,/ nulladm: Creates the file .... nulladm(8)

The DARPA port to RPC program number mapper portmap: .... portmap(8)

/standardinput and computes the number of disk blocks (including/ .... acctdusg(8)

an/ /to each file divided by the number of hard links then writes .... acctdusg(8)

Number/ chargefee: Charges the number of units specified bythe .... chargefee(8)

/number of units specified bythe Number parameter to the login/ .... chargefee(8)

lvextend: Increases the numberof physical extents/ .... lvextend(8)

lvreduce: Decreases the numberof physical extents/ .... lvreduce(8)

/the initial digits of telephone numbers used to establish remote/ .... Dialcodes(4)

to turn process accounting on or off, or to create a new/ /command .... turnacct(8)

Turns process accounting offSee acct(8) shutacct: .... shutacct(8)

Turns account processing on and offSee acctprc(8) accton: .... accton(8)

Turns file system quotas offSee quotaon(8) quotaoff: .... quotaoff(8)

remove: Deletes all ofthe /var/adm/acct/sum/wtmp*,/ .... remove(8)

Saves a core dump of the operating system savecore: .... savecore(8)

shutdown: Ends system operation .... shutdown(8)

/of the basic user database organized for efficient searches .... mkpasswd(8)

mirrors that are stale in one ormore logical volume /volume .... lvsync(8)

files from a remote magnetic tape orother specified storage/ /Reads .... rrestore(8)

group, and read (r) permission to otherusersSee acct(8) /owner and .... nulladm(8)

/named file and writes to standard output any inconsistencies.See/ .... grpck(8)

utmp formatted record to standard output See fwtmp(8) /Writesa .... acctwtmp(8)

/record for each user to standard output.See acctdisk(8) .... acctdusg(8)

ac: Outputs connect-session records .... ac(8)

summaries acctcon1, acctcon2: Outputs connect-time accounting .... acctcon(8)

last commands/ lastcomm : Outputs information about the .... lastcomm(8)

accounting information pac: Outputs printer/plotter .... pac(8)

accounting record/ acctcom : Outputs selected process .... acctcom(8)

password database printpw : Outputs the contents of the .... printpw(8)

specified by File and/ prctmp: Outputsthe session record file .... prctmp(8)

/write (w) permissionsto the file owner and group, and read (r)/ .... nulladm(8)

quot: Summarizes file system ownership .... quot(8)

accounting information pac: Outputs printer/plotter .... pac(8)

ping : Sends ICMP ECHO_REQUEST packets to network hosts .... ping(8)

Specifies additional device for paging and swapping swapon: .... swapon(8)
/of units specified bythe Number parameter to the login name/ .... chargefee(8)
/the file specified inthe File parameter, gives read (r) and/ .... nulladm(8)
or displays network interface parameters ifconfig: Configures .... ifconfig(8)
/specified by the File parameterSee acct(8) .... prtacct(8)
login name specified by the User parameterSee acct(8) /to the .... chargefee(8)
volume that can be used as part of a volume group /physical .... pvcreate(8)
/var/adm/acct/nite/lock* files as part of the daily cleanup/ /and .... remove(8)
pwck, grpck: Checks the password and group files for/ .... pwck(8)
: Outputs the contents of the password database printpw .... printpw(8)
the line printer ripple test pattern lptest: Generates .... lptest(8)
acctdisk, acctdusg : Perform disk-usage accounting .... acctdisk(8)
acctprc1, acctprc2, accton: Perform process accounting/ .... acctprc(8)
dumps dump, rdump: Performs incremental file system .... dump(8)
monacct: Collects daily or other periodic accountingrecords into/ .... monacct(8)
superblock update: Periodically updates the .... update(8)
owner and group, and read (r) permission to otherusersSee/ /file .... nulladm(8)
/gives read (r) and write (w) permissionsto the file owner and/ .... nulladm(8)
lvextend: Increases the numberof physical extents allocated to a/ .... lvextend(8)
lvreduce: Decreases the numberof physical extents allocated to a/ .... lvreduce(8)
volume/ pvmove: Moves allocated physical extentsfrom one physical .... pvmove(8)
/Changes the characteristics of a physical volume in a volume group .... pvchange(8)
as part of a/ pvcreate: Creates a physical volume that can be used .... pvcreate(8)
other/ /physical extentsfrom one physical volume to one or more .... pvmove(8)
group by removing one or more physical volumes from it /volume .... vgreduce(8)
Extend a volume group by adding physical volumes to it vgextend: .... vgextend(8)
/information about one or more physical volumes within a volume/ .... pvdisplay(8)
volume to one or more other physical volumes /one physical .... pvmove(8)
packets to network hosts ping : Sends ICMP ECHO_REQUEST .... ping(8)
exports: Defines remote mount points for NFS mount requests .... exports(4)
portmap: The DARPA port to RPC program number mapper .... portmap(8)
program number mapper portmap: The DARPA port to RPC .... portmap(8)
file specified by File and/ prctmp: Outputsthe session record .... prctmp(8)
of the accounting data of/ prdaily : Formats an ASCII file .... prdaily(8)
last : Displays information about previous logins .... last(8)
base printcap: printer capability data .... printcap(4)
printcap: printer capability data base .... printcap(4)
lpc: Line printer control program .... lpc(8)
lpd: line printer daemon .... lpd(8)
lptest: Generates the line printer ripple test pattern .... lptest(8)
information pac: Outputs printer/plotter accounting .... pac(8)
the password database printpw : Outputs the contents of .... printpw(8)
renice: Alters the priority of a running process .... renice(8)
called bythe runacct shell procedure and converts/ /usually .... acctcon2(8)
/as part of the daily cleanup procedure called by the runacct/ .... remove(8)
login/ /called bythe runacct shell procedure to write asequence of .... acctcon1(8)
Perform process accounting procedures /acctprc2, accton: .... acctprc(8)
to create a new /var/adm/pacctn process accounting file.See/ /or .... turnacct(8)
shutacct: Turns process accounting offSee acct(8) .... shutacct(8)
to/ /tothe accton command to turn process accounting on or off, or .... turnacct(8)
/acctprc2, accton: Perform process accounting procedures .... acctprc(8)

acctcom : Outputs selected process accounting record/ .... acctcom(8)

init: Process control initialization . ... init(8)

by the user, except the calling process /all processes started .... killall(8)

Controls the initialization process inittab: .... inittab(4)

Alters the priority of a running process renice: .... renice(8)

copies of files that could not be processed /: Contains .... &.Corrupt(4)

except/ killall: Terminates all processes started by the user, ... killall(8)

accton: Turns account processing on and offSee/ .... accton(8)

halt: Stops the processor .... halt(8)

/of login session records produced by the acctcon1 command/ .... acctcon2(8)

from accounting/ acctcms : Produces command usage summaries .... acctcms(8)

/about the status of the uucp program contacts with remote/ .... &.Status(4)

/: Contains the uucp program log files .... &.Log(4)

/: Contains the combined uucp program log files .... &.Old(4)

portmap: The DARPA port to RPC program number mapper .... portmap(8)

lpc: Line printer control program .... lpc(8)

files used by the uucp program /Contains administrative .... &.Admin(4)

definitions for the sendmail program aliases: Contains alias .... aliases(4)

work for the file transport program uusched : Schedules .... uusched(8)

used internally by file transport programs /Holds temporary files .... &.Workspace(4)

and controls Address Resolution Protocol (ARP) tables /Displays .... arp(8)

telnetd: The DARPA TELNET protocol server .... telnetd(8)

The DARPA Internet File Transfer Protocol server ftpd: .... ftpd(8)

The DARPA Trivial File Transfer Protocol server tftpd: .... tftpd(8)

trpt : Transliterates protocol trace .... trpt(8)

services: Defines the sockets and protocols used for Internet/ .... services(4)

protocols: Defines the Internet protocols used on the local host .... protocols(4)

protocols used on the local host protocols: Defines the Internet .... protocols(4)

mkproto: Constructs a prototype file system .... mkproto(8)

shell scripts acct/* : Provides accounting commands for .... acct(8)

accton command to turn/ turnacct : Provides an interface tothe .... turnacct(8)

check and interactive/ fsck : Provides file system consistency .... fsck(8)

total accountingfile specified/ prtacct: Formats and displays any .... prtacct(8)

characteristics of a physical/ pvchange: Changes the .... pvchange(8)

volume that can be used as part/ pvcreate: Creates a physical .... pvcreate(8)

about one or more physical/ pvdisplay: Displays information .... pvdisplay(8)

extentsfrom one physical volume/ pvmove: Moves allocated physical .... pvmove(8)

output any inconsistencies.See pwck(8) /and writes to standard .... grpck(8)

and group files for/ pwck, grpck: Checks the password .... pwck(8)

interactively nslookup : Queries Internet name servers .... nslookup(8)

with the messages in the mail queue /temporary files associated .... mqueue(4)

transfers/ Directories: Contains queued requests for file .... Directories(4)

ownership quot: Summarizes file system .... quot(8)

quotacheck: Checks filesystem quota consistency .... quotacheck(8)

quota consistency quotacheck: Checks filesystem .... quotacheck(8)

quotas offSee quotaon(8) quotaoff: Turns file system .... quotaoff(8)

on or off quotaon, quotaoff: Turns filesystem quotas .... quotaon(8)

Turns file system quotas offSee quotaon(8) quotaoff: .... quotaoff(8)

filesystem quotas on or off quotaon, quotaoff: Turns .... quotaon(8)

quotaoff: Turns file system quotas offSee quotaon(8) .... quotaoff(8)

quotaoff: Turns filesystem quotas on or off quotaon, ... quotaon(8) edquota: Edits user quotas .... edquota(8)

repquota: Summarizes filesystem quotas .... repquota(8)

when stopping the system rc0: Run command script executed .... rc0(8)

when entering a multiuser run/ rc2: Run command script executed .... rc2(8)

when entering a multiuser run/ rc3: Run command script executed .... rc3(8)

tapes written with the dump or rdump command, respectively /from .... restore(8)

storage device all files changed/ rdump: Copies tothe dump_file .... rdump(8)

system dumps dump, rdump: Performs incremental file .... dump(8)

inthe File parameter, gives read (r) and write (w)/ /specified .... nulladm(8)

/the file owner and group, and read (r) permission to/ .... nulladm(8)

standardinput and/ acctdusg: Reads a list of files from .... acctdusg(8)

magnetic tape orother/ rrestore: Reads files from a remote .... rrestore(8)

inputthat are in a/ acctprc1: Reads records from standard .... acctprc1(8)

records writtenby/ acctprc2: Reads, from standard input, the .... acctprc2(8)

reboot: Restarts the machine .... reboot(8)

checking file systems fastboot: Reboots the system without .... fastboot(8)

prctmp: Outputsthe session record file specified by File and/ .... prctmp(8)

/links then writes an individual record for each user to standard/ .... acctdusg(8)

errors : Contains a record of uucico daemon errors .... errors(4)

selected process accounting record summaries /: Outputs .... acctcom(8)

acctwtmp: Writesa utmp formatted record to standard output See/ .... acctwtmp(8)

are in a format/ acctprc1: Reads records from standard inputthat .... acctprc1(8)

/Examines standard inputor File records in the wtmp format for/ .... wtmpfix(8)

/asequence of login session records produced by the acctcon1/ .... acctcon2(8)

/Modify connect time accounting records to change formats and to/ .... fwtmp(8)

/Reads, from standard input, the records writtenby acctprc1 and/ .... acctprc2(8)

ac: Outputs connect-session records .... ac(8)

sa : Summarizes accounting records .... sa(8)

usage summaries from accounting records /: Produces command .... acctcms(8)

and to make corrections in the records /to change formats .... fwtmp(8)

/time total accounting records.See acctcon(8) .... acctcon2(8)

asequence of login and logout recordsSee acctcon(8) /to write .... acctcon1(8)

one or more physical/ vgreduce: Reduce a volume group by removing .... vgreduce(8)

devices rmt: Allows remote access to magnetic tape .... rmt(8)

by the uuxqt daemon to execute remote command requests /used .... &.Xqtdir(4)

/Lists modems used for uucp remote communications links .... Dialers(4)

the talk(1)command talkd: The remote communications server for .... talkd(8)

/numbers used to establish remote connections over a/ .... Dialcodes(4)

rexecd: The remote execution server .... rexecd(8)

rlogind: The remote login server .... rlogind(8)

rrestore: Reads files from a remote magnetic tape orother/ .... rrestore(8)

requests exports: Defines remote mount points for NFS mount .... exports(4)

requests mountd: Services remote NFS compatible mount .... mountd(8)

host showmount: Shows remote NFS compatible mounts on a .... showmount(8)

nfsd: The remote NFS compatible server .... nfsd(8)

rshd: The remote shell server .... rshd(8)

that require the resources of a remote system /running commands .... Execute(X.*)(4)

/A file containing the names of remote systems and users that can/ .... hosts.equiv(4)

data files during transfers to remote systems /(TM.*): Stores .... Temporary(TM.*)(4)

of the uucp program contacts with remote systems /about the status .... &.Status(4)

and command executions on remote systems /file transfers .... Directories(4)

data, and execute files to remote systems /uucp command, ... uucico(8)

Contains data to be sent to remote systems Data (D.*): .... Data(D.*)(4)

Logs access attempts by unknown remote systems remote.unknown: .... remote.unknown(4)

attempts by unknown remote/ remote.unknown: Logs access .... remote.unknown(4)

/var/adm/acct/sum/wtmp*,/ remove: Deletes all of the .... remove(8)

volumes from a volume/ lvremove: Removes one or more logical .... lvremove(8)

more volume groups/ vgremove: Removes the definition of one or .... vgremove(8)

volumes/ /Reduce a volume group by removing one or more physical .... vgreduce(8)

running process renice: Alters the priority of a .... renice(8)

consistency check and interactive repair /: Provides file system .... fsck(8)

nfsstat: Reports NFS statistics .... nfsstat(8)

quotas repquota: Summarizes filesystem .... repquota(8)

Directories: Contains queued requests for file transfers and/ .... Directories(4)

about the status of file transfer requests /Contains information .... xferstats(4)

daemon to execute remote command requests /files used by the uuxqt .... &.Xqtdir(4)

remote mount points for NFS mount requests exports: Defines .... exports(4)

remote NFS compatible mount requests mountd: Services .... mountd(8)

system /for running commands that require the resources of a remote .... Execute(X.*)(4)

Check for files and directories required by uucp uucheck: .... uucheck(8)

/Displays and controls Address Resolution Protocol (ARP) tables .... arp(8)

configuration file resolv.conf: resolver .... resolv.conf(4)

resolv.conf: resolver configuration file .... resolv.conf(4)

running commands that require the resources of a remote system /for .... Execute(X.*)(4)

with the dump or rdump command, respectively /from tapes written .... restore(8)

reboot: Restarts the machine .... reboot(8)

specified storage device.See restore(8) /magnetic tape orother .... rrestore(8)

from tapes written with the dump/ restore, rrestore: Restores files .... restore(8)

with the dump/ restore, rrestore: Restores files from tapes written .... restore(8)

server rexecd: The remote execution .... rexecd(8)

Generates the line printer ripple test pattern lptest: .... lptest(8)

rlogind: The remote login server .... rlogind(8)

magnetic tape devices rmt: Allows remote access to .... rmt(8)

chroot: Changes the root directory of a command .... chroot(8)

routing tables route: Manually manipulates the .... route(8)

routing information to the routed daemon /Specifies Internet .... gateways(4)

tables routed: Manages network routing .... routed(8)

gated : The gateway routing daemon .... gated(8)

gateways: Specifies Internet routing information to the routed/ .... gateways(4)

route: Manually manipulates the routing tables .... route(8)

routed: Manages network routing tables .... routed(8)

portmap: The DARPA port to RPC program number mapper .... portmap(8)

remote magnetic tape orother/ rrestore: Reads files from a .... rrestore(8)

tapes written with the/ restore, rrestore: Restores files from .... restore(8)

rshd: The remote shell server .... rshd(8)

stopping the system rc0: Run command script executed when .... rc0(8)

entering a multiuser run/ rc2: Run command script executed when .... rc2(8)

entering a multiuser run/ rc3: Run command script executed when .... rc3(8)

when entering a multiuser run level /script executed .... rc2(8)

when entering a multiuser run level /script executed .... rc3(8)

runacct : Runs daily accounting .... runacct(8)

cleanup procedure called by the runacct commandSee acct(8) /daily .... remove(8)

command is usually called bythe runacct shell procedure and/ /This .... acctcon2(8)
/command is normally called bythe runacct shell procedure to write/ .... acctcon1(8)
/(X.*): Contains instructions for running commands that require the/ .... Execute(X.*)(4)
renice: Alters the priority of a running process .... renice(8)
runacct : Runs daily accounting .... runacct(8)
rwhod: The system status server .... rwhod(8)
records sa : Summarizes accounting .... sa(8)
the operating system savecore: Saves a core dump of .... savecore(8)
operating system savecore: Saves a core dump of the .... savecore(8)
named file and writes to/ grpck: Scansthe /etc/group file or the .... grpck(8)
transport program uusched : Schedules work for the file .... uusched(8)
multiuser run/ rc2: Run command script executed when entering a .... rc2(8)
multiuser run/ rc3: Run command script executed when entering a .... rc3(8)
system rc0: Run command script executed when stopping the .... rc0(8)
accounting commands for shell scripts acct/* : Provides .... acct(8)
database organized for efficient searches /of the basic user .... mkpasswd(8)
ftpusers: The ftpd security file .... ftpusers(4)
spool/ uucleanup: Deletes selected old files from the uucp .... uucleanup(8)
record/ acctcom : Outputs selected process accounting .... acctcom(8)
sendmail.cf: Contains the sendmail configuration file data .... sendmail.cf(4)
alias definitions for the sendmail program /Contains .... aliases(4)
sendmail configuration file data sendmail.cf: Contains the .... sendmail.cf(4)
Internet sendmail: Sends mail over the .... sendmail(8)
to network hosts ping : Sends ICMP ECHO_REQUEST packets .... ping(8)
sendmail: Sends mail over the Internet .... sendmail(8)
Data (D.*): Contains data to be sent to remote systems .... Data(D.*)(4)
interface slattach: Attaches a serial line to a network .... slattach(8)
timed: Controls the time server daemon at system startup .... timed(8)
Internet Name Domain) name server file /the BIND (Berkeley .... named.*(4)
fingerd: The user information server for networks .... fingerd(8)
talkd: The remote communications server for the talk(1)command .... talkd(8)
comsat: The biff server .... comsat(8)
named: Internet domain name server .... named(8)
nfsd: The remote NFS compatible server .... nfsd(8)
rexecd: The remote execution server .... rexecd(8)
rlogind: The remote login server .... rlogind(8)
rshd: The remote shell server .... rshd(8)
rwhod: The system status server .... rwhod(8)
Internet File Transfer Protocol server ftpd: The DARPA .... ftpd(8)
NFS compatible asynchronous I/O server nfsiod: The local .... nfsiod(8)
The DARPA TELNET protocol server telnetd: .... telnetd(8)
Trivial File Transfer Protocol server tftpd: The DARPA .... tftpd(8)
nslookup : Queries Internet name servers interactively .... nslookup(8)
mount requests mountd: Services remote NFS compatible .... mountd(8)
and protocols used for Internet services /Defines the sockets .... services(4)
protocols used for Internet/ services: Defines the sockets and .... services(4)
File and/ prctmp: Outputsthe session record file specified by .... prctmp(8)
/and converts asequence of login session records produced by the/ .... acctcon2(8)
group to yes or no vgchange: Sets the availability of a volume .... vgchange(8)
speed, and line/ getty: Sets the terminal type, modes, ... getty(8)
lib_admin: Administers shared libraries .... lib_admin(8)

/is usually called bythe runacct shell procedure and converts/ .... acctcon2(8)

is normally called bythe runacct shell procedure to write/ /command .... acctcon1(8)

Provides accounting commands for shell scripts acct/* : .... acct(8)

rshd: The remote shell server .... rshd(8)

userlogged inSee acct(8) /file to show the last date each .... lastlogin(8)

compatible mounts on a host showmount: Shows remote NFS .... showmount(8)

mounts on a host showmount: Shows remote NFS compatible .... showmount(8)

accounting offSee acct(8) shutacct: Turns process .... shutacct(8)

shutdown: Ends system operation .... shutdown(8)

accounting/ ckpacct: Checks the size of the activeprocess .... ckpacct(8)

to a network interface slattach: Attaches a serial line .... slattach(8)

Internet/ services: Defines the sockets and protocols used for .... services(4)

Displays statistics on free disk space df: .... df(8)

mknod: Creates a special file .... mknod(8)

/Outputsthe session record file specified by File and created by/ .... prctmp(8)

displays any total accountingfile specified by the File/ /and .... prtacct(8)

parameter to the login name specified by the User/ /Number .... chargefee(8)

to/ /Charges the number of units specified bythe Number parameter .... chargefee(8)

/after a certain date in the specified filesystem.See dump(8) .... rdump(8)

gives/ nulladm: Creates the file specified inthe File parameter, ... nulladm(8)

/a remote magnetic tape orother specified storage device.See/ .... rrestore(8)

paging and swapping swapon: Specifies additional device for .... swapon(8)

information to the/ gateways: Specifies Internet routing .... gateways(4)

/Sets the terminal type, modes, speed, and line discipline .... getty(8)

selected old files from the uucp spool directory /Deletes .... uucleanup(8)

/logical volume mirrors that are stale in one or morevolume groups .... vgsync(8)

/logical volume mirrors that are stale in one ormore logical/ .... lvsync(8)

writtenby/ acctprc2: Reads, from standard input, the records .... acctprc2(8)

in the wtmp/ wtmpfix: Examines standard inputor File records .... wtmpfix(8)

acctprc1: Reads records from standard inputthat are in a/ .... acctprc1(8)

or the named file and writes to standard output any/ /file .... grpck(8)

/Writesa utmp formatted record to standard output See fwtmp(8) .... acctwtmp(8)

/record for each user to standard output.See acctdisk(8) .... acctdusg(8)

/Reads a list of files from standardinput and computes the/ .... acctdusg(8)

stanza: Stanza file format .... stanza(4)

stanza: Stanza file format .... stanza(4)

killall: Terminates all processes started by the user, except the/ .... killall(8)

the time server daemon at system startup timed: Controls .... timed(8)

functionsSee acct(8) startup: Turns on the accounting .... startup(8)

filesystems fstab: Static information about .... fstab(4)

mailstats : Displays statistics about mail traffic .... mailstats(8)

df: Displays statistics on free disk space .... df(8)

nfsstat: Reports NFS statistics .... nfsstat(8)

/Contains information about the status of file transfer requests .... xferstats(4)

/: Contains information about the status of the uucp program/ .... &.Status(4)

rwhod: The system status server .... rwhod(8)

Run command script executed when stopping the system rc0: .... rc0(8)

halt: Stops the processor .... halt(8)

icheck: File system storage consistency check .... icheck(8)

rdump: Copies tothe dump_file storage device all files changed/ .... rdump(8)

/magnetic tape orother specified storage device.See restore(8) .... rrestore(8)

transfers to/ Temporary (TM.*):	Stores data files during	Temporary(TM.*)(4)
trace messages	strace: Displays STREAMS event	strace(8)
strace: Displays	STREAMS event trace messages	strace(8)
in a format defined by the acct	structure in/ /inputthat are	acctprc1(8)
sysconfigtab:	Subsystem definition data base	sysconfigtab(4)
acctcms : Produces command usage	summaries from accounting records	acctcms(8)
process accounting record	summaries /: Outputs selected	acctcom(8)
Outputs connect-time accounting	summaries acctcon1, acctcon2:	acctcon(8)
sa :	Summarizes accounting records	sa(8)
quot:	Summarizes file system ownership	quot(8)
repquota:	Summarizes filesystem quotas	repquota(8)
/records writtenby acctprc1 and	summarizes them according to user/	acctprc2(8)
periodic accountingrecords into	summary files in the/ /or other	monacct(8)
update: Periodically updates the	superblock	update(8)
inetd: The internet	super-server	inetd(8)
device for paging and swapping	swapon: Specifies additional	swapon(8)
additional device for paging and	swapping swapon: Specifies	swapon(8)
writes buffered files to the/	sync: Updates the inode table and	sync(8)
mirrors that are stale/ lvsync:	Synchronizes logical volume	lvsync(8)
mirrors that are stale/ vgsync:	Synchronizes logical volume	vgsync(8)
configuration	sysconfig: Modifies the system	sysconfig(8)
configuration database	sysconfigdb: Maintains the system	sysconfigdb(8)
definition data base	sysconfigtab: Subsystem	sysconfigtab(4)
	syslogd: Logs system messages	syslogd(8)
cron: The	system clock daemon	cron(8)
sysconfigdb: Maintains the	system configuration database	sysconfigdb(8)
config: Builds	system configuration files	config(8)
sysconfig: Modifies the	system configuration	sysconfig(8)
fsck : Provides file	system consistency check and/	fsck(8)
fsdb: File	system debugger	fsdb(8)
rdump: Performs incremental file	system dumps dump,	dump(8)
dumpfs: Dump UFS file	system information	dumpfs(8)
syslogd: Logs	system messages	syslogd(8)
shutdown: Ends	system operation	shutdown(8)
quot: Summarizes file	system ownership	quot(8)
quotaoff: Turns file	system quotas offSee quotaon(8)	quotaoff(8)
the time server daemon at	system startup timed: Controls	timed(8)
rwhod: The	system status server	rwhod(8)
icheck: File	system storage consistency check	icheck(8)
systems fastboot: Reboots the	system without checking file	fastboot(8)
fasthalt: Halts the	system	fasthalt(8)
newfs: Constructs a new file	system	newfs(8)
require the resources of a remote	system /for running commands that	Execute(X.*)(4)
can execute commands on the local	system /systems and users that	hosts.equiv(4)
or more volume groups from the	system /the definition of one	vgremove(8)
Constructs a prototype file	system mkproto:	mkproto(8)
script executed when stopping the	system rc0: Run command	rc0(8)
a core dump of the operating	system savecore: Saves	savecore(8)
Tune up an existing UFS file	system tunefs:	tunefs(8)
containing the names of remote	systems and users that can/ /file	hosts.equiv(4)
files during transfers to remote	systems /(TM.*): Stores data	Temporary(TM.*)(4)

uucp program contacts with remote systems /about the status of the .... &.Status(4)

and command executions on remote systems /for file transfers .... Directories(4)

data, and executefiles to remote systems /Transfers uucp command, ... uucico(8)

data to be sent to remote systems Data (D.*): Contains .... Data(D.*)(4)

the system without checking file systems fastboot: Reboots .... fastboot(8)

contact attempts from unknown systems Foreign: Logs .... Foreign(4)

umount: Mounts and dismounts file systems mount, ... mount(8)

access attempts by unknown remote systems remote.unknown: Logs .... remote.unknown(4)

umount: Unmounts file systemsSee mount(8) .... umount(8)

to the/ sync: Updates the inode table and writes buffered files .... sync(8)

routed: Manages network routing tables .... routed(8)

Address Resolution Protocol (ARP) tables /Displays and controls .... arp(8)

Manually manipulates the routing tables route: .... route(8)

communications server for the talk(1)command talkd: The remote .... talkd(8)

server for the talk(1)command talkd: The remote communications .... talkd(8)

Allows remote access to magnetic tape devices rmt: .... rmt(8)

/files from a remote magnetic tape orother specified storage/ .... rrestore(8)

/rrestore: Restores files from tapes written with the dump or/ .... restore(8)

between the uucpprogram and TCP/IP /Manages communications .... uucpd(8)

remote connections over a telephone line /used to establish .... Dialcodes(4)

/Contains the initial digits of telephone numbers used to/ .... Dialcodes(4)

telnetd: The DARPA TELNET protocol server .... telnetd(8)

protocol server telnetd: The DARPA TELNET .... telnetd(8)

files during transfers to remote/ Temporary (TM.*): Stores data .... Temporary(TM.*)(4)

the/ /: Contains the log file and temporary files associated with .... mqueue(4)

/usr/spool/uucp/.Xqtdir: Contains temporary files used by the uuxqt/ .... &.Xqtdir(4)

/usr/spool/uucp/.Workspace: Holds temporary files used internally/ .... &.Workspace(4)

line discipline getty: Sets the terminal type, modes, speed, and .... getty(8)

by the user, except the/ killall: Terminates all processes started .... killall(8)

Generates the line printer ripple test pattern lptest: .... lptest(8)

Transfer Protocol server tftpd: The DARPA Trivial File .... tftpd(8)

/defined by the acct structure in the/usr/include/sys/acct.h header/ .... acctprc1(8)

/specified by File and created by theacctcon1 commandSee acct(8) .... prctmp(8)

file of the accounting data of theprevious daySee acct(8) /ASCII .... prdaily(8)

timedc: Controls the timed daemon .... timedc(8)

daemon at system startup timed: Controls the time server .... timed(8)

timedc: Controls the timed daemon .... timedc(8)

/format for corrupted date and timestamp entries.See fwtmp(8) .... wtmpfix(8)

intermediary/ acctmerg : Merges total accounting files into an .... acctmerg(8)

/command intoconnect time total accounting records.See/ .... acctcon2(8)

prtacct: Formats and displays any total accountingfile specified by/ .... prtacct(8)

turnacct: Provides an interface tothe accton command to turn/ .... turnacct(8)

all files changed/ rdump: Copies tothe dump_file storage device .... rdump(8)

strace: Displays STREAMS event trace messages .... strace(8)

trpt : Transliterates protocol trace .... trpt(8)

: Displays statistics about mail traffic mailstats .... mailstats(8)

Command (C.*): Contains file transfer directions for the/ .... Command(C.*)(4)

ftpd: The DARPA Internet File Transfer Protocol server .... ftpd(8)

tftpd: The DARPA Trivial File Transfer Protocol server .... tftpd(8)

about the status of file transfer requests /information .... xferstats(4)

/Contains queued requests for file transfers and command executions/ .... Directories(4)

/(TM.*): Stores data files during transfers to remote systems .... Temporary(TM.*)(4)

executefiles to remote/ uucico: Transfers uucp command, data, and .... uucico(8)

trpt : Transliterates protocol trace .... trpt(8)

: Schedules work for the file transport program uusched .... uusched(8)

files used internally by file transport programs /temporary .... &.Workspace(4)

server tftpd: The DARPA Trivial File Transfer Protocol .... tftpd(8)

trace trpt : Transliterates protocol trpt(8)

system tunefs: Tune up an existing UFS file .... tunefs(8)

file system tunefs: Tune up an existing UFS .... tunefs(8)

interface tothe accton command to turn process accounting on or/ /an .... turnacct(8)

tothe accton command to turn/ turnacct: Provides an interface .... turnacct(8)

offSee acctprc(8) accton: Turns account processing on and .... accton(8)

quotaon(8) quotaoff: Turns file system quotas offSee .... quotaoff(8)

quotaon, quotaoff: Turns filesystem quotas on or off .... quotaon(8)

functionsSee acct(8) startup: Turns on the accounting .... startup(8)

acct(8) shutacct: Turns process accounting offSee .... shutacct(8)

getty: Sets the terminal type, modes, speed, and line/ .... getty(8)

dumpfs: Dump UFS file system information .... dumpfs(8)

tunefs: Tune up an existing UFS file system .... tunefs(8)

systems mount, umount: Mounts and dismounts file .... mount(8)

mount(8) umount: Unmounts file systemsSee .... umount(8)

chargefee: Charges the number of units specified bythe Number/ .... chargefee(8)

/Logs access attempts by unknown remote systems .... remote.unknown(4)

Logs contact attempts from unknown systems Foreign: .... Foreign(4)

umount: Unmounts file systemsSee mount(8) .... umount(8)

superblock update: Periodically updates the .... update(8)

writes buffered files to/ sync: Updates the inode table and .... sync(8)

update: Periodically updates the superblock .... update(8)

lastlogin: Updatesthe/ .... lastlogin(8)

acctcms : Produces command usage summaries from accounting/ .... acctcms(8)

/Creates a version of the basic user database organized for/ .... mkpasswd(8)

/and summarizes them according to user ID and nameSee acctprc(8) .... acctprc2(8)

Generates disk accounting data by user ID diskusg : .... diskusg(8)

networks fingerd: The user information server for .... fingerd(8)

adduser: Adds a new user interactively .... adduser(8)

the login name specified by the User parameterSee acct(8) /to .... chargefee(8)

edquota: Edits user quotas .... edquota(8)

/an individual record for each user to standard output.See/ .... acctdusg(8)

/all processes started by the user, except the calling process .... killall(8)

/file to show the last date each userlogged inSee acct(8) .... lastlogin(8)

/the names of remote systems and users that can execute commands/ .... hosts.equiv(4)

/the data that the named daemon uses to initialize the BIND/ .... named.*(4)

shell/ acctcon2: This command is usually called bythe runacct .... acctcon2(8)

output See/ acctwtmp: Writesa utmp formatted record to standard .... acctwtmp(8)

directories required by uucp uucheck: Check for files and .... uucheck(8)

errors : Contains a record of uucico daemon errors .... errors(4)

file transfer directions for the uucico daemon /(C.*): Contains .... Command(C.*)(4)

Contains debug messages from the uucico daemon audit: .... audit(4)

data, and executefiles to remote/ uucico: Transfers uucp command, ... uucico(8)

files from the uucp spool/ uucleanup: Deletes selected old .... uucleanup(8)

executefiles/ uucico: Transfers uucp command, data, and .... uucico(8)

systems /about the status of the uucp program contacts with remote .... &.Status(4)
/: Contains the uucp program log files .... &.Log(4)
/: Contains the combined uucp program log files .... &.Old(4)
administrative files used by the uucp program /Contains .... &.Admin(4)
Dialers: Lists modems used for uucp remote communications links .... Dialers(4)
selected old files from the uucp spool directory /Deletes .... uucleanup(8)
files and directories required by uucp uucheck: Check for .... uucheck(8)
between the uucpprogram and/ uucpd: Manages communications .... uucpd(8)
communications between the uucpprogram and TCP/IP /Manages .... uucpd(8)
file transport program uusched : Schedules work for the .... uusched(8)
/temporary files used by the uuxqt daemon to execute remote/ .... &.Xqtdir(4)
database/ mkpasswd: Creates a version of the basic user .... mkpasswd(8)
of a volume group to yes or no vgchange: Sets the availability .... vgchange(8)
vgcreate: Creates a volume group .... vgcreate(8)
about volume groups vgdisplay: Displays information .... vgdisplay(8)
by adding physical volumes to it vgextend: Extend a volume group .... vgextend(8)
by removing one or more physical/ vgreduce: Reduce a volume group .... vgreduce(8)
of one or more volume groups/ vgremove: Removes the definition .... vgremove(8)
volume mirrors that are stale in/ vgsync: Synchronizes logical .... vgsync(8)
vipw: Edits the /etc/passwd file .... vipw(8)
volumes to it vgextend: Extend a volume group by adding physical .... vgextend(8)
more physical/ vgreduce: Reduce a volume group by removing one or .... vgreduce(8)
/Sets the availability of a volume group to yes or no .... vgchange(8)
vgcreate: Creates a volume group .... vgcreate(8)
that can be used as part of a volume group /a physical volume .... pvcreate(8)
or more physical volumes within a volume group /about one .... pvdisplay(8)
or more logical volumes from a volume group /Removes one .... lvremove(8)
of a physical volume in a volume group /the characteristics .... pvchange(8)
Creates a logical volume in a volume group lvcreate: .... lvcreate(8)
/the definition of one or more volume groups from the system .... vgremove(8)
Displays information about volume groups vgdisplay: .... vgdisplay(8)
lvcreate: Creates a logical volume in a volume group .... lvcreate(8)
the characteristics of a physical volume in a volume group /Changes .... pvchange(8)
one/ lvsync: Synchronizes logical volume mirrors that are stale in .... lvsync(8)
one/ vgsync: Synchronizes logical volume mirrors that are stale in .... vgsync(8)
of/ pvcreate: Creates a physical volume that can be used as part .... pvcreate(8)
/physical extentsfrom one physical volume to one or more other/ .... pvmove(8)
extents allocated to a logical volume /the numberof physical .... lvextend(8)
extents allocated to a logical volume /the numberof physical .... lvreduce(8)
are stale in one ormore logical volume /volume mirrors that .... lvsync(8)
the characteristics of a logical volume lvchange: Changes .... lvchange(8)
/Removes one or more logical volumes from a volume group .... lvremove(8)
by removing one or more physical volumes from it /a volume group .... vgreduce(8)
a volume group by adding physical volumes to it vgextend: Extend .... vgextend(8)
/about one or more physical volumes within a volume group .... pvdisplay(8)
to one or more other physical volumes /one physical volume .... pvmove(8)
information about logical volumes lvdisplay: Displays .... lvdisplay(8)
one or more physical volumes within a volume group /about .... pvdisplay(8)
fastboot: Reboots the system without checking file systems .... fastboot(8)
/parameter, gives read (r) and write (w) permissionsto the file/ .... nulladm(8)
/bythe runacct shell procedure to write asequence of login and/ .... acctcon1(8)

/by the number of hard links then writes an individual record for/ .... acctdusg(8)

sync: Updates the inode table and writes buffered files to the disk .... sync(8)

/file or the named file and writes to standard output any/ .... grpck(8)

standard output See/ acctwtmp: Writesa utmp formatted record to .... acctwtmp(8)

/Restores files from tapes written with the dump or rdump/ .... restore(8)

/from standard input, the records writtenby acctprc1 and summarizes/ .... acctprc2(8)

inputor File records in the/ wtmpfix: Examines standard .... wtmpfix(8)

accounting/ fwtmp, acctwtmp, wtmpfix: Modify connect time .... fwtmp(8)

about the status of file/ xferstats: Contains information .... xferstats(4)

availability of a volume group to yes or no vgchange: Sets the .... vgchange(8)

format/ /Examines standard inputor File records in the wtmp .... wtmpfix(8)

/inputor File records in the wtmp format for corrupted date/ .... wtmpfix(8)

consistency check and/ fsck : Provides file system .... fsck(8)

/runacct shell procedure to write asequence of login and logout/ .... acctcon1(8)

/shell procedure and converts asequence of login session/ .... acctcon2(8)

produced by the acctcon1 command intoconnect time total/ /records .... acctcon2(8)

Chapter 1

Commands

This chapter contains reference pages documenting all OSF/1 system administration and network management commands. The reference pages are arranged in alphabetical order (U.S. English).

ac(8)

ac

Purpose   Outputs connect-session records

Synopsis   /usr/sbin/ac [-dp] [-w *filename*] [*user(s)* ...]

The **ac** command prints the total connect time in hours to the nearest hundreth for all users, or the connect time for any user(s) specified with the **-p** flag.

Flags

-d   Outputs the total connect time for each midnight-to-midnight period for which a **wtmp** file exists. When *user(s)* is specified, this flag limits the output to the login names specified by any *user(s)* parameter(s).

-p   Outputs the connect time total by individual login name of the user specified with the **-p** flag and the *user(s)* parameter. Omission of this flag only permits a total for the midnight-to-midnight time period for all logged in users to be produced.

-w *filename*
            Specifies a **wtmp** file other than the **/var/adm/wtmp** file. The **wtmp** file you access for data may have been created automatically by some shell script administration command; for example, **runacct**, or manually by the system administrator when the original **/var/adm/wtmp** file becomes too large.

Description

The **ac** command prints to the default output device the total connect time in hours to the nearest hundreth for all users, or the connect time for any user(s) specified with the **-p** flag. It also prints the names of users specified by the *user(s)* parameter who have logged in during the life of the current **/var/adm/wtmp** file.

Connect-time records are written by the **init** and the **login** programs and are collected in the **/var/adm/wtmp** file, when such a file exists. When a **/var/adm/wtmp** file does not exist, no connect-time accounting records are written; consequently, when connect-time records are wanted, the system administrator should create a **/var/adm/wtmp** file that has an initial record length of 0 (zero). Records in **wtmp** files (there may be more than one such file) should be processed periodically to keep the files from becoming too large.

When you use the **runacct** command in a shell script, additional **wtmp** files can be automatically created whenever the current **wtmp** file becomes too large. You can output the contents of any of these other files when you specify the **-w** flag and the desired **wtmp** *filename*.

The **ac** command is run independently with respect to any accounting shell procedure created or run by any of the **acct/*** shell procedures or **runacct** commands.

Examples

1. To obtain an output of the total connect time for all users who have logged in during the life of the current **wtmp** data file, enter:

    /usr/sbin/ac

2. To obtain an output of the total connect time for **smith** and **jones** as recorded in the default **wtmp** data file, enter:

    /usr/sbin/ac smith jones

3. To obtain an output of the connect time subtotals for **smith** and **jones** as recorded in the default **wtmp** data file, enter:

    /usr/sbin/ac -p smith jones

Files

/usr/sbin/ac
>   Specifies the command path.

/var/adm/wtmp
>   The active data file for the collection of connect-time records

Related Information

Commands: **init(8), login(1)**

acct/*

Purpose   Provides accounting commands for shell scripts

Synopsis   **/usr/sbin/acct/chargefee** *User Number*

/usr/sbin/acct/ckpacct [*BlockSize*]

/usr/sbin/acct/dodisk [**-o**] [*File ....*]

/usr/sbin/acct/lastlogin

/usr/sbin/acct/monacct [*Number*]

/usr/sbin/acct/nulladm [*File ....*]

/usr/sbin/acct/prctmp *File ....*

/usr/sbin/acct/prdaily [[**-l**] [*mmdd*]] | [**-c**]

/usr/sbin/acct/prtacct [**-f** *Specification*] [**-v**] *File* [*'Heading'*]

/usr/sbin/acct/remove

/usr/sbin/acct/shutacct [*'Reason'*]

/usr/sbin/acct/startup

/usr/sbin/acct/turnacct *on* | *off* | *switch*

Description

There are 13 commands in the **acct/*** group that, along with other accounting commands, permit you to obtain a wide range of system accounting records and files. When used in shell scripts, many of the **acct/*** commands permit you to produce daily accounting records and files when called by the **runacct** command (a command outside of the **acct/*** group). Some of the **acct/*** commands are called when system activity is interrupted and must be restarted or when active accounting files become too large; still other **acct/*** commands may be used by a system administrator to perform occasional accounting procedures.

Most often, periodic accounting files are obtained by **acct/*** commands written to a **crontabs** file and which are processed by the **cron** daemon. These periodic accounting files consist of a collection of records that are produced at the end of any process and on a daily and monthly periodic basis.

You may specify a prime-time period for any 24-hour weekday. The prime time period is those contiguous hours of a weekday for which premium fees might be charged for resource use. Nonprime time hours are those contiguous hours that are not defined as prime time. Non-prime time also includes weekends and any holidays listed in the file **/usr/sbin/acct/holidays**.

Recommended accounting set-up procedures include entries in the **/usr/spool/cron/crontabs/adm** file to run two **acct/*** commands that are usually processed on a daily basis during nonprime time: 1) the **dodisk** command, which invokes the generation of disk-usage accounting files and 2) the **ckpacct** command, which is used to check the size of the **/var/adm/pacct** process accounting files. Another **crontabs** accounting command is **monacct**, which is used to produce monthly summary accounting files in the **/var/adm/acct/fiscal** accounting subdirectory from the daily accounting files. The following 13 commands may be used in shell scripts.

chargefee *User Number*

> The **chargefee** command is used by the system administrator to charge the number of units specified by the *Number* parameter to the login name specified by the *User* parameter. The *Number* value may be an integer or a decimal value. The **chargefee** command writes a record to the **/var/adm/fee** file. This information is then merged with other accounting records with the **acctmerg** command to create a daily **/var/adm/fee** report.

> The **chargefee** command uses the **printpw** command to get the list of all users stored in the password database.

ckpacct [*BlockSize*]

> The **ckpacct** command is used to check the size of the active process accounting file, **/var/adm/pacct**. Normally, the **cron** daemon processes this command from the **crontabs** file. When the size of the active data files exceeds the number of blocks specified by the *BlockSize* parameter, the **ckpacct** command is used to invoke the **turnacct switch** command to turn off process accounting. The default value for the *BlockSize* parameter is 500.

> When the number of free disk blocks in the **var** file system falls below 500, the **ckpacct** command is used to inhibit process accounting by invoking the **turnacct** *off* command. When at least 500 free disk blocks are again available, account processing is reactivated. This feature is sensitive to how frequently **ckpacct** is run.

> When the environment variable **MAILCOM** is set to **mail root adm**, a mail message is sent to the super-user (root) and to **adm** in case of an error.

dodisk [**-o**] [*File* ....]

> The **dodisk** command initiates disk-usage accounting by calling the **diskusg** command and the **acctdisk** command.

> When you specify the **-o** flag with the **dodisk** command, a more thorough but slower version of disk accounting by login directory is initiated with the **acctdusg** command. Normally, the **cron** daemon

runs the **dodisk** command. The following flag may be used with the **dodisk** command:

-o   Calls the **acctdusg** command instead of the **diskusg** command to initiate disk accounting by login directory.

By default, the **dodisk** command does disk accounting on special files recorded in the **/etc/fstab** file. But when you specify file names with the *File* parameter, disk accounting is done on only those files.

When you do not specify the **-o** flag, the *File* parameter should specify special filenames of mountable file systems. When you specify both **-o** and one or more *File(s)*, *File(s)* should specify mount points of mounted file systems.

lastlogin The **lastlogin** command updates the **/var/adm/acct/sum/loginlog** file to show the last date each user logged in. Normally, the **runacct** procedure, running under the **cron** daemon, calls this command and adds the information to the daily report; however, the **lastlogin** command can also be entered by the system administrator. The **lastlogin** commands uses the **printpw** command to get a list of all users whose name and user ID are stored in the password database file.

monacct [*Number*]

The **monacct** command collects daily or other periodic accounting records into summary files in the **/var/adm/acct/fiscal** subdirectory. After monthly summary files are produced, **monacct** removes the old accounting files from the **/var/adm/acct/sum** subdirectory and replaces them with the newly created summary files. The **cron** daemon should run this command once each month on the first day of the following month or some other specified day after all the dailys have been produced. (The **monacct** example shows how to enter this command for the **cron** daemon.)

The *Number* parameter is a numerical value in the range $1 < n < 12$ (where *n* is the month) that indicates the month for which daily files are processed. The default value used for the *Number* parameter is the current month. The **monacct** command stores the newly created summary files in the **/var/adm/acct/fiscal** subdirectory and restarts new summary files in **/var/adm/acct/sum**, the cumulative summaries to which daily record summaries are appended.

nulladm [*File* ....]

> The **nulladm** command creates the file specified in the *File* parameter, gives read (**r**) and write (**w**) permissions to the file owner and group, read (**r**) permission to other users, and ensures that the file owner and group is **adm**. Various accounting shell procedures invoke the **nulladm** command. The system administrator uses this command to set up active data files, such as the **/var/adm/wtmp** file.

prctmp *File* ....

> The system administrator may use the **prctmp** command to output the session record file specified by *File* and created by the **acctcon1** command (this is normally the **/var/adm/acct/nite/ctmp** file).

prdaily [[**-l**] [*mmdd*]] | [**-c**]

> The **prdaily** command is invoked from the **runacct** shell procedure to format an ASCII file of the accounting data of the previous day. The records making up this file are located in the **/var/adm/acct/sum/rprt***mmdd* files, where *mmdd* is the month and day for which the file is produced. Use the *mmdd* parameter to specify a date other than the current day. The following flags may be used with the **prdaily** command:
>
> | | |
> |---|---|
> | **-c** | Reports exceptional resource usage by command. May be used only on accounting records for the current day. |
> | **-l** [*mmdd*] | Reports exceptional usage by login ID for the specified date. |

prtacct [**-f** *Specification*] [**-v**] *File* ['*Heading*']

> The **prtacct** command formats and displays any total accounting file specified by the *File* parameter; records for these files are defined by a type **tacct** structure in the **tacct.h** include file. You can enter the **prtacct** command to output any **tacct** file to the default output device. For example, you may output a daily report keyed to connect time, to process time, to disk usage, and to printer usage. To specify a title for the report, specify a name for the *Heading* parameter with enclosed single or double quotes. The following flags may be used with the **prtacct** command:
>
> | | |
> |---|---|
> | **-f** *Specification* | Selects type **tacct** structure members to be output, using the structure-member selection mechanism specified for the **acctmerg** command. |
> | **-v** | Produces verbose output in which more precise notation is used for floating-point numbers. |
> | *Heading* | Specifies a heading for report members. |

acct(8)

The type **tacct** structure defines a total accounting record format, parts of which are used by various accounting commands. Members of the type **tacct** structure whose data types are specified as an array of two *double* elements have both prime-time and nonprime values. The type **tacct** structure has the following members.

uid_t ta_uid	User ID.
char ta_name[NSZ]	A field for the login name with the same number of characters **NSZ** as the *ut_user* member of the **utmp** structure.
double ta_cpu[2]	Cumulative CPU time in minutes.
double ta_kcore[2]	Cumulative k-core time in minutes.
double ta_io[2]	Cumulative number of characters transferred in blocks of 512 bytes.
double ta_rw[2]	Cumultive number of blocks read and written.
double ta_con[2]	Cumulative connect time in minutes.
double ta_du	Cumulative disk-usage time in minutes.
long ta_qsys	Queueing system (printer) fee in number of pages.
double ta_fee	Special services fee expressed in units.
long ta_pc	A count of the number of processes.
unsigned short ta_sc	A count of the number of login sessions.
unsigned short ta_dc	A count of the number of disk samples.

remove The **remove** command deletes all **/var/adm/acct/sum/wtmp***, **/var/adm/acct/sum/pacct***, and **/var/adm/acct/nite/lock*** files as part of the daily cleanup procedure called by the **runacct** command.

shutacct [*'Reason'*]

The **shutacct** command turns process accounting off and adds a *'Reason'* record to the **/var/adm/wtmp** file. This command is usually invoked during a system shutdown.

startup The **startup** command turns on the accounting functions and adds a reason record to the **/var/adm/wtmp** file. Usually it is called from the **/etc/rc** command file, when the system is started up. See the start-up example for the command line to add to the **/etc/rc** file when you do the set-up procedures.

turnacct *on* | *off* | *switch*

> The **turnacct** command provides an interface to the **accton** command to turn process accounting on or off, or to create a new **/var/adm/pacct***n* process accounting file. This command can only be executed by a superuser or by the **adm** login name. Only one of the arguments *on*, *off*, or *switch* may be used.
>
> | | |
> |---|---|
> | *on* | Turns process accounting on. |
> | *off* | Turns process accounting off. |
> | *switch* | The *switch* flag is used to create a new **/var/adm/pacct***n* file when the current **/var/adm/pacct***n* file is too large. The suffix *n* (where *n* is a positive integer) indicates the previous active **/var/adm/pacct***n* file. After the currently active **/var/adm/pacct***n* file is renamed, a new active **/var/adm/pacct** file is created and process accounting is restarted. |
>
> This command is usually called by the **ckpacct** command, running under the **cron** daemon, to keep the active **pacct** data file down to a manageable size.

Notes

You should not share accounting files among nodes in a distributed environment. Each node should have its own copy of the various accounting files.

When you are also using the **sa** command, **sa** does not know whether information is stored in the incremental **/var/adm/pacct***n* file or in any other **/var/adm/pacct***n* summary file by the **acct/*** commands (see the **turnacct** command).

Examples

1. To charge **smith** for **10** units of work on a financial report, enter:

   /usr/sbin/acct/chargefee smith 10

   A record is created in the **/var/adm/fee** file, which the **acctmerg** command is subsequently instructed to merge with records in other accounting files to produce the daily report.

2. To check the size of a **/var/adm/pacct***n* summary accounting file, add the following instruction to the **/usr/spool/cron/crontabs/adm** shell script:

   5 * * * * /usr/sbin/acct/ckpacct

   This example shows another instruction that the **cron** daemon reads and acts upon when it is included in the **/usr/spool/cron/crontabs/adm** shell script file. The **ckpacct** command is set to run at 5 minutes past every hour

(5 *) every day. This command is only one of many accounting instructions normally passed to the **cron** daemon from the **/usr/spool/cron/crontabs/adm** shell script file. See chapter 9 of the *OSF/1 System Administrator's Guide* for details.

3.   To initiate disk-usage accounting, add the following to the **/usr/spool/cron/crontabs/adm** shell script file:

0 2 * * 4 /usr/sbin/acct/dodisk

This example illustrates a shell script instruction that the **cron** daemon reads and then processes. The **dodisk** command runs at 2 AM (0 2) each Thursday (4). This command is one of many accounting instructions normally passed to the **cron** daemon from a **/usr/spool/cron/crontabs/adm** shell script file. See chapter 9 of the *OSF/1 System Administrator's Guide* for details.

4.   To produce a monthly accounting report, at the beginning of each month, add the following instruction to the **/usr/spool/cron/crontabs/adm** file:

15 5 1 * * /usr/sbin/acct/monacct

This example is an instruction that the **cron** deamon reads and then processes. The **monacct** command runs at 5:15 (15 5) the first day of each month (1). This command is only one of many accounting instructions normally passed to the **cron** daemon from the **/usr/spool/cron/crontabs/adm** shell script file. See chapter 9 of the *OSF/1 System Administrator's Guide* for details.

5.   To turn on the accounting functions when the system is started up, add the following to the **/etc/rc** file:

/bin/su - adm -c /usr/sbin/acct/startup

The startup shell procedure records the time and cleans up the records produced the previous day.

Files

/usr/sbin/acct/*

    Specifies the command path.

/usr/include/sys/acct.h, /usr/include/utmp.h

    Header files defining structures used to organize accounting information.

/var/adm/fee

    Accumulates the fees charged to each login name.

/var/adm/pacct

    Current database file for process accounting information.

/var/adm/pacct*n*

Another process accounting database file, which is produced when the /var/adm/pacct file gets too large.

/var/adm/wtmp

Login/logout database file.

/usr/sbin/acct/ptelus.awk

Shell procedure that calculates limits for exceptional usage by the login ID.

/usr/sbin/acct/ptecms.awk

Shell procedure that calculates limits of exceptional usage by command name.

/var/adm/acct/nite

Working directory that contains daily accounting database files.

/etc/fstab

Contains information about file systems.

/var/adm/acct/sum

Working subdirectory that contains accounting summary database files.

Related Information

Commands: **acctcms(8)**, **acctcom(8)**, **acctcon(8)**, **acctmerg(8)**, **acctprc(8)**, **fwtmp(8)**, **printpw(8)**, **runacct(8)**

Daemons: **cron(8)**

Calls: **acct(2)**

acctcms

Purpose   Produces command usage summaries from accounting records

Synopsis   **/usr/sbin/acct/acctcms** [**-acjnspot**] *file* ....

Flags

-a   Displays output in ASCII summary format rather than binary summary
            format. Each output line contains the following information under its
            own heading: command name, the number of times the command was
            run, total K-core time, total CPU time, total real time, mean memory size
            in kilobytes (KB), mean CPU time per command, CPU usage (called hog
            factor), the number of characters transferred, and the number of blocks
            read. All times are expressed in minutes.

            The **acctcms** command normally sorts its output in descending order by
            total K-core minutes. The unit *K-core minutes* is a measure of the amount
            of storage used (in KB) multiplied by the amount of time the buffer was
            in use. The hog factor is the total CPU time divided by the total real time.
            The default command summary output format has the following
            headings.

```
                              TOTAL COMMAND SUMMARY
COMMAND    NUMBER    TOTAL     TOTAL     TOTAL     MEAN    MEAN     HOG      CHAR     BLOCKS
NAME       CMDS      KOREMIN   CPU-MIN   REAL-MIN  SIZE-K  CPU-MIN  FACTOR   TRNSFD   READ
```

-c   Sorts in descending order by total CPU time rather than total K-core
            minutes.

-j   Combines all commands called only once by writing "*****other**" in the
            COMMAND NAME column.

-n   Sorts in decending order by the number of times each command was
            called.

-o   Displays a command summary of nonprime-time commands.

-p   Displays a command summary of prime-time commands.

-s   Assumes that any named file that follows this flag is in binary format.

-t   Processes all records as total accounting records. The default binary
            format splits each heading into prime time and nonprime-time parts.

Description

The **acctcms** command outputs data in a format called TOTAL COMMAND
SUMMARY. This command reads each file specified by the *file* parameter,
combines and sorts all records for identically named processes, and writes them in
a binary format to the output device. Files are usually organized in the **acct** file
format. When you use the **-o** and **-p** flags together, the **acctcms** command produces
a summary report that combines commands processed during both prime and
nonprime time. All the output summaries specify total usage, except for the number
of times run, CPU minutes, and real minutes, which are split into prime and
nonprime minutes.

Examples

To collect command accounting records from one or more source files into a
command summary file called **today** and to maintain a running total summary of
commands in a file called **cmtotal**, add the following lines to an accounting shell
script:

acctcms [source *File(s)* **....] > today**

cp total prev_tot

acctcms -s today prev_tot > cmtotal

acctcms -a -s cmtotal

First, the **acctcms** command is used to redirect command records in *File(s)* that
you specify to a file called **today**. Next the old **total** command summary file is
renamed **prev_tot**. Then the command summary records that are collected in the
today and the **prev_tot** files are redirected to a new command summary file called
cmtotal. These are all binary files. The last **acctcms** command outputs to the
default output device the contents of the **cmtotal** file in the ASCII default
command summary format previously described, so that the report may be viewed.

Files

/usr/sbin/acct/acctcms
> Specifies the command path.

/usr/sbin/acct/holidays
> This is where prime time is set.

/usr/include/sys/acct.h, **/usr/include/utmp.h**
> Accounting header files that define formats for writing accounting files.

acctcms(8)

Related Information

Commands: **acct(8)**, **runacct(8)**

Calls: **acct(2)**

acctcom

Purpose   Outputs selected process accounting record summaries

Synopsis   **/usr/sbin/acct/acctcom** -[q or o] -[**abhikmrtv**] -[**C** *seconds* **g** *group*
H *factor* **I** *number* **l** *line* **n** *pattern* **O** *seconds* **u** *user* **e** *time* **E** *time* **s** *time* **S** *time*]
[*file(s)*]

The **acctcom** command reads process accounting records from files specified by
the *file(s)* parameter from standard input or from the **/var/adm/pacct** file. Records
from the specified input source are written to the default output device.

Flags

-a
Lists average statistics about the processes selected. Statistics are
displayed at the end of the output records in the format *var=val* (where
var is the listed variable and *val* is a numerical value to the nearest
hundreth) and in the listed order.

Variable	Value
CMDS	The total number of commands listed in the named *file(s)*.
REAL	Average real time per process.
CPU	Average CPU time per process.
USER	Average user CPU time per process.
SYS	Average system CPU time per process.
CHAR	Average number of characters transferred.
BLK	Average number of blocks transferred.
USR/TOT	Average CPU factor (average user time divided by total CPU time).
HOG	Average hog factor (average CPU time divided by average elapsed time).

-b
Lists backward in time-ascending order, showing the most recent
commands first. This flag has no effect when the **acctcom** command
reads from the default input device. The column heading format is the
same as the default column heading format.

-C *seconds*
Lists processes whose total CPU time (system time + user time) exceeds
seconds. The column heading format is the same as the default column
heading format.

1–15

acctcom(8)

-e *time*   Lists processes starting at or before the specified START BEFORE time. You may use the **NLTIME** environment variable to specify the order of hours, minutes, and seconds. The default order is *hh:mm:ss*. The column heading format is as follows:

```
ACCOUNTING RECORDS FROM: day mon date hh:mm:ss yy
START BEFORE: day mon date hh:mm:ss yy
COMMAND                      START END     REAL    CPU     MEAN
NAME        USER TTYNAME     TIME  TIME  (SECS) (SECS) SIZE(K)
```

-E *time*   Lists processes ending at or before the specified END BEFORE time. You may use the **NLTIME** environment variable to specify the order of hours, minutes, and seconds. The default order is *hh:mm:ss*. When you specify the same time for both the **-E** and **-S** flags, the **acctcom** command displays processes that existed at the specified time. The column heading format is as follows:

```
ACCOUNTING RECORDS FROM: day mon date hh:mm:ss yy
END BEFORE   : day mon date hh:mm:ss yy
COMMAND                      START END     REAL    CPU     MEAN
NAME        USER TTYNAME     TIME  TIME  (SECS) (SECS)  SIZE(K)
```

-f   Adds columns to list the state of the **fork/exec** flag F (means of executing another process) and the system exit value STAT (0 or an error code) in the output by adding F and STAT columns, respectively, to the output column headings. The column heading format is as follows:

```
ACCOUNTING RECORDS FROM: day mon date hh:mm:ss yy
COMMAND                      START END     REAL    CPU     MEAN
NAME        USER TTYNAME     TIME  TIME  (SECS) (SECS) SIZE(K)F STAT
```

-g *group*   Lists processes belonging to *group*. You may specify either the group ID or the group name. The column heading format is the same as the default column heading format.

-h   The MEAN SIZE(K) column heading is replaced with the HOG FACTOR heading to list the fraction of total available CPU time consumed by the process (see HOG below). The column heading format is as follows:

```
ACCOUNTING RECORDS FROM: day mon date hh:mm:ss yy
COMMAND              START    END     REAL    CPU     HOG
NAME        USER TTYNAME     TIME  (SECS) (SECS) FACTOR
```

-H *hogfactor*

    Lists processes that exceed *hogfactor*. The column heading format is the same as the default column heading format.

-i   The `MEAN SIZE(K)` column heading is replaced with the `CHARS TRANSFD` heading to list the number of characters transferred during read or write I/O operations. The `BLOCKS READ` column is added to list the number of blocks transferred. The column heading format is as follows:

```
ACCOUNTING RECORDS FROM: day mon date hh:mm:ss yy
COMMAND                    START END    REAL   CPU  CHARS  BLOCKS
NAME      USER TTYNAME     TIME  TIME (SECS) (SECS) TRANSFD  READ
```

-I *number*

Lists processes transferring more than *number* characters. The column heading format is the same as the default column heading format.

-k   The `MEAN SIZE(K)` column heading is replaced with the `KCORE MIN` heading to list the total K-core minutes. The column heading format is as follows:

```
ACCOUNTING RECORDS FROM: day mon date hh:mm:ss yy
COMMAND                    START END    REAL   CPU KCORE
NAME      USER TTYNAME     TIME  TIME (SECS) (SECS)  MIN
```

-l *line*   Lists only processes belonging to workstation /**dev**/*line*. The column heading format is the same as the default column heading format.

-m   Lists mean process memory used. The **-h** flag or **-k** flag turns off the **-m** flag. The column heading format is the same as the default column heading format.

-n *pattern*

Lists all commands matching *pattern*, where *pattern* is a regular expression, similar to those use with the **ed** command. The column heading format is the same as the default column heading format.

selflag **-o** *file*

Copies all *selflag* process records to *file* in the **acct** binary format. The *selflag* process records are those that can be selected using the **-C, -e, -E, -g, -H, -I, -l, -n, -O, -s, -S,** and **-u** flags. If no *selflag* is specified, all process records are copied. No column heading format is printed except the date and time the accounting records are taken from.

```
ACCOUNTING RECORDS FROM: day mon date hh:mm:ss yy
```

-O *seconds*

Lists processes with CPU system time exceeding *seconds*. The column heading format is the same as the default column heading format.

-q   Does not produce a listing. Only outputs the average statistics that are produced at the end of a listing when the **-a** flag is used.

acctcom(8)

-r Lists CPU factor. The default heading `MEAN SIZE(K)` column is changed to `CPU FACTOR` (see `USR/TOT`). The column heading format is as follows:

```
ACCOUNTING RECORDS FROM: day mon date hh:mm:ss yy
COMMAND                     START END   REAL  CPU   CPU
NAME        USER TTYNAME    TIME  TIME (SECS)(SECS)FACTOR
```

-s *time* Lists only those processes that existed on or after the specified `END AFTER` time. You can use the **NLTIME** environment variable to specify the order of hours, minutes, and seconds. The default order is *hh:mm:ss*. The column heading format is as follows:

```
ACCOUNTING RECORDS FROM: day mon date hh:mm:ss yy
END AFTER    : day mon date hh:mm:ss yy
COMMAND                     START END   REAL  CPU   MEAN
NAME        USER TTYNAME    TIME  TIME (SECS)(SECS) SIZE(K)
```

-S *time* List only those processes starting at or after the specified `START AFTER` time. You can use the **NLTIME** environment variable to specify the order of hours, minutes, and seconds. The default timestamp order is *hh:mm:ss*. The column heading format is as follows:

```
ACCOUNTING RECORDS FROM: day mon date hh:mm:ss yy
START AFTER : day mon date hh:mm:ss yy
COMMAND                     START END   REAL  CPU   MEAN
NAME        USER TTYNAME    TIME  TIME (SECS)(SECS) SIZE(K)
```

-t Lists system and user CPU times under separate headings. The default column `CPU (SECS)` is changed to `CPU SYS` and lists the system CPU time. The default column `MEAN SIZE(K)` is changed to `(SECS) USER` and lists user CPU time. The column heading format is as follows:

```
ACCOUNTING RECORDS FROM: day mon date hh:mm:ss yy
COMMAND                     START END   REAL CPU  (SECS)
NAME        USER TTYNAME    TIME  TIME (SECS)SYS   USER
```

-u *user* Lists processes belonging to *user;* a user ID, a login name that is converted to a user ID, a **#** (number sign) to select processes run by the **root** user, or a ? (question mark) to select processes associated with unknown user IDs. The column heading format is the same as the default column heading format.

-v Eliminates column headings from the output. The column format is the same as the default column format.

Description

The **acctcom** command reads process accounting records from files specified by the *file(s)* parameter from standard input or from the **/var/adm/pacct** file. Records from the specified input source are written to the default output device.

The use of this command is not restricted to individuals with administrative authority. The **acctcom** command is stored in the **/usr/bin** directory for accessiblity to most users. When you do not specify a *file(s)* parameter and standard input is assigned to a workstation or to **/dev/null** (when a process runs in the background, for example), the **acctcom** command reads the **/var/adm/pacct** file.

When you specify *file(s)*, the **acctcom** process reads each file chronologically in time-descending order according to process completion time. Usually **/var/adm/pacct** is the current file that **acctcom** writes to the default output device. Because the **ckpacct** procedure keeps this file from growing too large, a busy system may have several **pacct** files. All but the current file has the following pathname: **/var/adm/pacct***n*, where *n* is a unique integer whose value is assigned to any additional **/var/adm/pacct***n* files in the order they are created.

Each record represents execution times for one completed process. The default output format includes the command name, username, tty namg, process start time, process end time, real seconds, CPU seconds, and mean memory size (in kilobytes). The process summary output has the following default column heading format.

```
ACCOUNTING RECORDS FROM:  day mon date hh:mm:ss yy

COMMAND                      START   END     REAL    CPU     MEAN
NAME        USER   TTYNAME   TIME    TIME    (SECS)  (SECS)  SIZE(K)
```

The date and timestamp format is *day mon date hh:mm:ss yy* where *day* is the day of the week, *mon* is the month, *hh:mm:ss* is the time expressed in hours (in 24-hour clock notation), minutes, and seconds, and *yy* is the year expressed as four digits.

By using appropriate flags, you may also output the state of the **fork/exec** flag, F; the system exit value, STAT; the ratio of total CPU time to elapsed time, HOG FACTOR; the product of memory used and elapsed time, KCORE MIN; the ratio of user time to total (system plus user) time, CPU FACTOR; the number of characters transferred during I/O operations, CHARS TRNSFD; and the total number of blocks read or written, BLOCKS READ.

Whenever a process is run under **root** or **su** authority, the command name is prefixed with a # (number sign). When a process is not assigned to a known tty; for example, when the **cron** daemon runs the process, a ? (question mark) is written in the TTYNAME column.

acctcom(8)

The **acctcom** command only reports on processes that have completed. Use the **ps** command to examine the status of active processes. When a specified time is later than the current time, it is interpreted as occurring on the previous day.

For any flag value that produces a date and timestamp in an output heading, the order of date and time information is locale dependent. The date and timestamps shown in the examples are for the default headings, but their order may be changed using the **NLTIME** environment variable to change the timestamp format.

Examples

1. To display information about processes that exceed 2.0 seconds of CPU time, enter:

    /usr/sbin/acct/acctcom -O 2 < /var/adm/pacct

    The process information is read from the **/var/adm/pacct** file.

2. To display information about processes belonging to the **Finance** group, enter:

    /usr/sbin/acct/acctcom -g Finance < /var/adm/pacct

    The process information is read from the **/var/adm/pacct** file.

3. To display information about processes belonging to tty **/dev/console** that run after 5:00 p.m., enter:

    /usr/sbin/acct/acctcom -l /dev/console -s 17:00

    The process information is read from the **/var/adm/pacct** file by default.

Files

/usr/sbin/acct/acctcom
    Specifies the command path

/var/adm/pacct
    The active process accounting database file.

/etc/passwd, **/etc/group**
    User and group database files.

/usr/include/sys/acct.h, **/usr/include/utmp.h**
    Accounting header files that define formats for writing accounting files.

Related Information

Commands: **acct(8)**, **ed(8)**, **ps(8)**, **runacct(8)**, **su**(1)

Calls: **acct(2)**

Daemons: **cron(8)**

acctcon1, acctcon2

Purpose Outputs connect-time accounting summaries

Synopsis **/usr/sbin/acct/acctcon1** [-l *file*] [-o *file*] [-p] [-t]
/usr/sbin/acct/acctcon2

Flags

-l *file* When this flag is used, **acctcon1** writes a columnar format called "line usage" to *file*. The **acctcon1** command rewrites records from the source file (usually **/var/adm/wtmp**) to *file* as line usage records for the accounting period during which the file **/var/adm/wtmp** is active.

The line-usage summary format lists the line name in a LINE column, the number of session minutes used in a MINUTES column, the percentage of total elapsed time used for the sessions in a PERCENT column, the number of sessions charged in a # SESS column, the number of logins in a # ON column, and the number of logouts in a # OFF column. The **acctcon1** command rewrites the **/var/adm/wtmp** input file records as shown in the following example ASCII line-usage heading format.

```
TOTAL DURATION:mm MINUTES
LINE   MINUTES   PERCENT   # SESS   # ON   # OFF
TOTALS
```

In the foregoing line-usage format example, *mm* is the total number of minutes used for connect sessions during the accounting period during which the file **/var/adm/wtmp** is active. The last line in the line-usage file totals the entries for each column. The line-usage format helps an administrator track line usage and identify bad lines. All hangups, terminations of the **login** command, and terminations of the login shell cause the system to write logout records, so that the number of logouts is often greater than the number of sessions.

-o *file* When this flag is used, **acctcon1** writes a file format called "overall record" from source file information (usually the **/var/adm/wtmp** file) to *file*. The destination file is an overall record for the accounting period during which the **/var/adm/wtmp** file is active. This file lists a starting time, an ending time, the number of restarts, and the number of date changes. The **acctcon1** command rewrites **/var/adm/wtmp** information to *file* as shown in the following example ASCII overall record format:

```
from  mon day date hh:mm:ss yy tz
to    mon day date hh:mm:ss yy tz
```

2	date changes	The number of times the date was changed.
21	acctg off	The number of times accounting functions were turned off.
25	run-level S	The number of times accounting functions ran in single-user mode.
108	system boot	The number of times the system was rebooted.
21	acctg on	The number of times accounting functions were turned on.
21	acctcon1	The number of times the **acctcon1** command was issued.

The default date and timestamp format is *mon day date hh:mm:ss yy tz* where *mon* is the month, *day* is the day of the week, *hh:mm:ss* is the time expressed in hours (in 24-hour notation), minutes, and seconds, *yy* is the year express as a 4-digit number and *tz* is the name of the time zone. In the overall-record format, from is the accounting period start time and to is the accounting period end time.

-p   Writes **/var/adm/wtmp** file information to the default output device. The output columnar format lists the line reference name **1** (see the following example list), the login name **2**, the time in seconds since the Epoch **3**, the date **4** through **5**, the 24-hour clock time **6**, the year **7**, and the name of the time zone **8**.

The input records from the **/var/adm/wtmp** source file are written to the destination, which is the default output device. The **acctcon1** command rewrites the **/var/adm/wtmp** input file records as shown in the following example:

1	2	3	4	5	6	7	8
pty/ttyp1	hoff	616883748	Jul	19	16:35:48	1990	EST
pty/ttyp1	hoff	616883825	Jul	19	16:37:05	1990	EST
pty/ttyp1	LOGIN	616883833	Jul	19	16:37:13	1990	EST
pty/ttyp1	tom	616883837	Jul	19	16:37:17	1990	EST

-t   The **acctcon1** command also maintains a list of ports on which users are logged in. When the **acctcon1** command reaches the end of its input, a session record is written for each port that still appears to be active. The **acctcon1** command assumes that the input source is a current file and uses current time as the ending time for each session still in progress.

The **-t** flag uses the last time found in the input as the ending time for any current processes. This, rather than current time, is necessary to have reasonable and repeatable values for noncurrent files. The output format is the same as the default output format.

Description

acctcon1

The **acctcon1** command is normally called by the **runacct** shell procedure to write a sequence of login and logout records (stored in the **/var/adm/wtmp** file). One record for each connect session is written to a specified destination as a sequence of login session records. The input records should be redirected from the **/var/adm/wtmp** source file as input to the destination, which is the default output device. The **acctcon1** command rewrites the **/var/adm/wtmp** input file records as shown in the following example of the ASCII default columnar output format:

1	2	3	4	5	6	7	8	9	10	11
285212673	1192	hoff	85	0	616883748	Jul	19	16:35:48	1990	EST
285212673	1033	tom	10	0	616883837	Jul	19	16:37:17	1990	EST
285212673	0	root	1345	2852	616883855	Jul	19	16:37:35	1990	EST
285212673	1120	jim	0	62	616888058	Jul	19	17:47:38	1990	EST

In the foregoing example output records have no column headings; the numbers in boldface type are for reference. The default format output columns have the following significance:

1. The device address expressed as a decimal equivalent of the major/minor device address at which the connection was activated.
2. The user ID assigned for the connect-session record.
3. The user login name under which the session took place.
4. The total number of prime-time seconds for the connect session.
5. The total number of nonprime-time seconds for the connect session.
6. The number of seconds since the Epoch. The Epoch is referenced absolutely to 0 hours, 0 minutes 0 seconds, 1 January 1970.
7. The month of the year expressed as an initial-capitalized, 3-letter string.
8. The day of the month expressed as a decimal number.
9. The connect-session starting time expressed in hours, minutes, and seconds.
10. The year expressed as a 4-digit number.
11. The name of the current time zone.

For any column entries referenced **7** through **11** in the foregoing example that produce date and timestamp information in an output file, the order of date and time information is locale dependent. The date and timestamps shown in the examples are for the default headings, but their order may be changed using the **NLTIME** environment variable to change the timestamp format.

acctcon2

The **acctcon2** command, also usually called by the **runacct** shell procedure, converts a sequence of login session records produced by the **acctcon1** command into connect time total accounting records. These records are often merged with other total accounting records with the **acctmerg** command to produce a daily report.

Examples

Individual Session Records

To convert login records (in the **/var/adm/wtmp** file) to a default format login session record report (written to a file called **/var/adm/logsess**), include the following line in an accounting shell script:

```
acctcon1 -t /var/adm/lineuse -o /var/adm/reboots < /var/adm/wtmp >
/var/adm/logsess
```

Three files are generated. The output file **/var/adm/logsess** lists ending date and 24-hour timestamp records that correspond with the last time that input was provided (obtained with the **-t** flag). Two other files are generated: a line-usage summary file (**/var/adm/lineuse**) obtained with the **-l** flag, and an overall record file (**/var/adm/reboots**) obtained with the **-o** flag, for the accounting period covered by the **/var/adm/wtmp** file.

Total Accounting Records

To convert a series of login session records (in the **/var/adm/logsess** file) to a total accounting record (stored in a **/var/adm/logacct** binary file), include the following line in a shell script after the **/var/adm/logsess** file is produced:

```
acctcon2 < /var/adm/logsess > /var/adm/logacct
```

Files

/usr/sbin/acct/acctcon1
> Specifies command path.

/usr/sbin/acct/acctcon2
> Specifies command path.

/var/adm/wtmp
> The active login/logout database file.

acctcon(8)

/usr/include/sys/acct.h, /usr/include/utmp.h
> Accounting header files that define formats for writing accounting files.

Related Information

Commands: **acctmerg(8), acct(8), fwtmp(8), init(8), login(1)**

Calls:**acct(2)**

acctcon1

Purpose   This command is normally called by the **runacct** shell procedure to write a sequence of login and logout records

See **acctcon(8)**

acctcon2

Purpose   This command is usually called by the **runacct** shell procedure and converts a sequence of login session records produced by the **acctcon1** command into connect time total accounting records.

See **acctcon(8)**

acctdisk, acctdusg

Purpose   Perform disk-usage accounting

Synopsis   **/usr/sbin/acct/acctdisk**

/usr/sbin/acct/acctdusg [**-u** *file*] [**-p** *file*]

The **acctdisk** and **acctdusg** commands are called from the **dodisk** shell procedure to do disk usage accounting.

Flags

-**p** *file*   Searches *file* as the alternate file for login names and numbers, instead of searching **/etc/passwd**.

-**u** *file*   Writes records of filenames for which it does not charge into *file*.

Description

Normally the **acctdisk** and **acctdusg** commands are called from the **dodisk** shell procedure to do disk usage accounting. The **dodisk** shell procedure is invoked when the **cron** daemon executes commands in the **/usr/spool/cron/crontabs/**[*filename*] file. In the usual case, the output of the **diskusg** command is the redirected input to the **acctdisk** command. When a more thorough, but slower, version of disk accounting is needed, specify the **-o** flag with the **dodisk** command. This is not normally done in the **/usr/spool/cron/crontabs/**[*filename*] file. When the **-o** flag is used, the **acctdusg** command replaces the **diskusg** command.

acctdisk

Normally, the **acctdisk** command reads a temporary output file produced by the **diskusg** or the **acctdusg** command from standard input, converts each record into a total disk accounting record, and writes it to standard output. These records are merged with other accounting records with the **acctmerg** command to produce a daily accounting report.

acctdusg

The **acctdusg** command is called when the **-o** flag is used with the **dodisk** command. This produces a more thorough, but slower, version of disk accounting records. Otherwise, the **dodisk** shell procedure invokes the **diskusg** command.

The **acctdusg** command reads a list of files from standard input (usually piped from a **find** / **-print** command), computes the number of disk blocks (including indirect blocks) allocated to each file divided by the number of hard links then writes an individual record for each user to standard output.

Find the user who is charged for the file as follows:

Compare each file pathname with the login directories of the users. The user who has the longest pathname component match is charged for the file. Therefore, the relevant information for charging users is **not** ownership of a file but the directory where it is stored.

The **acctdusg** command searches the **/etc/passwd** file, or the alternate password file specified with the **-p** flag, for login names, numbers and login directories. Each output record has the following format:

```
uid login #blocks
```

Examples

1. To start normal disk accounting procedures, add a line similar to the following to the **/usr/spool/cron/crontabs/**[*filename*] file.

    0 2 * * 4 /usr/sbin/acct/dodisk

    The foregoing example is a typical, periodically invoked command that the **cron** daemon reads and executes. The period is expressed by a six field entry having the format: *mm hh daymon monyr wkday cmd*. For any field requiring digits, numbers are integers. These six fields have the following significance:

Variable	Purpose
mm	Is a time variable that has the value 0 through 59 expressing minutes past the hour.
hh	Is a time variable for the hour of the day in 24-hour clock notation.
daymon	Is a time variable for the day of the month.
monyr	Is a time variable for month of the year.
wkday	Is a time variable for the day or days-of-the-week, where 0 is Sunday and inclusive days are separated with a hyphen (-).
cmd	Is the command the **cron** daemon must execute.

    Whenever you write any of the time variables described in the foregoing table, an unspecified value must be noted with an * (asterisk) to define an empty field.

In the foregoing example, the **dodisk** shell procedure runs at 02:00 hours (2) every Thursday (4). The **dodisk** shell procedure calls the **acctdusg** command to redirect its input to a temporary file and then calls the **acctdisk** shell procedure to redirect disk usage records from the temporary file as input to a /**var**/**adm**/**acct**/**nite**/[*filename*] file as ouput. The file stored in the /**var**/**adm**/**acct**/**nite** subdirectory is a permanent binary record of disk usage for the specified period.

2. To initiate a slower, more thorough disk accounting procedure, add a line similar to the following to the /**usr**/**spool**/**cron**/**crontabs**/[*filename*] file.

    ```
    0 2 * * 0-6  /usr/sbin/acct/dodisk  -o
    ```

    The **dodisk** shell procedure calls the **acctdusg** command and the **acctdisk** command to write disk usage records to the /**var**/**adm**/**acct**/**nite**/[*filename*] file just as in the previous example. The **dodisk** procedure runs at 2 a.m. every day (**0-6**) including Sunday.

Files

/usr/sbin/acct/acctdisk
> Specifies the command path.

/usr/sbin/acct/acctdusg
> Specifies the command path.

/etc/passwd
> User database file.

/var/adm/wtmp
> The active login/logout database file.

/usr/include/sys/acct.h, **/usr/include/utmp.h**
> Accounting header files that define formats for writing accounting files.

Related Information

Commands: **acct(8)**, **dodisk(8)**, **acctmerg(8)**, **diskusg(8)**, **runacct(8)**

Calls: **acct(2)**

Daemons: **cron(8)**

acctdusg

Purpose   Reads a list of files from standard input and computes the number of disk blocks (including indirect blocks) allocated to each file divided by the number of hard links then writes an individual record for each user to standard output.

See **acctdisk(8)**

acctmerg

Purpose   Merges total accounting files into an intermediary file or a daily accounting file

Synopsis   **/usr/sbin/acct/acctmerg -[ahipv]** [*specification*] **-[tu]** [*file* ....]

The **acctmerg** command combines total accounting records in **tacct** binary or **tacct** ASCII format.

Flags

-a [*specification*]
Produces output as ASCII records.

-h [*specification*]
Lists column headings. This flag implies **-a** but is effective with the **-p** or **-v** flags.

-i [*specification*]
Expects input files to have ASCII records that are converted to binary output records.

-p [*specification*]
Lists input but without processing.

-t   Produces a single record that contains the totals of all input.

-u   Summarizes by user ID rather than by user name. This is convenient when a single user ID is allocated to more than one user name.

-v [*specification*]
Produces output in ASCII, with more precise notation for floating-point values.

Description

The **acctmerg** command combines process, connect time, fee, disk usage, and queuing (printer) total accounting records in **tacct** binary or **tacct** ASCII format (see the **tacct** structure in the **acct.h** file format for a description of this total accounting format). The **acctmerg** command writes the results of record processing to standard output. The accounting file produced by the **acctmerg** command may have entries for as many as 18 columns. Column headings are printed only when you use the **-h** flag. The following table lists the column headings by number, the column heading by label, and the purpose of the entry.

1.	`UID`	User ID. This is the integer value of the user ID from the **/etc/passwd** file.
2.	`LOGNAME`	User login name. This is the alpha user login name from the **/etc/passwd** file.
3.	`PRI_CPU`	Prime-time CPU run time. This is the total time in seconds that prime-time CPU run time was charged to the user during the active accounting period.
4.	`NPRI_CPU`	Nonprime time CPU runtime. This is the total time in seconds that nonprime CPU run time was charged to the named user.
5.	`NPRI_MEM`	Prime time memory K-core. This is a measure of memory usage during prime time. This value expresses the amount of memory used and the elapsed amount of prime time during which it was used (K-core is the product of total CPU time in minutes and mean size of memory used).
6.	`NPRI_MEM`	Nonprime time memory K-core. This is a measure of memory usage during nonprime time.
7.	`PRI_RD/WR`	Prime-time read and write characters. This is the total number of characters transferred during prime-time operation.
8.	`NPRI_RD/WR`	Nonprime-time read and write characters. This is the total number of characters transferred during nonprime-time operation.
9.	`PRI_BLKIO`	Prime-time number of I/O blocks. This is the total number of I/O blocks transferred during prime-time read and write operations. The number of bytes in an I/O block is implementation dependent.
10.	`NPRI_BLKIO`	Nonprime time number of I/O blocks. This is the total number of I/O blocks transferred during nonprime-time read and write operations.
11.	`PRI_CONNECT`	Prime-time connect duration. This is the total number of prime-time seconds during which a connection existed.
12.	`NPRI_CONNECT`	Nonprime-time connect duration. This is the total number of nonprime-time seconds during which a connection existed.
13.	`DSK_BLOCKS`	Disk blocks used. This is the total number of disk blocks used.

14.   PRINT   Number of pages printed. This is the total number of pages
                        queued to any printers in the system.

15.   FEES   Special fee charge units. This is the number of integer units
                        to charge for any special fee. This value is the one supplied
                        when the **/usr/sbin/acct/chargefee** command is processed
                        during the active accounting period.

16.   PROCESSES   Number of processes. This is the total number of processes
                        spawned by the user during the active accounting period.

17.   SESS   Number of logins. This is the total number of times the user
                        logged in during the active accounting period.

18.   DSAMPS   Number of disk accounting samples. This is the total number
                        of times during the active accounting period that the disk
                        accounting command was used to get the total number of
                        disk blocks listed in the DSK_BLOCKS column. When the
                        value in the DSK_BLOCKS column is divide by this
                        number, the average number of disk blocks used during the
                        accounting period is obtained.

Total accounting records are read from standard input and any additional files (up
to nine) you specify with the *file* parameter. File records are merged according to
identical keys, usually the user ID and user login name. To optimize processing
performance, output is written in binary, unless the **-a** or **-v** flag is used.

Normally the **acctmerg** command is called from the **runacct** shell procedure,
either to produce an intermediate file (**/var/adm/acct/nite/daytacct**, for example)
when one or more source accounting files is full, or to merge intermediate files into
a cumulative total (**/var/adm/acct/sum/tacct**, is another example). The cumulative
total daily files are the source from which the **monacct** command produces an
ASCII monthly summary file, which is written to the **/var/adm/acct/fiscal**
subdirectory.

Optional *Specification* allows you to select input or output column entries, as
illustrated in Example 1. Field specifications are a comma-separated string of field
numbers. Filed numbers are referenced in boldface type in the first column of the
foregoing list together with their respective column headings. When you specify
field numbers they should be listed in the order specified by the boldfaced heading
reference numbers.

Inclusive field ranges may also be specified, with array sizes properly taken into
account except for the *ta_name* number of characters. For example, **-h2-3,11,15-
13,2** displays the LOGNAME (**2**), PRI_CPU (**3**), PRI_CONNECT time (**11**),
FEES (**15**), PRINT (**14**), DISK_BLOCKS (**13**), and again LOGNAME (**2**), in that
order, with the described column headings (**-h**). The default specification is to
output all 18 columns (1-18 or 1-), which produces rather wide output records that
contain all the available accounting data.

acctmerg(8)

Queuing system, disk usage, or fee data can be converted into **tacct** records with the **acctmerge** command, using the **-i** flag and the *specification* parameter.

Examples

1.   To merge inclusive fields from an ASCII disk accounting file called **dacct** into an existing total accounting file named **tacct** as binary information, but with entries for fields 1, 2, 13, and 18 only, enter the following line.

   acctmerg -i 1 -2,13,18 <dacct | acctmerg tacct >output

   The **acctmerg** command reads the columnar entries for UID (**1**), LOGNAME (**2**), DSK_BLOCKS (**13**), and DSAMPS (**18**) from the **dacct** file as input, merges this information as **tacct** binary records, and writes the result to standard output as ASCII.

2.   To repair file **jan2.rpt** in inclusive **tacct** columnar format, enter the following initial command, edit the **jan2.tmp** file, and then enter the last command:

   acctmerg -v <jan2.rpt >jan2.tmp

   Edit **jan2.tmp** as desired....

   acctmerg -i >jan2.tmp >jan2.rpt

   The first command redirects the content of file **jan2.rpt** to file **jan2.tmp**, with ASCII output and floating-point values. After you edit file **jan2.tmp**, the last command redirects file **jan2.tmp** as ASCII input to file **jan2.rpt** as output, with output records in binary.

Files

/usr/sbin/acct/acctmerg
Specifies the command path.

/usr/include/sys/acct.h, /usr/include/utmp.h
Accounting header files that define formats for writing accounting files.

/usr/sbin/acct/holidays
This is where prime-time is set.

/var/adm/acct/nite/daytacct
Intermediate daily total accounting file.

/var/adm/acct/sum/tacct
Cumulative total accounting file.

Related Information

Commands: **acct(8)**, **acctcms(8)**, **acctcom(8)**, **acctcon(8)**, **acctdisk(8)**, **acctprc(8)**, **fwtmp(8)**, **runacct(8)**

Calls: **acct(2)**

accton

Purpose   Turns account processing on and off

See **acctprc(8)**

acctprc1, acctprc2, accton

Purpose   Perform process accounting procedures

Synopsis   **/usr/sbin/acct/acctprc1** [*InFile*]

                /usr/sbin/acct/acctprc2

                /usr/sbin/acct/accton [*OutFile*]

Description

The three **acctprc** commands, **acctprc1, acctprc2,** and **accton,** are used in the **runacct** shell procedure to produce process-accounting reports.

acctprc1 [*InFile*]

The **acctprc1** command is used to read records from standard input that are in a format defined by the **acct** structure in the **/usr/include/sys/acct.h** header file. This process adds the login names that correspond to user IDs, and then writes corresponding ASCII records to standard output. For each process, the record format includes the following 7 unheaded columns.

1   User ID. The user ID column includes both traditional and assigned user identification numbers listed in the **/etc/passwd** file.

2   Login name. The login name is the one used for the user ID in the **/etc/passwd** file.

3   Prime time CPU time. The number of seconds the process consumed when exectuted during prime-time hours. Prime and nonprime-time hours are defined in the **/usr/sbin/acct/holidays** file.

4   Nonprime-time CPU time. The number of seconds the process consumed when executed during nonprime-time hours.

5   Total number of characters transferred.

6   Total number of blocks read and written.

7   Mean memory size (in kilobyte units).

When specified, *InFile* contains a list of login sessions in a format defined by the **utmp** structure in the **/usr/include/utmp.h** header file. The login session records are sorted according to user ID and login name. When *InFile* is not specified, **acctprc1** gets login names from password file **/etc/passwd**. The information in *InFile* is used to distinguish different login names that share the same user ID.

acctprc(8)

acctprc2

The **acctprc2** command reads, from standard input, the records written by **acctprc1**, summarizes them according to user ID and name, and writes sorted summaries to standard output as total accounting records in the **tacct** format (see the **acctmerg** command).

acctton [*OutFile*]

When no parameters are specified with the **accton** command, account processing is turned off. When you specify an existing *OutFile* file, process accounting is turned on, and the kernel adds records to that file. You must specify an *Outfile* to start process accounting. Many shell script procedures expect the file name **/var/adm/pacct**, the standard process accounting file.

Examples

1. To add a user name to each process-accounting record in a binary file and then write these modified binary-file records to an ASCII file named **out.file**, enter the following line to an accounting shell script:

   /usr/sbin/acct/acctprc1 < /var/adm/pacct >out.file

   A user name is added to each record. The raw data in the **pacct** file is converted to ASCII and added to file **out.file**.

2. To produce a total binary accounting record of the ASCII output file **out.file** produced in example 1, enter the following line to an accounting shell script:

   /usr/sbin/acct/acctprc2 < out.file > /var/adm/acct/nite/daytacct

   The resulting binary total accounting file, written in the **acct** format, contains records sorted by user ID. This sorted user ID file, is usually merged with other total accounting records when an **acctmerg** command is processed to produce a daily summary accounting record called **/var/adm/acct/sum/daytacct.**

3. To turn on process accounting, enter:

   /usr/sbin/acct/accton /var/adm/pacct

4. To turn off process accounting, enter:

   /usr/sbin/acct/accton

Files

Commands: **acct(8)**, **acctcms(8)**, **acctmerg(8)**, **runacct(8)**

Calls: **acct(2)**

acctprc1

Purpose   Reads records from standard input that are in a format defined by the **acct** structure in the **/usr/include/sys/acct.h** header file.

See **acctprc(8)**

acctprc2

Purpose   Reads, from standard input, the records written by **acctprc1** and summarizes them according to user ID and name

See **acctprc(8)**

acctwtmp

Purpose   Writes a **utmp** formatted record to standard output

See **fwtmp(8)**

adduser

Purpose   Adds a new user interactively

Synopsis   **adduser**

Description

The **adduser** command is an interactive program for adding new user accounts to your system. The program prompts you for specific information and informs you of its activity and error conditions.

Only the **superuser** can execute this command.

The program follows this sequence:

It queries for a login name for the new user. Enter the login name. If this entry already exists in the **passwd** file, the program informs you of this and repeats the prompt for a login name. If the entry does not already exist, the program creates one for the new user.

It queries for a full name of the new user. Enter the user's full name. This is sometimes called the "gecos" entry and is displayed by the **finger** command.

It queries for a login group for the new user and specifies the default group, users. To accept the default, press the **Return** key. To select a different group, enter the name of that group. Be aware that the specified group must currently exist. If it does not exist, the program exits. If you encounter this problem, add the new group to the **/etc/group** file, then reinvoke the **adduser** program.

It queries for other groups of which the new user will be a member. Again, the group you specify must already exist. If you specify a group to which the user already belongs, the program informs you of this.

It queries for a home directory for the new user and specifies the default directory, /usr/users. To accept the default, press the **Return** key. To select a different home directory, enter the path of that directory. Be aware that the path that you specify must exist within a mounted file system.

It displays a message that it is adding the new user. At this point, the program creates a UID, makes an entry for the user in the **passwd** file, creates the home directory, creates the mail directory,

adduser(8)

sets ownership and access permissions on the new user's home and mail directories, and creates (or copies) the required startup files (**.cshrc**, **.login**, and **.profile**) for the new user in the home directory.

When you exit from the **adduser** program, invoke the **passwd** command and enter a password for the new user.

Files

/usr/sbin/adduser
Specifies the command path.

Related Information

Commands: **passwd(1)**, **finger(1)**, **chsh(1)**, **chfn(1)**, **vipw(8)**

Calls: **passwd(2)**

arp

Purpose   Displays and controls Address Resolution Protocol (ARP) tables

Synopsis   **arp** *hostname*
arp -a [*system*] [*core*]
arp -d *hostname*
arp -f *filename*
arp -s *hostname hardware_addr* [**temp**] [**pub**] [**trail**]

The **arp** command displays and modifies the ARP tables that map Internet addresses to network hardware addresses.

Flags

hostname
> With no flags, the program displays the current ARP entry for *hostname*. The host may be specified by name or by number, using Internet dot notation.

-a [*system*] [*core*]
> Displays all of the current ARP entries by reading the table from the file *core* (default **/dev/kmem**) based on the kernel file *system* (default **/vmunix**).

-d *hostname*
> Deletes the entry for *hostname* if the user issuing the command has superuser authority.

-f *filename*
> Reads entries from *filename* and adds those entries to the ARP tables. Entries in the file are in the following form:
>
> *hostname hardware_addr* [**temp**] [**pub**] [**trail**]
>
> where:
>
> *hostname*
>> Specifies the remote host identified by the entry.
>
> *hardware_addr*
>> Specifies the hardware address of the remote host. The address is given as 6 hexadecimal bytes separated by colons.

temp	Specifies that this ARP table entry is temporary. When this argument is not used, the table entry is permanent.
pub	Indicates that the table entry will be published and that the current system will act as an ARP server, responding to requests for *hostname* even though the host address is not its own.
trail	Indicates that the trailer encapsulation may be sent to this host.

-s *hostname hardware_addr* [**temp**] [**pub**] [**trail**]

Creates a single ARP entry for *hostname*. The arguments are explained in the discussion of the **-f** flag.

Description

The **arp** command displays or modifies the current ARP entry for the host specified by *hostname*. The host may be specified by name or number, using Internet dot notation.

The ARP tables can be displayed by any user, but only the superuser can modify them.

Examples

1. To display the ARP address mapping tables for the local host that has one interface defined, enter:

    arp -a

    milan.ber.org   (555.555.5.555)   at   0:dd:0:39:af:0   shaw.cjr.org (555.555.5.555) at 8:0:2b:15:42:83 trailers

2. To add a single entry for the remote host **laszlo** to the ARP mapping tables temporarily, enter:

    arp -s laszlo 0:dd:0:a:85:0 temp

    Note that you must have superuser authority to execute this command.

3. To add multiple entries to the ARP mapping tables from the file **newentries**, enter:

    arp -f newentries

    Note that you must have superuser authority to execute this command.

Files

/usr/sbin/arp
    Specifies the command path

Related Information

Commands: **arp(4)**, **ifconfig(8)**, **netstat(1)**

Specification: RFC826.

cfgmgr

Purpose   Configuration manager daemon

Synopsis   **cfgmgr** [**-c** *database*] [**-d -f -v**]

Flags

-c *database*
:   Specifies the configuration database to use instead of the default file, **/etc/sysconfigtab**.

-d
:   Specifies that debugging information should be produced during operation.

-f
:   Specifies that the **cfgmgr** should not detach from the current controlling tty (session).

-v
:   Specifies that more verbose information should be produced during operation.

Description

The configuration manager, **cfgmgr** manages dynamically configurable subsystems. **cfgmgr** is usually started at system startup time. When **cfgmgr** is started, it configures all subsystems marked in the configuration database as automatic. **cfgmgr** then listens on a communications socket for command requests from the **sysconfig** command. When a SIGHUP signal is received by **cfgmgr**, it rereads the configuration database.

The **cfgmgr** logs operational output information and error messages to the **syslogd** daemon. The amount of operational information can be controlled by the **-d** and the **-v** flags.

Files

/sbin/cfgmgr
:   Specifies the command path

/etc/sysconfigtab
:   Specifies the command path for the configuration database file

Related Information

Commands: **sysconfig(8)**, **sysconfigdb(8)**, **syslogd(8)**

Files: **sysconfigtab(4)**

chargefee

Purpose   Charges the number of units specified by the *Number* parameter to the login name specified by the *User* parameter

See **acct(8)**

chroot

Purpose   Changes the root directory of a command

Synopsis   **chroot** *directory* [*command*]

Description

Only **root** can use the **chroot** command. The **chroot** command changes the root directory from / to the specified *directory* when the *command* executes. Consequently, the root of any path (as indicated by the first / (slash) in the pathname) changes to *directory* and is always relative to the current root. Even if the **chroot** command is in effect, *directory* is relative to the current root of the running process.

Several programs may not operate properly after **chroot** executes. For example, the **ls -l** command fails to give user and group names if the current root location and the **/etc/passwd** file are on different file systems. Utilities that depend on description files produced by the **ctab** command may also fail if the required description files are on a different file system than the new root file system. You must ensure that all vital data files are present in the new root file system and that the relevant pathnames for the data files correspond to the new root file system.

Examples

1.   To run a subshell with another file system as the root, enter:

   chroot /dev/ra1a /bin/sh

   This command specifies a change from the current root file system to **/dev/ra1a** while **/bin/sh** executes. When **/bin/sh** executes, the original root file system is inaccessible. The file system on **/dev/ra1a** must contain the standard directories of a root file system. In particular, the shell looks for commands in **/bin** and **/usr/bin** on the new root file system.

   Running the **/bin/sh** command creates a subshell, which runs as a separate process from the original shell. Press **<Ctrl-d>** to exit the subshell and to return to the original shell. This restores the environment of the original shell, including the meanings of the current directory (.) and the root directory (/).

2.   To run a command in another root file system and save the output on the initial root file system, enter:

chroot /dev/ra1a /bin/cc -E /u/bob/prog.c > prep.out

This command runs the **/bin/cc** command with **/dev/ra1a** as the specified root file system. It compiles the **/dev/ra1a/u/bob/prog.c** file, reads the **#include** files from the **/dev/ra1a/usr/include** directory, and puts the compiled text in the **prep.out** file on the initial root file system.

3.   To create a file relative to the original root rather than the new one, use this syntax and enter:

chroot *directory* [*command*] > *file*

Files

/usr/sbin/chroot
          Specifies the command path.

Cautions

If special files in the new root have different major and minor device numbers than the initial root directory, it is possible to overwrite the file system.

Related Information

Commands: **cc(1)**, **cpp(1)**, **ls(1)**, **sh(1)**

Files: **ctab(4)**

Calls: **chdir(2)**, **chroot(2)**

ckpacct

Purpose   Checks the size of the active process accounting file **/var/adm/pacct**
See **acct(8)**

clri

Purpose   Clears i-nodes

Synopsis   **clri** *filesystem i-number* ...

Description

The **clri** command is obsoleted for normal file system repair work by the **fsck** command.

The **clri** command writes zeros on the i-nodes with the decimal *i-numbers* on the specified filesystem. After **clri** has finished its work, any blocks in the affected file are defined as "missing" when you run **icheck** on the filesystem.

Read and write permission is required on the specified file system device. The i-node becomes allocatable.

The primary purpose of this routine is to remove a file which does not appear in any directory. If you use the command to remove an i-node which does appear in a directory, take care to track down the entry and remove it. Otherwise, when the i-node is reallocated to some new file, the old entry will still point to that file. If you then remove the old entry, you will destroy the new file, and the new entry will again point to an unallocated i-node. Consequently, the entire cycle repeats itself.

You must be **root** to use this command.

Bugs

If the file is open, **clri** is likely to be ineffective.

Related Information

Files

/usr/sbin/clri
        Specifies the command path

Commands: **icheck(8)**

comsat

Purpose   The biff server

Synopsis   **comsat**

The **comsat** server receives reports of incoming mail and notifies users who request this service.

Description

The **comsat** server is invoked by the **inetd**(8) daemon when it receives messages on a datagram port associated with the **biff**(1) service specification in **/etc/services**(4). The datagram contains a 1-line message of the form:

user@mailbox-offset

If the *user* specified is logged in and the associated terminal has the owner execute bit turned on (with **biff y**), *offset* is used as a seek offset into the file named in *mailbox*. The first 7 lines or 560 characters of the message are printed on the user's system. The message excludes mail header lines other than the **From, To, Date,** or **Subject** lines.

Files

/usr/sbin/comsat
> Specifies the command path.

/etc/utmp
> Includes information about logged-in users and their associated ttys.

Related Information

Commands: **biff**(1), **inetd**(8)

Files: **services(4), inetd.conf(4)**

config

Purpose   Builds system configuration files

Synopsis   **config** [**-p**] [**-s**] *system_name*

Flags

      -p   Configure the system for profiling. You must have sources to use this flag.

      -s   Build the system from sources.

Description

The **config** command builds a set of system configuration files from a short file that describes the sort of system that is being configured. It also takes as input a file which tells **config** what files are needed to generate a system. This can be augmented by a configuration-specific set of files that give alternate files for a specific machine.

Run the **config** command from the **conf** subdirectory of the system source (usually **/sys/conf**). Its argument is the name of a system configuration file containing device specifications, configuration options and other system parameters for that specific system configuration. **config** assumes that there is already a directory "*../system_name*" created. It places all its output files in that directory. The output of **config** consists of a number of files; each machine type has its own specific set of files. All machine types have a **makefile** which is used by **make** during the system build. Typically, there are also a set of header files which contain definitions of the number of various devices that will be compiled into the system, and a set of swap configuration files contain definitions for the disk areas to be used for swapping, the root file system, argument processing, and system dumps.

After running **config**, you run **make depend** in the directory where the new makefile was created. **config** prints a reminder of this when it completes.

If any other error messages are produced by **config**, the problems in the configuration file should be corrected and **config** should be run again. Attempts to compile a system that had configuration errors are likely to be unsuccessful.

Files

/sys/conf/makefile.*machine type*
> Generic makefile for the specific machine type

/sys/conf/files
> List of common files used to build the system

/sys/conf/files.*machine type*
> List of machine specific files

/sys/conf/devices.*machine type*
> Name to major device mapping file for the *machine type*

/sys/conf/files.*NAME*
> List of files specific to *NAME* system.

Bugs

The line numbers reported in error messages are usually off by one.

Related Information

Commands: **make(1)**

cron

Purpose   The system clock daemon

Synopsis   **/usr/sbin/cron**

Description

The **cron** daemon runs shell commands at specified dates and times. Commands that are to run according to a regular or periodic schedule are found within the **crontab** files. Commands that are to run once only are found within the **at** files. You submit **crontab** and **at** file entries by using the **crontab** and **at** commands. Because the **cron** process exits only when killed or when the system stops, only one **cron** daemon should exist on the system at any given time. Normally, you start the **cron** daemon from within a run command file.

During process initialization and when **cron** detects a change, it examines the **crontab** and **at** files. This strategy reduces the overhead of checking for new or changed files at regularly scheduled intervals.

The **cron** daemon executes a **sync** system call (approximately once a minute) to ensure that all information in memory that should be on disk (buffered output) is written out. These periodic updates minimize the possibility of file system damage in the event of a crash. The **cron** command creates a log of its activities. The **cron** daemon starts each job with the following process attributes stored with the job by the invoking process:

> Login user ID
> Effective and real user IDs
> Effective and real group IDs
> Supplementary groups

It also establishes the followinig attributes from the authentication profile of the account associated with the login user ID of the invoking process:

> Audit control and disposition masks
> Kernel authorizations

Files

/usr/sbin/cron
>   Specifies the command path.

Diagnostics

>   The **at** and **batch** programs will refuse to accept jobs submitted from processes whose login user ID is diffferent from the real user ID.

Related Information

>   Commands: **at(1)**, **crontab(1)**, **rc0(8)**, **rc2(8)**, **rc3(8)**
>
>   Calls: **sync(2)**

df

Purpose   Displays statistics on free disk space

Synopsis   **df** [**-i -k**] *file* | *file system* ...

Flags

-i   Includes statistics on the number of free inodes.

-k   Causes the numbers to be reported in kilobytes. By default, all reported numbers are in 512-byte blocks.

Description

The **df** command displays statistics on the amount of free disk space on the specified *file system* or on the file system of which the specified *file* is a part. If neither a file nor a file system is specified, statistics for all mounted file systems are displayed.

Files

/usr/bin/df
Specifies the command path

Related Information

Commands: **quota(8)**, **mount(8)**, **quot(8)**

Files: **fstab(4)**

diskusg

Purpose   Generates disk accounting data by user ID

Synopsis   **/usr/sbin/acct/diskusg** [**-U** *number*] [**-sv**] [**-p** *pw_file*] [**-u** *ufile*] [**-i** *ignlist*]
[*file* ...]

The **diskusg** command generates intermediate disk accounting information and
writes one record per user to standard output.

Flags

-U *number*
> Sets the number of internal allocated user structures to *number*, one for
> each user. The default is 1000.

-i *ignlist*
> Ignores the data in the *ignlist* file system. The *ignlist* parameter specifies
> a list of file system names that are separated with commas or are
> enclosed within quotation marks.

-p *pw_file*
> Uses *pw_file* as the alternate password file used to generate login names.
> The default password file is **/etc/passwd**.

-s   Combines all records for a single user into a single record. Input data
> must be already in the previously described format. In combination with
> this option specified *file* arguments are regular files containing data in the
> described output format. When *file* is not specified, input data are taken
> from standard input.

-u *ufile*   Writes a record to *ufile* for each file that has changed its user ID to no
> one. Each record consists of the special file name, the inode number, and
> the user ID.

-v   Writes a list of all files charged to user no one to standard error.

Description

The **diskusg** command generates intermediate disk accounting information from
data in files specified with the *file* parameter, which is the name of the raw device
the data files reside on, or from standard input, and writes one record per user to
standard output. This command is normally called from the **dodisk** shell procedure
when the **cron** daemon executes commands in
/usr/spool/cron/crontabs/[*Filename*]. The output, produced when this command is

diskusg(8)

executed, is redirected as input to the **acctdisk** command. When the **-o** flag is used with the **dodisk** command, the **acctdusg** command replaces the **diskusg** command. Records output by this command provide the following output.

1   User ID. The assigned user number.
2   Login name. The user login name.
3   Number of blocks. The total number of disk blocks allocated to this user.

The output of this command becomes the input of the **acctdisk** command, which converts the information to a total accounting record. This total accounting record is merged with other total accounting records to produce a daily report.

The **diskusg** command normally reads only the inodes of file systems specified by the *file* parameter, which provides the special file names of the raw devices. When you need a more thorough accounting of disk usage, see the **acctdusg** command.

This command is for local devices only.

Examples

1.   To generate daily disk accounting information, add a line similar to the following to the **/usr/spool/cron/crontabs/adm** file.

0 2 * * 4 /usr/sbin/acct/dodisk

The foregoing example is a typical, periodically invoked command that the **cron** daemon reads and executes. The period is expressed by a 6-field entry having the format: *mm hh daymon monyr wkday cmd* (where numbers are integers and *mm* has a value 0 through 59 expressing minutes past the hour, *hh* is the hour of the day in 24-hour clock notation, *daymon* is day of the month, *monyr* is month of the year, *wkday* is the day or days of the week, where 0 is Sunday and inclusive days are separated with a - (hyphen), and *cmd* is the command the **cron** daemon must execute. Unspecified times must use the * (asterisk) to define an empty field.

In the foregoing example, the **dodisk** shell procedure runs at 02:00 hours (**2**) every Thursday (**4**). Normally, the **dodisk** shell procedure calls the **diskusg** command to redirect its output to a temporary file and then calls **acctdisk** to redirect disk usage records from the temporary file as input to the **/var/adm/acct/nite/**[*filename*] file as ouput. The file stored in the **/var/adm/acct/nite** subdirectory is a permanent binary record of disk usage for the specified period.

Files

/usr/sbin/acct/diskusg
    Specifies the command path.

/usr/include/sys/acct.h, /usr/include/utmp.h
    Accounting header files that define formats for writing accounting files.

/etc/passwd
    User database file.

Related Information

Commands: **acct(8)**,   **acctmerg(8)**,   **acctdusg(8)**,   **acctdisk(8)**,   **dodisk(8)**,
runacct(8)

Calls: **acct(2)**

dodisk

Purpose   Initiates disk-usage accounting by calling the **diskusg** command and the **acctdisk** command

See **acct(8)**

dump, rdump

Purpose   Performs incremental file system dumps

Synopsis   **/usr/sbin/dump** [*key* [*argument* ....] *filesystem*]

/usr/sbin/rdump -f *dump_file* [*otherkey* [*argument* ....] *filesystem*]

The **dump** command copies to the default **/dev/rmt0h**, or to the alternate storage device specified with the **-f** flag, all files changed after a certain date in the specified local *filesystem*.

rdump

The **rdump** command copies to the *dump_file* storage device all files changed after a certain date in the specified *filesystem*.

Flags

-0-9   Specifies the dump level. All files modified since the last timestamp whose names are currently stored in the **/etc/dumpdates** file for a named *filesystem* at levels less than the one specified are dumped to tape. When no timestamp entry is defined for a dump level, the Epoch is assumed; thus, the value **-0** for this *key* causes the entire file system to be dumped to the storage medium.

-b *blocks_per_write*
            Expresses the number of blocks in 1024 bytes to write to the storage medium. When the *blocks_per_write* parameter is not expressed, **dump** or **rdump** makes a dynamically conservative estimate.

-c   The dump medium is a non-9-track cartridge tape.

-d *density*
            Specifies the write density of the storage medium. The *density* parameter is expressed in bits per inch (bpi). This information is used in calculating the amount of medium used per each volume of the storage medium. The default write density is 1600 bpi.

-f *dump_file*
            Writes the dump to the *dump_file* storage device instead of the default tape drive. When the name of *dump_file* is **-**, the **dump** process writes to standard output.

            When the **rdump** command is invoked, the *dump_file* parameter must specify both the remote machine and the storage device in the format *machine:device*, where *machine* is the name or reference designation of

1–67

dump(8)

the host machine and *device* is the name or reference designation of the storage device.

-n   Notifies, by means of a command similar to **wall**(8), all operators in the group named **operator**, which is specified in the **/etc/group** file whenever **dump** or **rdump** requires operator attention (to change a tape, for example).

-s *size*   Specifies the size of a dump tape in feet. The number of feet is expressed by the *size* parameter. When the amount of tape specified by *size* has been written, either process waits for the current reel to be changed (see the **-n** flag). The default tape size is 2300 feet.

-u   Writes the time of the beginning of the dump as the timestamp entry in the **/etc/dumpdates** file for the *filesystem* record when the dump successfully completes.

-w   Tells an operator what file systems must be dumped to the storage device. This information is obtained from the **/etc/dumpdates** and **/etc/fstab** files. The **-w** *key* tells either process to print to the standard output, a record for each *filesystem* listed in the **/etc/dumpdates** file.

-B   Specifies a block-mode device.

-N   Tells the operator not to rewind a tape.

-S *full_tape_size*
     Specifies output file size in blocks (together with the **-B** flag) or in feet.

-T *tape_number*
     Specifies tape number, which is used in the dialog with the operator as the number of the first tape.

-W   Similar to **-w**, but for any *filesystem* listed in the **/etc/dumpdates** file, prints an output record and highlights this record with the character > (greater than), all files that must be dumped. When **-W** is specified, all other options are ignored, and **dump** exits immediately.

Description

The **dump** and **rdump** commands are used to dump local files from a single file system defined by the *filesystem* parameter to a local or remote storage device, respectively, where *filesystem* contains the files you want to back up.

The **dump** and **rdump** commands perform similar functions with respect to storage of files contained in the named *filesystem*. However, the **rdump** command requires that the **-f** flag be used with any *otherkey* and the special *dump_file* parameters.

Both commands copy all files in *filesystem* whose dump level is less than a specified value, and that have changed after a specified date to the default storage device or to an alternate storage device. The dump level and date are specified in the local **/etc/dumpdates** file. The *key* and *argument* parameters specify one or more various options that may be used to write files to the storage medium. Characters permitted by the *key* parameter are similar to flags that consist of any of the characters **0123456789bcdfnsuwBNSTW** only, which may be used in any logical combination, but must be preceded with the - (dash) character; the *argument* parameter specifies other options that tell these **dump** and **rdump** processes what to do. These options are described under **FLAGS**. Not all *keys* permit *argument* options to be specified.

The **/etc/dumpdates** file consists of 3-column record lines that specify the *filesystem* name, a dump level, and a standard timestamp. These processes enter a timestamp into the *filesystem* record after each file in the named *filesystem* is successfully backed up. The 3-column record in the **/etc/dumpdates** file contains the following information:

1. File system name

> Lists the *filesystem* device name.

2. Dump level   This is an integer between 1 and 9 that defines a hierachy for files in *filesystem*. This hierachy indicates which files should be written to the storage medium when the **dump** or **rdump** command is executed. Level 0 defines all the files in *filesystem*. When a level is assigned, all files equal to and less than that level in *filesystem* are backed up.

3. Timestamp   The timestamp tells the **dump** or **rdump** process when *filesystem* had its last backup. This timestamp is written by the **dump** or **rdump** process after the specified *filesystem* backup is completed. When there is no timestamp, the **dump** or **rdump** process assumes the beginning of time (called the Epoch).

The **/etc/dumpdates** file is written in ASCII and consists of a single record per line. This file may be edited to change any record field, when necessary.

When no *argument* is specified, *key* is assumed to be **-9u** so that all files in the default file system named **/dev/rrz0g**, which were modified since the last dump, are dumped to the default storage medium named **/dev/rmt0h**.

Either process requires operator intervention when any of these conditions occur: end-of-tape, end-of-dump, tape-write error, tape-open error, and when the number of disk-read errors is greater than 32. In addition to alerting all operators specified by the **-n** *key*, these processes interact with an operator at the terminal from which **dump** or **rdump** was invoked when either program can no longer proceed.

All queries written to standard output by the **dump** or **rdump** process must be answered by typing **yes** or **no** to the standard input.

dump(8)

Because a dump to any storage medium requires excessive time to process, each process checks itself at the start of each storage volume. When a volume write fails, **dump** or **rdump** restarts itself from the last successful checkpoint, with operator permission, after the currently written storage medium is properly removed and another (replacement) storage medium has been mounted.

These processes also tell an operator what is going on at periodic intervals when writing to the storage medium. This information consists of somewhat conservative estimates for the number of blocks to write, the number of storage media that must be used for the dump, the time to complete the dump, and the time until the storage medium must be replaced with another one to complete the dump. Output is verbose, so that others know that the terminal controlling **dump** is busy. When processing takes place, the following conditions apply:

1. Fewer than 32 read errors during a **dump** or **rdump** tape-dump process are ignored. Each renewal of the storage medium requires a new dump process, so that parent processes for storage media already written are in effect until the entire storage medium is written.

2. When the **dump** command has the **W** or **w** *key* set, no records are written to the standard output for a *filesystem* that has no current record in the **/etc/dumpdates** file, even when listed in **/etc/fstab** file.

3. When no *argument* is specified, the *key* parameter is assumed to be **-9u** so that the default file system is dumped to a default storage medium named **/dev/rmt0h** (usually a tape).

dump

The **dump** command copies to the default **/dev/rmt0h**, or to the alternate storage device specified with the **-f** flag, all files changed after a certain date in the specified local *filesystem*.

rdump

The **rdump** command copies to the *dump_file* storage device all files changed after a certain date in the specified *filesystem*. This command is similar in operation to **dump**, except that the **-f** flag is always specified (see **Flags**) together with any *otherkey* you may wish to specify. The *dump_file* parameter should always be specified by machine name and device name as *machine:device name*.

The **rdump** command starts remote server **/usr/sbin/rmt** on the client machine to access the storage medium.

The **dump** command exits with 0 status on success. Start up errors are indicated with an exit code of 1; abnormal termination is indicated with an exit code of 3.

Examples

To perform a tape dump, enter commands simmilar to the following examples.

1. Start with a full level 0 dump by entering:
    dump -0un -s 26500 -d 6250 filesystem

    In the foregoing example, **0** specifies that all files in **filesystem** must be dumped to tape; **u** specifies that after a successful **filesystem** write to tape, a new timestamp should be entered on the **filesystem** record line in the **/etc/dumpdates** file, and **n** specifies that operators must be notified. The size of the tape is 26,500 feet and has a write density of 6250 bpi.

2. To do a daily tape dump of any active file systems using a modified Tower of Hanoi algorithm, use the following sequence of dump levels:
    3 2 5 4 7 6 9 8 9 9....

    The sequence **3 2 5 4 7 6 9 8 9 9** is used for a daily tape dump. This sequence specifies a set of 10 tapes per dumped file system and is used on a cyclical basis. Each week, a level 1 dump is taken and the daily Hanoi sequence repeats with **3**.

3. For weekly tape dumps, a set of 5 tapes per dumped file system is also used on a cyclical basis. Each month a level 0 dump is taken on a set of fresh tapes that is saved forever.

4. To dump a local file system to a remote storage tape, enter a command similar to the following:
    rdump -3u -f tape_server:/dev/rmt0h filesystem

    In the foregoing example, **3** specifies the dump level of all files in **filesystem** that must be dumped to tape **/dev/rmt0h** on system **tape_server**, and **u** specifies that after a successful **filesystem** write to tape, a new timestamp should be entered on the **filesystem** record line in **/etc/dumpdates**.

Files

/usr/sbin/dump

Specifies the command path.

/dev/rrz0g

Default file system to dump to tape.

/dev/rmt0h

Default tape unit to use for the tape dump.

/etc/dumpdates

The dump date record database.

dump(8)

/etc/fstab
Table of file systems.

/etc/group
Lists group operator.

Related Information

Commands: **restore(8)**, **rrestore(8)**, **rmt(8)**

dumpfs

Purpose   Dump UFS file system information

Synopsis   **dumpfs** *filesystem* ... | *device*

Description

The **dumpfs** command prints out the super block and cylinder group information for the specified UFS file system(s) or special device. The listing is very long and detailed. This command is useful for getting information about the file system block size and minimum free space percentage, for example.

Files

/usr/sbin/dumpfs
    Specifies the command path.

Related Information

Commands: **fsck(8)**, **newfs(8)**, **tunefs(8)**

Files: **disktab(4)**

edquota

Purpose   Edits user quotas

Synopsis   **edquota** [-**p** *proto_user*] [-**u**] *username* ...

edquota [-**p** *proto_group*] -**g** *groupname* ...

edquota [-**u** I -**g**] -**t**

Flags

-**g**   Edits the quotas of one or more groups, specified by *groupname* ... on the command line. When used with -**t**, changes the grace period for all filesystems with group quotas specified in **/etc/fstab**.

-**p**   Causes **edquota** to initialize the specified quotas by duplicating the quotas of the specified prototypical *proto_user* (if used with the -**u** flag or no other flags) or *proto_group* (if used with the -**g** flag). *proto_user* or *proto_group* must have a previously defined and valid quota file.   This is the normal mechanism used to initialize quotas for group of users.

-**t**   Changes the default grace period for which users may exceed their soft limits. By default, or when you specify -**t** with the -**u** flag, the grace period is set for all filesystems with user quotas specified in **/etc/fstab**; when you specify -**t** with the -**g** flag, the grace period is set for all the filesystems with group quotas specified in **/etc/fstab**.

-**u**   Edits the quotas of one or more users, specified by *username* ... on the command line. -**u** is the default. When used with -**t**, changes the grace period for all filesystems with user quotas specified in **/etc/fstab**.

Description

The **edquota** command is a quota editor. By default, or if you specify -**u**, user quotas of the *username*s you specify are edited. If you specify -**g**, group quotas of the *groupname*s you specify are edited.

For each user or group, the program creates a temporary file with an ASCII representation of the current disk quotas for that user or group, then invokes an editor that you use to modify the file.

Using the editor, you can then modify quotas, add new quotas, and so on. Setting a quota to **0** (zero) indicates that no quota should be imposed. Setting a hard limit to **1** (one) indicates that no allocations should be permitted. Setting a soft limit to **1** (one) with a hard limit of **0** (zero) indicates that allocations should be permitted on only a temporary basis (see the **-t** flag). The current usage information in the file is for informational purposes; only the hard and soft limits can be changed.

When you exit the editor, **edquota** reads the temporary file and modifies the binary quota files to reflect the changes made.

The **vi** editor is invoked by default. To override the default, specify a different editor for the **EDITOR** environment variable in your login file.

Use the **-p** flag to initialize quotas for the users or groups by specifying a *proto_user* or *proto_group* whose quotas are to be duplicated.

Users are permitted to exceed their soft limits for a grace period that may be specified for each filesystem. Once the grace period has expired, the soft limit is enforced as a hard limit. The default grace period for a filesystem is specified in **/usr/include/ufs/quota.h**.

Use the **-t** flag to change the grace period. By default, or when invoked with **-u**, **-t** sets the grace period for all filesystems with user quotas specified in **/etc/fstab**. When invoked with the **-g** flag, **-t** sets the grace period for all filesystems with group quotas specified in **/etc/fstab**.

For each filesystem, the program creates a temporary file with an ASCII representation of the current grace period for that user or group, then invokes an editor that you use to modify the grace period. The grace period may be specified in days, hours, minutes, or seconds. Setting a grace period to **0** (zero) indicates that the default grace period should be imposed. Setting a grace period to **1** second indicates that no grace period should be granted. When you exit the editor, **edquota** reads the temporary file and modifies the **quota.h** file to reflect the changes made.

Only the superuser can edit quotas.

Files

/usr/sbin/edquota
>   Specifies the command path

[*filesystem_root*]/**quota.user**
>   Contains user quotas for *filesystem*

[*filesystem_root*]/**quota.group**
>   Contains user quotas for *filesystem*

/etc/fstab
>   Contains filesystem names and locations

edquota(8)

Related Information

Commands: **quota**(1), **quotacheck**(8), **quotaon**(8), **repquota**(8).

Functions: **quotactl**(2).

Files: **fstab**(4). Functions: **setluid**(3).

fastboot

Purpose   Reboots the system without checking file systems

Synopsis   **fastboot** [**-l -n -q**]

Flags

-l   Does not log the reboot or place a shutdown record in the accounting file

-n   Does not sync the disks or log the reboot

-q   Performs a quick reboot without first shutting down running processes; does not log the reboot

Description

The **fastboot** command reboots the system without checking file systems. The program creates the **fastboot** file then invokes the **reboot** program. The system start-up script contains instructions to look for the **fastboot** file. If present, the script removes the file and skips the invocation of the **fsck** command.

You must have **root** privileges to use this command.

Files

/usr/sbin/fastboot
            Specifies the command path

Related Information

Commands: **fsck(8)**, **rc**_n_**(8)**, **reboot(8)**, **shutdown(8)**, **syslogd(8)**

Calls: **sync(2)**, **syslog(3)**

fasthalt

Purpose   Halts the system

Synopsis   **fasthalt** [-l -n -q]

Flags

-l   Does not log the halt using **syslog**

-n   Prevents the sync before stopping, and does not log the halt using **syslog**

-q   Causes a quick halt, does not log the halt using **syslog**, and makes no attempt to kill all processes

Description

The **fasthalt** command halts the system and flags a subsequent reboot to skip the execution of **fsck**. The program creates the **fastboot** file, then invokes the **halt** program. The system start-up script contains instructions to look for the **fastboot** file. If present, the script removes the file and skips the invocation of the **fsck** command.

If the command is invoked without the **-l**, **-n**, or **-q** flag, the **halt** program logs the shutdown using the **syslogd** command and places a record of the shutdown in the login accounting file, **/var/adm/wtmp**. Using the **-q** and the **-n** flags imply the **-l** flag.

You must have **root** privileges to use this command.

Files

/usr/sbin/fasthalt
Specifies the command path

/usr/sbin/syslogd
Specifies the path of the syslog daemon

Related Information

Commands: **fsck(8)**, **halt(8)**, **syslogd(8)**

Calls: **halt(2)**, **sync(2)**, **syslog(3)**

fingerd

Purpose   The user information server for networks

Synopsis   **fingerd** [-s]

The **fingerd** program allows users to get information about remote systems or users when they execute; for example, **finger** *user@host*.

Flags

-s   Turns on socket level debugging.

Description

The **fingerd** program is a protocol that provides an interface to the **finger(1)** command. **fingerd** is invoked by **inetd(8)**, which listens for **finger** requests at port 79. When it receives control, **fingerd** reads a single command line, terminated by a newline, and passes it to the **finger** command, which generates a report. **fingerd** closes its port connection when output from **finger** is finished.

Files

/usr/sbin/fingerd
          Specifies the command path

/etc/passwd
          User database

/var/adm/utmp
          who file

$HOME/.plan
          Plans for requested user

$HOME/.project
          Projects for requested user

/usr/bin/whois
          whois command

/usr/bin/who
          who command

Related Information

Commands: **finger(1)**, **inetd(8)**, **syslogd(8)**, **who(1)**

Specification: RFC742

fsck

Purpose   Provides file system consistency check and interactive repair

Synopsis   **fsck** [*options*] [*file system*]

fsck [*common_options*] [**-t ufs** I **s5fs** [*fs_type_options*] [*file system*]]

fsck [*common_options*] [**-T ufs** I **s5fs** [*fs_type_options*] [*file system*]]

Description

Since OSF/1 supports multiple file system types, **fsck** is a front-end program used to manage each file system type on your system. See the subsequent major sections of this reference page for information about using **fsck** for each specific file system type.

The ufs is the default file system type in OSF/1. If a system has only ufs file system, no changes are needed to manage the file systems on the system.

If fsck is invoked with zero or more options (but no **-t** or **-T** options), and no file system names are specified, the file systems listed in **/etc/fstab** are checked. Depending on the file system types of the file systems listed in **/etc/fstab**, the file system type dependent fsck programs are invoked using the option list. A file system dependent **fsck** program is invoked only if there are file systems in **/etc/fstab** that are of that file system type. If the **fsck** program of the default file system type (ufs) fails; that is, the program terminates with a non-zero value, **fsck** terminates with the exit value of the default file system type **fsck**. This ensures that the auto-reboot dependencies such as those commonly used in the run command script continue to function. However, if a non-default file system type **fsck** program terminates with a non-zero value, **fsck** continues to execute the remaining file system type dependent **fsck** programs as necessary before terminating. It then returns the first non-zero exit value from the non-default file system type **fsck** programs.

If **fsck** is invoked with zero or more options (but no **-t** or **-T** options) and file systems are specifed, each file system is searched for in **/etc/fstab.** If it is in **/etc/fstab,** the listed file system type is used to determine which file system type dependent **fsck** program will be invoked with the supplied options on the device. If a file system is not listed in **/etc/fstab**, that file system will be checked using the default file system type **fsck** program. File systems of different file system types may be listed in any order on the command line. Each file system dependent **fsck** program will be invoked once with the appropriate list of file systems.

fsck(8)

The front-end **fsck** program interprets the **-t** and the **-T** flags. Any options specified before the **-t** and the **-T** flags are common options which are passed onto all file system dependent **fsck** programs to be run. Options following the **-t** and the **-T** flags are passed along only to the **fsck** programs of the specified file system types.

-t   Specifies the file system type to check. The immediately following argument is the name of the file system type. If any options follow, they are applied only in the specified file system type dependent **fsck** program. If any file systems follow before another **-t** option, the file systems are treated as of the specified file system type.

-T   Specifies to which file system type the following options apply. The immediately following argument is the name of the file system type. If any options follow, they are applied only in the specified file system type dependent **fsck** program. If any file systems follow, if there is a previous **-t** option, the file systems are treated as file systems of the file system type specified by that **-t** option. If there is no previous **-t** option, each file system is looked up in **/etc/fstab** to determine its file system type. If a file system is not listed in **/etc/fstab**, it is assumed to be a file system of the default type. ufs is the default file system type on OSF/1. You must be **root** to use this command.

Examples

Assume that **/etc/fstab** contains the following ufs and s5fs file systems: */dev/ufs_dev* is a device listed in **/etc/fstab** as containing a ufs file system; */dev/s5fs_dev* is a device listed in **/etc/fstab** as containing a s5fs file system; */dev/unlisted* is a device that is not listed in **/etc/fstab**; **ufs_fsck** is the ufs **fsck** program; **s5fs_fsck** is the **fsck** program that checks System V file systems.

1.   To invoke the front-end **fsck** program which invokes the **ufs_fsck** and the **s5fs_fsck** file system dependent **fsck** programs (both of which check the **/etc/fstab** file), enter:

    fsck

2.   To check a specific ufs file system, a System V file system, and an unlisted file system, enter:

    fsck /dev/ufs_dev /dev/s5fs_dev /dev/unlisted

    The **ufs_fsck** program checks the /dev/ufs_dev and /dev/unlisted file systems. The **s5fs_fsck** program checks the /dev/s5fs_dev file system.

3. To check all ufs file systems and apply the **-p** flag, and to check all System V file systems and apply the **-D** flag, enter:

   fsck -T ufs -p -T s5fs -D

   The **fsck** program invokes the **ufs_fsck** program (which checks the usf file systems and applies the **-p** flag) and the **s5fs_fsck** program (which checks the System V file systems and applies the **-D** flag.

4. To check all ufs file systems and apply the **-p** flag, enter:

   fsck -t ufs -p

   The **fsck** program invokes the **ufs_fsck -p** command. s5fs_fsck is not invoked (although there are System V file systems listed in **/etc/fstab**) since only the **-t ufs** file system specification was given in the command line.

5. To check an unlisted System V file system, enter:

   fsck -t s5fs /dev/unlisted

   The **fsck** program invokes **s5fs_fsck** which checks the /dev/unlisted file system.

6. To check a file system which is not listed in the **/etc/fstab** file, enter:

   fsck /dev/unlisted

   The **fsck** program invokes the **ufs_fsck** program which checks the /dev/unlisted file system.

FILE SYSTEM DEPENDENT fsck - FOR UFS FILE SYSTEMS

Synopsis   **fsck** **-p** [**-m** *mode*]

fsck [**-b** *block#*] [**-c**] [**-y**] [**-n**] [**-m** *mode*] [*file system*] ...

Description

The first form of **fsck** preens a standard set of file systems or the specified file systems. It is normally used in the run command script during automatic reboot. Here **fsck** reads the **/etc/fstab** table to determine which file systems to check. Only partitions in **fstab** that are mounted "rw," "rq" or "ro" and that have non-zero pass number are checked. File systems with pass number 1 (normally just the root file system) are checked one at a time. When pass 1 completes, all remaining file systems are checked, running one process per disk drive. The disk drive containing each file system is inferred from the longest prefix of the device name that ends in a digit; the remaining characters are assumed to be the partition designator.

The system takes care that only a restricted class of innocuous inconsistencies can happen unless hardware or software failures intervene. These inconsistencies include unreferenced inodes, link counts in inodes that are too large, missing blocks in the free map, blocks in the free map that are also in files, and wrong counts in the super-block.

The preceding inconsistencies are the only ones that **fsck** with the **-p** flag corrects; if it encounters other inconsistencies, it exits with an abnormal return status and an automatic reboot will then fail. For each corrected inconsistency one or more lines are printed identifying the file system on which the correction takes place, and the nature of the correction. After successfully correcting a file system, **fsck** prints the number of files on that file system, the number of used and free blocks, and the percentage of fragmentation.

If sent a QUIT signal, **fsck** finishes the file system checks, then exits with an abnormal return status that causes an automatic reboot to fail. This is useful when you want to finish the file system checks during an automatic reboot but do not want the machine to come up multiuser after the checks complete.

Without the **-p** option, **fsck** audits and interactively repairs inconsistent conditions for file systems. If the file system is inconsistent, you are prompted for concurrence before each correction is attempted. Note that some of the corrective actions which are not correctable under the **-p** option will result in some loss of data. The amount and severity of data lost can be determined from the diagnostic output. The default action for each consistency correction is to wait for you to respond **yes** or **no**. If you do not have write permission on the file system **fsck** defaults to a **-n** action.

The **fsck** has more consistency checks than its predecessors **check, dcheck, fcheck,** and **icheck** combined.

The following flags are interpreted by **fsck.**

-b   Use the block specified immediately after the flag as the super block for the file system. Block 32 is usually an alternate super block.

-l   Limit the number of parallel checks to the number specified in the following argument. By default, the limit is the number of disks, running one process per disk. If a smaller limit is given, the disks are checked round-robin, one file system at a time.

-m   Use the mode specified in octal immediately after the flag as the permission bits to use when creating the lost+found directory rather than the default 1777. In particular, systems that do not want to have lost files accessible by all users on the system should use a more restrictive set of permissions such as 700.

-y   Assume a yes response to all questions asked by **fsck**; this should be used with great caution as this is a free license to continue after essentially unlimited trouble has been encountered.

-n   Assume a no response to all questions asked by **fsck** except for "CONTINUE?", which is assumed to be affirmative; do not open the file system for writing.

-c   If the file system is in the old (static table) format, convert it to the new (dynamic table) format. If the file system is in the new format, convert it to the old format provided the old format can support the file system configuration. In interactive mode, **fsck** will list the direction the conversion is to be made and ask whether the conversion should be done. If a negative answer is given, no further operations are done on the file system. In preen mode, the direction of the conversion is listed and done if possible without user interaction. Conversion in preen mode is best used when all the file systems are being converted at once. The format of a file system can be determined from the first line of output from **dumpfs**.

If no file systems are given to **fsck**, then a default list of file systems is read from the file **/etc/fstab**.

Inconsistencies checked are as follows:

1.   Blocks claimed by more than one inode or the free map.

2.   Blocks claimed by an inode outside the range of the file system.

3.   Incorrect link counts.

4.   Size checks: directory size not of proper format; partially truncated file.

5.   Bad inode format.

6.   Blocks not accounted for anywhere.

7.   Directory checks: file pointing to unallocated inode; inode number out of range; . (dot) or .. (dot dot) not the first two entries of a directory or having the wrong inode number.

8.   Super Block checks: more blocks for inodes than there are in the file system.

9.   Bad free block map format.

10.   Total free block and/or free inode count incorrect.

Orphaned files and directories (allocated but unreferenced) are, with your concurrence, reconnected by placing them in the **lost+found** directory. The name assigned is the inode number. If the **lost+found** directory does not exist, it is created. If there is insufficient space its size is increased.

fsck(8)

Because of inconsistencies between the block device and the buffer cache, the raw device should always be used.

Files

/usr/sbin/fsck

> Specifies the command path

/etc/fstab

> Contains default list of file systems to check

Related Information

Commands: **fsdb(8)**, **newfs(8)**, **reboot(8)**

Files: **fs(5)**, **fstab(5)**

FILE SYSTEM DEPENDENT fsck - FOR SYSTEM V FILE SYSTEMS

Synopsis **fsck** [*options*]

fsck -T s5fs [*options*]

fsck -t s5fs [*options*] [*file system*]

Description

If there are System V file systems listed in **/etc/fstab**, the first and second forms of **fsck** cause all of these file systems to be checked.

If **fsck** is invoked with the **-t s5fs** flag but with no file systems listed, all of the System V file systems listed in **/etc/fstab** are checked. If a file system is listed as an argument, it will be checked as a System V file system.

The **fsck** command audits and interactively repairs inconsistent conditions for System V file systems. If the file system is found to be consistent, the number of files, blocks used, and blocks free are reported. If the file system is inconsistent, you are prompted for concurrence before each correction is attempted. Note that most corrective actions will result in some loss of data. The amount and severity of data loss can be determined from the diagnostic output. The default action for each correction is to wait for you to respond yes or no before any action is taken. If you do not have write permission, **fsck** defaults to the action of the **-n** option.

The **fsck** program interprets the following flags:

-y   Assumes a "yes" response to all questions asked by **fsck**.

-n   Assumes a "no" response to all questions asked by **fsck**; do not open the file system for writing.

-sb:c   Ignores the actual free list and (unconditionally) reconstructs a new one by rewriting the super-block of the file system. The file system must be unmounted while this is done.

The **-sb:c** flag allows for the creation of an optimal free-list organization. The following forms are supported:

-s

-sBlocks-per-cylinder:Blocks-to-skip

If **b:c** is not given, the values used when the file system was created are used. If these values were not specified, then a reasonable default value is used.

-S   Conditionally reconstructs the free list. This flag is like **-sb:c** except that the free list is rebuilt only if there are no discrepancies discovered in the file system. Using **-S** forces a "no" response to all questions asked by **fsck**. This flag is useful for forcing free list reorganization on uncontaminated file systems.

-C   If **fsck** cannot obtain enough memory to keep its tables, it uses a scratch file. If you specify the **-C** flag, the file named in the next argument is used as the scratch file, if needed. Without the **-C** flag, **fsck** prompts you for the name of the scratch file. The file chosen should not be on the file system being checked, and if it is not a special file or did not already exist, it is removed when **fsck** exits.

-q   Quiet fsck. Do not print size-check messages. Unreferenced fifos and symlinks will silently be removed. If **fsck** requires it, counts in the super block will be automatically fixed and the free list salvaged.

-D   Directories are checked for bad blocks. Useful after system crashes.

-f   Fast check. Check block and sizes and check the free list. The free list will be reconstructed, if necessary.

The **fsck** program checks the following inconsistencies:

1.   Blocks claimed by more than one inode or the free list.

2.   Blocks claimed by an inode or the free list outside the range of the file system.

3.   Incorrect link counts.

4.   Size checks: Incorrect number of blocks, directory size not 16-byte aligned.

5.   Bad inode format.

6.   Blocks not accounted for anywhere.

7.   Directory checks: File pointing to unallocated inoder, inode number out of range.

8.   Super Block checks: More than 65536 inodes, more blocks for inodes than there are in the file system.

9.   Bad free block list format.

10.   Total free block and/or free inode count incorrect.

Orphaned files and directories (allocated but unreferenced) are, with your concurrence, reconnected by placing them in the lost+found directory, if the files are nonempty. You are notified if the file or directory is or is not empty. Empty files or directories are removed, if you do not specify the **-n** flag. **fsck** forces the reconnection of nonempty directories. The name assigned is the inode number. The only restriction is that the lost+found directory must preexist in the root of the file system being checked and must have empty slots in which entries can be made. This is accomplished by making lost+found, copying a number of files to the directory, and then removing them (before **fsck** is executed).

Because of inconsistencies between the block device and the buffer cache, the raw device should always be used.

Files

/usr/sbin/fsck
        Specifies the command path

/etc/fstab
        Contains the default list of System V file systems to check

Related Information

Commands: **newfs(8)**

Files: **fstab(4)**

fsdb

Purpose   File system debugger

Synopsis   **fsdb** [*options*] *special*

Flags

-?   Display usage

-o   Override some error conditions

-p'string'
            Set prompt to string

-w   Open for write

Description

Since **fsdb** reads the disk raw, it is able to circumvent normal file system security. Extreme caution is advised in determining its availability on the system. Suggested permissions are 600, owned by **bin**.

You must be **root** to use this command.

The **fsdb** command can be used to repair a damaged file system after a crash. It has conversions to translate block and i-numbers into their corresponding disk addresses. Also included are mnemonic offsets to access different parts of an inode. These greatly simplify the process of correcting control block entries or descending the file system tree.

The **fsdb** command contains several error-checking routines to verify inode and block addresses. These can be disabled if necessary by invoking **fsdb** with the **-o** option.

The **fsdb** command reads a block at a time and works with raw as well as block I/O. A buffer management routine is used to retain commonly used blocks of data in order to reduce the number of read system calls. All assignment operations result in an immediate write-through of the corresponding block. Note that in order to modify any portion of the disk, **fsdb** must be invoked with the **-w** option.

Wherever possible, **adb**-like syntax was adopted to promote the use of **fsdb** through familiarity.

Numbers are considered hexadecimal by default. However, you have control over how data is to be displayed or accepted. The **base** command displays or sets the input/output base. Once set, all input will default to this base and all output will be shown in this base. The base can be overriden temporarily for input by preceding hexadecimal numbers with '0x', preceding decimal numbers with '0t', or octal numbers with '0'. Hexadecimal numbers beginning with a-f or A-F must be preceded with '0x' to distinguish them from commands.

Disk addressing by **fsdb** is at the byte level. However, **fsdb** offers many commands to convert a desired inode, directory entry, block, superblock etc. to a byte address. Once the address has been calculated, **fsdb** will record the result in **dot**.

Several global values are maintained by **fsdb**: The current base (referred to as **base**); the current address (referred to as **dot**); the current inode (referred to as **inode**); the current count (referred to as **count**); and the current type (referred to as **type**). Most commands use the preset value of **dot** in their execution. For example,

> 2:inode

will first set the value of **dot** to 2, ':' will alert the start of a command, and the **inode** command will set **inode** to 2. A count is specified after a ','. Once set, **count** will remain at this value until a new command is encountered which will then reset the value back to 1 (the default). So, if

> 2000,400/X

is typed, 400 hex longs are listed from 2000, and when completed, the value of **dot** will be 2000 + 400 * sizeof (long). If you press the **<Return>** key, the output routine uses the current values of **dot**, **count**, and **type** and displays 400 more hex longs. An asterisk (*) causes the entire block to be displayed.

End of fragment, block and file are maintained by **fsdb**. When displaying data as fragments or blocks, an error message is displayed when the end of fragment or block is reached. When displaying data using the **db**, **ib**, *directory*, or **file** commands, an error message is displayed if the end of file is reached. This is mainly needed to avoid passing the end of a directory or file and getting unknown and unwanted results.

An example showing several commands and the use of **<Return>** follows:

> **> 2:ino; 0:dir?d**

or

> **> 2:ino; 0:db:block?d**

The two examples are synonymous for getting to the first directory entry of the root of the file system. Once there, subsequent use of the **<Return>** key (or +, -) advances to subsequent entries. The following display is again synonymous:

> **> 2:inode; :ls**

or

> **> :ls /**

Expressions

The symbols recognized by **fsdb** are:

<Return>
> update the value of **dot** by the current value of *type* and display using the current value of *count*.

#
> numeric expressions may be composed of +, -, *, and % operators (evaluated left to right) and may use parentheses. Once evaluated, the value of **dot** is updated.

, count
> count indicator. The global value of *count* will be updated to *count*. The value of *count* remains until a new command is run. A count specifier of '*' will attempt to show the information of a block. The default for *count* is 1.

?f
> display in structured style with format specifier *f*

/f
> display in unstructured style with format specifier *f*

.
> the value of **dot**.

+e
> increment the value of **dot** by the expression *e*. The amount actually incremented is dependent on the size of *type*:

> $$dot = dot + e * sizeof\ (type)$$

> The default for *e* is 1.

-e
> decrement the value of **dot** by the expression *e* (see +).

*e
> multiply the value of **dot** by the expression *e*. Multiplication and division don't use *type*. In the above calculation of **dot**, consider the size of (*type*) to be 1.

%e
> divide the value of **dot** by the expression *e* (see *).

<*name* restore an address saved in register *name*. *name* must be a single letter or digit.

> *name* save an address in register *name*. *name* must be a single letter or digit.

=*f* display indicator. If *f* is a legitimate format specifier, then the value of **dot** is displayed using format specifier *f*. Otherwise, assignment is assumed.

= *[s] [e]* assignment indicator. The address pointed to by **dot** has its contents changed to the value of the expression *e* or to the ASCII representation of the quoted ("") string *s*. This may be useful for changing directory names or ASCII file information.

=+ *e* incremental assignment. The address pointed to by **dot** has its contents incremented by expression *e*.

=- *e* decremental assignment. The address pointed to by **dot** has its contents decremented by expression *e*.

Commands

A command must be prefixed by a ':' character. Only enough letters of the command to uniquely distinguish it are needed. Multiple commands may be entered on one line by separating them by a space, tab or ';'.

In order to view a potentially unmounted disk in a reasonable manner, **fsdb** offers the **cd**, **pwd**, **ls**, and **find** commands. The functionality of these commands substantially matches those of its **UNIX** counterparts. The '*', '?', and '[-]' wild card characters are available.

base=b display or set base. As stated above, all input and output is governed by the current **base**. If the '=b' is left off, the current **base** is displayed. Otherwise, the current **base** is set to *b*. Note that this is interpreted using the old value of **base**, so to ensure correctness use the '0', '0t', or '0x' prefix when changing the **base**. The default for **base** is hexadecimal.

block convert the value of **dot** to a block address.

cd*dir* change the current directory to directory *dir*. The current values of *inode* and **dot** are also updated. If no *dir* is specified, then change directories to inode 2 ("/").

cg convert the value of *dot* to a cylinder group.

directory
If the current *inode* is a directory, then the value of *dot* is converted to a directory slot offset in that directory and *dot* now points to this entry.

file the value of *dot* is taken as a relative block count from the beginning of the file. The value of *dot* is updated to the first byte of this block.

find *dir [-name n] [-inum i]*

find files by name or i-number. *find* recursively searches directory *dir* and below for filenames whose i-number matches *i* or whose name matches pattern *n*. Note that only one of the two options (-name or -inum) may be used at one time. Also, the -print is not needed or accepted.

fill=*p*   fill an area of disk with pattern *p*. The area of disk is delimited by *dot* and *count*.

fragment

convert the value of *dot* to a fragment address. The only difference between the *fragment* command and the *block* command is the amount that is able to be displayed.

inode   convert the value of *dot* to an inode address. If successful, the current value of *inode* will be updated as well as the value of *dot*. As a convenient shorthand, if ':inode' appears at the beginning of the line, the value of *dot* is set to the current *inode* and that inode is displayed in inode format.

ls *[-R] [-l] pat1 pat2 ...*

list directories or files. If no file is specified, the current directory is assumed. Either or both of the options may be used (but, if used, *must* be specified before the filename specifiers). Also, as stated above, wild card characters are available and multiple arguments may be given. The long listing shows only the i-number and the name; use the *inode* command with '?i' to get more information.

override toggle the value of override. Some error conditions may be overriden if override is toggled on.

prompt *p*

change the fsdb prompt to *p*. *p* must be surrounded by (")s.

pwd   display the current working directory.

quit   quit *fsdb*.

sb   the value of *dot* is taken as a cylinder group number and then converted to the address of the superblock in that cylinder group. As a shorthand, ':sb' at the beginning of a line will set the value of *dot* to *the* superblock and display it in superblock format.

!   escape to shell

Inode Commands

In addition to the above commands, there are several commands that deal with inode fields and operate directly on the current *inode* (they still require the ':'). They may be used to more easily display or change the particular fields.

The value of *dot* is only used by the ':db' and ':ib' commands. Upon completion of the command, the value of *dot* is changed to point to that particular field. For example,

> **:ln=+1**

would increment the link count of the current *inode* and set the value of *dot* to the address of the link count field.

at   access time.

bs   block size.

ct   creation time.

db   use the current value of *dot* as a direct block index, where direct blocks number from 0 - 11. In order to display the block itself, you need to 'pipe' this result into the *block* or *fragment* command. For example,

> **1:db:block,20/X**

would get the contents of data block field 1 from the inode and convert it to a block address. 20 longs are then displayed in hexadecimal (see Formatted Output section).

gid   group id.

ib   use the current value of *dot* as an indirect block index where indirect blocks number from 0 - 2. This will only get the indirect block itself (the block containing the pointers to the actual blocks). Use the *file* command and start at block 12 to get to the actual blocks.

ln   link count.

mt   modification time.

md   mode.

maj   major device number.

min   minor device number.

nm   although listed here, this command actually operates on the directory name field. Once poised at the desired directory entry (using the *directory* command), this command will allow you to change or display the directory name. For example,

> **> 7:dir:nm="foo"**

will get the 7th directory entry of the current *inode* and change its name to foo. Note that names cannot be made larger than the field is set up for. If an attempt is made, the string is truncated to fit and a warning message to this effect is displayed.

sz   file size.

uid   user id.

Formatted Output

There are two styles and many format types. The two styles are structured and unstructured. Structured output is used to display inodes, directories, superblocks and the like. Unstructured just displays raw data. The following table shows the different ways of displaying:

?

c	display as cylinder groups
i	display as inodes
d	display as directories
s	display as superblocks

/

b	display as bytes
c	display as characters
o O	display as octal shorts or longs
d D	display as decimal shorts or longs
x X	display as hexadecimal shorts or longs

The format specifier immediately follows the '/' or '?' character. The values displayed by '/b' and all '?' formats are displayed in the current *base*. Also, *type* is appropriately updated upon completion.

Examples

> **2000+400%(20+20)=D**

will display 2010 in decimal (use of *fsdb* as a calculator for complex arithmetic).

> **386:ino?i**

display i-number 386 in an inode format. This now becomes the current *inode*.

> **:ln=4**

changes the link count for the current *inode* to 4.

> **:ln=+1**

increments the link count by 1.

> **:ct=X**

display the creation time as a hexadecimal long.

> **:mt=t**

display the modification time in time format.

> **0:file/c**

displays, in *ASCII*, block zero of the file associated with the current *inode*.

> **2:ino,*?d**

displays the first blocks worth of directory entries for the root inode of this file system. It will stop prematurely if the eof is reached.

> **5:dir:inode; 0:file,*/c**

changes the current inode to that associated with the 5th directory entry (numbered from zero) of the current *inode*. The first logical block of the file is then displayed in *ASCII*.

> **:sb**

displays the superblock of this file system.

> **1:cg?c**

displays cylinder group information and summary for cylinder group 1.

> **2:inode; 7:dir=3**

changes the i-number for the seventh directory slot in the root directory to 3.

> **7:dir:nm="name"**

changes the name field in the directory slot to *name*.

> **2:db:block,*?d** displays the third block of the current *inode* as directory entries.

> **3c3:fragment,20:fill=0x20**

get fragment 3c3 and fill 20 *type* elements with 0x20.

> **2050=0xffff**

set the contents of address 2050 to 0xffffffff. 0xffffffff may be truncated depending on the current *type*.

> **1c92434="this is some text"**

will place the ASCII for the string at 1c92434.

Files

/usr/sbin/fsdb
> Specifies the command path

Related Information

> Commands: **fsck(8)**

ftpd

Purpose   The DARPA Internet File Transfer Protocol server

Synopsis   **ftpd** [**-dl**] [**-t***timeout*] [**-T***maxtimeout*]

Flags

-d   Debugging information is written to the **syslogd**(8).

-l   Each FTP session is logged in the syslog.

-t*time-out*
         The inactivity time-out period will be set to *time-out* seconds.

-T*maxtime-out*
         The maximum timeout period allowd may be set to *timeout* seconds with
         this option.

Description

The **ftpd** command is the DARPA (Defense Advanced Research Projects Agency)
Internet File Transfer Protocol server process. The server uses the TCP protocol
and listens at the port specified in the FTP service specification; see **services (5).**

If the **-d** flag is specified, debugging information is written to the **syslogd**(8).

If the **-l** flag is specified, each ftp session is logged in the syslog.

The FTP server will time out an inactive session after 15 minutes. If the **-t** flag is
specified, the inactivity time-out period will be set to *time-out* seconds. A client
may also request a different time-out period; the maximum period allowed may be
set to *time-out* seconds with the **-T** flag. The default limit is 2 hours.

The FTP server currently supports the following ftp requests; case is not
distinguished.

Request	Description
ABOR	Abort previous command
ACCT	Specify account (ignored)
ALLO	Allocate storage (vacuously)
APPE	Append to a file
CDUP	Change to parent of current working directory
CWD	Change working directory
DELE	Delete a file
HELP	Give help information
LIST	Give list files in a directory (**ls -lgA**)

MKD	Make a directory
MDTM	Show last modification time of file
MODE	Specify data transfer mode
NLST	Give name list of files in directory
NOOP	Do nothing
PASS	Specify password
PASV	Prepare for server-to-server transfer
PORT	Specify data connection port
PWD	Print the current working directory
QUIT	Terminate session
REST	Restart incomplete transfer
RETR	Retrieve a file
RMD	Remove a directory
RNFR	Specify rename-from filename
RNTO	Specify rename-to filename
SITE	Nonstandard commands (see next section)
SIZE	Return size of file
STAT	Return status of server
STOR	Store a file
STOU	Store a file with a unique name
STRU	Specify data transfer structure
SYST	Show operating system type of server system
TYPE	Specify data transfer type
USER	Specify username
XCUP	Change to parent of current working directory (deprecated)
XCWD	Change working directory (deprecated)
XMKD	Make a directory (deprecated)
XPWD	Print the current working directory (deprecated)
XRMD	Remove a directory (deprecated)

The following nonstandard or UNIX compatible commands are supported by the **SITE** request.

Request	Description
UMASK	Change umask (for example: **SITE UMASK 002**)
IDLE	Set idle timer (for example: **SITE IDLE 60**)
CHMOD	Change mode of a file (for example: **SITE CHMOD 755** filename)
HELP	Give help information (for example: **SITE HELP**)

The remaining **ftp** requests specified in Internet RFC959 are recognized, but not implemented. **MDTM** and **SIZE** are not specified in RFC959, but will appear in the next updated FTP RFC.

The **ftp** server will abort an active file transfer only when the **ABOR** command is preceded by a Telnet Interrupt Process (IP) signal and a Telnet Synch signal in the command Telnet stream, as described in Internet RFC959. If a **STAT** command is received during a data transfer, preceded by a Telnet IP and Synch, transfer status will be returned.

The **ftpd** command interprets filenames according to the ''globbing'' conventions used by **csh**(1). This allows users to utilize the metacharacters ''*?[]{ }~''.

The **ftpd** command authenticates users according to four rules:

1.   The username must be in the password database, **/etc/passwd**, and not have a null password. In this case, a password must be provided by the client before any file operations may be performed.

2.   The username must not appear in the **/etc/ftpusers** file.

3.   The user must have a standard shell returned by **getusershell**(3).

4.   If the username is **anonymous** or **ftp**, an anonymous **ftp** account must be present in the password file (user **ftp**). In this case, the user is allowed to log in by specifying any password (by convention this is given as the client host's name).

In the last case, **ftpd** takes special measures to restrict the client's access privileges. The server performs a **chroot**(2) command to the home directory of the **ftp** user. In order that system security is not breached, it is recommended that the **ftp** subtree be constructed with care; the following rules are recommended.

~ftp   Make the home directory owned by **ftp** and unwritable by anyone.

~ftp/bin   Make this directory owned by the superuser and unwritable by anyone. The program **ls**(1) must be present to support the list command. This program should have mode 111.

~ftp/etc   Make this directory owned by the superuser and unwritable by anyone. The files **passwd**(5) and **group**(5) must be present for the **ls** command to be able to produce owner names rather than numbers. The password field in **passwd** is not used, and should not contain real encrypted passwords. These files should be mode 444.

~ftp/pub   Make this directory mode 777 and owned by **ftp**. Users should then place files that are to be accessible via the anonymous account in this directory.

Files

/usr/sbin/ftpd
        Specifies the command path.

Cautions

The anonymous account is inherently dangerous and should be avoided when possible.

The server must run as the superuser to create sockets with privileged port numbers. It maintains an effective user ID of the logged in user, reverting to the superuser only when binding addresses to sockets. The possible security holes have been extensively scrutinized, but are possibly incomplete.

Related Information

Commands: **ftp(1)**

Routines: **getusershell(3)**

Daemons: **syslogd(8)**

fwtmp, acctwtmp, wtmpfix

Purpose   Modify connect time accounting records to change formats and to make corrections in the records

Synopsis   **/usr/sbin/acct/fwtmp** [**-ic**]

/usr/sbin/acct/wtmpfix [*File* . . .]

/usr/sbin/acct/acctwtmp *'Reason'*

Flags

-i   The **fwtmp** command accepts ASCII records in the type **utmp** structure format as input.

-c   The **fwtmp** command converts output to type **utmp** structure formatted binary records.

-ic   The **fwtmp** command converts ASCII type **utmp** structure formatted input records to binary output records.

Description

fwtmp [**-ic**]

The **fwtmp** command reads records from standard input and writes records to standard output. Normally, information in record fields of the **/var/adm/wtmp** file is entered as binary data by the **init** and **login** programs during the life of the **/var/adm/wtmp** file. These **/var/adm/wtmp** file records have nine fields formatted according to members of a type **utmp** structure defined in the **utmp.h** include file. The **fwtmp** command is also capable of writing properly formatted ASCII records from standard input into a file when you use the **-i** flag.

Whenever you enter properly formatted ASCII records for conversion to binary records using the **-i** flag from the standard input device, you must enter data for each field of the 9-field record in the same order as that of type **utmp** structure members using a space as a field separator. The first column of the following table lists record fields in the order they should be entered, the next column lists the type **utmp** structure member name, and the last column tells you the purpose and entry character length.

1. **1 ut_user**
   The user login name, which must have exactly **sizeof(ut_user)** characters.

2. **ut_id** The **inittab** ID, which must have exactly **sizeof(ut_id)** characters.

3. **ut_line** The device name, which must have exactly **sizeof(ut_line)** characters.

4. **ut_pid** The process ID, which must have 5 decimal places.

5. **ut_type** The type of entry, which must have 2 decimal places. The type of entry may have any one of several symbolic constant values. The symbolic constants are defined in the **utmp.h** header file.

6. **ut_exit.e_termination**
   The process termination status, which must have 4 decimal places.

7. **ut_exit.e_exit**
   The process exit status, which must have 4 decimal places.

8. **ut_time**
   The starting time, which must have 10 decimal places.

9. **ut_host** The hostname, which must have exactly **sizeof(ut_host)** characters.

All record field entries you make from standard input must be separated by a space. Also you must fill all string fields with blank characters up to the maximum string size. All decimal values must have the specified number of decimal places with preceding 0s (zeros) to fill empty digit positions. The actual size of character arrays can be found in the **utmp.h** include file.

acctwtmp *'Reason'*
   The **acctwtmp** command is called by the **runacct** shell procedure to write a **utmp** formatted record to standard output with the current date and time together with a *'Reason'* string (**sizeof(ut_line)** characters or less) that you must also enter.

wtmpfix [*File . . .*]
   The **wtmpfix** command is called by the **runacct** shell procedure to examine standard input or *File* records in the **wtmp** format for corrupted date and timestamp entries. Whenever a corrupted entry is detected, the **wtmpfix** command corrects date and timestamp inconsistencies and writes corrected records to standard output. Whenever the **acctcon1** command runs, and a date and timestamp in a **/var/adm/wtmp** file is incorrect, an error is generated when the first corrupted entry is encountered. The **acctcon1** process is aborted whenever such an error is detected.

The **wtmpfix** command also checks the validity of the name field to ensure that the name consists only of alphanumeric characters, a $ (dollar sign), or spaces.

Whenever an invalid name is detected, the **wtmpfix** command changes the login name to **INVALID** and writes a diagnostic message to standard error. In this way, the **wtmpfix** command reduces the likelihood that the **acctcon2** command may fail.

Each time a date is entered (on system startup or with the **date** command) a pair of date-change records is written to the **/var/adm/wtmp** file. The first date-change record is the old date, which is entered with the string **old time** (the **OTIME_MSG** string) in the **ut_line** field and the flag **OLD_TIME** in the **ut_type** field. The second record is the new date, which is entered with the string **new time** (the **NTIME_MSG** string) in the **ut_line** field and the flag **NEW_TIME** in the **ut_type** field. The **wtmpfix** command uses these records to synchronize all date and time stamps in the **/var/adm/wtmp** file. The date-change record pair is then removed.

Examples

1. To convert binary **/var/adm/wtmp** records in type **utmp** structure format to an ASCII file called **dummy.file**, enter a command similar to the following:

    /usr/sbin/acct/fwtmp < /var/adm/wtmp > dummy.file

    The content of binary file **/var/adm/wtmpfile** as input is redirected to **dummy.file** as ASCII output.

2. To convert records in an ASCII type **utmp** structure formatted file to a binary output file called **/var/adm/wtmp**, enter an **fwtmp** command with the **-ic** flag similar to the following:

    /usr/sbin/acct/fwtmp -ic < dummy.file > /var/adm/wtmp

    The content of ASCII file **dummy.file** as input is redirected to binary file **/var/adm/wtmp** as output.

Files

/usr/sbin/acct/fwtmp
> Specifies the command path.

/usr/sbin/acct/wtmpfix
> Specifies the command path.

/usr/sbin/acct/acctwtmp
> Specifies the command path.

/usr/include/utmp.h
> Header file defining structures used to organize login information.

/var/adm/utmp
> Database file for currently logged in users.

/var/adm/wtmp
> Login/logout database file.

Related Information

Commands: **acct(8)**, **acctcon(8)**, **acctmerg(8)**, **date(1)**, **runacct(8)**

Calls: **acct(2)**

gated

Purpose   The gateway routing daemon

Synopsis   **gated** [**-teiHprRu**]

The gated daemon processes multiple routing protocols according to the configuration set in **gated.conf** file.

Flags

-e	Logs all external errors due to EGP, exterior routing errors, and EGP state changes.
-H	Traces all HELLO packets received.
-i	Logs all internal errors and interior routing errors.
-p	Traces all EGP packets sent and received.
-R	Traces all RIP packets received.
-r	Logs all routing changes.
-t	If used alone, the **-t** flag starts the **-i**, **-e**, **-r**, and **-p** trace flags.

When used with another flag, the **-t** flag has no effect and only the accompanying flags are recognized. Note that when other flags are used, the **-t** flag must be used with them and must be the first flag given in the command line.

-u   Logs all routing updates sent.

The **gated** daemon always logs fatal errors. If no log file is specified and none of the preceding trace flags are set, all messages are sent to the **/dev/null** file.

Description

The **gated** daemon manages multiple routing protocols, including the Routing Information Protocol (RIP), Exterior Gateway Protocol (EGP), and Local Network Protocol (HELLO). The **gated** process can be configured to perform all or any combination of these routing protocols. It replaces daemons that use the HELLO routing protocol; for example, **routed (8)** and **egpup (8).** The configuration for the **gated** daemon is by default stored in the **/etc/gated.conf** file, and can be changed at compile time in the file **defs.h.** The **gated** daemon stores its process ID in the **/etc/gated/pid** file.

When a routing update indicates that the route in use is being deleted, the **gated** daemon waits for 2 minutes before deleting the route. Be aware that unpredictable results may occur when the **gated** and **routed** daemons are run together on the same host.

Start the **gated** daemon with a log file that you specify on the command line. You can also enter one or more trace flags on the command line or specify the flags in the **traceflags** stanza of the **gated.conf** configuration file. When trace flags are specified without a log file, all trace output is sent to the controlling terminal.

By default, the **gated** daemon forks and detaches itself from the controlling terminal.

When certain networks are restricted from using the Internet network, the **gated** daemon uses both the **syslogd** daemon at the **LOG_WARNING** log level and the **LOG_DAEMON** facility to record all invalid networks.

If you use the EGP when you supply the default route (by the RIP or HELLO gateway) and all EGP neighbors are lost, the default route is not advertised until at least one EGP neighbor is regained.

The RIP both propagates and listens to host routes. This allows the **gated** daemon to handle point-to-point links with consistency. The **gated** daemon also supports the **RIP_TRACE** commands.

The **gated** daemon detects changes made to the network interfaces and its own start-up flags while it is running. Thus, you need not restart the **gated** daemon if you change the configuration. However, if the net mask, subnet mask, broadcast address, or interface metric is changed, use the **ifconfig**(8) command to mark the interface **down** and then **up** 30 seconds later.

Subnet interfaces are supported. Subnet information is passed through interfaces to other subnets of the same network.

The **gated** daemon listens to host and network **REDIRECT** signals. The daemon tries to take an action for its own internal tables. This action is parallel to the action the kernel takes on the **REDIRECT** signal.

In addition, the **gated** daemon cancels (times out) all routes learned from **REDIRECT** signals in 6 minutes. The daemon then deletes the route from the kernel routing tables, which keeps the routing tables consistent.

No routing protocol announces routes learned from **REDIRECT** signals.

The **gated** EGP code verifies that all networks sent and received are valid class A, B, or C networks as specified by the EGP. The **gated** daemon does not contribute

gated(8)

information about networks that do not meet EGP specifications. If an EGP update packet contains information about a network that is not class A, B, or C, the **gated** daemon considers the update to be in error and ignores it.

Signals

The **gated** server performs the following actions when you use the **kill**(1) command to send it the **SIGHUP** and **SIGINT** signals.

SIGHUP   When a **SIGHUP** signal is sent to a **gated** daemon that was invoked with trace flags and a log file, tracing is toggled off and the log file is closed. At this point the log file can be moved or deleted. When the next **SIGHUP** signal is sent to the **gated** daemon, tracing is toggled on. The **gated** daemon reads the **/etc/gated.conf** configuration file and sets the trace flags to those specified by the **traceflags** stanza.

If no **traceflags** stanza exists, tracing resumes and uses any trace flags specified on the command line. Trace output is sent to the log file specified on the command line. The output is appended if the log file already exists, and the file is created if it does not exist.

SIGINT   Sending the **gated** daemon a **SIGINT** signal causes a memory dump to be scheduled within the next 60 seconds. The memory dump is written to a file named **/usr/temp/gated_dump**. The **gated** daemon processes all pending routing updates before performing the memory dump.

The memory dump contains a snapshot of the current **gated** daemon status, including the interface configurations, EGP neighbor status, and the routing tables. If the **/usr/tmp/gated_dump** file already exists, the memory dump is appended to the existing file.

Internal Metrics for the gated Daemon

The **gated** daemon stores all metrics internally as a time delay in milliseconds to preserve the granularity of HELLO time delays. The internal delay ranges from 0 to 30,000 milliseconds, with 30,000 representing infinity. Metrics from other protocols are translated to and from a time delay as they are received and transmitted. EGP distances are not comparable to HELLO and RIP metrics but are stored as time delays internally for comparison with other EGP metrics. The conversion factor between EGP distances and time delays is 100.

RIP and interface metrics are translated to and from the internal time delays with the use of the following translation tables. The first two columns represent the time delay to RIP metric translation, while the second two columns represent the RIP metric to time delay translation.

Time Delay				
Minimum	Maximum	RIP Metric	RIP Metric	Time Delay
0	0	0	0	0
1	100	1	1	100
101	148	2	2	148
149	219	3	3	219
220	325	4	4	325
326	481	5	5	481
482	713	6	6	713
714	1057	7	7	1057
1058	1567	8	8	1567
1568	2322	9	9	2322
2323	3440	10	10	3440
3441	5097	11	11	5097
5098	7552	12	12	7552
7553	11,190	13	13	11,190
11,191	16,579	14	14	16,579
16,580	24,564	15	15	24,564
24,565	30,000	16	16	30,000

Cautions

Unpredictable results may occur when the **gated** and **routed** daemons are run together on the same host.

Files

/usr/sbin/gated
    Specifies the command path

/etc/gated.conf
    Contains the **gated** configuration information

/etc/gated.pid
    Contains the **gated** process ID

/usr/tmp/gated_dump
    Specifies the memory dump file

Related Information

Commands: **kill, routed(8)**

getty

Purpose   Sets the terminal type, modes, speed, and line discipline

Synopsis   **getty** [**-h**] [**-t** *time*] *line_speed_label terminal line_discipline*

getty -c *file*

Flags

-h   Hold the carrier during the initialization phase;do not hang up.

-t *time* Set the *time* period to the specified number of seconds. Drop the line after that amount of time if nothing is typed.

-c   Check the specified **gettydefs** file.

Description

The **getty** command sets and manages terminals by setting up speed, terminal flags, and the line discipline. If command flags are provided, **getty** adapts the system to those specifications. **getty** prints the login prompt, waits for the user to enter a username, and invokes the **login** command.

getty uses the **/etc/gettydefs** file for terminal information. The *line_speed_label* argument is a pointer into the **/etc/gettydefs** file where the definitions for speed and other associated flags are located. The *terminal* argument specifies the name of the terminal type. The *line_discipline* argument specifies the name of the line discipline.

The second syntax for the **getty** command provides a check option. When **getty** is invoked with the **-c** option and *filename* argument, it checks the specified file in the same way it scans **gettydefs** for terminal information, then prints the results to standard output.

Files

/etc/getty
          Specifies the command path

/etc/gettydefs
          Specifies the terminal line database file

Related Information

Commands: **init(8)**, **login(1)**, **stty(1)**

grpck

Purpose   Scans the **/etc/group** file or the named *file* and writes to standard output any inconsistencies.

See **pwck(8)**

halt

Purpose   Stops the processor

Synopsis   **halt** [**-l -n -q -y**]

The **halt** command writes data to the disks and then stops the processor(s), but does not reboot the machine. Only **root** can run this command.

Flags

-l   Does not log the halt using **syslog**

-n   Prevents the sync before stopping, and does not log the halt using **syslog**

-q   Causes a quick halt, does not log the halt using **syslog**, and makes no attempt to kill all processes

-y   Halts the system from a dial-up operation

Description

Use the **halt** command if you are not going to restart the machine immediately. When the system displays the   ....Halt completed.... message, you can turn off the power.

If the command is invoked without the **-l**, **-n**, or **-q** flag, the **halt** program logs the shutdown using the **syslogd** command and places a record of the shutdown in the login accounting file, **/var/adm/wtmp**. Using the **-q** and the **-n** flags imply the **-l** flag.

Examples

1.   To halt the system without logging the shutdown in the log file, enter:

        halt -l

2.   To halt the system quickly, enter:

        halt -q

3.   To halt the system from a dial-up, enter:

        halt -y

Cautions

Do not use this command if other users are logged into the system, or if the system is operating at a multiuser run level.

Files

/usr/sbin/halt
> Specifies the command path

/usr/sbin/syslogd
> Specifies the syslog daemon

/var/adm/wtmp
> Specifies the login accounting file

Related Information

Commands: **fasthalt(8), reboot(8), shutdown(8), syslogd(8)**

Calls: **halt(2), reboot(2), sync(2), syslog(3)**

icheck

Purpose   File system storage consistency check

Synopsis   **icheck** [**-b** *numbers*] [*file system*]

Description

The **icheck** command is obsoleted for normal consistency checking by **fsck**.

The **icheck** command examines a file system, builds a bit map of used blocks, and compares this bit map against the free map maintained on the file system. If the file system is not specified, a set of default file systems is checked. The normal output of **icheck** includes a report of the following items:

> The total number of files and the numbers of regular, directory, block special and character special files.

> The total number of blocks in use and the numbers of single-, double-, and triple-indirect blocks and directory blocks.

> The number of free blocks.

> The number of blocks missing; that is, not in any file or in any free map.

A list of block numbers follows the **-b** option; whenever any of the named blocks turn up in a file, a diagnostic is produced.

The **icheck** command is faster if the raw version of the special file is used since it reads the i-list many blocks at a time.

Files

/usr/sbin/icheck
Specifies the command path.

Diagnostics

For duplicate blocks and bad blocks which lie outside the file system, **icheck** announces the difficulty, the i-number, and the kind of block involved. If a read error is encountered, the block number of the bad block is printed and **icheck** considers it to contain zero.

Bugs

Since **icheck** is inherently two-pass in nature, extraneous diagnostics may be produced if applied to active file systems. It believes even preposterous super-blocks and consequently can get core images.

Related Information

Commands: **clri(8)**, **fsck(8)**, **ncheck(8)**

ifconfig

Purpose   Configures or displays network interface parameters

Synopsis   **ifconfig** *interface_id* [*address_family*] [*address* [*dest_address*]] [*parameters*]

The **ifconfig** command assigns and displays an address to a network interface, and configures network interface parameters.

Description

You use the **ifconfig** command at boot time to define the network address of each interface. You can also use the **ifconfig** command at other times to redefine the address of an interface or to set other operating parameters.

Any user can query the status of a network interface; only the superuser can modify the configuration network interfaces.

You specify an interface with the **ifconfig** *interface_id* syntax. (See your hardware documentation for information on obtaining an interface ID.)

If you do not specify an address or optional parameters, the **ifconfig** program displays the current configuration for the specified network interface only.

If a protocol family is specified by the *address_family* parameter, **ifconfig** reports only the configuration details specific to that protocol family.

When changing an interface configuration, an address family, which may alter the interpretation of succeeding parameters, must be specified. This family is required because an interface can receive transmissions in different protocols, each of which may require a separate naming scheme.

For the **inet** family, the *address_family* parameter is either a hostname or an Internet address in the standard dotted-decimal notation.

For the Xerox Network Systems family, addresses are *net:a.b.c.d.e.f* , where *net* is the assigned network number (in decimal), and each of the 6 bytes of the host number, *a* to *f*, are specified in hexadecimal. The host number may be omitted on 10-Mbps (Megabits per second) Ethernet interfaces, which use the hardware physical address, and on interfaces other than the first.

The destination address (*dest_address*) argument specifies the address of the correspondent on the remote end of a point-to-point link.

Parameters

netmask *mask*

Specifies how much of the address to reserve for subdividing networks into sub-networks. This parameter can only be used with an address family of **inet**.

The *mask* variable includes both the network part of the local address and the subnet part, which is taken from the host field of the address. The *mask* can be specified as a single hexadecimal number beginning with **0x**, in the standard Internet dotted-decimal notation, or beginning with a name.

The *mask* contains 1s (ones) for the bit positions in the 32-bit address that are reserved for the network and subnet parts, and 0s (zeros) for the bit positions that specify the host. The *mask* should contain at least the standard network portion.

trailers
Requests the use of a trailer link-level encapsulation when sending messages.

If a network interface supports **trailers**, the system will, when possible, encapsulate outgoing messages in a manner that minimizes the number of memory-memory copy operations performed by the receiver. On networks that support the Address Resolution Protocol (see **arp**), this flag indicates that the system should request that other systems use **trailers** when sending to this host. Similarly, trailer encapsulations will be sent to other hosts that have made such requests. Currently used by Internet protocols only.

-trailers
Disables the use of a trailer link-level encapsulation. The use of **-trailers** may be disabled by default (check your vendor documentation).

up
Marks an interface as working (**up**). This parameter is used automatically when setting the first address for an interface, or can be used to enable an interface after an **ifconfig down** command. If the interface was reset when previously marked with the parameter **down** (see the following section for a description of this parameter), the hardware will be reinitialized.

down
Marks an interface as not working (**down**), which keeps the system from trying to transmit messages through that interface. If possible, the **ifconfig** command also resets the interface to disable reception of messages. Routes that use the interface, however, are not automatically disabled.

arp   Enables the use of the Address Resolution Protocol (ARP) in mapping between network-level addresses and link-level addresses. This parameter is on by default.

-arp   Disables the use of the ARP. Use of this parameter is not recommended, however, as your system will then only be able to communicate with other hosts that are configured with the parameter **-arp**.

-broadcast

Specifies the address to use to represent broadcasts to the network. The default broadcast address is the address with a host part consisting of all 1s (ones). Note that the computation of the host part is dependent on **netmask** (see the description of the **netmask** parameter).

debug   Enables driver-dependent debug code. This might turn on extra console error logging. (See your hardware documentation for further information.)

-debug   Disables driver-dependent debug code.

dest_address

Specifies the correspondent on the other end of a point-to-point link.

ipdst   Specifies an Internet host willing to receive IP packets encapsulating packets bound for a remote network. For an Network Systems (NS) case, an apparent point-to-point link is constructed, and the address specified will be taken as the NS address and network of the destinee.

alias   Establishes an additional network address for this interface. This is sometimes useful when changing network numbers and one wishes to accept packets addressed to the old interface.

delete   Removes the network address specified. This would be used if you incorrectly specified an alias, or if it was no longer needed. If you have incorrectly set an NS address having the side effect of specifying the host portion, removing all NS addresses will allow you to respecify the host portion.

metric *number*

Sets the routing metric, or number of hops, for the interface to the value of *number*. The default value is 0 (zero) if *number* is not specified, indicating that both hosts are on the same network. The routing metric is used by the **routed** daemon, with higher metrics indicating that the route is less favorable.

Examples

To query the status of serial line interface **sl0**, enter:

$ ifconfig sl0

sl0: flags=51<UP,POINTOPOINT,RUNNING>
    inet 192.9.201.3 ---> 192.9.354.7 netmask 0xffffff00

To configure the local loopback interface, enter:

 # ifconfig lo0 inet 127.0.0.1 up

Only a user with superuser authority can modify the configuration of a network interface.

Files

/usr/sbin/ifconfig
    Specifies the command path

Related Information

Commands: **netstat(1)**

inetd

Purpose   The internet super-server

Synopsis   **inetd** [**-d**] [*configfile*]

Flags

> **-d**   Dumps debugging messages to **syslogd(8)** and to standard error.
>
> *configfile*
>
> > By default, this file is **/etc/inetd.conf**. It contains configuration
> > information that the daemon reads at startup.

Description

> The **inetd** daemon should be run at boot time by **inetd** in **etc/init.d.** It then listens
> for connections on certain Internet sockets. When a connection is found on one of
> its sockets, it decides what service the socket corresponds to, and invokes a
> program to service the request. After the program is finished, it continues to listen
> on the socket (except in some cases that are later in this manpage. Essentially,
> **inetd** allows running one daemon to invoke several others, reducing load on the
> system.
>
> Upon execution, **inetd** reads its configuration information from a configuration file,
> which, by default, is **/etc/inetd.conf**. There must be an entry for each field of the
> configuration file, with entries for each field separated by a tab or a space.
> Comments are denoted by a # (number sign) at the beginning of a line. There must
> be an entry for each field. The fields of the configuration file are as follows:
>
> *ServiceName SocketType ProtocolName Wait/Nowait UserName*
> *ServerPath ServerArgs*
>
> The *ServiceName* entry is the name of a valid service in the **/etc/services/** file . For
> **Internal** services (discussed below), the service name *must* be the official name of
> the service (that is, the first entry in **/etc/services**).
>
> The *SocketType* should be one of **stream**, **dgram**, **raw**, **rdm**, or **seqpacket**,
> depending on whether the socket is a stream, datagram, raw, reliably delivered
> message, or sequenced packet socket.
>
> The *ProtocolName* must be a valid protocol as given in **/etc/protocols**. Examples
> might be **tcp** or **udp**.
>
> The *Wait/Nowait* entry is applicable to datagram sockets only (other sockets should
> have a *NOWAIT* entry in this space). If a datagram server connects to its peer,

freeing the socket so *intend* can received further messages on the socket, it is said to be a multithreaded server, and should use the **nowait** entry. For datagram servers that process all incoming datagrams on a socket and eventually time out, the server is said to be single-threaded, and should use a wait entry. **Comsat** (**biff**) and **talk** are both examples of the latter type of datagram server. **tftpd** is an exception; it is a datagram server that establishes pseudoconnections. It must be listed as wait in order to avoid a race; the server reads the first packet, creates a new socket, and then forks and exits to allow **inetd** to check for new service requests to spawn new servers.

The *UserName* entry should contain the username of the user as whom the server should run. This allows for servers to be given less permission than root. The *ServerPath* entry should contain the pathname of the program that is to be executed by **inetd** when a request is found on its socket. If **inetd** provides this service internally, this entry should be **internal**.

The arguments to the *ServerPath* should be just as they normally are, starting with argv[0], which is the name of the program. If the service is provided internally, the word ''internal'' should take the place of this entry.

The **inetd** daemon provides several trivial services internally by use of routines within itself. These services are **echo**, **discard**, **chargen** (character generator), **daytime** (human-readable time), and **time** (machine-readable time, in the form of the number of seconds since midnight January 1, 1900). All of these services are **tcp** based. For details of these services, consult the appropriate RFC from the Network Information Center.

The **inetd** daemon rereads its configuration file when it receives a hangup signal, **SIGHUP**. Services may be added, deleted, or modified when the configuration file is reread.

Files

/usr/sbin/inetd
> Specifies the command path.

Related Information

Commands: **comsat(8)**
Daemons: **fingerd(8)**, **ftpd(8)**, **rexecd(8)**, **rlogind(8)**, **rshd(8)**, **telnetd(8)**, **tftpd(8)**

init

Purpose   Process control initialization

Synopsis   **init** [0s23]

Description

The **init** program initializes the system by creating and controlling processes. The processes run by **init** at each run level are defined in the **inittab** file. **init** reads entries contained within the **inittab** file and acts on them.

The **init** command considers the system to be in a run level at any given time; each run level has a specific group of processes that run at that level. **init** operates in one of four run levels: **0**, **s**, **2**, or **3**. The run level changes when a privileged user invokes **init**. The new **init** sends appropriate signals to the original **init** that tell it which run level to change to.

The **init** command is run as the last step of the boot process after the root file system is mounted. **init** attempts to locate the **inittab** file and looks for an entry with the initdefault keyword. If the entry is there, **init** uses the run level specified as the initial run level to enter. If the entry is not in the **inittab** file, or the **inittab** file is not found, **init** requests that the user enter a run level from the system console, **/dev/console**. If the user enters the letter **s**, **init** enters single user state, assigns the virtual console terminal to the user's terminal and opens it for reading and writing. The **su** command is invoked and the system displays a message on the console stating the location of the virtual console.

To change the run level, the user enters one of the digits **0**, **2**, or **3**, or the letter **s**.

0   shuts down and halts the system.

s   changes the run level to a single user state with only the essential kernel services.

2   changes the run level to a multiuser state with local processes and daemons.

3   changes the run level to a multiuser state with remote processes and daemons.

If this is the first post-boot execution of **init** to a run level other than single user, it searches the **inittab** file for entries at the new run level that have the **boot** or **bootwait** keywords. **init** acts on these entries before processing other entries in the **inittab** file if the run level entered matches the entry. Any special initialization of the system, such as checking and mounting file systems, takes place before users are allowed on the system. **init** then scans the **inittab** file to find all entries that are to be handled for that level.

Before starting a new process, **init** reads each entry in the **inittab** file, and for each entry that should be respawned, **init** forks a child process. After spawning all required processes, **init** waits for one of its descendant processes to stop, a power-fail signal, or a signal that it should change the run level. When one of the preceding three conditions occurs, **init** reexamines the **inittab** file. You can add new entries to the **inittab** file by editing the file but **init** does not reexamine the file until one of the three conditions actually occurs. To provide for immediate reexamination of the file, run the **init -q** command.

Files

/sbin/init

Specifies the command path

/tcb/files/inittab

Specifies the **init** command control file

tcb/files/sysinitrc

Specifies the boot time script used by systems that do not support **inittab**

/var/adm/wtmp

Specifies the permanent login accounting file

Related Information

Commands: **getty(8)**, **rc0(8)**, **rc2(8)**, **rc3(8)**, **shutdown(8)**

Calls: **kill(2)**, **reboot(2)**

Files: **inittab(4)**

killall

Purpose   Terminates all processes started by the user, except the calling process

Synopsis   **killall** [- | - *signal_name* | - *signal_number*]

            killall -l

Flags

-    The hyphen character (without an argument) sends a **SIGTERM** signal initially and then sends a **SIGKILL** signal to all processes that survive for 30 seconds after receipt of the first signal. This gives processes that catch the **SIGTERM** signal an opportunity to clean up.

-signal_name
    The hyphen character (with a signal name argument) sends the specified signal to processes.

-signal_number
    The hyphen character (with a signal number argument) sends the specified signal, either a name, stripped of the **SIG** prefix (such as **KILL**), or a number (such as **9**). For information about signal names and numbers, see the **signal** system call.

-l   Lists signal names in numerical order (as given in the **/usr/include/signal.h** file), stripped of the common **SIG** prefix.

Description

This command provides a convenient means of killing all processes created by the shell that you control. When started by the superuser, the **killall** command kills all processes that can be terminated, except those processes that started it, the kernel processes, and processes **0** and **1** (**init**)

Examples

1.   To stop all background processes that have started, enter:

    killall

    This sends all background processes signal 9 (the **kill** signal, also called **SIGKILL**).

2. To stop all background processes, giving them a chance to clean up, enter:

    killall -

    This sends signal 15 (**SIGTERM**), waits 30 seconds, and then sends signal 9 (**SIGKILL**).

3. To send a specific signal to the background processes, enter:

    killall -2

    This sends signal **2** (**SIGINT**) to the background processes.

4. To list the signal names in numerical order, stripped of the **SIG** prefix, enter:

    killall -l

    This displays a list of signals, which may vary from system to system.

Files

/usr/sbin/killall   Specifies the command path

Related Information

Calls: **kill(2)**, **sigaction(2)**, **signal(2)**

kloadsrv

Purpose   Loads kernel modules into the kernel

Synopsis   **kloadsrv** [**-f**] [**-d** *debug-level*] [**-p** *kernel-package-name*] [*kernel-object-filename*]

Flags

-**p** *kernel-package-name*
    Specify the default kernel package name, in order to override the default kernel package name, **kernel**.

-**f**   Remain in the forground.

-**d** *debug-level*
    Specify the debug level. The debug level is a small integer. Zero disables debugging. Non-zero values from one to higher levels cause **kloadsrv** to print various log messages.

Description

The **kloadsrv** command is the kernel load server and is responsible for loading kernel modules into the kernel. It is typically started during system startup. During its initialization, **kloadsrv** builds the initial export list for the kernel, by reading the kernel object file, by default: /**vmunix**. Each symbol exported by the kernel must belong to some package. Any symbol not in a package is placed in the default kernel package, whose name by default is **kernel**. Once **kloadsrv** has successfully initialized itself, it puts itself into the background and enters its server loop, where it waits to receive and respond to kernel load requests.

The **kloadsrv** command optionally accepts the name of the kernel object file, in order to override the default kernel object file, /**vmunix**.

Files

/sbin/kloadsrv

   Specifies the command path.

/vmunix The default kernel object file from which the initial kernel export list is built.

/var/run/kloadsrv.pid

   The file that contains the process ID of the current invocation of the kernel load server.

Related Information

Commands: **cfgmgr(8)**, **sysconfig(8)**, **sysconfigdb(8)**

Calls: **ldr_kernel_process(2)**, **ldr_xattach(2)**, **ldr_xdetach(2)**, **ldr_xload(2)**, **ldr_xunload(2)**, **ldr_xentry(2)**, **ldr_xlookup_package(2)**, **ldr_inq_module(2)**, **ldr_inq_region(2)**, **ldr_next_module(2)**

last

Purpose   Displays information about previous logins

Synopsis   /usr/bin/last [-N] [*Name*...] [*Tty*...]

Flags

-N   Limits the output to *N* number of record lines.

Description

The **last** command displays, in reverse chronological order, all previous logins and logouts entered in the currently active **/var/adm/wtmp** file. The list of output records may be restricted to *N* number of record lines when the -N flag is used with this command. This command also lists login or logout by user specified with the *Name* parameter, and login or logout from terminals specified with the *Tty* parameter. *Tty* terminals references may be fully named (**tty0**, for example) or abbreviated (**0**, for example). For each process, the following information is listed according to session, with the most recent session listed first:

1.   Time session began.

2.   Duration of session.

3.   The tty terminal on which session took place.

The following information is included when applicable:

1.   Terminations when rebooting.

2.   Continuing sessions.

When the **last** command is interrupted, an indication of how far the search has progressed in the **/var/adm/wtmp** file is provided. When **last** is interrupted with a **quit** signal, an indication as to how far the search has progressed is provided, but the search continues.

To obtain information about the mean time between reboots, use the word **shutdown** as the *Name* parameter.

Examples

1. To list all recorded logins and logouts according to user **root** from the **console** terminal, enter:

    last root console

    Provides a list of logins and logouts made from the **console** terminal by the user whose name is **root**.

2. To list the time between system reboots, enter:

    last shutdown

    The pseudouser named **shutdown** is used to list the mean time betwen system reboots.

Files

/usr/bin/last
> Specifies the command path.

/usr/include/utmp.h
> Header file defining structures used to organize login information.

/var/adm/wtmp
> The login/logout database file.

Related Information

Commands: **lastcomm(8)**

lastcomm

Purpose   Outputs information about the last commands executed

Synopsis   /usr/bin/lastcomm [*Command*] [*Name*] [*Tty*]

Description

The **lastcomm** command outputs information about all previously executed commands that are recorded in the **/var/adm/pacct** file in reverse chronological order.

You may specify a particular command with the *Command* parameter, a particular user with the *Name* parameter, and a particular terminal as the command source with the *Tty* parameter. Output is then restricted to the specified parameters. A *Tty* terminal may be named fully (for example, **tty0**) or abbreviated (for example, **0**).

The following information is displayed for each process:

1. Name of the command under which the process was called.

2. Any flags collected when the command was executed. The following flags are valid:

    -S   Command issued by the superuser.
    -F   Command ran after a fork, but without an **exec** system call following it.

3. Name of the user who issued the command.

4. The terminal the command was started from.

5. Seconds of CPU time used.

6. Time the process started.

Examples

1. To display information about all previously executed commands recorded in the **/var/adm/pacct** file, enter:

    lastcomm

2. To display information about commands named **a.out** executed by the **root** user on terminal **ttyd0**, enter:

    lastcomm a.out root ttyd0

Files

/usr/bin/lastcomm
> Specifies the command path.

/var/adm/pacct
> The current accounting file.

Related Information

Commands: **last(8)**

lastlogin

Purpose   Updates the **/var/adm/acct/sum/loginlog** file to show the last date each user logged in

See **acct(8)**

lib_admin

Purpose   Administers shared libraries

Synopsis   **/sbin/lib_admin** [**-i**] [**-p**] [**-o** *global_file*] [**-v**] *database*

Flags

-i   Do not install any libraries. This flag overrides the **install** attribute from the *database* file.

-p   Do not preload any libraries. This flag overrides the **preload** attribute from the *database* file.

-o *global_file*
            Create the loader global data file with the specified output file name rather than with the default file, **/etc/ldr_global.dat**. Note that the standalone loader (**/sbin/loader**) only looks for its loader global data file using the default pathname.

-v   Run in verbose mode and print more information about each install or preload operation as it occurs.

Description

You use the **lib_admin** program to manage the set of shared libraries available to all applications programs. **lib_admin** installs a list of shared libraries into the Global Known Package table, thus making them available to the the program loader in resolving unresolved symbols during program loading. In addition, **lib_admin** can optionally preload specified libraries, resulting in faster startup of programs using those libraries.

The **lib_admin** command normally runs from **/etc/init** during system initialization to install and preload the shared libraries needed by the other commands. You can, however, run the **lib_admin** command at any time to change the set of libraries that are installed or preloaded on the system.

The **lib_admin** command creates an output file, the *loader global data file*, which contains the Global Known Package table and the cache of preloaded library information. By default, this file is named **/etc/ldr_global.dat**. The standalone loader (**/sbin/loader**) maps the loader global data file to obtain access to the Global Known Package table and preload cache.

A *database* file drives the actions of the **lib_admin** command. This file lists all of the shared libraries and the default installation options for each library. The database file is in "attributes file" format and consists of a series of entries, one per shared library. Entries are separated by one or more blank lines. Each entry has the following format:

library_name:
> *attribute=value*
> *attribute=value*

where:

library_name is specified as an absolute pathname; that is, a pathname beginning with '/'. A colon (:) marks the end of the *library_name* specification.

The following *attribute=value* specifications are valid:

> The **install** attribute takes either a **true** or **false** value, specifying whether or not the library is to be installed.

> The **preload** attribute takes either a **true** or **false** value, specifying whether or not the library is to be preloaded.

For example, an entry in *database* for a library named */usr/lib/this1* could look like this:

```
/usr/lib/this1:
     install=true
     preload=false
```

Files

/sbin/lib_admin
> Specifies the command path

/etc/ldr_global.dat
> The default loader global data file

/etc/ldr*XXXXXXXX.X*
> Binary data files containing the regions of preloaded libraries

Related Information

Commands: **init(8)**

Calls: **ldr_install(2)**, **ldr_remove(2)**, **load(2)**, **exec(2)**, **exec_with_loader(2)**

Files: **stanza(4)**

lpc

Purpose   Line printer control program

Synopsis   **/usr/sbin/lpc** [*command* [*argument* ...]]

Description

The **lpc** command is used by the system administrator to control the operation of the line printer system. For each line printer configured in the **/etc/printcap** file, the **lpc** command may be used for disabling or enabling a printer; disabling or enabling the printer spooling queue; rearranging the order of jobs in a spooling queue or finding the status of printers, their associated spooling queues, and the printer daemons.

Without arguments, **lpc** prompts for commands from the standard input. When arguments are supplied,**lpc** interprets the first argument as a command and any remaining arguments as command parameters. The standard input may be redirected so that **lpc** reads commands from a file. The following is the list of recognized **lpc** commands:

? [*command* ....]
>   Prints a short description of each command specified in the argument list or, when no arguments are supplied, a list of the recognized commands.

help [*command* ....]
>   Prints a short description of each command specified in the argument list or, when no arguments are supplied, a list of the recognized commands.

abort {**all** | *printer* ....}
>   Terminates an active spooling daemon running on the local host, and then disables printing. This prevents new daemons from being started by **lpr** or **lp** for the specified printers.

clean { **all** | *printer* ....}
>   Removes any temporary files, data files, and control files that cannot be printed (files that do not form a complete printer job) from the specified printer queue(s) on the local machine.

disable {**all** | *printer* ....}
>   Turns the specified printer queues off. This prevents new printer jobs from being entered into the queue by **lpr** or **lp**.

down { **all** | *printer*} *message* ....
>   Turns the specified printer queue off, disables printing, and puts a message in the printer status file. The message does not need to be quoted

because remaining arguments are treated the same as **echo**. The **down** command is normally used to take a printer down and let others know why. (The **lpq** command indicates that the printer is down and prints a status message.)

enable { **all** | *printer* .... }

Enables spooling on the local queue for the listed printers. This allows **lpr** or **lp** to put new jobs in the spool queue.

exit   Exit from **lpc**.

quit   Exit from **lpc**.

restart { **all** | *printer* .... }

Attempts to start a new printer daemon. This is useful when some abnormal condition causes the daemon to terminate unexpectedly and leave jobs in the queue. **lpq** reports that there is no daemon present when this condition occurs. When a daemon is stuck, you must first kill it and then restart.

start { **all** | *printer* .... }

Enables printing and starts a spooling daemon for the listed printers.

status { *printer* .... }

Displays the status of daemons and queues on the local machine. When printer name paramaters are not supplied, information about all printers is provided.

stop { **all** | *printer* .... }

Stops a spooling daemon after the current job has completed and disables printing.

topq *printer* [*jobnum* ....] [*user* ....]

Places jobs in the order listed at the top of the printer queue.

up { **all** | *printer* ... }

Enables all printing and starts a new printer daemon. Cancels the effect of the **down** command.

Files

/usr/sbin/lpc

Specifies the command path.

/etc/printcap

Specifies the printer description file.

/usr/spool/*

Specifies print spool directories.

/usr/spool/*/lock
> Specifies the lock file for queue control.

Diagnostics

The following diagnostic messages are possible.

`?Ambiguous command`
> Abbreviation matches more than one command.

`?Invalid command`
> No match was found.

`Privileged command`
> Command may be executed by the superuser only.

Related Information

Commands: **cancel(1), lp(1), lpd(8), lpr(1), lpq(1), lprm(1), lpstat(1)**

lpd

Purpose   line printer daemon

Synopsis   /usr/sbin/lpd [-l]

Flags

-l   Tells the **lpd** daemon to log valid requests received from the network. This flag is useful for debugging.

Description

The **lpd** program is the line printer daemon (spool area handler), which is normally invoked at boot time. This daemon makes a single pass through the **printcap**(5) file to find out about any existing printers to print all files previously not printed before a shutdown. The daemon then uses system calls **listen**(2) and **accept**(2) to receive requests to print files in the queue, to transfer files to the spooling area, and to display the queue or remove jobs from the queue. For each case, the daemon forks a child to handle the request so that the parent can continue to listen for more requests. The Internet port number used to rendezvous with other processes is identified with the **getservbyname**(3) system call and is specified in **/etc/devices** by its printer service record entry.

Access control is provided by the following means:

1.   All requests must originate from one of the machines listed in the **/etc/hosts.equiv** or **/etc/hosts.lpd** file.

2.   When an **rs** capability, which restricts remote users to those with local accounts, is specified in the **/etc/printcap** file for the printer being accessed, an **lpr** or **lp** request is honored only for those users having accounts on the same machine as the printer.

The **minfree** file, which is a simple ASCII file, in each spool directory contains the number of disk blocks to leave free so that the line printer queue will not completely fill the disk.

The **lock** file in each **/usr/spool** subdirectory is used to prevent more than one active **lpd** daemon and to store information about the daemon process for other printer spooling commands.

After the **lpd** daemon has successfully set the lock in the **lock** file, it scans the **/usr/spool** subdirectory for files beginning with the charcters cf. Records in each of the cf files specify files to be printed or specify one or more non-printing actions to be performed. Each such record begins with a key character that specifies what to do with the remainder of the line. In the following table, the columns list the beginning key character, the key-character name, and its purpose.

J	**Job Name**	String to be used for the job name on the burst page.
C	**Classification**	String to be used for the classification line on the burst page.
L	**Literal**	The record line provides identification information from the **etc/passwd** file and initiates banner page printing.
T	**Title**	String to be used as the title for the **pr** command.
H	**Hostname**	Name of the machine where the **lpr** daemon or the **lp** command was invoked.
P	**Person**	Login name of the person who invoked the **lpr** or **lp** commands. This record is used to verify ownership by the **lprm** or **cancel** commands.
M	**Notify**	Sends mail to the specified user when the current print job completes.
f	**Formatted File**	Name of an already formatted file to print.
l	**Formatted File**	Similar to **f**, but passes control characters and does not make page breaks.
p	**File Name**	Name of a file to print using the **pr** command as a filter.
t	**Troff File**	The file contains **troff** output (**cat** phototypesetter commands).
n	**Ditroff File**	The file contains DVI (device-independent) troff output.
d	**DVI File**	The file contains **Tex**(l) output (DVI format from Stanford).
g	**Graph File**	The file contains data produced by the **plot**(3X) command.
c	**Cifplot File**	The file contains data produced by the **cifplot** command.
v	**Raster Image**	The file contains a raster image.
r	**Fortran**	The file contains text data with Fortran carriage control characters.
1	**Troff Font R**	Name of another font file to use in place of the default font file.
2	**Troff Font I**	Name of another font file to use in place of the default font file.
3	**Troff Font B**	Name of another font file to use in place of the default font file.
4	**Troff Font S**	Name of another font file to use in place of the default font file.
W	**Width**	Changes the page width (in characters) used by the **pr** command and by text filters.

I	Indentation	The number of character spaces to indent the output (spacing is from the ASCII character set).
U	Unlink	Name of file to remove on completion of printing.
N	Filename	The name of the file undegoing printing, or when blank, for the standard input (when the **lpr** or **lp** command is invoked in a pipeline or when the command is invoked from the standard input).

Whenever a file cannot be opened for printing, a message is logged via the **syslog**(3) subroutine using the **LOG_LPR** facility. When this is the case, the **lpd** daemon tries to reopen a file, which it expects is referenced by a correct pathname, up to 20 times. When a file cannot be opened after 20 tries, **lpd** goes to the next the file.

The **lpd** daemon uses the **flock**(2) system call to provide exclusive access to the lock file and to prevent multiple daemons from being simultaneously activated. When the daemon should be killed or dies unexpectedly, the lock file need not be removed.

The 2-line **/usr/spool/lock** file is stored in readable ASCII form and contains two lines. The first line specifies the process ID of the daemon and the second line specifies the control file-name of the job currently undergoing printing. The second line is updated to reflect the current status of the **lpd** daemon for commands **lpq**, **lprm**, **cancel**, and **lpstat**.

Files

/usr/sbin/lpd
> Specifies the command path.

/etc/printcap
> Printer description file.

/usr/spool/*
> Spool directories. The location of spool directories is a convention, but not necessary (see the **/etc/printcap** file).

/usr/spool/*/minfree
> Minimum free disk space to leave.

/dev/lp* Line printer devices.

/dev/printer
> Socket for local requests.

/etc/hosts.equiv
> Lists machine names allowed access to a printer.

/etc/hosts.lpd
> Lists machine names allowed access to a printer, but which are not under same administrative control.

Related Information

Commands: **cancel(8)**, **lp(1)**, **lpc**(8), **pac(8)**, **lpr(1)**, **lpq(1)**, **lpstat(1)**, **lprm(1)**

Calls: **syslog**(3)

lptest

Purpose   Generates the line printer ripple test pattern

Synopsis   **lptest** [*length* [*count*]]

Flags

length   Specifies the output line length when the 79-character default line length is inappropriate.

count   Specifies the number of output lines to be generated when the default 200-line length is inappropriate. When *count* is specified, *length* must also be specified.

Description

The **lptest** command writes a traditional *ripple test* pattern to the standard output. In 96 lines, a pattern containing all 96 printable ASCII characters in each column position of the line is printed. In the pattern, each printed character is displaced rightward one character-column on each successive line. Originally created to test printers, the ripple test pattern is also useful for testing terminals, driving terminal ports during debugging, and for any other diagnostic task where a quick output of randomized data is needed.

Files

/usr/sbin/lptest
      Specifies the command path.

lvchange

Purpose   Changes the characteristics of a logical volume

Synopsis   **lvchange** [**-a** *Availability*] [**-d** *Schedule*] [**-p** *Permission*] [**-r** *Relocate*] [**-s** *Strict*]
[**-v** *Verify*] *LogicalVolumePath*

Flags

-a *Availability*

Sets the availability of the logical volume. The *Availability* parameter is represented by one of the following:

y   Makes a logical volume available; that is, an open of the logical volume will succeed.

n   Makes a logical volume temporarily unavailable; that is, an open of the logical volume will fail.

-d *Schedule*   Sets the scheduling policy when a logical extent with more than one mirror is written. The *Schedule* parameter is represented by one of the following:

p   Establishes a parallel scheduling policy.

s   Establishes a sequential scheduling policy. Use this value with care because, in most cases, it leads to performance loss.

-p *Permission* Sets the access permission to read-write or read-only. The *Permission* parameter is represented by one of the following:

w   Sets the access permission to read-write.

r   Sets the access permission to read-only.

-r *Relocate*   Sets the bad block relocation policy. The *Relocate* parameter is represented by one of the following:

y   Causes bad block relocation to occur.

n   Prevents bad block relocation from occurring.

-s *Strict*   Determines the strict allocation policy. Mirrors of a logical extent can be allocated to share or not to share the same physical volume. This flag only make sense when the physical volumes (of the volume group that owns the logical volume to be changed) reside on different physical disks. The *Strict* parameter is represented by one of the following:

	y	Sets a strict allocation policy; mirrors of a logical extent can not share the same physical volume.
	n	Does not set a strict allocation policy; mirrors of a logical extent can share the same physical volume.
-v *Verify*		Sets the write-verify state for the logical volume. The *Verify* parameter is represented by one of the following:
	y	Causes all writes to the logical volume to be verified with a follow up read.
	n	Prevents all writes to the logical volume from being verified with a follow up read.

Description

The **lvchange** command changes the characteristics of a logical volume. You include the optional command flags and parameters on the command line to specify the type and extent of change. Each current characteristic for a logical volume remains in effect until you explicitly change it with the corresponding flag. All flags except the **-s** flag take effect immediately. The change you make with the **-s** flag takes effect only when new extents are allocated using the **lvextend** command. The *LogicalVolumePath* parameter must be a logical volume name.

Examples

1. To change the permission of logical volume lv03, enter:

   lvchange -p r /dev/vg01/lv03

   Logical volume lv03 now has read-only permission.

2. To change the allocation policy of logical volume lv07, enter:

   lvchange -s n /dev/vg01/lv07

Files

/usr/sbin/lvchange
   Specifies the command path.

Related Information

Commands: **lvcreate(8)**, **lvdisplay(8)**, **lvextend(8)**

lvcreate

Purpose   Creates a logical volume in a volume group

Synopsis   **lvcreate** [**-d** *Schedule*] [**-l** *LogicalExtentsNumber*] [**-m** *MirrorCopies*][**-n** *LogicalVolumeName*] [**-p** *Permission*] [**-r** *Relocate*] [**-s** *Strict*] [**-v** *Verify*] *VolumeGroupName*

Flags

-d *Schedule*

Sets the scheduling policy when one logical extent with more than one mirror is written. *Schedule* is represented by one of the following:

p   Establishes a parallel scheduling policy.

s   Establishes a sequential scheduling policy. This value should be used with care since, in most cases, it will lead to performance loss.

The default for *Schedule* is **p**.

-l *LogicalExtentsNumber*

Allocates *LogicalExtentsNumber* number of logical extents to the *LogicalVolumePath*. *LogicalExtentsNumber* must be a number between **1** and **65535,** which is the implementation limit.

The default for *LogicalExtentsNumber* is **0**

-m *MirrorCopies*

Sets the number of physical extents allocated for each logical extent.

MirrorCopies (that is, mirrors) can be a value of either **1** or **2**; this means that, beyond the original copy, one or two mirror copies will contain the same data as the original one.

The default for *MirrorCopies* is **0**.

-n *LogicalVolumeName*

Specifies that the new logical volume must be created with the name *LogicalVolumeName* supplied by you. This name must be a simple file name and not a path name.

-p *Permission*

Sets the access permission to read-write or read-only. *Permission* is represented by one of the following:

w Sets the access permission to read-write.

r Sets the access permission to read-only

The default for *Permission* is **w**.

-r *Relocate*

Sets the bad block relocation policy. Relocation is represented by one of the following:

y Causes bad block relocation to occur.

n Prevents bad block relocation from occurring.

The default for *Relocate* is **y**.

-s *Strict* Determines the strict allocation policy. Mirror copies of a logical extent can be allocated to share or not to share the same physical volume. This flag only makes sense when the physical volumes (of the volume group that owns the logical volume to be changed) reside on different physical disks. The *Strict* parameter is represented by one of the following:

y Sets a strict allocation policy; mirrors for a logical extent cannot share the same physical volume.

n Does not set a strict allocation policy; mirrors for a logical extent can share the same physical volume.

The default for *Strict* is **y**.

-v *Verify* Sets the write-verify state for the logical volume. The *Verify* parameter is represented by one of the following:

y Causes the verification of all write operations to the logical volume.

n Prevents the verification of all write operations to the logical volume.

The default for *Verify* is **n**.

Description

The **lvcreate** command creates a new logical volume within the volume group represented by the *VolumeGroupName* parameter.

If *LogicalVolumeName* is provided by the user, the new logical volume is created with the given name. If *LogicalVolumeName* is not provided, a system generated name is provided. The system generated name will be of the form "lvol#", where # is the minor number of the new logical volume.

The name of the new logical volume is displayed.

The default settings provide the most commonly used characteristics, but use flags to tailor the logical volume to the requirements of your system. Once a logical volume is created, its characteristics can be changed with the **lvchange**, **lvextend** and **lvreduce** commands.

Examples

1. To make a logical volume in volume group vg02, enter:

    lvcreate /dev/vg02

2. To make a logical volume in volume group vg03 with non-strict allocation policy, enter:

    lvcreate -s n /dev/vg03

    A new logical volume in volume group vg03 is created with non-strict allocation policy.

Files

/usr/sbin/lvcreate
> Specifies the command path.

Related Information

Commands: **lvchange(8)**, **lvextend(8)**, **lvreduce(8)**, **pvchange(8)**

lvdisplay

Purpose   Displays information about logical volumes

Synopsis   **lvdisplay** [**-v**] *LogicalVolumePath* ...

Flags

-v   Lists the map and additional information about the distribution of the logical volume across the physical volumes of the volume group.

Distribution of logical volume:
Lists the distribution of the logical volume *LogicalVolumePath* within the volume group.

PV Name:
The name of the physical volume to which the logical extents are allocated

LE on PV:
The number of logical extents that are allocated on the physical volume

PE on PV:
The number of physical extents that are allocated on the physical volume

Logical extents:
Displays the following information for each logical extent:

LE: The logical extent number

PV1:   The physical volume name that corresponds to the location of the first physical extent of the logical extent

PE1:   The first physical extent number allocated to the logical extent

Status 1: The status of the first physical extent: stale or current

PV2:   The physical volume name that corresponds to the location of the second physical extent (first copy) of the logical extent

PE2:   The second physical extent number allocated to the logical extent

Status 2: The status of the second physical extent: stale or current

PV3: The physical volume name that corresponds to the location of the third physical extent (second copy) of the logical extent

PE3: The third physical extent number allocated to the logical extent

Status 3: The status of the third physical extent: stale or current

Description

The **lvdisplay** command displays the characteristics and status of each logical volume specified by the *LogicalVolumePath* parameter. If you use the **-v** (verbose) option, the program displays physical volume (PV) distribution information, and map information about the physical extents that correspond to the logical extents of the logical volume(s).

If you enter the **lvdisplay** command without any flags, the program displays information about the following characteristics:

LV Name: The name of the logical volume

VG Name: The name of the volume group

LV Permission:
The access permission: read-only or read-write

LV Status: The state of the logical volume: available/stale, available/syncd, or unavailable

Available/stale indicates that the logical volume is available but contains physical extents that are not current. Available/syncd indicates that the logical volume is available and synchronized. Closed indicates that the logical volume is not available for use.

Write verify: The write verify state of the logical volume: on or off

Mirror Copies:
The number of physical extents allocated for each logical extent

Schedule: The sequential or parallel scheduling policy

Current LE: The number of logical extents currently in the logical volume

Allocated PE:
The number of physical extents allocated to the logical volume

Bad Blocks: The bad block relocation policy

lvdisplay(8)

Allocation: The current allocation state: strict or non-strict

A strict allocation specifies that mirror copies for a logical extent are not allocated on the same physical volume. A non-strict allocation specifies that physical extents that belong to the same logical extent can be allocated on the same physical volume. If the allocation does not meet the criteria for strict, it is considered to be non-strict.

Examples

1. To display information about the logical volume, lv03, enter:

   lvdisplay /dev/vg01/lv03

   The program displays information about lv03, its logical and physical extents, and the volume group to which it belongs.

2. To display all the available information about the logical volume, lv03, enter:

   lvdisplay -v /dev/vg01/lv03

   The program displays the characteristics, status and distribution map of lv03.

Files

/usr/sbin/lvdisplay
   Specifies the command path.

Related Information

Commands: **lvchange(8)**, **lvcreate(8)**, **lvextend(8)**, **lvreduce(8)**, **pvdisplay(8)**, **vgdisplay(8)**

lvextend

Purpose   Increases the number of physical extents allocated to a logical volume

Synopsis   **lvextend** {**-l** *LogicalExtentsNumber* | **-m** *MirrorCopies*} *LogicalVolumePath*
[*PhysicalVolumePath* ...]

Flags

-**l** *LogicalExtentsNumber*

Increases the number of logical extents allocated to the
LogicalVolumePath.
LogicalExtentsNumber must be greater than the number of logical
extents previously allocated to *LogicalVolumePath* and less than **65535**
which is the implementation limit.

LogicalExtentsNumber represents the new total number of logical extents
that can be allocated to *LogicalVolumePath*. The change is accomplished
by allocating the number of additional logical extents represented by the
difference between *LogicalExtentsNumber* and the previous number of
extents.

The mirror policy and mirror copies number for the new logical extents is
the same as previously established for the *LogicalVolumePath*.

Either this option or the **-m** option must be supplied.

-**m** *MirrorCopies*

Sets the number of physical extents allocated for each logical extent.

MirrorCopies (that is, mirrors) can be either 1 or 2. This means that
beyond the original copy, one or two mirror copies will contain the same
data as the original copy.

MirrorCopies must be greater than the current number of mirrors for the
logical volume.

The data in the new copies are synchronized. The synchronization
process can be time consuming, depending on the hardware
characteristics and the amount of data.

If the allocation policy for the logical volume is strict and the specified
physical volume already contains logical extents of the logical volume,
the request will be rejected.

Either this option or the **-l** option must be supplied.

lvextend(8)

Description

The **lvextend** command changes either the number of logical extents allocated to a logical volume specified with the *LogicalVolumePath* parameter or the number of physical extents allocated to each logical extent in the logical volume. The change is determined according to which command flags you use.

To limit the allocation to specific physical volumes, use the names of one or more physical volumes in the *PhysicalVolumePath* parameter; otherwise, all of the physical volumes in a volume group are available for allocating new physical extents.

Examples

1. To increase the number of the logical extents of logical volume lv03 up to one hundred, enter:

    lvextend -l 100 /dev/vg01/lv03

2. To get two mirrors (that is, three copies) for each logical extent of logical volume lv05, enter:

    lvextend -m 2 /dev/vg01/lv05

    Each logical extent of logical volume lv05 is now doubly mirrored.

Files

/usr/sbin/lvextend
Specifies the command path.

Related Information

Commands: **lvcreate(8)**, **lvdisplay(8)**, **lvreduce(8)**, **pvchange(8)**, **pvdisplay(8)**

lvreduce

Purpose   Decreases the number of physical extents allocated to a logical volume

Synopsis   **lvreduce** {**-m** *MirrorCopies* | **-l** *LogicalExtentsNumber*} [**-f**] *LogicalVolumePath*

Flags

-f   Forces the reduction of the number of logical extents without first requesting confirmation. This option can be used only if the **-l** flag has been used.

-m *MirrorCopies*
            Sets the number of physical extents allocated for each logical extent.

            MirrorCopies (that is, mirrors) can be either 0 or 1. This means that beyond the original copy, no other (0) or one (1) mirror copy will contain the same data as the original copy.

            MirrorCopies must be less than the current number of mirrors for the logical volume. Either this option or the **-l** option must be supplied.

-l *LogicalExtentsNumber*
            Decreases the number of logical extents allocated to the *LogicalVolumePath*. *LogicalExtentsNumber* must be less than the number of logical extents previously allocated to *LogicalVolumePath*.

            LogicalExtentsNumber represents the new total number of logical extents within *LogicalVolumePath*. The change is accomplished by deallocating the number of logical extents represented by the difference between the previous number of extents and *LogicalExtentsNumber*.

            The **lvreduce** command asks for confirmation if you do not use the **-f** flag.

            You must use either this option (**-l**) or the **-m** option.

Description

            The **lvreduce** command changes either the number of logical extents allocated to a logical volume specified with the *LogicalVolumePath* parameter or the number of physical extents allocated to each logical extent in the logical volume. The change is determined according to which command flags you use.

lvreduce(8)

Cautions

The Logical Volume Manager does not store any information about which physical extents contain useful data; therefore, using the **-l** option might lead to the loss of useful data.

Examples

1. To decrease the number of the logical extents of logical volume lv03 to one hundred, enter:

    lvreduce -l 100 /dev/vg01/lv03

2. To get one mirror (that is, two copies) for each logical extent of logical volume lv05, enter:

    lvreduce -m 1 /dev/vg01/lv05

    Each logical extent of logical volume lv05 is now singly mirrored.

Files

/usr/sbin/lvreduce
    Specifies the command path.

Related Information

Commands: **lvcreate(8), lvdisplay(8), lvextend(8), pvchange(8), pvdisplay(8)**

lvremove

Purpose   Removes one or more logical volumes from a volume group

Synopsis   **lvremove** [**-f**] *LogicalVolumePath* ...

Flags

    -f   Specifies that no user confirmation is required

Description

The **lvremove** command removes the logical volume(s) specified by the *LogicalVolumePath* parameter. You must close the logical volume(s) before removing them. For example, if the logical volume contains a file system, you must unmount the file system.

Cautions

This command destroys all data in the logical volume(s).

Examples

1.   To remove logical volume lv05 without requiring user confirmation, enter:

     lvremove -f /dev/vg01/lv05

     The program removes the logical volume from the volume group.

Files

    /usr/sbin/lvremove
          Specifies the command path.

Related Information

Commands: **lvchange(8)**, **umount(8)**

lvsync

Purpose   Synchronizes logical volume mirrors that are stale in one or more logical volume

Synopsis   **lvsync** *LogicalVolumePath* ...

Description

The **lvsync** command synchronizes the physical extents. The physical extents are mirrors of the original physical extent that are stale in the logical volume(s) specified by the *LogicalVolumePath* parameter. The synchronization process can be time consuming, depending on the hardware characteristics and the amount of data.

Examples

1.   To synchronize the mirrors on logical volume lv05, enter:

   lvsync /dev/vg01/lv05

Files

/usr/sbin/lvsync
         Specifies the command path.

Related Information

Commands: **lvdisplay(8)**, **vgsync(8)**

mailstats

Purpose   Displays statistics about mail traffic

Synopsis   **/usr/sbin/mailstats** [**-S** *File*]

Flags

     -S *File*   Specifies to use the *File* parameter as the input statistics file instead of the **/var/adm/sendmail/sendmail.st** file

Description

This command reads the information in the **/var/adm/sendmail/sendmail.st** file (or in the file specified with the **-S** flag), formats it, and writes it to standard output. Note also that you can change the location of the **sendmail.st** file by editing its pathname in the **sendmail.cf** file.

Examples

The format of the information is shown in the following example, in which the first field (**M**) contains a number that indicates the position of that mailer in the **sendmail.cf** file, starting at 0 (zero). For example, the first mailer in the **sendmail.cf** file corresponds to the number 0 in the **mailstats** display, the second mailer corresponds to the number 1, and so on.

```
Statistics from Wed Aug 29 16:42:25 1990
M       msgsfr      bytes_from      msgsto      bytes_to
1         50           77K            1           3K
6         43           59K           58          99K
```

The fields in the report have the following meanings:

M   Indicates the position of the mailer in the **sendmail.cf** file.

msgsfr   Contains the number of messages received by the local machine from the indicated mailer.

bytes_from
     Contains the number of bytes in the messages received by the local machine from the indicated mailer.

msgsto   Contains the number of messages sent from the local machine using the indicated mailer.

mailstats(8)

        bytes_to Contains the number of bytes in the messages sent from the local machine using the indicated mailer.

        If **sendmail** transmits mail directly to a file, such as the **dead.letter** file or an alias target, the message and byte counts are credited to the **prog** mailer, as defined in the **sendmail.cf** file. However, **mailstats** will still default to **var/adm/sendmail/sendmail.st**.

Files

        /usr/sbin/mailstats
                Specifies the command path

        /var/adm/sendmail/sendmail.st
                Contains system statistics

        /var/adm/sendmail/sendmail.cf
                Contains configuration information for **sendmail**

Related Information

        Commands: **sendmail(8)**

mklost+found

Purpose   Makes a **lost+found** directory for **fsck**

Synopsis   **/usr/sbin/mklost+found**

Description

The **mklost+found** command creates a **lost+found** directory in the current directory. **mklost+found** also creates (and then removes) a number of empty files so that there will be empty slots for **fsck**. The **fsck** command reconnects any orphaned files and directories by placing them in the **lost+found** directory with an assigned inode number. **mklost+found** is not normally needed since **mkfs** automatically creates the **lost+found** directory when a new file system is created.

Files

/usr/sbin/mklost+found
        Specifies the command path

Related Information

Commands: **fsck(8)**, **mkfs(8)**

mknod

Purpose   Creates a special file

Synopsis   **mknod** *special file* [**b** *major_device# minor_device#* | **c** *major_device# minor_device#*]

mknod *file name* **p**

Flags

b   Indicates that the special file corresponds to a block-oriented device (disk or tape)

c   Indicates that the special file corresponds to a character-oriented device

p   Creates named pipes (FIFOs)

Description

The **mknod** command makes a directory entry. The first argument is the name of the *special device file*. Select a name that is descriptive of the device.

The **mknod** command has two forms. In the first form, the second argument is the **b** or **c** flag. The last two arguments are numbers specifying the *major device*, which helps the operating system find the device driver code, and the *minor device*, the unit drive, or line number, which may be either decimal or octal.

The assignment of major device numbers is specific to each system. You can determine the device numbers by examining the **conf.c** system source file. If you change the contents of the **conf.c** file to add a device driver, you must rebuild the kernel.

In the second form of **mknod**, you use the **p** flag to create named pipes (FIFOs).

Only the superuser can create a character or device special file.

Examples

1.   To create the special file for a new drive, /dev/ra2, with a major device number of 1 and a minor device number of 2, enter:

mknod /dev/ra2 b 1 2

This command creates the special file, /dev/ra2, which is a block special file with major device number 1 and minor device number 2.

2.   To create a named pipe, enter:

mknod pipe p

This command creates the FIFO called *pipe* in your current directory.

Files

/usr/sbin/mknod

Specifies the command path

conf.c   Specifies the system device numbers specification file

mkpasswd

Purpose Creates a version of the basic user database organized for efficient searches

Synopsis **mkpasswd -v** [*tempfile*]

Flags

-v Specifies that each stored entry be listed on standard output

Description

The **mkpasswd** command creates an auxiliary version of the basic user database in a form organized for efficient searches. The command reads the user attributes in the **/etc/passwd** file and creates a version in the **/etc/passwd.**xx file, or the file you specify with the *tempfile* argument, by applying a hashing algorithm with look-aside search capabilities. The hashing algorithm minimizes the search time needed for the **getpwuid** subroutine and the **getpwnam** subroutine to retrieve information.

Following an edit of the **/etc/passwd** file, the **vipw** command calls the **mkpasswd** command to create a version of the database in the **ptmp** temporary file.

To use the **ptmp** file, you must have write access to the file as well as to the **ptmp.pag** file and the **ptmp.dir** file. If they do not exist, you must have write access to the **/etc** directory. For this reason, it may be better for an individual to use the **/tmp** directory or the **/usr/tmp** file.

Only the **root** user should have execute access to this command. The command should be **setgid** to the **passwd** group to have access to the user database. The **passwd** group should have access to all of the following files.

Files Accessed:

Mode	File
r	**/etc/passwd**
rw	**/etc/passwd.pag**
rw	**/etc/passwd.dir**
rw	*tempfile*
rw	*tempfile***.pag**
rw	*tempfile***.dir**

Example

To organize the basic user database for efficient searches and store it in the **ptmp** file, enter:

mkpasswd /usr/tmp

An auxiliary version of the basic user database is created with a hashing algorithm.

Exit Values

The **mkpasswd** command exits with a nonzero exit code if any errors are detected.

Files

/usr/sbin/mkpasswd
  Specifies the command path

Related Information

Command: **vipw(8)**

mkproto

Purpose   Constructs a prototype file system

Synopsis   **/usr/sbin/mkproto** *special proto*

Description

The **mkproto** command is used to bootstrap a new file system. First a new file system is created using **newfs**. **mkproto** is then used to copy files from the old file system into the new file system according to the directions found in the prototype file *proto*. The prototype file contains tokens separated by spaces or newlines. The first tokens comprise the specification for the root directory. File specifications consist of tokens, giving the mode, the user ID, the group ID, and the initial contents of the file. The syntax of the contents field depends on the mode.

The mode token for a file is a 6-character string. The first character specifies the type of the file. (The characters **-bcd** specify regular, block-special, character-special, and directory files, respectively.) The second character of the type is either a **u** or a **-** (dash) to specify **setuid** mode or not. The third character is either a **g** or a **-** (dash) for the **setgid** mode. The rest of the mode is a 3-digit octal number, giving the owner, group, and other read, write, execute permissions. (See the **chmod(1)** command for more information.)

Two decimal number tokens come after the mode; they specify the user and group IDs of the owner of the file. If the file is a regular file, the next token is a pathname from which the contents and size are copied. If the file is a block-special or a character-special file, two decimal number tokens follow, giving the major and minor device numbers. If the file is a directory, **mkproto** makes the entries . (dot) and .. (dot dot) and then reads a list of names and (recursively) file specifications for the entries in the directory. The scan is terminated with the token **$**.

The following listing shows a sample prototype specification.

```
d--777 3 1
usr    d--777 3 1
       sh    ---755 3 1 /bin/sh
       ken   d--755 6 1
             $
       b0    b--644 3 1 0 0
       c0    c--644 3 1 0 0
       $
$
```

Files

/usr/sbin/mkproto
Specifies the command path

Related Information

Commands: **fsck(8)**, **fsdb(8)**, **mkfs(8)**, **newfs(8)**

monacct

Purpose   Collects daily or other periodic accounting records into summary files in the **/var/adm/acct/fiscal** subdirectory

See **acct(8)**

mount, umount

Purpose   Mounts and dismounts file systems

Synopsis   **/usr/sbin/mount**

/usr/sbin/mount -p

/usr/sbin/mount -a[fv] [**-t** *type*]

/usr/sbin/mount [**-frv**] [**-o** *option* ,...] [**-t** *type*] *file_system directory*

/usr/sbin/mount [**-vf**] *file_system*

/usr/sbin/mount [**-vf**] *directory*

/usr/sbin/umount [**-h** *host*]

/usr/sbin/umount -a[v] [**-t** *type*]

/usr/sbin/umount [**-v**] [*file_system* l *directory*] ...

Flags

mount Flags

-a   Attempts to mount all the file systems described in **/etc/fstab**. In this case, *file_system* and *directory* are taken from **/etc/fstab**. If a *type* is specified, all of the file systems in **/etc/fstab** with that type will be mounted. File systems are not necessarily mounted in the order listed in **/etc/fstab**.

-f   Fakes a new **/etc/mtab** entry, but does not actually mount any file systems.

-o *option*[*,option* ...]
         Specifies *options*, a list of comma-separated words from the following list. Some options are valid for all file system types, while others apply to a specific type only.

         Options valid on all file systems (the default is **rw,noquota**):

         quota   Usage limits enforced.

         noquota Usage limits not enforced.

         rw   Read/write.

         ro   Read-only.

suid   Set-user-ID execution allowed.

nosuid   Set-user-ID execution not allowed.

The following options are specific to **nfs** (NFS) file systems:

bg   If the first mount attempt fails, retries in the background.

fg   Retries in foreground.

retry=n Sets the number of mount failure retries to n.

rsize=n Sets the read buffer size to n bytes.

wsize=n Sets the write buffer size to n bytes.

timeo=n Sets the NFS time-out to n tenths of a second.

retrans=n

Sets the number of NFS retransmissions to n.

port=n Sets the server IP port number to n.

soft   Returns an error if the server does not respond.

hard   Retries request until the server responds.

The defaults are as follows:

fg,retry=1,timeo=7,retrans=4,port=NFS_PORT,hard

Defaults for **rsize** and **wsize** are set by the kernel.

The **bg** option causes **mount** to run in the background if the server's **mountd** does not respond. **mount** attempts each request **retry=**n times before giving up. Once the file system is mounted, each NFS request made in the kernel waits **timeo=**n tenths of a second for a response. If no response arrives, the time-out is multiplied by 2 and the request is retransmitted. When **retrans=**n retransmissions have been sent with no reply, a **soft** mounted file system returns an error on the request and a **hard** mounted file system retries the request. File systems that are mounted **rw** (read/write) should use the **hard** option. The number of bytes in a read or write request can be set with the **rsize** and **wsize** options.

-p   Prints the list of mounted file systems in a format suitable for use in **/etc/fstab**.

-r   Mounts the specified file system read-only. This is a shorthand for the following:

           mount -o ro *file_system directory*

           Physically write-protected and magnetic tape file systems must be mounted read-only, or errors will occur when access times are updated, whether or not any explicit write is attempted.

-t *type*   Specifies the file system type. The accepted types are: **ufs**, **s5fs**, **nfs**, and **mfs**; see **fstab** for a description of the legal file system types.

-v   Displays a message indicating which file system is being mounted (Verbose).

umount Flags

-a   Attempts to unmount all the file systems currently mounted (listed in **/etc/mtab**). In this case, *file_system* is taken from **/etc/mtab**.

-h   Unmounts all file systems listed in **/etc/mtab** that are remotely mounted from *host*.

-t   Unmounts all file systems listed in **/etc/mtab** that are of the specified *type*.

-v   Displays a message indicating the file system being unmounted (Verbose).

Description

The **mount** command announces to the system that a file system, *file_system*, is to be attached to the file tree at *directory*, which must already exist. It becomes the name of the newly mounted root. The contents of *directory* are hidden until the file system is unmounted. If *file_system* is of the form *host:path*, the file system type is assumed to be Network File System (NFS).

The **umount** command announces to the system that the file system, *file_system*, previously mounted on *directory* should be removed. Either the file system name or the mounted-on directory may be used.

mount(8)

The **mount** and **umount** commands maintain a table of mounted file systems in **/etc/mtab**, described in **mtab**. If invoked without an argument, **mount** displays the table. Note that since **/etc/mtab** can be modified by commands other than **mount** and **umount**, its contents may not accurately reflect what is actually mounted. If invoked with only one of *file_system* or *directory*, **mount** searches **/etc/fstab** for an entry whose *directory* or *file_system* field matches the given argument. For example, **mount /usr** and **mount /dev/xy0g** are shorthand for **mount /dev/xy0g /usr** if the following line is in **/etc/fstab**:

```
/dev/xy0g /usr 5.2 rw 1 1
```

Examples

1. To mount a local disk, enter:

   mount /dev/xy0g /usr

2. To mount all System V.2 file systems, enter:

   mount -at 5.2

3. To mount a remote file system, enter:

   mount -t nfs serv:/usr/src /usr/src

4. To mount a remote file system, enter:

   mount serv:/usr/src /usr/src

5. To mount remote file system with a hard mount, enter:

   mount -o hard serv:/usr/src /usr/src

6. To save the current mount state, enter:

   mount -p > /etc/fstab

Files

/usr/sbin/mount
　　　　Specifies the command path

/usr/sbin/umount
　　　　Specifies the command path

/etc/mtab

/etc/fstab

Notes

Mounting file systems full of garbage will crash the system.

No more than one user should mount a disk partition read/write or the file system may become corrupted.

If the directory on which a file system is to be mounted is a symbolic link, the file system is mounted on the directory to which the symbolic link refers, rather than being mounted on top of the symbolic link itself.

Related Information

Commands: **mountd**(8), **nfsd**(8).

Functions: **mount**(M), **umount**(3).

Files: **fstab**(4).

mountd

Purpose   Services remote NFS compatible mount requests

Synopsis   **/usr/sbin/mountd** [**-n**] [*exportsfile*]

Flags

-n   The optional **-n** option allows non-root mount requests to be served. This should only be specified if there are clients such as PC's that require it.

exportsfile
The optional *exportsfile* argument specifies an alternate location for the **exports** file. The **etc/exports** file is the default.

Description

The **mountd** daemon is the server for NFS protocol mount requests from clients. The **mountd** daemon responds to requests from remote computer systems to mount directories. When getting the signal **SIGHUP**, **mountd** rereads the **exports** file.

Files

/usr/sbin/mountd
Specifies the command path

/etc/exports
Contains a list of directories that can be exported

/etc/services
Shows the network services available on this system

Related Information

nfsstat (1), nfsd (8), portmap (8), exports (4), showmount (8)

named

Purpose   Internet domain name server

Synopsis   **named** [**-d** *debuglevel*] [**-p** *port#*] [{**-b**} *bootfile*]

Flags

-d   Print debugging information. A number after the **d** determines the level of messages printed.

-p   Use a different port number. The default is the standard port number as listed in the **/etc/services** file.

-b   Use an alternate boot file. Allows you to specify a file with a leading dash. The usage of the **-b** option is not required.

Any additional argument is taken as the name of the boot file. The boot file contains information about where the name server is to get its initial data. If multiple boot files are specified, only the last is used. Lines in the boot file cannot be continued on subsequent lines.

Description

The **named** daemon is the Internet domain name server. See RFC883 for more information on the Internet name-domain system. Without any arguments, **named** will read the default boot file **/etc/named.boot**, read any initial data, and listen for queries.

The following is an example of part of a **named.boot** file, created by the network administrator.

```
;
;       boot file for name server
;
directory       /usr/local/domain
; type       domain                 source host/file              backup file
cache        .                                                    root.cache
primary      Berkeley.EDU           berkeley.edu.zone
primary      32.128.IN-ADDR.ARPA    ucbhosts.rev
secondary    CC.Berkeley.EDU        128.32.137.8 128.32.137.3 cc.zone.bak
secondary    6.32.128.IN-ADDR.ARPA  128.32.137.8 128.32.137.3 cc.rev.bak
primary      0.0.127.IN-ADDR.ARPA                                 localhost.rev
forwarders 10.0.0.78 10.2.0.78
; slave
```

The **directory** line causes the server to change its working directory to the directory specified. This can be important for the correct processing of **$INCLUDE** files in primary zone files.

The **cache** line specifies that data in **root.cache** is to be placed in the backup cache. Its main use is to specify data such as locations of root domain servers. This cache is not used during normal operation, but is used as "hints" to find the current root servers. The file root.cache is in the same format as "berkeley.edu.zone". There can be more than one "cache" file specified. The cache files are processed in such a way as to preserve the time-to-live's of data dumped out. Data for the root nameservers is kept artificially valid if necessary.

The first "primary" line states that the file "berkeley.edu.zone" contains authoritative data for the "Berkeley.EDU" zone. The file "berkeley.edu.zone" contains data in the master file format described in RFC883. All domain names are relative to the origin, in this case, "Berkeley.EDU" (see below for a more detailed description).

The second "primary" line states that the file "ucbhosts.rev" contains authoritative data for the domain "32.128.IN-ADDR.ARPA," which is used to translate addresses in network 128.32 to hostnames. Each master file should begin with an SOA record for the zone (see below).

The first "secondary" line specifies that all authoritative data under "CC.Berkeley.EDU" is to be transferred from the name server at 128.32.137.8. If the transfer fails it will try 128.32.137.3 and continue trying the addresses, up to 10, listed on this line.

The secondary copy is also authoritative for the specified domain. The first non-dotted-quad address on this line will be taken as a filename in which to backup the transfered zone. The name server will load the zone from this backup file if it exists when it boots, providing a complete copy even if the master servers are unreachable. Whenever a new copy of the domain is received by automatic zone transfer from one of the master servers, this file will be updated. The second "secondary" line states that the address-to-hostname mapping for the subnet 128.32.136 should be obtained from the sume list of master servers as the previous zone.

The "forwarders" line specifies the addresses of sitewide servers that will accept recursive queries from other servers. If the boot file specifies one or more forwarders, then the server will send all queries for data not in the cache to the forwarders first. Each forwarder will be asked in turn until an answer is returned or the list is exhausted. If no answer is forthcoming from a forwarder, the server will continue as it would have without the forwarders line unless it is in "slave" mode.

The forwarding facility is useful to cause a large sitewide cache to be generated on a master, and to reduce traffic over links to outside servers. It can also be used to allow servers to run that do not have access directly to the Internet, but wish to act as though they do.

The ''slave'' line (shown commented out) is used to put the server in slave mode. In this mode, the server will only make queries to forwarders. This option is normally used on machine that wish to run a server but for physical or administrative reasons cannot be given access to the Internet, but have access to a host that does have access.

The ''sortlist'' line can be used to indicate networks that are to be preferred over other, unlisted networks. Queries for host addresses from hosts on the same network as the server will receive responses with local network addresses listed first, then addresses on the sort list, then other addresses. This line is only acted on at initial startup. When reloading the nameserver with a SIGHUP, this line will be ignored.

The master file consists of control information and a list of resource records for objects in the zone of the forms:

> **$INCLUDE** *<filename> <opt_domain>*
> **$ORIGIN** *<domain>*
> *<domain> <opt_ttl> <opt_class> <type>*
> *<resource_record_data>*

where *domain* is "." for root, "@" for the current origin, or a standard domain name. If *domain* is a standard domain name that does not end with ''.'', the current origin is appended to the domain. Domain names ending with ''.'' are unmodified.

The *opt_domain* field is used to define an origin for the data in an included file. It is equivalent to placing a $ORIGIN statement before the first line of the included file. The field is optional. Neither the *opt_domain* field nor $ORIGIN statements in the included file modify the current origin for this file.

The *opt_ttl* field is an optional integer number for the time-to-live field. It defaults to zero, meaning the minimum value specified in the SOA record for the zone.

The *opt_class* field is the object address type; currently only one type is supported, **IN**, for objects connected to the DARPA Internet.

The *type* field contains one of the following tokens; the data expected in the *resource_record_data* field is in parentheses.

A   a host address (dotted quad)

NS   an authoritative name server (domain)

MX a mail exchanger (domain)

CNAME the canonical name for an alias (domain)

SOA marks the start of a zone of authority (domain of originating host, domain address of maintainer, a serial number and the following parameters in seconds: refresh, retry, expire and minimum TTL (see RFC883))

MB a mailbox domain name (domain)

MG a mail group member (domain)

MR a mail rename domain name (domain)

NULL a null resource record (no format or data)

WKS a well know service description (not implemented yet)

PTR a domain name pointer (domain)

HINFO host information (cpu_type OS_type)

MINFO mailbox or mail list information (request_domain error_domain)

Resource records normally end at the end of a line, but may be continued across lines between opening and closing parentheses. Comments are introduced by semicolons and continue to the end of the line.

Each master zone file should begin with an SOA record for the zone. An example SOA record is as follows:

```
@   IN  SOA ucbvax.Berkeley.EDU. rwh.ucbvax.Berkeley.EDU. (
                2.89; serial
                10800    ; refresh
                3600; retry
                3600000 ; expire
                86400 ) ; minimum
```

The SOA lists a serial number, which should be changed each time the master file is changed. Secondary servers check the serial number at intervals specified by the refresh time in seconds; if the serial number changes, a zone transfer will be done to load the new data. If a master server cannot be contacted when a refresh is due, the retry time specifies the interval at which refreshes should be attempted until successful. If a master server cannot be contacted within the interval given by the expire time, all data from the zone is discarded by secondary servers. The minimum value is the time-to-live used by records in the file with no explicit time-to-live value.

The boot file directives ''domain'' and ''suffixes'' have been made obsolete by a more useful resolver based implementation of suffixing for partially qualified domain names. The prior mechanisms could fail under a number of situations, especially when then local nameserver did not have complete information.

The following signals have the specified effect when sent to the server process using the **kill**(1) command.

SIGHUP   Causes server to read named.boot and reload database.

SIGINT   Dumps current data base and cache to /var/tmp/named_dump.db

SIGIOT   Dumps statistics data into /var/tmp/named.stats if the server is compiled -DSTATS. Statistics data is appended to the file.

SIGSYS   Dumps the profiling data in /var/tmp if the server is compiled with profiling (server forks, chdirs and exits).

SIGTERM Dumps the primary and secondary database files. Used to save modified data on shutdown if the server is compiled with dynamic updating enabled.

SIGUSR1 Turns on debugging; each SIGUSR1 increments debug level. (SIGEMT on older systems without SIGUSR1)

SIGUSR2 Turns off debugging completely. (SIGFPE on older systems without SIGUSR2)

Files

/usr/sbin/named
> Specifies the command path

Related Information

/etc/namedb/named.boot name server configuration boot file
/var/run/named.pid   the process id
/var/tmp/named.run   debug output
/var/tmp/named_dump.db dump of the name server database
/var/tmp/named.stats   nameserver statistics data

kill(1), **gethostbyname(3N)**, **signal(3c)**, **resolver(3)**, **resolver(5)**, **hostname(7)**, RFC882, RFC883, RFC973, RFC974, *Name Server Operations Guide for BIND*

ncheck

Purpose   generate names from i-numbers

Synopsis   **ncheck** [**-i** *numbers*] [**-a**] [**-s**] [**-m**] *file systems* ...

Flags

-a   Allows printing of the names . (dot and .. (dot dot), which are ordinarily suppressed.

-i*numbers*
            Reduces the report to only those files whose i-numbers follow.

-m   Allows printing of the mode, UID, and GID of files. This flag takes effect only if either the **-i** or the **-s** flag is also specified on the command line.

-s   Reduces the report to special files and files with set-user-ID mode

Description

For most normal file system maintenance, the function of **ncheck** is subsumed by the **fsck** command. The **ncheck** command with no options generates a list of all files on every specified file system. The list includes the pathname and the corresponding i-number of each file. A /. (slash dot) follows the name of each directory file.

Issuing the command with the **-i** option reduces the report to only those files whose i-numbers follow. Issuing the command with the **-a** option allows for the printing of the names . (dot) and .. (dot dot) which are ordinarily suppressed. Issuing the command with the **-s** option reduces the report to special files and files with set-user-ID mode. This flag is intended to discover concealed violations of security policy.

Since the report is generated in an order that is not particularly useful, you should probably sort it prior to reading it.

Diagnostics

When the filesystem structure is improper, ?? (question mark question mark) denotes the parent of a parentless file. A pathname beginning with ... (dot dot dot) denotes a loop.

Files

/usr/sbin/ncheck
> Specifies the command path

Related Information

Commands: **sort(1)**, **fsck(8)**, **icheck(8)**

newfs

Purpose   Constructs a new file system

Synopsis   /usr/sbin/newfs [-T ufs | s5fs] [-N] [*newfs-options*] *special disk-type*

Flags

-T ufs | s5fs
> Since OSF/1 supports multiple file system types, a new flag, **-T** is used to choose between the ufs and System V file systems. If **-T** is not specified, a ufs file system is created by default.

-N   Causes the file system parameters to be printed out without really creating the file system.

Description

You must be **root** to use this command.

The **newfs** command creates a new file system on the specified *special disk-type*. If the disk has been labeled using **disklabel**, **newfs** builds a file system on the specified device, basing its defaults on the information in the disk label. If the disk has not been labeled using **disklabel**, **newfs** looks up the specified disk type in the disk description file **/etc/disktab** to get default information on the specified special device. Typically the defaults are reasonable, however **newfs** has numerous options to allow the defaults to be selectively overridden.

The following sections describe the file system dependencies for the ufs file systems (the default) and for System V file systems. Each section defines the command syntax and the particular options that apply to that specific file system type.

File System Dependent newfs - For UFS File Systems

Synopsis   /usr/sbin/newfs [-N] [*newfs-options*] *special disk-type*

Flags

The following *newfs-options* define the general layout policies.

-b*block-size*
> The block size of the file system in bytes.

-f*frag-size*   The fragment size of the file system in bytes.

-m*%free_space*

The percentage of space reserved from normal users; the minimum free space threshold (*minfree*). The default value is 10%. See **tunefs(8)** for more details on how to set this option.

-o*opt_preference*

The file system can either be instructed to try to minimize the *time* spent allocating blocks, or to try to minimize the *space* fragmentation on the disk. If the value of *minfree* is less than 10%, the default is to optimize for space; if the value of *minfree* is greater than or equal to 10%, the default is to optimize for time. See **tunefs(8)** for more details on how to set this option.

-a*maxcontig*

This specifies the maximum number of contiguous blocks that will be laid out before forcing a rotational delay (refer to the **-d** option). The default value is 1. See **tunefs(8)** for more details on how to set this option.

-d*rotdelay*   This specifies the expected time (in milliseconds) to service a transfer completion interrupt and initiate a new transfer on the same disk. The default is 4 milliseconds. See **tunefs(8)** for more details on how to set this option.

-e*maxbpg*   This indicates the maximum number of blocks any single file can allocate out of a cylinder group before it is forced to begin allocating blocks from another cylinder group. The default is about one-quarter of the total blocks in a cylinder group. See **tunefs(8)** for more details on how to set this option.

-i*#bytes/inode*

This specifies the density of inodes in the file system. The default is to create an inode for each 2048 bytes of data space. If fewer inodes are desired, a larger number should be used; to create more inodes a smaller number should be given.

-c*#cylinders/group*

The number of cylinders per cylinder group in a file system. The default value is 16.

-s*size*   The size of the file system in sectors.

The following options override the standard sizes for the disk geometry. Their default values are taken from the disk label. Changing these defaults is useful only when using **newfs** to build a file system whose raw image will eventually be used on a different type of disk than the one on which it is initially created (on a write-once disk, for example). Note that changing any of these values from their defaults makes it impossible for **fsck** to find the alternate superblocks if the standard superblock is lost.

-r*revolutions/minute*
> The speed of the disk in revolutions per minute.

-S*sector-size*
> The size of a sector in bytes (almost never anything but 512).

-u*sectors/track*
> The number of sectors per track available for data allocation by the file system. This does not include sectors reserved at the end of each track for bad block replacement (see **-p**).

-t*#tracks/cylinder*
> The number of tracks per cylinder available for data allocation by the file system.

-p*spare_sectors/track*
> Spare sectors (bad sector replacements) are physical sectors that occupy space at the end of each track. They are not counted as part of the sectors per track (**-u**) since they are not available to the file system for data allocation.

-x*spare_sectors/cylinder*
> Spare sectors (bad sector replacements) are physical sectors that occupy space at the end of the last track in the cylinder. They are deducted from the sectors per track (**-u**) of the last track of each cylinder since they are not available to the file system for data allocation.

-l*hardware_sector_interleave*
> Used to describe perturbations in the media format to compensate for a slow controller. Interleave is physical sector interleave on each track, specified as the denominator of the ratio: sectors read/sectors passed over.
>
> Thus, an interleave of 1/1 implies contiguous layout, while 1/2 implies logical sector 0 (zero) is separated by one sector from logical sector 1.

-k*sector0-skew/track*
> Used to describe perturbations in the media format to compensate for a slow controller. Track skew is the offset of sector 0 (zero) on track N relative to sector 0 (zero) on track N-1 on the same cylinder.

File System Dependent newfs - For System V File Systems

Synopsis   /usr/sbin/newfs -T s5fs [*options*] *special disk-type*

Flags

The following **newfs** options are specific to the System V file system:

-b*block-size*   The block size of the filesystem in bytes. Valid block sizes are 512, 1024 and 2048. The default is 512.

-s*size*   The size of the file system in number of block-size blocks.

-C*blocks/cyliner*
                      The number of blocks/cylinder.

-G*gap*   The rotational gap.

-I*inodes*   The number of inodes.

-P*proto_name*
                      The name of the prototype file to use for creating the file system.

The **newfs** program waits 10 seconds before starting to construct the file system. During this 10-second pause the command can be aborted by pressing the **<Delete>** key.

The specified special device should either be previously labeled using **disklabel(8)** or its disk-type must be in **/etc/disktab**. If the block-size and/or the size of the file system is specified, the specified values override what is in the disklabel or in **/etc/disktab**.

If no prototype file is specified, **newfs** builds a file system with a single empty directory on it. The boot program block (block zero) is left uninitialized.

If a prototype file is specified, **newfs** takes its directions from that file. The prototype file contains tokens separated by spaces or new-lines. A sample prototype specification follows; line numbers have been added to aid in the explanation:

```
 1.    file_name
 2.    512 4872 110
 3.    d--777 3 1
 4.    usr d--777 3 1
 5.    sh  ---755 3 1 /sbin/sh
 6.    ken d--755 6 1
 7.    $
 8.    b0   b--644 3 1 0 0
 9.    c0   c--644 3 1 0 0
10.    $
11.    $
```

Historically line 1 (as shown in the preceding example) is the name of a file to be copied onto block zero as the bootstrap program. Since OSF/1 does not support using the System V file system as a root file system, this file name is ignored by **newfs** and no data is copied onto block zero of the specified special device.

Line 2 specifies the block size of the file system in bytes, the size of the file system in number of blocks of the just specified block size and the number of inodes in the file system.

Lines 3 to 9 tell **newfs** about files and directories to be included in this file system. Line 3 specifies the root directory. Lines 4 to 6 and 8 to 9 specify other directories and files. The $ on line 7 tells **newfs** to end the branch of the file system it is on, and continue from the next higher directory.

The $ on lines 10 and 11 end the process, since no additional specifications follow.

File specifications give the mode, the user ID, the group ID, and the initial contents of the file. Valid syntax for the contents field depends on the first character of the mode.

The mode for a file is specified by a 6-character string. The first character specifies the type of the file. The character range is -bcd to specify regular, block special, character special and directory files, respectively. The second character of the mode is either u or - to specify set-user-id mode or not. The third is g or - for the set-group-id mode. The rest of the mode is a 3-digit octal numbr giving the owner, group, and other read, write, execute permissions. Refer to **chmod(1)** for additional information.

Two decimal number tokens come after the mode; they specify the user and group IDs of the owner of the file. If the file is a regular file, the next token of the specification may be a path name from which the contents and size are copied. If the file is a block or character special file, two decimal numbers follow which give the major and minor device numbers. If the file is a directory, **newfs** makes the entries . (dot) and .. (dot dot) and then reads a list of names and file specifications recursively for the entries in the directory. As noted previously, the scan is terminated with the token $.

Files

/usr/sbin/newfs
> Specifies the command path

/etc/disktab
> Provides disk geometry and file system partition information

Related Information

Commands: **chmod(1)**, **disklabel(8)**, **fsck(8)**, **tunefs(8)**

Files: **disktab(4)**, **fstab(4)**

nfsd

Purpose   The remote NFS compatible server

Synopsis   **nfsd** [*msk mtch numprocs*]
                nfsd [*numprocs*]

Description

The **nfsd** daemon runs on a server machine to service NFS requests from client machines. At least one **nfsd** must be running for a machine to operate as a server.

msk mtch

These arguments permit restriction of NFS services to a subset of the host addresses. The *msk* and *mtch* are applied to the client host address as follows:

If ((*host_address* & *msk*) == *mtch*)
   - service the client request
else
   - drop the request

numprocs

Specifies how many servers to fork off. If *numprocs* is not specified, it defaults to 1.

Cautions

The client host address restrictions specified here are unrelated to the mount restrictions specified in **/etc/exports** for **mountd(8)**.

Examples

1.   In the following example, **4** daemons are run that accept requests from any client on subnet **131.104.48**.

```
nfsd   255.255.255.0      131.104.48.0      4
```

2.   In the following example, **6** daemons are run that accept requests from clients with addresses in the range **131.104.0.***n* to **131.104.15.***n*.

```
nfsd   255.255.240.0      131.104.0.0       6
```

3.   In the following example, any client with only **4** servers is served.

```
nfsd    0    0    4
```

In the following example, any client with only **4** servers is served.

```
nfsd 4
```

A server should typically run enough daemons to handle the maximum level of concurrency from its clients, typically 4 to 6.

The **nfsd** daemon listens for service requests at the port indicated in the NFS server specification; see *Network File System Protocol Specification, RFC1094.*

Files

/usr/sbin/nfsd
    Specifies the command path

Related Information

Commands: **nfsstat (8) nfssvc (2)**

Daemons: **mountd (8), portmap(8)**

nfsiod

Purpose   The local NFS compatible asynchronous I/O server

Synopsis   **nfsiod** [*numdaemons*]

Description

The **nfsiod** daemon runs on an NFS compatible client machine to service asynchronous I/O requests to its server. It improves performance, but is not required for correct operation. The *numdaemons* option defines how many **nfsiod** daemons to start; if unspecified, only a single daemon will be started. A client should typically run enough daemons to handle their maximum level of concurrency, typically 4 to 6.

Files

/usr/sbin/nfsiod
          Specifies the command path

Related Information

Commands: **nfsstat (1)**

Daemons: **async_daemon (2), mountd (8), portmap (8)**

nfsstat

Purpose   Reports NFS statistics

Synopsis   **nfsstat** [**-i** *interval*] [*system*] [*corefile*]

Description

The **nfsstat** command delves into the system and normally reports certain statistics kept about NFS client and server activity. If **-i***interval* is specified, then successive lines are summaries over the last *interval* seconds. The **nfsstat -i 5** command will print what the NFS compatible system is doing every 5 seconds.

A second argument is taken to be the file containing the system's namelist. Otherwise, **/vmunix** is used. A third argument tells **nfsstat** where to look for *corefile*. Otherwise, **/dev/kmem** is used.

Files

/usr/bin/nfsstat
        Specifies the command path

Related Information

Commands: **netstat (1), vmstat (1)**

nslookup

Purpose   Queries Internet name servers interactively

Synopsis   **nslookup** [-*option* ...] [*host-to-find* [*server*]]

Description

The **nslookup** command is a program that is used to query Internet domain name servers. The **Nslookup** command has two modes: interactive and noninteractive. Interactive mode allows the user to query name servers for information about various hosts and domains or to print a list of hosts in a domain. Noninteractive mode is used to print just the name and requested information for a host or domain.

ARGUMENTS

Interactive mode is entered in the following cases:

1.   When no arguments are given (the default name server will be used).

2.   When the first argument is a - (dash) and the second argument is the hostname or Internet address of a name server.

Noninteractive mode is used when the name or Internet address of the host to be looked up is given as the first argument. The optional second argument specifies the hostname or address of a name server.

The options listed under the **set** command can be specified in the **.nslookuprc** file in the user's home directory if they are listed one per line. Options can also be specified on the command line if they precede the arguments and are prefixed with a - (dash). For example, to change the default query type to host information, and the initial time-out to 10 seconds, enter:

nslookup -query=hinfo -timeout=10

INTERACTIVE COMMANDS

Commands may be interrupted at any time by entering a **<Ctrl-c>**. To exit, enter a **<Ctrl-d>** (EOF) or type exit. The command line length must be less than 256 characters. To treat a built-in command as a hostname, precede it with an escape character (backslash). Note that an unrecognized command will be interpreted as a hostname.

host [*server*]   Look up information for *host* using the current default server or using *server* if specified. If *host* is an Internet address and the query type is A or PTR, the name of the host is returned. If *host* is a name and does not have a trailing period, the default domain name is appended to the name. (This behavior depends on the state of the **set** options **domain, srchlist, defname,** and **search**). To look up a host not in the current domain, append a . (dot) to the name.

server *domain*
lserver *domain*

Change the default server to *domain*. **lserver** uses the initial server to look up information about *domain* while **server** uses the current default server. If an authoritative answer cannot be found, the names of servers that might have the answer are returned.

root

Changes the default server to the server for the root of the domain name space. Currently, the host **ns.nic.ddn.mil** is used. (This command is a synonym for **lserver ns.nic.ddn.mil.**) The name of the root server can be changed with the **set root** command.

finger [*name*] [> *filename*]

finger [*name*] [>> *filename*]

Connect with the finger server on the current host. The current host is defined when a previous lookup for a host was successful and returned address information (see the **set querytype=A** command). *name* is optional. The > and >> (redirection symbols) can be used to redirect output in the usual manner.

ls [*option*] *domain* [> *filename*]
ls [*option*] *domain* [>> *filename*]

List the information available for *domain*, optionally creating or appending to *filename*. The default output contains hostnames and their Internet addresses. *option* can be one of the following:

-t *querytype*
Lists all records of the specified type (see *querytype* later in this manpage).

-a Lists aliases of hosts in the domain. This option is a synonym for **-t CNAME**.

-d Lists all records for the domain. This option is a synonym for **-t ANY**.

-h Lists CPU and operating system information for the domain. This option is a synonym for **-t HINFO**.

-s   Lists well-known services of hosts in the domain. This option is a synonym for **-t WKS**.

When output is directed to a file, # (number signs) are printed for every 50 records received from the server.

view *filename*
Sorts and lists the output of previous **ls** command(s) with **more**(1).

help

?   Prints a brief summary of commands.

exit   Exits the program.

set *keyword*[=*value*]
This command is used to change state information that affects the lookups. Valid keywords are

    all   Prints the current values of the frequently used options to **set**. Information about the current default server and host is also printed.

    class=*value*
        Changes the query class to one of

        IN   The Internet class.

        CHAOS   The Chaos class.

        HESIOD   The MIT Athena Hesiod class.

        ANY   Wildcard (any of the above).

        The class specifies the protocol group of the information. (Default = **IN**, abbreviation = **cl**)

    [no]debug
        Turns debugging mode on. A lot more information is printed about the packet sent to the server and the resulting answer. (Default = **nodebug**, abbreviation = **[no]deb**)

    [no]d2   Turns exhaustive debugging mode on. Essentially all fields of every packet are printed. (Default = **nod2**)

    domain=*name*
        Changes the default domain name to *name*. The default domain name is appended to a lookup request depending on the state of

the **defname** and **search** options. The domain search list contains the parents of the default domain if it has at least two components in its name. For example, if the default domain is **CC.Berkeley.EDU**, the search list is **CC.Berkeley.EDU** and **Berkeley.EDU**. Use the **set srchlist** command to specify a different list. Use the **set all** command to display the list.

(Default = value from hostname, **/etc/resolv.conf** or **LOCALDOMAIN**, abbreviation = **do**) **srchlist**=*name1*/*name2*/... Change the default domain name to *name1* and the domain search list to *name1*, *name2*, and so on. A maximum of 6 names separated by | (slashes) can be specified: For example,

> **set srchlist=lcs.MIT.EDU/ai.MIT.EDU/MIT.EDU**

sets the domain to **lcs.MIT.EDU** and the search list to the three names. This command overrides the default domain name and search list of the **set domain** command. Use the **set all** command to display the list.
(Default = value based on hostname, **/etc/resolv.conf** or **LOCALDOMAIN**, abbreviation = **srchl**)

[no]defname

If set, appends the default domain name to a single-component lookup request (that is, one that does not contain a dot).
(Default = **defname**, abbreviation = **[no]def**)

[no]search

If the lookup request contains at least one . (dot) but does not end with a trailing dot, append the domain names in the domain search list to the request until an answer is received.
(Default = **search**, abbreviation = **[no]sea**)

port=*value*

Changes the default TCP/UDP name server port to *value*.
(Default = **53**, abbreviation = **po**)

querytype=*value*
type=*value*

Change the type of information query to one of

A   The host's Internet address.

CNAME   The canonical name for an alias.

HINFO   The host CPU and operating system type.

MINFO	The mailbox or mail list information.
MX	The mail exchanger.
NS	The name server for the named zone.
PTR	The hostname if the query is an Internet address; otherwise the pointer to other information.
SOA	The domain's start-of-authority information.
TXT	The text information.
UINFO	The user information.
WKS	The supported well-known services.

Other types (.BANY,.BAXFR, .BMB,.BMD,.BMF,.BNULL) are described in the RFC1035 document.
(Default = **A**, abbreviations = **q, ty**)

[no]recurse

Tells the name server to query other servers if it does not have the information.
(Default = **recurse**, abbreviation = **[no]rec**)

retry=*number*

Sets the number of retries to *number*. When a reply to a request is not received within a certain amount of time (changed with **set time-out**), the timeout period is doubled and the request is present. The retry value controls how many times a request is resent before giving up.
(Default = **4**, abbreviation = **ret**)

root=*host*

Changes the name of the root server to *host*. This affects the **root** command.
(Default = **ns.nic.ddn.mil.**, abbreviation = **ro**)

timeout=*number*

Changes the initial timeout interval for waiting for a reply to *number* seconds. Each retry doubles the timeout period.
(Default = 5 seconds, abbreviation = ti)

[no]vc   Always use a virtual circuit when sending requests to the server.
(Default = novc, abbreviation = [no]v)

[no]ignoretc

Ignore packet truncation errors.
(Default = noignoretc, abbreviation = [no]ig)

Files

/usr/bin/nslookup
Specifies the command path

/etc/resolv.conf
Initial domain name and name server addresses

$HOME/.nslookuprc
User's initial options

/usr/share/misc/nslookup.help
Summary of commands

Diagnostics

If the lookup request was not successful, an error message is printed. Possible errors are

```
Timed out
```
The server did not respond to a request after a certain amount of time (changed with **set timeout=***value*) and a certain number of retries (changed with **set retry=***value*).

```
No response from server
```
No name server is running on the server machine.

```
No records
```
The server does not have resource records of the current query type for the host, although the hostname is valid. The query type is specified with the **set querytype** command.

```
Nonexistent domain
```
The host or domain name does not exist.

```
Connection refused
Network is unreachable
```
The connection to the name or finger server could not be made at the current time. This error commonly occurs with **ls** and **finger** requests.

```
Server failure
```
The name server found an internal inconsistency in its database and could not return a valid answer.

```
Refused
```
The name server refused to service the request.

```
Format error
```
The name server found that the request packet was not in the proper format. It may indicate an error in **nslookup**.

Related Information

resolver(3), resolver(5), named(8),

Specifications: RFC1034, RFC1035

nulladm

Purpose   Creates the file specified in the *File* parameter, gives read (**r**) and write (**w**) permissions to the file owner and group, and read (**r**) permission to other users

See **acct(8)**

pac

Purpose   Outputs printer/plotter accounting information

Synopsis   **/usr/sbin/pac** [**-c**] [**-m**] [**-p** *price*] [**-P** *printer*] [**-r**] [**-s**] [*name*]

Flags

-c   Sorts output according to the computed cost instead of alphabetically according to user.

-m   Groups all printing charges for the user specified by *name*, without regard for the host machine from which printing was invoked.

-p *price*   Uses the dollar amount charged per unit of output specified by *price*. The default dollar amount charged is $0.02 per unit when a dollar amount is not specified by an entry in the **/etc/qconfig** file or there is no **/etc/qconfig** file.

-P *printer*

Specifies the printer for which accounting records are produced. Alternatively, the system selects the printer named with the **PRINTER** environment variable, or the default printer **lp0**.

-r   Reverses the sorted order, so that records are listed alphabetically from z to a, or in descending order by computed cost when this flag is used with the **-c** flag.

-s   Writes printer accounting information to a summary file. You must specify the **-P** flag and *printer* name when this flag is used. Output is made to a file in the **/var/adm/printer** subdirectory. The file name is:

printer.acct_sum (where *printer* is the specified printer name)

Output is in three unheaded columns in the format:

```
pages/feet   machinename:username    runs
```

Description

When printer accounting is enabled in the **/etc/printcap** file, and you use the **pac** command in a shell script or from the standard input, **pac** outputs printer/plotter accounting records to the standard output for each user of the printer specified with the **-P** flag and *printer* name or for users specified with the *name* parameter. The unit used for printer accounting is the number of pages printed. However, for raster devices (such as laser printers, typesetters, and plotters) length in feet of paper (film, for example) is the unit used. Output units are expressed both as the number of units used and the charge in dollars according to the price specified with **-p** flag and *price* amount per unit. The printer/plotter accounting output has the following column headings and format.

```
              Login              pages/feet       runs        price
   aife:billb                        19.00          2      $   0.38
   alewife.osf.org:hermi             22.00          3      $   0.44
   amalthea:willie                   53.00         12      $   1.06
   riafsl.osf.org:root                1.00          1      $   0.02
   robin:hoffmann                   834.00        202      $  16.68
   robin:root                        69.00         20      $   1.38
   sailor:brezak                    184.00         17      $   3.68
```

There are four fields, each with its own column heading, in each record of the default output produced by the **pac** command: 1) the machine from which the print command was entered and login name is entered in the `Login` column; 2) the number of pages or feet of paper output is entered in the `page/feet` column; 3) the number of times the printer was used is entered in the `runs` column; and 4) the cost computed at the default or specified price is entered in the `price` column.

Examples

To print printer/plotter accounting information for all users of default printer **lp0** to the standard output device, enter:

/usr/sbin/pac

Output is sorted alphabetically according to machine name and username. The number of printed pages or feet of output paper used and the charge per foot of paper or page is computed at the default dollar amount of $0.02 per page because no flags are specified. The assumption here is that the **PRINTER** environment variable is unspecified and no dollar amount for cost per page is specified in the **/etc/qconfig** file, or there is no **/etc/qconfig** file.

To write printer/plotter accounting records in a summary file enter the following line as a superuser or as **adm**.

/usr/sbin/pac -P*printer* **-s** (where *printer* is the printer name)

Summary information is written to the file:

/var/adm/printer/*printer***.acct_sum**

To produce printer/plotter accounting information for **smith**, **jones** and **greene** for pages printed with the printer whose reference name is **lp12**, enter:

/usr/sbin/pac -Plp12 smith jones greene

pac(8)

Files

/usr/sbin/pac
Specifies the command path

/var/adm/*printer***.acct**,

/var/adm/*printer***.acct_sum**

Related Information

Commands: **acct(8)**, **acctcms(8)**, **acctcom(8)**, **acctcon(8)**, **acctmerg(8)**, **acctprc(8)**, **runacct(8)**

ping

Purpose   Sends ICMP ECHO_REQUEST packets to network hosts

Synopsis   **ping** [-**dfnqrvR**] [-**c** *count*] [-**i** *wait*] [-**l** *preload*] [-**p** *pattern*] [-**s** *packetsize*]

Flags

-**c** *count*   Stops after sending (and receiving) *count* ECHO_RESPONSE packets.

-**d**   Set the SO_DEBUG option on the socket being used.

-**f**   Floods **ping**. Outputs packets as fast as they come back or 100 times per second, whichever is more. For every ECHO_REQUEST sent, a . (dot) is printed, while for ever ECHO_REPLY received a backspace is used. This provides a rapid display of how many packets are being dropped. Only the superuser may use this option. *This can be very hard on a network and should be used with caution.* (see **Cautions**)

-**i** *wait*   Waits *wait* seconds between sending each packet. The default is to wait for 1 second between each packet. This option is incompatible with the -**f** option.

-**l** *preload*
    If *preload* is specified, **ping** sends that many packets as fast as possible before falling into its normal mode of behavior.

-**n**   Numeric output only. No attempt will be made to look up symbolic names for host addresses.

-**p** *pattern*
    You may specify up to 16 pad bytes to fill out the packet you send. This is useful for diagnosing data-dependent problems in a network. For example, -**p ff** will cause the sent packet to be filled with all 1s (ones).

-**q**   Quiets output. Nothing is displayed except the summary lines at start-up time and when finished.

-**R**   Records route. Includes the RECORD_ROUTE option in the ECHO_REQUEST packet and displays the route buffer on returned packets. Note that the IP header is only large enough for nine such routes. Many hosts ignore or discard this option.

-**r**   Bypasses the normal routing tables and directly sends to a host on an attached network. If the host is not on a directly attached network, an error is returned. This option can be used to send **ping** to a local host through an interface that has no route through it (for example, after the interface was dropped by **routed**(8)).

-**s** *packetsize*
Specifies the number of data bytes to be sent. The default is 56, which translates into 64 ICMP data bytes when combined with the 8 bytes of ICMP header data.

-**v**
Specifies verbose output. ICMP packets other than ECHO_RESPONSE that are received are listed.

Description

The **ping** command uses the ICMP (Internet Control Message Protocol) protocol's mandatory ECHO_REQUEST datagram to elicit an ICMP ECHO_RESPONSE from a host or gateway. ECHO_REQUEST datagrams (pings) have an IP (Internet Protocol) and ICMP header, followed by a *struct timeval* and then an arbitrary number of pad bytes used to fill out the packet.

When using **ping** for fault isolation, it should first be run on the local host to verify that the local network interface is up and running. Then, hosts and gateways further and further away should be sent the **ping** command. Round-trip times and packet loss statistics are computed. If duplicate packets are received, they are not included in the packet loss calculations, although the round-trip time of these packets is used in calculating the minimum, average, and maximum round-trip time numbers. When the specified number of packets have been sent (and received) or if the program is terminated with a **SIGINT**, a brief summary is displayed.

This program is intended for use in network testing, measurement, and management. Because of the load it can impose on the network, it is unwise to use **ping** during normal operations or from automated scripts.

ICMP Packet Details

An IP header without options is 20 bytes. An ICMP ECHO_REQUEST packet contains an additional 8 bytes worth of ICMP header followed by an arbitrary amount of data. When a *packetsize* is given, this indicates the size of this extra piece of data (the default is 56). Thus, the amount of data received inside of an IP packet of type ICMP ECHO_REPLY will always be 8 bytes more than the requested data space (the ICMP header).

If the data space is at least 8 bytes large, **ping** uses the first 8 bytes of this space to include a timestamp, which it uses in the computation of round-trip times. If less than 8 bytes of pad are specified, no round-trip times are given.

Duplicate and Damaged Packets

The **ping** command will report duplicate and damaged packets. Duplicate packets should never occur, and seem to be caused by inappropriate link-level retransmissions. Duplicates may occur in many situations and are rarely (if ever) a good sign, although the presence of low levels of duplicates may not always be cause for alarm.

Damaged packets are obviously serious cause for alarm and often indicate broken hardware somewhere in the **ping** packet's path (in the network or in the hosts).

Trying Different Data Patterns

The (inter)network layer should never treat packets differently depending on the data contained in the data portion. Unfortunately, data-dependent problems have been known to sneak into networks and remain undetected for long periods of time. In many cases the particular pattern that will have problems is something that does not have sufficient transitions, such as all 1s (ones) or all 0s (zeros), or a pattern right at the edge, such as almost all 0s (zeros). It is not necessarily enough to specify a data pattern of all 0s (zeros) (for example) on the command line because the pattern that is of interest is at the data-link level, and the relationship between what you enter and what the controllers transmit can be complicated.

This means that if you have a data-dependent problem you will probably have to do a lot of testing to find it. If you are lucky, you may manage to find a file that either cannot be sent across your network or that takes much longer to transfer than other similar length files. You can then examine this file for repeated patterns that you can test using the **-p** option of **ping**.

TTL Details

The TTL value of an IP packet represents the maximum number of IP routers that the packet can go through before being thrown away. In current practice you can expect each router in the Internet to decrement the TTL field by exactly 1 (one).

The TCP/IP specification states that the TTL field for TCP packets should be set to 60, but many systems use smaller values (4.3BSD uses 30, 4.2BSD used 15).

The maximum possible value of this field is 255, and most UNIX compatible systems set the TTL field of ICMP ECHO_REQUEST packets to 255. This is why you will find you can use the **ping** command on some hosts, but not reach them with **telnet** or **ftp**.

In normal operation, **ping** prints the TTL value from the packet it receives. When a remote system receives a **ping** packet, it can do one of three things with the TTL field in its response:

1. Not change it; this is what Berkeley UNIX compatible systems did before the 4.3BSD release. In this case, the TTL value in the received packet will be 255 minus the number of routers in the round-trip path.

ping(8)

2. Set it to 255; this is what current Berkeley UNIX compatible systems do. In this case, the TTL value in the received packet will be 255 minus the number of routers in the path *from* the remote system *to* the host that received the **ping** command.

3   Set it to some other value. Some machines use the same value for ICMP packets that they use for TCP packets; for example, either 30 or 60. Others may use completely wild values.

Cautions

Many hosts and gateways ignore the RECORD_ROUTE option.

Flooding the **ping** command is not recommended in general, and flooding **ping** on the broadcast address should only be done under very controlled conditions.

Files

/usr/sbin/ping
        Specifies the command path

Related Information

Commands: **netstat(1)**, **ifconfig(8)**

Daemons: **routed(8)**

portmap

Purpose   The DARPA port to RPC program number mapper

Synopsis   **portmap**

Description

The **portmap** daemon is a server that converts Remote Procedure Call (RPC) program numbers into Defense Advanced Research Projects Agency (DARPA) protocol port numbers. It must be running in order to make RPC calls.

When an RPC server is started, it will tell **portmap** what port number it is listening to, and what RPC program numbers it is prepared to serve. When a client wishes to make an RPC call to a given program number, it will first contact **portmap** on the server machine to determine the port number where RPC packets should be sent.

The **portmap** daemon must be started before any RPC servers, including **mountd** and **nfsd**, are invoked. Note that if **portmap** crashes, all servers must be restarted.

Files

/usr/sbin/portmap
    Specifies the command path

Related Information

Files: **servers(5)**
Daemons: **inetd(8)**

prctmp

Purpose   Outputs the session record file specified by *File* and created by the **acctcon1** command

See **acct(8)**

prdaily

Purpose   Formats an ASCII file of the accounting data of the previous day

See **acct(8)**

printpw

Purpose   Outputs the contents of the password database

Synopsis   **/usr/sbin/acct/printpw** [-acdgsu]

Flags

    -a   Outputs all information. Use of this flag is the same as specifying all flags with **-cdgsu**.

    -c   Outputs username and the comment string.

    -d   Output username and the login directory.

    -g   Outputs username and the group ID numerical value.

    -s   Output username and the login shell.

    -u   Output username and the UID numerical value.

Description

The **printpw** command outputs the contents of the **/etc/password** database file in ASCII format to the standard output. When **printpw** is called with no option, all usernames in the database are output.

The **/etc/password** database file is accessed through the standard library function **getpwent**. On secure systems or on systems with an installed Yellow Pages service that have changed this library function, **printpw** produces the same information.

When **printpw** is called in combination with any flag, one or more additional columns separated with **:** (colon) is output.

Examples

To output the username, UID, and login directory of all users in the password database file, enter:

    /usr/sbin/acct/printpw **-ud**

Files

/usr/sbin/acct/printpw
> Specifies the command path

/etc/passwd
> The password database file.

Related Information

Commands: **chargefee(8)**, **lastlogin(8)**

prtacct

Purpose   Formats and displays any total accounting file specified by the *File* parameter

See **acct(8)**

pvchange

Purpose   Changes the characteristics of a physical volume in a volume group

Synopsis   **pvchange -x** *Extensibility PhysicalVolumePath*

Flags

-x *Extensibility*

Sets the allocation permission for additional physical extents on the physical volume specified by the *PhysicalVolumePath* parameter. The *Extensibility* parameter is represented by one of the following:

y   Allows the allocation of additional physical extents on the physical volume.

n   Prohibits the allocation of additional physical extents on the physical volume. You can, however, access the logical volumes that reside on the physical volume.

Description

The **pvchange** command changes the characteristics and state of a physical volume in a volume group by setting the allocation permission for additional physical extents on the physical volume to either allowed or prohibited.

Examples

1.   To prohibit the allocation of additional physical extents to physical volume hdisk03, enter:

       pvchange -x n /dev/hdisk03

       Additional physical extents to hdisk03 are prohibited.

2.   To allow the allocation of additional physical extents to physical volume hdisk03, enter:

       pvchange -x y /dev/hdisk03

       Additional physical extents to hdisk03 are allowed.

pvchange(8)

Files

/usr/sbin/pvchange
Specifies the command path

Related Information

Commands: **pvdisplay(8)**

pvcreate

Purpose   Creates a physical volume that can be used as part of a volume group

Synopsis   **pvcreate** [**-b**] [**-f**] [**-t** *DiskType*] *PhysicalVolumePath*

Flags

-b   Used to specify (on standard input) the numbers that correspond to the indexes of all known bad blocks on the physical volume, *PhysicalVolumePath*, that you are creating. Specify the indexes with decimal, octal, or hexadecimal numbers using the C language conventional formats; use the newline, tab, or formfeed character to separate each number. If you do not use this flag, it is presumed that the physical volume contains no bad blocks.

-f   Forces the creation of a physical volume (thus deleting any file system present) without first requesting confirmation. Currently BSD and System V file systems are recognized.

-t *DiskType*
Used to retrieve configuration information about the physical volume from the **/etc/disktab** file. Specify the device (rz23, for example) with the *DiskType* parameter.

NOTE: If the physical volume does not contain any disklabel, the command will complain. The command must then be executed one more time with this flag set.

Description

The **pvcreate** command initializes a direct access storage device (a raw block device) for use as a physical volume in a volume group. The *PhysicalVolumePath* parameter specifies the pathname of the raw device to be used.

If *PhysicalVolumePath* contains a file system, you are asked for confirmation if your command entry does not include the **-f** flag. The request for confirmation avoids the accidental deletion of a file system. Currently, BSD and System V file systems are recognized.

The operation will be denied if *PhysicalVolumePath* belongs to another volume group. Only physical volumes not belonging to other volume groups can be created.

If *PhysicalVolumePath* contains a disk label, it will be updated to reflect that *PhysicalVolumePath* is now a physical volume that can be installed in a volume group.

After you create a physical volume with the **pvcreate** command, you can add it to a new volume group with the **vgcreate** command, or to an existing volume group with the **vgextend** command.

You can not add a raw device to a volume group if it has not been initialized with the **pvcreate** command.

Examples

1. To create a physical volume on the raw device /dev/hdisk1 that contains a disklabel, and to force the creation without confirmation, enter:

    pvcreate -f /dev/hdisk1

2. To create a physical volume on the raw device /dev/hdisk1 that does not contain a disklabel, and to get confirmation by default, enter:

    pvcreate -t rz23 /dev/hdisk1

3. To create a physical volume on the raw device /dev/hdisk1, specifying that a bad blocks list (7, 13, 95, and 133) must be read from standard input, enter:

    echo 7 13 95 133 | pvcreate -b /dev/hdisk1

Files

/usr/sbin/pvcreate

Specifies the command path

/etc/disktab

Specifies the database containing the disk geometry and disk partition characteristics for all disk devices on the system

Notes

We strongly recommend that you check the manufacturer's listing, or run diagnostics testing for bad blocks on the device prior to creating a physical volume. If bad blocks are present, use the **-b** flag when creating the physical volume.

Related Information

Commands: **echo(1)**, **vgcreate(8)**, **vgextend(8)**

pvdisplay

Purpose   Displays information about one or more physical volumes within a volume group

Synopsis   **pvdisplay** [**-v**] *PhysicalVolumePath* ...

Flags

-v   Lists additional information for each logical volume and for each physical extent on the physical volume.

Distribution of physical volume:
Lists the logical volumes that have extents allocated on *PhysicalVolumePath*.

LV Name:
The name of the logical volume which has extents allocated on *PhysicalVolumePath*.

LE of LV:
The number of logical extents within the logical volume that are contained on this physical volume

PE for LV:
The number of physical extents within the logical volume that are contained on this physical volume

Physical extents:
Displays the following information for each physical extent:

PE: The physical extent number

Status: The current state of the physical extent: free, used, or stale

LV: The name of the logical volume to which the extent is allocated

LE: The index of the logical extent to which the physical extent is allocated

Description

The **pvdisplay** command displays information about the physical volume(s) specified with the *PhysicalVolumePath* parameter. If you use the **-v** (verbose) flag, the program displays a map of the logical extents that correspond to the physical extents of each physical volume.

If you use the **pvdisplay** command without any flags, the program displays the characteristics of each physical volume that you specified with the *PhysicalVolumePath* parameter, namely:

PV Name: The name of the physical volume

VG Name: The name of the volume group

PV Status: The state of the physical volume: available or unavailable

Allocatable: The allocation permission for the physical volume

VGDA: The number of volume group descriptors on the physical volume

Cur LV: The number of logical volumes using the physical volume

PE Size: The size of physical extents on the volume

Total PE: The total number of physical extents on the physical volume

Free PE: The number of free physical extents on the physical volume

Allocated PE:

 The number of physical extents on the physical volume that are allocated to logical volumes

Stale PE: The number of physical extents on the physical volume that are not current

Examples

1. To display the status and characteristics of physical volume hdisk3, enter:

 pvdisplay /dev/hdisk3

2. To display the status, characteristics, and allocation map of physical volume hdisk3, enter:

 pvdisplay -v /dev/hdisk3

Files

/usr/sbin/pvdisplay
    Specifies the command path

Related Information

Commands: **lvdisplay(8), pvchange(8), vgdisplay(8)**

pvmove

Purpose   Moves allocated physical extents from one physical volume to one or more other physical volumes

Synopsis   **pvmove**   [**-n**   *LogicalVolumeName*]   *SourcePhysicalVolumePath* [*DestinationPhysicalVolumePath* ...]

Flags

> **-n** *LogicalVolumeName*
>> Moves only the physical extents allocated to the logical volume (specified with the *LogicalVolumeName* parameter) and located on the source physical volume (specified with the *SourcePhysicalVolumePath* parameter) to the specified destination physical volume.

Description

The **pvmove** command moves allocated physical extents and the data they contain from the source physical volume, *SourcePhysicalVolumePath*, to one or more other physical volumes. To limit the transfer to specific physical volumes, specify the names of one or more physical volumes with the *DestinationPhysicalVolumePath* parameter. If you do not specify the destination volume(s), all of the physical volumes in the volume group are available as destination volumes for the transfer. All physical volumes must be within the same volume group. You must not include the *SourcePhysicalVolumePath* in the list of *DestinationPhysicalVolumePath* parameters.

The **pvmove** command will only succeed if there is enough space on the *DestinationPhysicalVolumePath* to hold all the extents of the *SourcePhysicalVolumePath*.

pvmove(8)

Examples

1.   To move physical extents from hdisk1 to hdisk6 and hdisk7, enter:

pvmove /dev/hdisk1 /dev/hdisk6 /dev/hdisk7

The program moves the physical extents from one physical volume to two others within the same volume group.

2.   To move physical extents in logical volume lv02 from hdisk1 to hdisk6, enter:

pvmove -n /dev/vg01/lv02 /dev/hdisk1 /dev/hdisk6

Only those physical extents contained in lv02 are moved from one physical volume to another.

Files

/usr/sbin/pvmove
        Specifies the command path

Related Information

Commands: **pvdisplay(8)**

pwck, grpck

Purpose   Checks the password and group files for inconsistencies

Synopsis   **pwck** [**/etc/passwd**] [*file*]

grpck [**/etc/group**] [*file*]

Description

The **pwck** command scans the **/etc/passwd** file or the named *file* and writes to standard output any inconsistencies. The scan checks the number of fields, login name, user ID, group ID, and existence of a login directory and optional program name.

The **grpck** command scans the **/etc/group** file or the named *file* and writes to standard output any inconsistencies. The scan checks the number of fields, group name, group ID, and whether all login names appear in the password file. **grpck** writes to standard output any group entries that do not have login names.

Example

To verify the password information in the **/etc/passwd** file for consistency, enter:

pwck /etc/passwd

Files

/usr/sbin/pwck
> Specifies the command path

/usr/sbin/grpck
> Specifies the command path

/etc/passwd
> Specifies the password file that contains the user IDs

/etc/group
> Specifies the group file that contains group IDs

Related Information

Commands: **adduser(8)**, **groups(1)**, **passwd(1)**, **vipw(8)**

quot

Purpose   Summarizes file system ownership

Synopsis   **quot** [**-c -f -n** *file system* ...]

Flags

-c   Prints three columns giving file size in blocks, number of files of that size, and cumulative total of blocks in an equal or smaller file size.

-f   Prints a count of number of files as well as space owned by each user.

-n   Causes the pipeline **ncheck file system | sort +0n | quot -n file system**. A list of all files and their owners is displayed.

Description

The **quot** command prints the number of blocks in the named *file system* currently owned by each user. If no *file system* is named, a default name is assumed. You must be **root** to use this command.

Example

To display the number of files in the **/dev/hd1** file system as well as the space owned by each user, enter:

quot -f /dev/hd1

Files

/usr/sbin/quot
    Specifies the command path

/etc/passwd
    Specifies the password file used to get user names

Related Information

Commands: **ls(1), du(1)**

quotacheck

Purpose   Checks filesystem quota consistency

Synopsis   **quotacheck** [**-guv**] *filesystem* ...

quotacheck -a [**-guv**]

Flags

-a   Checks all filesystems identified in **/etc/fstab** as read/write with disk quotas.

-g   Checks group quotas only.

-u   Checks user quotas only.

-v   Reports discrepancies between the calculated and   recorded disk quotas.

Description

The **quotacheck** command examines each specified *filesystem*, builds a table of current disk usage, and compares this table against that stored in the disk quota file for the filesystem. If any inconsistencies are detected, both the quota file and the current system copy of the incorrect quotas are updated (the latter only occurs if an active filesystem is checked).

quotacheck must be run by a user with superuser authority.

By default both user and group quotas listed in **/etc/fstab** are checked. The **-g** flag specifies that only group quotas should be checked; the **-u** flag specifies that only user quotas should be checked.

quotacheck does not report on any inconsistencies, or any of its activities, unless you use the **-v** flag.

quotacheck runs parallel passes on the filesystems required, using the pass numbers in **/etc/fstab** in a manner identical to **fsck**. **quotacheck** expects each filesystem to be checked to have quota files named **quota.user** and **quota.group** in the root directory. (These default file locations may be overridden in **etc/fstab**.) If these files are not present, **quotacheck** creates them.

The **quotacheck** command is normally run at boot time from the **/etc/rc.local** file (see **rc**) before enabling disk quotas with **quotaon**.

quotacheck(8)

The **quotacheck** command accesses the raw device in calculating the actual disk usage for each user. Thus, the filesystems checked should be quiescent while **quotacheck** is running.

Files

/usr/sbin/quotacheck
> Specifies the command path

/usr/sbin/fsck
> Specifies the filesystems check program

[*filesystem_root*]/**quota.user**
> Contains user quotas for *filesystem*

[*filesystem_root*]/**quota.group**
> Contains user quotas for *filesystem*

/etc/fstab
> Contains filesystem names and locations

Related Information

Commands: **edquota**(8), **fsck**(8), **quota**(1), **quotaon**(8), **repquota**(8).

Functions: **quotactl**(2).

Files: **fstab**(4).

quotaoff

Purpose   Turns file system quotas off

See **quotaon(8)**

quotaon, quotaoff

Purpose   Turns filesystem quotas on or off

Synopsis   **quotaon** [**-guv**] *filesystem* ...

quotaon -a [**-guv**]

quotaoff [**-guv**] *filesystem* ...

quotaoff -a [**-guv**]

Flags

-a   Turns on (with **quotaon**) or turns off (with **quotaoff**) quotas for all filesystems identified in **/etc/fstab** as read/write with quotas.

-g   Turns on or off group quotas only.

-u   Turns on or off user quotas only.

-v   Prints a message for each filesystem whose quotas are turned on or off.

Description

The **quotaon** command announces to the system that disk quotas should be enabled on one or more *filesystem*s. The filesystems specified must have entries in **/etc/fstab** and be mounted at the time.

The **quotaoff** command announces to the system that the *filesystem*s specified should have any disk quotas turned off.

quotaon and **quotaoff** must be run by a user with superuser authority.

These commands expect each filesystem to have quota files named **quota.user** and **quota.group** in the root directory. (These default file locations may be overridden in **etc/fstab**.)

By default both user and group quotas are turned on or off. The **-g** flag specifies that only group quotas should be affected; the **-u** flag specifies that only user quotas should be affected.

Files

/usr/sbin/quotaon
Specifies the command path

/usr/sbin/quotaoff
Specifies the command path

[*filesystem_root*]/**quota.user**
Contains user quotas for *filesystem*

[*filesystem_root*]/**quota.group**
Contains user quotas for *filesystem*

/etc/fstab
Contains filesystem names and locations

Related Information

Commands: **edquota**(8), **fsck**(8), **quota**(1), **quotacheck**(8), **repquota**(8).

Functions: **quotactl**(2).

Files: **fstab**(4).

rc0

Purpose   Run command script executed when stopping the system

Synopsis   **rc0**

Description

The **rc0** script contains run commands that enable a smooth shutdown and bring the system to a single-user state; run levels 0 and s. In addition to commands listed in within the script itself, **rc0** contains instructions to run commands found in the **/sbin/rc0.d** directory. The script defines the conditions under which the commands execute; some commands run if the system is being shut down while others run if the system is being shut down and rebooted to single user.

By convention, files in the **/sbin/rc0.d** directory begin with either the letter "K" or the letter "S" and are followed by a two-digit number and a filename; for example:

> **K00enlogin   K05lpd   K60cron   K30nfs**

In general, the system starts commands that begin with the letter "S" and stops commands that begin with the letter "K." The numbering of commands in the **/sbin/rc0.d** directory is important since the numbers are sorted and the commands are run in ascending order. Files in the **/sbin/rc0.d** directory are normally links to files in the **/etc/init.d** directory.

An entry in the **inittab** file causes the system to execute the **rc0** script; for example:

```
ss:Ss:wait:/sbin/rc0 shutdown < /dev/console > /dev/console 2>&1
s0:0:wait:/sbin/rc0 off < /dev/console > /dev/console 2>&1
```

The following operations are typical of those that result from executing the **rc0** script and the commands located in the **/sbin/rc0.d** directory:

> Notify users that the system is shutting down.
> Sync the disks
> Stop system services and daemons
> Stop processes
> Kill processes
> Unmount file systems
> Invoke init if the system is being shut down to single user

The **killall** command sends a SIGTERM signal to stop running processes; SIGKILL follows to kill all processes except the process which initiated the call. The **umount -a** command unmounts all file systems except the root file system.

Files

/sbin/rc0 Specifies the command path

/sbin/rc0.d
      Specifies the directory of commands that corresponds to the run level

Related Information

Commands: **init(8)**, **killall(8)**, **shutdown(8)**

rc2

Purpose   Run command script executed when entering a multiuser run level

Synopsis   **rc2**

Description

The **rc2** script contains run commands that enable initialization of the system to a multiuser state; run level 2. In addition to commands listed within the script itself, **rc2** contains instructions to run certain commands found in the **/sbin/rc2.d** directory. The script defines the conditions under which the commands execute; some commands run if the system is booting, other commands execute if the system is changing run levels.

By convention, files in the **/sbin/rc2.d** directory begin with either the letter "K" or the letter "S" and are followed by a two-digit number and a filename; for example:

K00lpd   S00savecore   S25uucp

In general, the system starts commands that begin with the letter "S" and stops commands that begin with the letter "K." Commands that begin with the letter "K" run only when the system is changing run levels from a higher to a lower level. Commands that begin with the letter "S" run in all cases. The numbering of commands in the **/sbin/rc2.d** directory is important since the numbers are sorted and the commands are run in ascending order. Files in the **/sbin/rc2.d** directory are normally links to files in the **/etc/init.d** directory.

An entry in the **inittab** file causes the system to execute the **rc2** run commands, for example:

```
s2:23:wait:/sbin/rc2 < /dev/console > /dev/console 2>&1
```

The following operations are typical of those that result from executing the **rc2** script and the commands located in the **/sbin/rc2.d** directory. The operation depends on which state the system is entering or exiting.

Setting the time zone
Checking the current run level
Stopping network services and daemons
Starting (or stopping) system services and daemons
Starting the **cron** daemon
Setting up paging and dump facilities
Setting up **uucp** files

Setting the TIMEZONE variable is one of the first operations completed by the **rc2** script. This action provides the default time zone for subsequent commands.

Files

/sbin/rc2 Specifies the command path

/sbin/rc2.d
Specifies the directory of commands that correspond to the run level

Related Information

Commands: **init(8)**

rc3

Purpose   Run command script executed when entering a multiuser run level

Synopsis   **rc3**

Description

The **rc3** script contains run commands that enable initialization of the system to a multiuser state; run level 3. In addition to commands listed within the script itself, **rc3** contains instructions to run certain commands found in the **/sbin/rc3.d** directory. The script defines the conditions under which the commands execute; some commands run if the system is booting, other commands execute if the system is changing run levels.

By convention, files in the **rc3.d** directory begin with either the letter "S" or the letter "K" and are followed by a two-digit number and a filename; for example:

S00inet   S55inetd   S70mount   S65lpd

In general, the system starts commands that begin with the letter "S" and stops commands that begin with the letter "K." Commands that begin with the letter "K" run only when the system is changing run levels from a higher to a lower level. Commands that begin with the letter "S" run in all cases. The numbering of commands in the **/sbin/rc3.d** directory is important since the numbers are sorted and the commands are run in ascending order. Files in the **/sbin/rc3.d** directory are normally links to files in the **/etc/init.d** directory.

An entry in the **inittab** file causes the system to execute the **rc3** run commands, for example:

```
s3:3:wait:/sbin/rc3 < /dev/console > /dev/console 2>&1
```

The following operations are typical of those that result from executing the **rc3** script and the commands located in the **/sbin/rc3.d** directory. The operation depends on which state the system is entering or exiting.

Setting the time zone
Checking the current run level
Starting network services and daemons
Starting (or stopping) system services and daemons
Mounting file systems

Setting the TIMEZONE variable is one of the first operations completed by the **rc3** script. This action provides the default time zone for subsequent commands.

Files

/sbin/rc3 Specifies the command path

/sbin/rc3.d
   Specifies the directory of commands that correspond to the run level

Related Information

Commands: **init(8)**

rdump

Purpose   Copies to the *dump_file* storage device all files changed after a certain date in the specified *filesystem*.

See **dump(8)**

reboot

Purpose Restarts the machine

Synopsis **reboot** [**-l -n -q**]

Flags

-l	Does not log the reboot using **syslog**
-n	Does not sync the disks or log the reboot using **syslog**
-q	Performs a quick reboot without first shutting down running processes; does not log the reboot using **syslog**

Description

The **reboot** command normally stops all running processes, syncs the disks, logs the reboot, and writes a shutdown entry in the login accounting file, **/var/adm/wtmp**. If you specify the **-l** flag, logging is omitted. If you specify the **-n** flag, the logging and disk sync are omitted. If you specify the **-q** flag, the shutdown is abrupt; processes are not stopped prior to the shutdown, and the logging is omitted.

When the system is running and multiple users are logged in, use the **shutdown -r** command to perform a reboot operation. If no users are logged in, use the **reboot** command.

The **reboot** command uses the **sync** call to synchronize the disks, and to to perform other shutdown activities such as resynchronizing the hardware time-of-day clock. After these activities, the system reboots. By default, the system starts and the file systems are automatically checked. If the start-up activities are successful, the system comes up in the default run-level. You must have **root** privileges to use this command.

Examples

1. To enable the default reboot action, enter:

    reboot

    This command causes the system to stop all running processes, sync the disks, log the shutdown, and perform other routine shutdown and reboot activities.

reboot(8)

2. To shut down the system without logging the reboot, enter:

   reboot -l

   This command shuts down the system and performs all shutdown and reboot activities, **except** logging the shutdown.

3. To reboot the system abruptly, enter:

   reboot -q

   This command reboots the system abruptly without shutting down running processes.

Files

/usr/sbin/reboot
: Specifies the command path

/var/adm/wtmp
: Specifies the login accounting file

/usr/sbin/syslogd
: Specifies the path of the syslog daemon

Cautions

Using the **-n** might result in file system damage.

Related Information

Commands: **fsck(8)**, **halt(8)**, **init(8)**, **shutdown(8)**, **syslogd(8)**

Calls: **sync(2)**, **syslog(3)**

remove

Purpose   Deletes all of the **/var/adm/acct/sum/wtmp***, **/var/adm/acct/sum/pacct***, and **/var/adm/acct/nite/lock*** files as part of the daily cleanup procedure called by the **runacct** command

See **acct(8)**

renice

Purpose   Alters the priority of a running process

Synopsis   **renice** *priority* [**-p** *pid* ...] [**-g** *pgrp* ...] [**-u** *user* ...]

Flags

    -g   Interprets arguments following the flag as process group IDs

    -u   Interprets arguments following the flag as usernames

    -p   Resets **renice** argument interpretation to default process IDs

Description

The **renice** command alters the scheduling priority of one or more running processes. The arguments are interpreted as process IDs, process group IDs, or user names. When you issue the **renice** command with the **-g** flag, all processes in the process group have their scheduling priority altered. When you run the **renice** command with the **-u** flag, all processes owned by the user have their scheduling priority altered. By default, the processes affected are specified by their process IDs.

The following priorities are particularly useful:

20   Runs affected processes when no other processes are running on the system

0   Runs at the base scheduling priority

Negative numbers
   Runs affected processes very quickly.

The preceding values are mapped by the command to those actually used by the kernel.

Note that users who do not have **root** privileges cannot increase the scheduling priorities of their own processes (even if they had originally decreased those priorities).

Examples

1. To change the priority of process IDs 987 and 32, and all processes owned
    the **daemon** and **root** users, enter:

    renice +1 987 -u daemon root -p 32

Files

/usr/sbin/renice
> Specifies the command path

Related Information

Calls: **getpriority(2)**, **setpriority(2)**

repquota

Purpose   Summarizes filesystem quotas

Synopsis   **repquota** [**-guv**] *filesystem* ...

          repquota -a [**-guv**]

Flags

-a   Prints quota for all the filesystems listed in **/etc/fstab**.

-g   Prints group quotas only.

-u   Prints user quotas only.

-v   Prints a header line before the information for each filesystem.

Description

The **repquota** command prints a summary of the disk usage and quotas for the specified *filesystem*s. By default, both user and group quota are displayed (if they exist).

For each user or group, the current number of files and amount of space (in kilobytes) is printed, as well as any quotas created with **edquota**.

repquota must be run by a user with superuser authority.

Files

/usr/sbin/repquota
         Specifies the command path

[*filesystem_root*]/**quota.user**
         Contains user quotas for *filesystem*

[*filesystem_root*]/**quota.group**
         Contains user quotas for *filesystem*

/etc/fstab
         Contains filesystem names and locations

Related Information

Commands: **edquota**(8), **fsck**(8), **quota**(1), **quotacheck**(8), **quotaon**(8).

Functions: **quotactl**(2).

Files: **fstab**(4).

restore, rrestore

Purpose   Restores files from tapes written with the **dump** or **rdump** command, respectively

Synopsis   **/usr/sbin/restore** [*key* [*argument* ...]]

/usr/sbin/rrestore -f *dump_file* [*key* [*argument* ...]]

The **restore** and **rrestore** commands are used to read files from a local or remote tape, respectively, to local file systems.

Flags

Function Flags

-i   This flag permits interactive restoration of files read from the tape. After reading directory information from the tape device, the **restore** or **rrestore** commands provide a shell-like interface that allows you to select the files you want to read. Some of the interactive commands require as an *arg* parameter a subdirectory or filename. When the *arg* parameter is unspecified, the default directory is the current one. The interactive commands are explained in the following list:

ls [*arg*]   Lists files in the the current directory or the directory specified with the *arg* parameter. Directory entries are appended with a / (slash) character. Entries that have been marked for reading are prepended with a * (asterisk) character. When the **-v** modifier flag is used, the inode number of each entry is also listed.

cd [*arg*]   Changes the current directory to the directory specified with the *arg* parameter.

pwd   Prints the pathname of the current directory to the standard output device.

add [*arg*]   Adds the files in the current directory or the files specified by *arg* to the list of files to be read from the tape (except when the **-h** flag is used). Files on the list of files to be read are prepended with the * (asterisk) character when they are listed with the **ls** interactive command.

delete [*arg*]   Deletes all the files in the current directory or the files specified by the *arg* parameter from the list of files to be read from the tape. Except when the **-h** flag is specified, all files and all files in subdirectories of a directory specified with the *arg* parameter are deleted.

An expedient way to select wanted files from any directory whose files are stored on the tape is to add the directory to the list of files to be read and then delete the ones that are not wanted.

extract Reads all files on the list of files to be read from the tape. The **restore** or **rrestore** command asks which volume you want to mount and whether the access modes of **.** (dot) are affected.

A fast way to read a few files from the tape device is to start with the last volume and work toward the first volume.

setmodes Sets owner, access modes, and file creation times for all directories that have been added to the files-to-read list; nothing is read from the tape. This interactive command is useful for cleaning up files after a **restore** or **rrestore** command has been prematurely aborted.

verbose Toggles the **-v** modifier (see the **-v** flag below). When set, the verbose flag causes the **ls** command to list the inode numbers of all files in the list of files to read. This interactive command also causes the **restore** or **rrestore** command to output information about each file to the output device when the file is read.

help Lists a summary of the available interactive commands.

? Same as the **help** interactive command.

what Outputs the tape header information to the standard output device.

quit Exits immediately, even when the all the files on list of files to read have not been read.

debug Toggles the debugging mode.

xit Same as **quit** command.

-r The tape is read and all files are loaded into the current working directory. The **-r** function flag should only be used to restore a complete dump into an empty file system, or to restore a previous incremental **dump** or **rdump** to the file system after a full level 0 (zero) restoration of files. For example:

/sbin/newfs /dev/rrp0g eagle

/sbin/mount /dev/rp0g /mnt

cd mnt restore -r

These four line entries are a typical sequence of commands to restore a complete set of files from tape to the disk whose device name is **/dev/rrp0g** and whose parameters are described in the **/etc/disktab** file under the name **eagle**. The file system name is **/dev/rp0g** and the directory where the file system is mounted and to which the files are written from the default tape device is called **/mnt**.

Other **restore** or **rrestore** operations may be called to restore additional files from a previous incremental **dump** or **rdump** to the tape device. Note that the **restore** or **rrestore** process writes a file named **restoresymtab** to the current directory. The **restoresymtab** file is used by these processes to provide information for incremental file restorations only; this scratch file has no other use and so should be removed when files from the last incremental storage medium has been restored.

-R   The **restore** or **rrestore** command requests a particular tape of a multivolume set on which to restart a full restore (see the **-r** flag). This allows **restore** or **rrestore** to be interrupted and then restarted.

-t *name* ...

The files specified by the *name* parameter are listed when they are stored on the tape. When a *name* parameter is not specified, all files in the root directory stored on the tape are listed, except when the **-h** flag is specified.

x *name* ...

The files specified by the *name* parameter are read from the tape device. When the *name* parameter matches a directory whose contents are stored on the tape, and the **-h** flag is not specified, the directory is recursively searched until all files have been read. The file owner, time of modification, and access mode are restored when possible. When no file is specified with the *name* parameter, the root directory is read from the tape device. Reading of the root directory results in storage of the entire file content from the tape, except when the **-h** flag has been specified.

Modifier Flags

-b *block_size*

The argument that follows this modifier flag is used as the block size of the tape (in kilobytes). When this modifier flag is not specified, **restore** or **rrestore** determines tape block size dynamically.

-c   Reads an old style dump tape (pre-4.2BSD file system).

-d   Debug mode. **restore** or **rrestore** performs many internal checks about the consistency of internal structures and prints debugging information to the standard output.

-f *dump_file*

> When an argument follows the **-f** modifier flag, it is used as the name of the archive device, replacing the default tape device **/dev/rmt0h**. When the argument is the character **-** (dash), **restore** or **rrestore** reads from standard input. Thus, **dump** and **restore** or **rdump** and **rrestore** may be used in a pipeline expression to copy file systems with the following typical command:

> **dump -0f - /usr | (cd /mnt; restore -xf -)**

-F *command_file*

> The argument that follows the **-F** modifier flag is used as the name of the file from which interactive input is read. As described in the foregoing list of **Function Flags** for the **-i** function flag, normally standard input is read. The **-F** modifier flag allows the interactive mode of the **restore** or **rrestore** command to be obtained from a previously written command file (similar to a shell script).

> In the application described here, the following are affected:

> 1. The interactive interface

> 2. A prompt for the next volume number

> 3. A prompt to set the access mode for **.** (dot)

> Error recovery interaction and the verification of operator readiness are not affected. For example, when the file named **inputfile** contains the following interactive command lines (the commands are taken from the **Function Flags** list):

> **add**

> **delete foo**

> **add foo/bar**

> **extract**

> **1**

> **yes**

> **quit**

> The command:

> **restore -iF inputfile**

> uses the interactive mode to automatically mark everything for reading (**add**), to unmark the subdirectory (**delete foo**), to mark the file **foo/bar** (**add foo/bar**), to read the marked files (**extract**), to specify volume 1 (**1**) of the default tape, to set the access mode for dot, **.** (**yes**), and then quit (**quit**).

-h	When this modifier flag is specified, **restore** or **rrestore** reads files from the specified directory, rather than files that it references. This prevents hierarchical restoration of complete subtrees from the tape.
-m	When this modifier is specified, **restore** or **rrestore** reads according to inode numbers rather than filename. This read operation is useful when only a few files are restored and you want to avoid rewriting the complete pathname to each file.
-N	Tells **restore** not to write to disk. This flag does not permit the process to act on files in the current directory.
-s	The argument that follows this modifier flag is used as the number (1 is the origin) of the file to restore. This flag is used to write more than one dump file from the tape.
-v	Normally the **restore** or **rrestore** commands do not notify you about their progress in reading from the storage device. When this modifier flag is used, the name of each file read from the tape is written to the standard output device.
-y	When this modifier is specified, **restore** or **rrestore** does not query whether a tape error should cause the read operation to abort, but instead the process attempts to skip over the bad block(s) and continue the read operation.
-Y	Overwrites existing files without any query.
-Z	When this flag is used, the **restore** or **rrestore** does not overwrite existing files.

Description

These commands read a tape or file previously written with the **dump** or **rdump** command. The **restore** and **rrestore** processes are controlled with the *key* parameter. Each *key* parameter is a flag that specifies an option, which may be used whenever files are restored from tape media.

restore

The *key* characters **bcdfhimrstvxyFNRYZ** consist of function *key* flags and modifier *key* flags, which may be used in any logical combination, but with a preceding - (dash) character. Function *key* flag characters are **irtx** and **R**; all other characters are modifier *key* flags. The *key* flags are expressed by a string of characters containing at most one function flag and possibly one or more of the modifier flags. Other arguments specified with these commands are the file or subdirectory name that specifies files to be restored. The function *key* and modifier *key* character flags are described under **FLAGS**.

Unless the **-h** modifier flag is specified (see the **-h** flag), inclusion of a directory name refers to all files and recursively, all files in all subdirectories of that directory.

rrestore

The **rrestore** command reads files from a remote magnetic tape or other specified storage device. The files were previously saved to tape with a **dump** or **rdump** command. The **rrestore** command is identical in operation to **restore**, except the **-f** function flag must be specified, and the *dump_file* parameter must have the form

machine:device

The **rrestore** command starts remote server **/usr/sbin/rmt** on the client machine to access the storage medium.

Files

/usr/sbin/restore
Specifies the command path

/usr/sbin/rrestore
Specifies the command path

/dev/rmt0h
The default storage device.

/tmp/rstdir*
A file that lists directories stored on the default tape.

/tmp/rstmode*
Owner, premission mode, and timestamps for stored directories.

./restoresymtab
Holds information required during incremental **restore** or **rrestore** operations.

Diagnostics

Detects bad **key** characters.

Detects read errors. When the **-y** modifier flag has been specified, or you respond with **y**, the process attempts to continue the **restore** operation.

When a previous **dump** or **rdump** writes over more than one storage device, **restore** or **rrestore** asks you to change a filled volume.

When the **-x** or **-i** function flag has been specified, **restore** or **rrestore** also asks what volume you wish to mount.

restore(8)

A fast way to read a few files is to first mount the last volume, and then mount other previous volumes working toward the first volume.

There are numerous consistency checks that can be listed by **restore**. Most checks are self-explanatory.

Common Errors

Common errors are listed as follows:

```
Converting to new filesystem format.
```

A tape previously written from an old file system has been loaded. On reading, the old file system was automatically converted to a new filesystem format.

filename: not found on tape

One or more filenames specified by the *filename* parameter was listed in the tape directory, but was not found on the tape. This is caused by storage device read errors when searching for a named file, or when a previously written tape was created on an active file system.

```
expected next file inumber, got inumber
```

A file that was not listed in the directory was detected. This can occur when using a tape previously created on an active file system.

```
Incremental tape too low
```

When doing incremental restore, a tape that was written before the previous incremental tape, or one that has too low an incremental level has been loaded.

```
Incremental tape too high
```

When doing incremental **restore** or **rrestore**, a storage process does not begin its coverage where the previous incremental tape left off, or one that has too high an incremental level has been loaded.

```
Tape read error while restoring < filename >.
Tape read error while skipping over inode < inumber >
Tape read error while trying to resynchronize
```

A tape read error has occurred. When a filename is specified, its contents are probably partially wrong. When an inode is being skipped, or the tape is trying to resynchronize, no files read from tape have been corrupted although some files may not be found on the tape.

```
resync restore, skipped < num > blocks
```

After a tape read error, **restore** or **rrestore** may have to resynchronize itself. This message lists the number of blocks that were skipped.

Notes

The **restore** or **rrestore** process may become confused when doing incremental reads from tapes that were previously written from an active file system.

A level **0** (zero) tape **dump** or **rdump** must be done after a full restore. Because **restore** or **rrestore** runs without kernel privileges, it has no control over inode allocation; thus, a full restore must be done to get a new set of directories that reflect new inode numbering, even when the content of files are unchanged.

Related Information

Commands: **dump(8)**, **rdump(8)**, **mount(8)**, **umount(8)**, **mkfs(8)**

rexecd

Purpose   The remote execution server

Synopsis   **rexecd**

Description

The **rexecd** daemon is the server for the **rexec**(3) routine. The server provides remote execution facilities with authentication based on usernames and passwords.

The **rexecd** daemon listens for service requests at the port indicated in the **exec** service specification; see **services** (4). When a service request is received, the following protocol is initiated:

1.   The server reads characters from the socket up to a null ('\0') byte. The resultant string is interpreted as an ASCII number, base 10.

2.   If the number received in step 1 is nonzero, it is interpreted as the port number of a secondary stream to be used for the **stderr**. A second connection is then created to the specified port on the client's machine.

3.   A null-terminated username of at most 16 bytes is retrieved on the initial socket.

4.   A null-terminated, unencrypted password of at most 16 bytes is retrieved on the initial socket.

5.   A null-terminated command to be passed to a shell is retrieved on the initial socket. The length of the command is limited by the upper bound on the size of the system's argument list.

6.   The **rexecd** server then validates the user as is done at login time and, if the authentication was successful, changes to the user's home directory, and establishes the user and group protections for the user. If any of these steps fail, the connection is aborted with a diagnostic message returned.

7.   A null byte is returned on the initial socket and the command line is passed to the normal login shell of the user. The shell inherits the network connections established by **rexecd**.

Diagnostics

Except for the last diagnostic message listed, all diagnostic messages are returned on the initial socket, after which any network connections are closed. An error is indicated by a leading byte with a value of 1 (0 is returned in step 7 above upon successful completion of all the steps prior to the command execution).

`Username too long.`
The name is longer than 16 bytes.

`Password too long.`
The password is longer than 16 bytes.

`Command too long.`
The command line passed exceeds the size of the argument list (as configured into the system).

`Login incorrect.`
No password file entry for the username existed.

`Password incorrect.`
The wrong password was supplied.

`No remote directory.`
The **chdir** command to the home directory failed.

`Try again.`
A **fork** by the server failed.

`shellname: ...`
The user's login shell could not be started. This message is returned on the connection associated with **stderr** and is not preceded by a flag byte.

Cautions

Indicating `Login incorrect` as opposed to `Password incorrect` is a security breach that allows people to probe a system for users with null passwords.

Files

/usr/sbin/rexecd
Specifies the command path

Related Information

Routines: **rexec(3)**

rlogind

Purpose The remote login server

Synopsis rlogind [-aln]

Flags

-a Requests the addresses for the hostname, verifying that the name and address correspond. Normal authentication is bypassed if the address verification fails.

-l Prevents authentication based on the user's **$HOME/.rhosts** file, unless the user is logging in as the superuser.

-n Disables transport-level, keep-alive messages. The messages are enabled by default.

Description

The **rlogind** daemon is the server for the **rlogin(1)** program. The server provides a remote login facility with authentication based on privileged port numbers from trusted hosts.

The **rlogind** daemon listens for service requests at the port indicated in the login service specification; see **services(4)**. When a service request is received, the following protocol is initiated:

1. The server checks the client's source port. If the port is not in the range 512 to 1023, the server aborts the connection.

2. The server checks the client's source address and requests the corresponding hostname (see **gethostbyaddr(3), hosts(4)** and **named(8))**. If the hostname cannot be determined, the dot-notation representation of the host address is used. If the hostname is in the same domain as the server (according to the last two components of the domain name), or if the **-a** flag is given, the addresses for the hostname are requested, verifying that the name and address correspond. Normal authentication is bypassed if the address verification fails.

Once the source port and address have been checked, **rlogind** proceeds with the authentication process described in **rshd(8).** It then allocates a pseudoterminal (see **pty (4)),** and manipulates file descriptors so that the slave half of the pseudoterminal becomes the **stdin, stdout,** and **stderr** for a login process. The login process is an instance of the **login(1)** program invoked with the **-f** option if authentication has succeeded. If automatic authentication fails, the user is prompted to log in as if on a standard terminal line. The **-l** option prevents any authentication based on the user's **.rhosts** file, unless the user is logging in as the superuser.

The parent of the login process manipulates the master side of the pseudoterminal, operating as an intermediary between the login process and the client instance of the **rlogin** program. In normal operation, the packet protocol described in **pty**(4) is invoked to provide **<Ctrl-s>/<Ctrl-q>** type facilities and propagate interrupt signals to the remote programs. The login process propagates the client terminal's baud rate and terminal type, as found in the **TERM** environment variable; see **environ (7)**. The screen or window size of the terminal is requested from the client, and window size changes from the client are propagated to the pseudoterminal.

Transport-level, keep-alive messages are enabled unless the **-n** flag is present. The use of keep-alive messages allows sessions to be timed out if the client crashes or becomes unreachable.

Note that the authentication procedure used here assumes the integrity of each client machine and the connecting medium. This is insecure, but is useful in an *open* environment.

Diagnostics

All initial diagnostic messages are indicated by a leading byte with a value of 1 (one), after which any network connections are closed. If there are no errors before **login** is invoked, a null byte is returned as an indication of success.

`Try again.`
A **fork** by the server failed.

Files

/usr/sbin/rlogind
Specifies the command path

Related Information

Commands: **login(1)**

Routines: **ruserok(3)**

Daemons: **rshd(8)**

rmt

Purpose   Allows remote access to magnetic tape devices

Synopsis   **rmt** [*debug-output-file*]

Description

The **rmt** command is started as a server process when requests from an **rdump** or **rrestore** call enter the system to operate a storage device through an interprocess communications connection. After the remote programs have finished, **rmt** exits and will be started again at the next request. The **rmt** command is normally invoked with an **rexec** or **rcmd** system call.

This process performs the commands described in the following table and responds with a status indication to tell a user the result of the commanded process. When the **rmt** command is called with a filename specified as the *debug-output-file* parameter, all status responses are passed to the *debug-output-file* in ASCII and in one of two possible formats. Consequently, a system administrator can debug both software and hardware problems associated with previously issued backup commands to storage devices.

Responses to successful commands are in the format:

A*number*\n

Where **A** identifies a normal response, *number* is an integer that defines the number of the response as an ASCII integer, and \n is a newline in the C-language idiom.

Responses to unsuccessful commands are in the format:

E*error_number error_message*\n

Where **E** identifies a response to an error, *error_number* is one of the possible error numbers values described in **intro**(2), *error_message* is the corresponding error-message string, which is output in response to a call to **perror**(3), and \n is a newline.

Debug information returned by **rmt** is stored in the named *debug-output-file* file. The **rmt** command is called from the **rdump** or **rrestore** process with no file argument only when the *debug-output-file* parameter is specified. To activate the debug option of **rmt** your system administrator should rename the original **rmt** to **rmt.ORG**, for example, and create a new shell executable **rmt** that calls **rmt.ORG** *debug-output-file*.

All numerical arguments of the following commands are transferred as ASCII strings:

O *device flag*   Opens the *device*, which must be a full pathname. The *flag* parameter is a flag value suitable for the **open** system call. When the *device* is successfully opened, the response is **A0\n**.

C *device*   Closes the current open *device*. When this command is successful, the response is **A0\n**.

L *offset whence*   Performs a seek operation. The *offset* and *whence* parameters have the same significance as the *offset* and *whence* parameters of the **lseek** system call. When this command successfully completes, the response is **A***n***\n**, where *n* has the same value returned by a normally successful **lseek** system call.

W *count*   Writes data to the *device* (see the **O** command above). The **rmt** command reads *count* bytes from the connection. This process is aborted when an **EOF** (End-of-File) is detected before the number of characters specified by *count* is transferred. The response to this command is **A***n***\n**, where *n* is the number of characters written.

R *count*   Reads *count* bytes of data from the open device. When the value of *count* exceeds the size of the data buffer (10 kilobytes), the number of characters read is truncated to the data buffer size. The **rmt** command then does the requested read operation. The response to this command is **A***n***\n**, where *n* is the number of characters read.

I *operation count*   Performs an **ioctl** system call on the open *device*. The *operation* parameter is a value passed to the **mt_op** member of a type **mtop** structure for an **MTIOCTOP ioctl** (magnetic tape operation) command. Valid values for the magnetic tape operations are defined in the **/usr/include/sys/mtio.h** include file. The *count* parameter is the value to pass to the **mt_count** member of the type **mtop** structure and specifies the number of operations performed on the tape drive. The response to this command is **A***n***\n**,where *n* is the **count**.

S   Returns the status of the open *device*, which is obtained with a **MTIOCGET ioctl** system call. A successful response to this command is **A***n***\n**, where *n* is the size of the status buffer, together with the contents of the status buffer in binary.

rmt(8)

Files

/usr/sbin/rmt
>   Specifies the command path

/usr/include/errno.h
>   Describes the possible error numbers.

/usr/include/sys/mtio.h
>   A header file that defines magnetic tape operations.

Related Information

Commands: **rdump(8)**, **rrestore(8)**.

System calls: **rcmd(3)**, **rexec(3)**, **open(2)**, **ioctl(2)**

route

Purpose   Manually manipulates the routing tables

Synopsis   **route** [-**nqv**] *command* [[*modifiers*] *args*]

Flags

-**n**   Prevents attempts to print host and network names symbolically when reporting actions.

-**v**   Causes additional details to be printed.

-**q**   Suppresses all output.

Description

The **route** command is a program used to manually manipulate the network routing tables. It normally is not needed, as a system routing table management daemon, such as **gated** or **routed**, should tend to this task.

The **route** command accepts five commands: **add**, to add a route, **flush**, to remove all routes, **delete**, to delete a specific route, **change**, to change aspects of a route (such as its gateway), and **monitor**, to report any changes to the routing information base, routing lookup misses, or suspected network partionings.

The **monitor** command has the syntax:
        route [-**n**] **monitor**

The **flush** command has the syntax:
        route [-**n**] **flush** [*family*]

where the address family may be specified by any of the -**xns** or -**inet** keywords.

The other commands have the following syntax:

        route [-**n**] *command* [-**net**|.-**host**] *destination gateway*

where *destination* is the destination host or network, and *gateway* is the next hop and gateway to which packets should be addressed. Routes to a particular host are distinguished from those to a network by interpreting the Internet address associated with *destination*. The optional keywords -**net** and -**host** force the destination to be interpreted as a network or a host, respectively. Otherwise, if the *destination* has a local address part of **INADDR_ANY**, or if the *destination* is the symbolic name of a network, then the route is assumed to be to a network; otherwise, it is presumed to be a route to a host.

For example, **128.32** is interpreted as **-host 128.0.0.32, 128.32.130** is interpreted as **-host 128.32.0.130; -net 128.32** is interpreted as **128.32.0.0**, and **-net 128.32.130** is interpreted as **128.32.130.0**.

If the route is via an interface rather than via a gateway, the **-interface** modifier should be specified; the gateway given is the address of this host on the common network, indicating the interface to be used for transmission.

The optional modifier **-xns** specifies that all subsequent addresses are in the XNS address families, and the names must be numeric specifications rather than symbolic names.

The optional modifiers **-rtt, -rttvar, -sendpipe, -recvpipe, -mtu, -hopcount, -expire**, and **-ssthresh** provide initial values to metrics maintained in the routing entry. These may be individually locked by preceding each such modifier to be locked by the **-lock** meta-modifier, or one can specify that all ensuing metrics may be locked by the **-lockrest** meta-modifier.

All symbolic names specified for a *destination* or *gateway* are looked up first as a hostname using **gethostbyname (3N)**. If this lookup fails, **getnetbyname (3N)** is then used to interpret the name as that of a network.

The **route** command uses a routing socket and the new message types RTM_ADD, RTM_DELETE, and RTM_CHANGE. As such, only the superuser may modify the routing tables.

If the **flush** command is specified, **route** will flush the routing tables of all gateway entries. One can choose to flush only those routes whose destinations are of a given address family by specifying an optional keyword describing which address family.

Examples

1. To add gateway **555.555.44.5** as a default gateway, enter: **route add default 555.555.44.5**

2. To add a route to host **milan** via gateway **555.555.44.5**, enter: **route add -host milan 555.555.44.5 -hopcount 2** where **2** is the distance in hops to the host.

3. To delete an existing route **555.555.44.5** to host **milan**, enter: **route delete -host milan 555.555.44.5**

Diagnostics

1. `Add [host | network] %s: gateway %s flags %x`
   The specified route is being added to the tables. The values printed are from the routing table entry supplied in the **ioctl** call. If the gateway address used was not the primary address of the gateway (the first one returned by **gethostbyname**), the gateway address is printed numerically as well as symbolically.

2. `Delete [ host | network ] %s: gateway %s flags %x`
   As above, but when deleting an entry.

3. `%s %s done`
   When the **-f** flag is specified, each routing table entry deleted is indicated with a **message** of this form.

4. `Network is unreachable`
   An attempt to add a route failed because the gateway listed was not on a directly connected network. The next hop gateway must be given.

5. `Not in table`
   A delete operation was attempted for an entry that was not present in the tables.

6. `Routing table overflow`
   An add operation was attempted, but the system was low on resources and was unable to allocate memory to create the new entry.

Files

/usr/sbin/route
   Specifies the command path

Related Information

netintro(4), **routed(8)**, **gated(8)**

routed

Purpose   Manages network routing tables

Synopsis   **routed** [**-dgqst**] [*logfile*]

The **routed** daemon manages the network routing tables.

Flags

-d   Enables additional debugging information, such as bad packets received, to be logged.

-g   Causes the routing daemon to run on a gateway host. This flag is used on internetwork routers to offer a route to the default destination.

-q   Inhibits the **routed** daemon from supplying Routing Information Protocol (RIP) data. The **-q** flag conflicts with the **-s** flag. Do not use the **-q** and **-s** flags together.

-s   Causes **routed** to supply RIP information even if it is not functioning as an Internet router. The **-s** flag conflicts with the **-q** flag. Do not use the **-s** and **-q** flags together.

-t   Causes all packets sent or received to be written to standard output. The **routed** daemon remains under control of the host that started it; therefore, an interrupt from the controlling host stops the **routed** process.

Description

Use the **routed** daemon to manage the RIP only. Use **gated** to manage RIP plus other protocols.

When **routed** starts, it finds any interfaces to directly connected hosts and networks that are configured into the system and marked as **up**. If multiple interfaces are present, **routed** assumes that the local host forwards packets between networks. The **routed** daemon transmits an RIP request packet on each interface (using a broadcast packet if the interface supports it) and then enters a loop, listening for RIP routing requests and response packets from other hosts. In addition, if **routed** is to supply RIP information to other hosts, it periodically sends RIP update packets (containing copies of its routing tables) to any directly connected hosts and networks.

When **routed** receives a RIP request packet and can supply RIP routing information, (the **-s** flag is set), it generates a reply (response packet) based on the information maintained in the kernel routing tables. The response packet contains a list of known routes, each marked with a *hop count metric* (the number of host-to-host connections in the route). The metric for each route is relative to the sending host. A metric of 16 or greater is considered to be infinite, or beyond reach.

Updating Routing Tables

If RIP processing is enabled, **routed** uses information contained in the RIP response and update packets from other hosts to update its routing tables. However, **routed** uses the information in the RIP routing packet to update the tables only if at least one of the following conditions exists:

- No routing table entry exists for the destination network or host, and the metric associated with the route is finite (that is, the metric is less than 16).

- The source host of the packet is the router in the existing routing table entry.

- The routing table entry is old and the new information is about a route that is at least as efficient as the existing route.

- The new route is shorter than the one that is currently stored in the routing tables. (Note that **routed** determines relative route length by comparing the new metric with the one stored in the routing table.)

When **routed** updates its internal routing tables, it generates an RIP update packet to all directly connected hosts and networks. Before updating the kernel routing tables, **routed** pauses for a brief period to allow any unstable conditions to stabilize.

Besides processing incoming RIP packets, **routed** also checks the internal routing table entries periodically. The metric for any entry that has not been updated for 3 minutes is set to infinity and marked for deletion. The deletion is delayed for 60 seconds so that information about the invalidated route can be distributed throughout the network. A host that acts as an RIP router supplies its routing tables to all directly connected hosts and networks every 30 seconds.

Using Gateways

In addition to managing routes to directly connected hosts and networks, **routed** maintains information about *distant* and *external* gateways. At startup, **routed** reads the **/etc/gateways** file to learn about these gateways.

The **/etc/gateways** file contains information about routes through distant and external gateways to hosts and networks that can be advertised through RIP. These routes are either static routes to specific destinations, or default routes that apply when a static route to a destination is unspecified.

Gateways that supply RIP routing information are marked **active** in the **/etc/gateways** file. The **routed** daemons distributes RIP routing information to active gateways; if no RIP routing information is received from the gateway for a period of time, **routed** deletes the associated route from the routing tables.

Gateways that do not exchange RIP routing information are marked **passive** in the /etc/**gateways** file. **Routed** maintains information about *passive* gateways indefinitely, and includes information about them in any RIP routing information transmitted.

Gateways are identified as *external* to inform **routed** that another routing process installs the route.

Information about *external* gateways is not maintained in the routing tables. Note that routes through external gateways must be to networks only.

If a *logfile* is specified, **routed** writes information about its actions to the specified log file. The log contains information about any changes to the routing tables and a history of recent route change messages sent and received that are related to changed routes.

Signals

The following signals have the specified effect when sent to the **routed** process using the **kill**(1) command:

SIGUSR1 Displays internal routing tables.

SIGHUP, SIGTERM, or **SIGQUIT**

Broadcasts RIP packets with hop counts set to infinity. Essentially, these signals disable the local host as a router. On a second **SIGHUP, SIGTERM,** or **SIGQUIT, routed** terminates.

Files

/usr/sbin/routed
Specifies the command path

/etc/gateways
Routes through distant and external gateways

/etc/networks
Contains the network name database

Cautions

1.   The **gated** and **routed** daemons should not both be run on the same host, as this may produce unpredictable results.

2.   Routes through external gateways must be to networks only.

Related Information

Commands: **route(8)**

rrestore

Purpose   Reads files from a remote magnetic tape or other specified storage device.

See **restore(8)**

rshd

Purpose   The remote shell server

Synopsis   **rshd** [**-aln**]

Flags

-a   The addresses for the hostname are requested, verifying that the name and address correspond.

-l   Prevents the **ruserok** command from doing any validation based on the user's **.rhosts** file, unless the user is the superuser.

-n   Disables transport-level, keep-alive messages.

Description

The **rshd** daemon is the server for the **rcmd(3)** routine and, consequently, for the **rsh(1)** program. The server provides remote execution facilities with authentication based on privileged port numbers from trusted hosts.

The **rshd** daemon listens for service requests at the port indicated in the **cmd** service specification; see **services(4).** When a service request is received, the following protocol is initiated:

1.   The server checks the client's source port. If the port is not in the range 512 to 1023, the server aborts the connection.

2.   The server reads bytes from the socket up to a null (`\0`) byte. The resultant string is interpreted as an ASCII number, base 10.

3.   If the number received in step 2 is nonzero, it is interpreted as the port number of a secondary stream to be used for the **stderr** option. A second connection is then created to the specified port on the client's machine. The source port of this second connection is also in the range 512 to 1023.

4.   The server checks the client's source address and requests the corresponding hostname (see **gethostbyaddr**(3), **hosts**(4), and **named**(8)). If the hostname cannot be determined, the dot-notation representation of the host address is used. If the hostname is in the same domain as the server (according to the last two components of the domain name), or if the **-a** flag is given, the addresses for the hostname are requested, verifying that the name and address correspond. If address verification fails, the connection is aborted with the message, Host address mismatch.

5.   A null-terminated username of at most 16 bytes is retrieved on the initial socket. This username is interpreted as the user identity on the client 's machine.

6.   A null-terminated username of at most 16 bytes is retrieved on the initial socket. This username is interpreted as a user identity to use on the server's machine.

7.   A null-terminated command to be passed to a shell is retrieved on the initial socket. The length of the command is limited by the upper bound on the size of the system's argument list.

8.   The **rshd** daemon then validates the user using **ruserok(3),** which uses the file **/etc/hosts.equiv** and the **.rhosts** file found in the user's home directory. The **-l** flag prevents **ruserok(3)** from doing any validation based on the user's **.rhosts** file, unless the user is the superuser.

9.   A null byte is returned on the initial socket and the command line is passed to the normal login shell of the user. The shell inherits the network connections established by **rshd**.

Transport-level, keep-alive messages are enabled unless the **-n** flag is present. The use of keep-alive messages allows sessions to be timed out if the client crashes or becomes unreachable.

Cautions

The authentication procedure used here assumes the integrity of each client machine and the connecting medium. This is insecure, but is useful in an *open* environment.

Diagnostics

Except for the last diagnostic message listed, `all diagnostic messages are returned` on the initial socket, after which any network connections are closed. An error is indicated by a leading byte with a value of 1 (0 is returned in step 9 above upon successful completion of all the steps prior to the execution of the login shell).

`Locuser too long.`
The name of the user on the client's machine is longer than 16 characters.

`Remuser too long.`
The name of the user on the remote machine is longer than 16 characters.

`Command too long.`
The command line passed exceeds the size of the argument list (as configured into the system).

`Login incorrect.`
No password file entry for the username existed.

`No remote directory.`
The **chdir** command to the home directory failed.

`Permission denied.`
The authentication procedure previously described failed.

`Can't make pipe.`
The pipe needed for the **stderr** option, but it was not created.

`''Can't fork; try again.''`
A **fork** by the server failed.

`<shellname>: ...`
The user's login shell could not be started. This message is returned on the connection associated with the **stderr** option, and is not preceded by a flag byte.

Files

/usr/sbin/rshd
> Specifies the command path

Related Information

rsh(1), rcmd(3), ruserok(3)

runacct

Purpose   Runs daily accounting

Synopsis   /usr/sbin/acct/**runacct** [*mmdd*] [*State* . . .]

Description

The **runacct** command is the daily accounting shell procedure. This shell procedure is normally invoked from the **cron** daemon to process connection, fee, disk usage, queueing (printer), and process accounting database files for the current day. The **runacct** shell procedure produces a /**var/adm/acct/nite/dayacct** binary daily accounting file and also produces summary files, which the **prdaily** shell procedure uses to generate ASCII daily file /**var/adm/acct/sum/rprt***mmdd* or to generate files used for billing for the use of various system resources. The /**var/adm/acct/nite/dayacct** binary daily accounting file is used by the **acctmerg** command.

The **acctmerg** command adds records from the **dayacct** file to the /**var/adm/acct/sumtacct** file. The /**var/adm/acct/sumtacct** file is a cumulative summary of system resources used during the accounting period. The **sumtacct** file is used by the **monacct** command to produce the monthly accounting summary file, /**var/adm/acct/fiscal**.

The **runacct** command has two parameters that you may enter from the keyboard whenever you must restart the **runacct** shell procedure. The date parameter, *mmdd*, is used to specify the day and month for which you want to rerun the accounting shell procedure. The *State* parameter is used to restart the **runacct** shell procedure from any of its 13 states. Recovery from a run failure and the **runacct** shell procedure restart is described under the **Restarting Runacct** heading on the next page.

The **runacct** command protects active accounting and summary files whenever a run-time error occurs. During execution, the state-to-state progress of the **runacct** shell process is recorded by writing descriptive messages to the /**var/adm/acct/nite/active** file. Whenever the **runacct** shell process detects a run-time error, a **mail** message is sent to the superuser (root) and to the user named **adm** when environment variable MAILCOM is set to **mail root adm**. After writing the mail message the **runacct** shell procedure aborts.

The **runacct** shell procedure also creates the temporary file named **lock** in subdirectory /**var/adm/acct/nite**. This file is used to prevent simultaneous calls to the **runacct** shell procedure. The **runacct** shell procedure also uses the **lastdate** file, in the same subdirectory, to prevent more than one invocation of the **runacct** command per day.

The **runacct** States

The **runacct** shell procedure is processed in 13 separate restartable states. When the **runacct** process completes each state, the name of the the next state to undergo execution is written to the **/var/adm/acct/nite/state** file. The **runacct** procedure processes the various states named in the second column in the order listed in the first column of the following table.

1. **SETUP**
Moves the active accounting files to working files and restarts the active files.

2. **WTMPFIX**
Verifies the integrity of the **/var/adm/wtmp** file and corrects date changes when necessary.

3. **CONNECT1**
Calls the **acctcon1** command to write connect session records.

4. **CONNECT2**
Converts connect session records from the **/var/adm/wtmp** file to total accounting records in total format defined by **tacct** structure members in the private **tacct.h** header file.

5. **PROCESS**
Converts process accounting records from the **/var/adm/pacct*** file(s) into total accounting records (see **CONNECT2** above).

6. **MERGE**
Merges the connect and process total accounting records.

7. **FEES**
Converts the output obtained with the **chargefee** command into total accounting records (see **CONNECT2** above) and merges them with other total accounting records.

8. **DISK**
Merges disk accounting records with connect, process, and fee total accounting records.

9. **QUEUEACCT**
Sorts queue (printer) accounting records, converts them into total accounting records (see **CONNECT2** above), and merges them with other total accounting records.

10. **MERGETACCT**
Merges the daily total accounting records in the **/var/adm/acct/nite/dayacct** file with summary total accounting records in the **/var/adm/acct/sum/tacct** file.

11. **CMS**
Produces command summaries in the file **/var/adm/acct/sum/cms**.

12. **USEREXIT**
When the shell procedure **/var/adm/siteacct** exists, and the **runacct** shell procedure enters this state, the **/var/adm/siteacct** is called to perform site-dependent account record processing.

13. **CLEANUP**
Deletes all temporary files and exits.

runacct(8)

Restarting **runacct**

To restart the **runacct** shell process after it fails, do the following:

1. Check the **/var/adm/acct/nite/active** file for diagnostic messages.

2. Repair records in any damaged database files, such as **/var/adm/pacct** or **/var/adm/wtmp**.

3. Remove the **/var/adm/acct/nite/lock** and **/var/adm/acct/nite/lastdate** files.

4. Before restarting the **runacct** shell procedure, you must specify the *mmdd* parameter of the **runacct** command. This parameter specifies the month and day for which the **runacct** command is to rerun the accounting shell process. The **runacct** shell procedure determines the entry point for processing by reading the **/var/adm/acct/nite/statefile** file. To override this default action, specify a *state* listed above on the **runacct** command line.

    It is not a good idea to restart the **runacct** command in the **SETUP** state. Instead, perform set-up actions manually and restart accounting in the **WTMPFIX** state by entering the following command:

    runacct mmdd WTMPFIX

Should the **runacct** process fail during its **PROCESS** state, remove the last **/var/adm/acct/nite/ptacct*.***mmdd* file before restarting the **runacct** shell process because the file does not complete until the next state is entered.

Examples

1. To start daily accounting procedures for the use of various system resources, add the following command line to a **crontabs** file so that the **runacct** shell procedure is automatically called by the **cron** daemon.

    0 4 * * 1-6 /usr/sbin/acct/runacct 2 > /var/adm/acct/nite/accterr

    This example shows the instructions that the **cron** daemon reads and then executes. The **runacct** shell procedure runs at 4:00 a.m. (**0 4**) every Monday through Saturday (**1-6**) and redirects errors from the standard error output (**2 >**) to the **/var/adm/acct/nite/accterr** file. This command typifies accounting instructions normally passed to the **cron** daemon from the **runacct** shell procedure. (See Chapter 9 of the *OSF/1 System Administrator's Guide* for more information about running accounting processes.)

2. To start daily accounting procedures for system resources from the command line (start the **runacct** command), enter:

    nohup /usr/sbin/acct/runacct 2> /var/adm/acct/nite/accterr&

    Although it is preferable to have the **cron** daemon start the **runacct** procedure automatically (see example 1), you may enter the command from the keyboard. The **runacct** command will run in the background (**&**), ignoring all **INTERRUPT** and **QUIT** signals (**nohup**), and write all standard error output (**2>**) to the **/var/adm/acct/nite/accterr** file.

3. To restart the system accounting procedures for a specific date, enter a command similar to the following:

   nohup /usr/sbin/acct/runacct 0601 2>> /var/adm/acct/nite/accterr&

   In this example, the **runacct** command is   on the first day of June (**0601**). The **runacct** process reads the **/var/adm/acct/nite/statefile** file to find the state from which to start. The **runacct** process runs in the background (**&**) and ignores all **INTERRUPT** and **QUIT** signals (**nohup**). The standard error output (**2**) is appended (**>>**) to the end of the file named **/var/adm/acct/nite/accterr**.

Files

/usr/sbin/acct/runnact
> Specifies the command path

/var/adm/wtmp
> The active login/logout database file.

/var/adm/pacct
> The active process accounting database file.

/var/adm/acct/nite/daytacct
> The active disk-usage accounting database file.

/var/adm/qacct
> The active queue (printer) accounting file.

/var/adm/fee
> The file containing records of fees charged to users.

/var/adm/acct/sum/*
> The command and total accounting summary files.

/var/adm/acct/nite/ptacct*.*mmdd*
> The concatenated version of the **pacct** files.

/var/adm/acct/nite/active
> The **runacct** error message file.

/var/adm/acct/nite/lock
> Prevents more than one invocation of the **runacct** shell procedure.

/var/adm/acct/nite/lastdate
> Contains the last date the **runacct** shell procedure was run.

/var/adm/acct/nite/statefile
> Contains the next state to process.

runacct(8)

/var/adm/siteacct

A shell procedure containing site-dependent accounting commands.

/usr/include/sys/acct.h

Accounting header file that defines formats for writing accounting files.

Related Information

Commands: **acct(8)**, **acctcms(8)**, **acctcom(8)**, **acctcon(8)**, **acctmerg(8)**, **acctprc(8)**, **fwtmp(8)**

Calls: **acct(2)**

Daemons: **cron**

rwhod

Purpose   The system status server

Synopsis   **rwhod**

Description

The **rwhod** daemon is the server that maintains the database used by the **rwho(1)** and **ruptime(1)** programs. Its operation is predicated on the ability to **broadcast** messages on a network.

The **rwhod** server operates as both a producer and consumer of status information. As a producer of information, it periodically queries the state of the system and constructs status messages, which are broadcast on a network. As a consumer of information, it listens for other **rwhod** servers' status messages, validating them, then recording them in a collection of files located in the **/var/rwho** directory.

The server transmits and receives messages at the port indicated in the **rwho** service specification; see **services**(4). The messages sent and received, are of the form:

```
struct   outmp {
         char    out_line[8];                /* tty name */
         char    out_name[8];                /* user id */
         long    out_time;                   /* time on */
};

struct   whod {
         char    wd_vers;
         char    wd_type;
         char    wd_fill[2];
         int     wd_sendtime;
         int     wd_recvtime;
         char    wd_hostname[32];
         int     wd_loadav[3];
         int     wd_boottime;
         struct  whoent {
                 struct  outmp we_utmp;
                 int     we_idle;
         } wd_we[1024 / sizeof (struct whoent)];
};
```

All fields are converted to network byte order prior to transmission. The load averages are as calculated by the **w**(1) program, and represent load averages over the 5-, 10-, and 15-minute intervals prior to a server's transmission; they are multiplied by 100 for representation in an integer. The hostname included is that returned by the **gethostname(2)** system call, with any trailing domain name omitted. The array at the end of the message contains information about the users logged in to the sending machine. This information includes the contents of the **utmp(5)** entry for each nonidle terminal line and a value indicating the time in seconds since a character was last received on the terminal line.

Messages received by the **rwho** server are discarded unless they originated at an **rwho** server's port. In addition, if the host's name, as specified in the message, contains any unprintable ASCII characters, the message is discarded. Valid messages received by **rwhod** are placed in files named **whod.hostname** in the **/var/rwho** directory. These files contain only the most recent message, in the format previosly described.

Status messages are generated approximately once every 3 minutes. **rwhod** performs an **nlist**(3) on **/vmunix** every 30 minutes to guard against the possibility that this file is not the system image currently operating.

Files

/usr/sbin/rwhod
> Specifies the command path

Related Information

Commands: **rwho(1)**, **ruptime(1)**

sa

Purpose   Summarizes accounting records

Synopsis   /usr/sbin/sa [**-abcdDfijkKlmnorstu**] [**-v** *Number*] [**-S** *SaveFile*] [**-U** *UserFile*] [*File*]

The **sa** command helps you manage the large volume of accounting information that is generated each day when system accounting has been enabled by the system administrator or by the superuser.

Flags

-a   Outputs all command names (including those containing unprintable characters and commands used only once) in the last column. In the default format, such commands are summed and the total is written as the entry *****other**.

-b   Sorts **cpu** output column **3** according to the sum of user and system CPU time divided by the amount of CPU time required to execute the command entered in the last column (**6**) as many times as is entered in the first column (**1**).

-c   Adds three percentage columns to the default format to list percentages as follows:

    1.   Lists the percentage of the number of times each command was executed with respect to the total number of times all commands were executed (see **1a** below).

    2.   Lists the percentage of the amount of real time required to execute each command the number of times entered in the first column with respect to the total real time required to execute the total of all commands entered in the last column (see **2a** below).

    3.   Lists the percentage of the amount of command CPU time required to execute each command the number of times entered in the first column with respect to the total CPU time required to execute the total of all commands entered in the last column (see **3a** below).

-d   Sorts **avio** output column (**4**) in descending order according to the average number of disk I/O operations.

-D   Substitutes **tio** column (**4a**) for the **avio** (**4**) column and sorts **tio** output column **4a** in descending order according to the total number of disk I/O operations.

-f   Used with the **-v** flag to inhibit interactive threshold comparison of commands.

-i   Reads raw database file **/var/adm/pacct** only. Does not include records from summary database file **/var/adm/savacct**.

-j   Outputs the average number of seconds per command in default columns **2**, **3**, and **4** instead of the total time in minutes for the number of calls entered in column **1** for each command.

-k   Sorts and outputs records according to the value in the **k** output column **5** in descending order.

-K   Substitutes **k*sec** column (**5a**) for the **k** (**5**) column and sorts the **k*sec** output column in descending order according to the value of the memory time integral.

-l   Separates **cpu** column **3** into two columns. The new column entries are column **3a**, which lists the **s** (system) part of the CPU minutes, and column **3b**, which lists the **u** (user) part of the CPU minutes.

-m   Outputs a 5-column file, which provides the information in the following table. This table lists the reference column numbers, which are not printed, from left to right, the identification suffix, when one is used, or **none** when one is not, and the purpose of the column. Columns identical with columns in the default output format described in the table under Description also have a * (asterisk) in the reference number column.

1	none	Username or user ID as written in the **/etc/passwd** file.
2	none	The total number of processes executed by the user during the accounting period.
3*	cpu	Same as column 3 in the default output file.
4*	tio	Same as column 4a in the default output file.
5a*	k*sec	Same as column 5a in the default output file.

-n   Outputs the default format sorted in descending order according to the number of times each command was called.

-o   Substitutes, in the default output format, the ratio of user CPU time (**u**) to system CPU time (**s**) as **u/s** in column **3** in place of the total user and system CPU time (**cpu**) for the number of calls entered in the first column.

-r   The default format, described under Description, is resorted in ascending order according to the values entered in column **3**, **cpu** time. This sort is the reverse of the default sort.

-s   Merges information in accounting database file **/var/adm/pacct** with summary files you specify with the **-U** and **-S** flags, or merges the database file information with information in default files

/var/adm/usracct or /var/adm/savacct. After the merge, database file
/var/adm/pacct is truncated. The use of this flag also implies the use of
the **-a** flag.

-S *SaveFile*

Uses *SaveFile* as the command summary file in place of file
/var/adm/savacct.

-t   Adds the **re/cp** column (**3d**) to the default format. Entries in this column
express the ratio of real time to total (**cpu**) time, which is the sum of user
and system time for each command entered in the last column.

-u   Suspends all other flags and prints the user numeric ID, the CPU time,
memory usage, number of I/O operations, and the command name for
each command.

-U *UserFile*

Uses *UserFile* as the user summary file in place of file **/var/adm/usracct**
to record per-user statistics output with the **-m** flag.

-v *Number*

Prints, as a query, the name of each command used *Number* times or
fewer to the standard output as follows:

command--

where *command--* is the name of the command written to the standard
output by **sa.**

When you respond by typing **y** to the standard input, the command record
is omitted from a default-formatted list at the end of the interactive
command queries written to the standard output. The columnar values of
the omitted record are totaled in an added record whose command name
is ****junk**** in the last column of that list. When you type any other
character, the record for the queried command name remains in the
default output list at the end of the interactive commands written to the
standard input.

Description

When you use the **-s** flag with the **sa** command, the information in **/var/adm/pacct**
is condensed into summary file **/var/adm/savacct**, which contains a count of the
number of times each command was called and the amount of time system
resources were used.

Condensed information for each user is stored in **/var/adm/usracct**. This
condensed-information file conserves storage space because on a large system the
/var/adm/pacct daily process file can grow by as many as 100 blocks per day.
Summary files are normally read before accounting files are, so that files produced
by **sa** include all available information.

When a filename is given as the last argument, the named file is treated as the process accounting file. The **/var/adm/pacct** file is the default process accounting file.

When the **sa** command is invoked with no flags, the default output summary is an unheaded 6-column file consisting of, in some cases, information having an identification suffix in the column. The identification suffix may be changed from the default (no flags specified) output format by using various flags.

The following table lists left-to-right reference column numbers (not printed) for the default format in the left column, the identification suffix for the entry when one is used, or **none** when one is not in the middle column, and the purpose of the information in that column in the right column.

Columns having more than one identification suffix description (**2** and **2a**, for example) use the alternate suffix designation in the same **sa** output printout column for each of the listed alternate entries for the column. For example, the second column has two possible suffix designations: **re** and **%**. The **re** reference in the middle column describes the information in the second column of the output printed by the **sa** command when this suffix is used. Correspondingly, the **%** reference describes the information in the **sa** output when the **%** suffix is used.

1	**none**	The number of times the command entered in the last column (**6**) was called.
1a	**%**	When the **-c** flag is used, **sa** adds this column after column **1** to list the number of times the command was called (entered in column **1**) as a percentage of the total number of times all commands entered in the last column were called.
2	**re**	The number of real-time (elapsed) minutes required to execute the command entered in the last column (**6**) as many times as is entered in the first column (**1**).
2a	**%**	When the **-c** flag is used, **sa** also adds this column after column **2** to list the amount of real time (entered in column **2**) required to process the command entered in the last column (**6**) as many time as is entered in the first column (**1**), as a percentage of the total amount of real time requried to process all of the commands listed in the last column.
3	**cpu**	The number of CPU (user plus system) minutes used to execute the command entered in the last column (**6**) as many times as is entered in the first column (**1**).

3a	u	The number of user CPU minutes used.
3b	s	The number of system CPU minutes used.
3c	u/s	When the **-o** flag is used, substitutes **u/s** column (**3c**) for the **cpu** (**3**) column and sorts the **u/s** output column in descending order according to the ratio of user CPU time to system CPU time.
3d	%	When the **-c** flag is used, **sa** also adds this column after column **3** to list the amount of CPU time (entered in column 3) requred to process the command, entered in the last column, the number of times, entered in the first column, as a percentage of the total CPU time required to process all of the commands listed in the last column.
3e	re/cpu	When the **-t** flag is used, adds the **re/cpu** column to the default output format. Entries in this column express the ratio of real CPU process time to total CPU time (**cpu**), which includes user and system time. These entries appear after entries for the **cpu** (**3**) column. The default output sort remains unchanged.
4	avio	The average number of input/output operations for each listed command.
4a	tio	The total number of input/output operations for each listed command.
5	k	The average number of kiloblocks (blocks x 1024) of memory used for each command process.
5a	k*sec	CPU storage-time integral in K-core seconds (seconds x 1024).
6	none	The command name (a trailing * [asterisk] indicates a forked program).

Other considerations for entries in the printed **sa** output are as follows:

1.   All times are expressed to nearest one hundreth. The default format is sorted in descending order according to the values entered in column **3**, **cpu** time.

2.   You should not share accounting files among nodes in a distributed environment. Each node should have its own copy of the various accounting files.

3.   When you are also using **/usr/sbin/acct/*** accounting commands, do not delete accounting records in the **/var/adm/pacct** process accounting source file because these records also provide information for summary data files when the **-s** option is used.

sa(8)

Examples

1. To summarize accounting records for all commands entered in the **/var/adm/pacct** process database file, enter:

   sa -a

   Commands used only once are summed with the entry ***other** in the last column of the default output format.

2. To summarize accounting records according to the average number of kiloblocks of memory used for each command, enter:

   sa -k

Files

/usr/sbin/sa

Specifies the command path

/var/adm/pacct

Process accounting database file.

/var/adm/savacct

System process accounting summary file.

/var/adm/usracct

User process accounting summary file.

Related Information

Commands: **acct(8)**, **acctcms(8)**, **acctcom(8)**, **acctcon(8)**, **acctmerg(8)**, **acctprc(8)**, **fwtmp(8)**, **runacct(8)**

savecore

Purpose   Saves a core dump of the operating system

Synopsis   **savecore** [**-cfv**] *directory* [*system*]

The **savecore** command saves the most recent core dump of the system and writes a reboot message in the shutdown log.

Flags

-c   Does not copy the dump, but simply marks it invalid.

-f   Copies the dump even if it appears to be invalid. If both **-c** and **-f** are specified, **-f** is ignored.

-v   Prints more verbose information.

Description

The **savecore** command is usually invoked during system startup (before the dump partition is accessed).

savecore checks that a dump has been made recently (during the last 3 days) and that there is enough space to save it (see the following information about **minfree**). These conditions are overridden by the **-f** flag.

Both the dump and the system (default **/vmunix**) are saved to files in *directory* under the names **vmcore.***n* and **vmunix.***n*. The variable *n* is the number specified by the file *directory*/*bounds* and incremented by **savecore** (if this value does not exist, it is created and initialized with the value 0). The file **directory/minfree** specifies the minimum number of kilobytes left on the filesystem containing *directory* after the dump is taken (default is 0).

savecore also logs a reboot message using facility **LOG_CRIT** (see **syslog**). If the system crashed as a result of a panic, **savecore** logs the panic string too.

If the core dump was from a system other than **/vmunix**, the name of that system must be supplied as the *system* argument.

savecore(8)

Files

/usr/sbin/savecore
> Specifies the command path.

/vmunix Specifies the current system.

directory/bounds
> Specifies the number of next dump files.

directory/minfree
> Specifies the minimum number of kilobytes to be left after a dump.

sendmail

Purpose   Sends mail over the Internet

Synopsis   **sendmail** [-*flags*] [*address ...*]
newaliases
mailq [-v]

Description

The **sendmail** command sends a message to one or more recipients, routing the message over whatever networks are necessary. sendmail does internetwork forwarding as necessary to deliver the message to the correct place.

sendmail is not intended as a user interface routine. other programs provide user-friendly front ends; sendmail is used only to deliver preformatted messages.

With no flags, sendmail reads its standard input up to an end-of-File or a line consisting only of a single . (dot), and sends a copy of the message found there to all of the addresses listed. It determines the network(s) to use based on the syntax and contents of the addresses.

Local addresses are looked up in a file and aliased appropriately. Aliasing can be prevented by preceding the address with a backslash. Normally the sender is not included in any alias expansions; for example, if **john** sends to **group**, and **group** includes **john** in the expansion, then the letter will not be delivered to **john**.

Flags are:

-ba   Goes into ARPANET mode. All input lines must end with a **CR-LF**, and all messages will be generated with a **CR-LF** at the end. Also, the **From:** and **Sender:** fields are examined for the name of the sender.

-bd   Runs as a daemon. This requires Berkeley IPC. The **sendmail** command will fork and run in the background, listening on socket 25 for incoming SMTP (Simple Mail Transfer Protocol) connections. This is normally run when going to multiuser mode.

-bi   Initializes the alias database.

-bm   Delivers mail in the usual way (default).

-bp   Prints a listing of the queue.

-bs   Use the SMTP protocol as described in RFC821 on standard input and output. This flag implies all the operations of the **-ba** flag that are compatible with SMTP.

-bt   Run in address test mode. This mode reads addresses and shows the steps in parsing; it is used for debugging configuration tables.

-bv   Verifies names only. Does not try to collect or deliver a message. Verify mode is normally used for validating users or mailing lists.

-bz   Creates the configuration freeze file.

-C_file_   Uses alternate configuration file. The **sendmail** command refuses to run as root if an alternate configuration file is specified. The frozen configuration file is bypassed.

-d_X_   Sets debugging value to X. A useful value is 21.n, where n is any nonzero integer less than 100. This produces information regarding address parsing and is typically used with the **-bt** flag. Higher values of n produce more verbose information.

-F_fullname_
         Sets the full name of the sender.

-f_name_ Sets the name of the "from" person (that is, the sender of the mail). **-f** can only be used by trusted users (normally **root, daemon,** and **network**) or if the person you are trying to become is the same as the person you are.

-h_N_   Set the hop count to N. The hop count is incremented every time the mail is processed. When it reaches a limit, the mail is returned with an error message, the victim of an aliasing loop. If not specified, `Received` lines in the message are counted.

-n   Does not do aliasing.

-o_x value_ Sets x to the specified _value_. Processing flags are described after the **-v** flag.

-q[_time_] Processes saved messages in the queue at given intervals. If _time_ is omitted, processes the queue once. The **time** command is given as a tagged number, with **s** being seconds, **m** being minutes, **h** being hours, **d** being days, and **w** being weeks. For example, **-q1h30m"** or **"-q90m** would both set the timeout to one hour thirty minutes. If the **time** command is specified, the **sendmail** command will run in background. This flag can be used safely with **-bd**.

-r_name_ An alternate and obsolete form of the **-f** flag.

-t   Reads message for recipients. **To:, Cc:,** and **Bcc:** lines will be scanned for recipient addresses. The **Bcc:** line will be deleted before transmission. Any addresses in the argument list will be suppressed; that is, they will not receive copies even if listed in the message header.

-v   Goes into verbose mode. Alias expansions will be announced, and so forth.

There are also a number of processing flags that may be set. Normally, these will only be used by a system administrator. Flags may be set either on the command line using the **-o** flag or in the configuration file. These are described in detail in the *Sendmail Installation and Operation Guide*.

The flags are as follows:

-A*file*   Uses alternate alias file.

-c   On mailers that are considered "expensive" to connect to, does not initiate immediate connection. This requires queueing.

-d*x*   Set the delivery mode to *x*. Delivery modes are **i** for interactive (synchronous) delivery, **b** for background (asynchronous) delivery, and **q** for queue only (that is, actual delivery is done the next time the queue is run).

-D   Tries to automatically rebuild the alias database if necessary.

-e*x*   Sets error processing to mode *x*. Valid modes are

> **m**   Mails the error message to the user's mailbox.
>
> **w**   Writes the error message to the terminal or mails it if the user is not logged in.
>
> **p**   Displays the error message on the terminal (default).
>
> **q**   Throws away the error message and returns the exit status only.
>
> **e**   Mails the error message to the user's mailbox, but always exits with a zero exit status (normal return).
>
> If the text of the message is not mailed by modes **m** or **w** and if the sender is a local user, a copy of the message is appended to the **dead.letter** file in the sender's home directory.

-F*mode*   The mode to use when creating temporary files.

-f   Saves UNIX compatible style **From:** lines at the front of messages.

-g*N*   The default group ID to use when calling mailers.

-H*file*   The SMTP help file.

-i   Does not take dots on a line by themselves as a message terminator.

-L*number*

> Specifies the log level to be the value supplied in the *number* argument. Each number includes the activities of all numbers of lesser value and adds the activity that it represents. Valid levels and the activities that they represent are as follows:

0   Prevents logging.

1   Logs major problems only.

2   Logs message collections and failed deliveries.

3   Logs successful deliveries.

4   Logs messages deferred (for example, because the host is down).

5   Logs messages that are placed in the queue (normal event).

6   Logs unusual but benign incidents (for example, trying to process a locked file).

9   Logs internal queue ID to external message ID mappings. This can be useful for tracing a message as it travels between several hosts.

12   Logs messages that are of interest when debugging.

16   Logs verbose information regarding the queue.

-m   Sends to me (the sender) also if I am in an alias expansion.

-o   If set, this message may have old style headers. If not set, this message is guaranteed to have new style headers (that is, commas instead of spaces between addresses). If set, an adaptive algorithm is used that will correctly determine the header format in most cases.

-Q*queuedir*

Selects the directory in which to queue messages.

-r*timeout*

The time-out on reads. If none is set, **sendmail** will wait forever for a mailer. This flag violates the word (if not the intent) of the SMTP specification, so the time-out should probably be fairly large.

-S*file*   Saves statistics in the **named** file.

-s   Always instantiate the queue file, even under circumstances where it is not strictly necessary. This provides safety against system crashes during delivery.

-T*time*   Sets the time-out on undelivered messages in the queue to the specified time. After delivery has failed (for example, because of a host being down) for this amount of time, failed messages will be returned to the sender. The default is 3 days.

-t*stz,dtz* Sets the name of the time zone.

-u*N*   Sets the default user ID for mailers.

-v   Runs in verbose mode.

In aliases, the first character of a name may be a vertical bar to cause interpretation of the rest of the name as a command to pipe the mail to. It may be necessary to quote the name to keep **sendmail** from suppressing the blanks from between arguments. For example, a file may contain a common alias such as:

```
msgs: "|/usr/bin/msgs -s"
```

Aliases may also have the syntax ''`:include:`*filename*'' to ask **sendmail** to read the named file for a list of recipients. For example, an alias such as:

```
poets: ":include:/usr/local/lib/poets.list"
```

would read **/usr/local/lib/poets.list** for the list of addresses making up the group.

The **sendmail** command returns an exit status describing what it did. The codes are defined in **<sysexits.h>**

EX_OK	Successful completion on all addresses.
EX_NOUSER	Username not recognized.
EX_UNAVAILABLE	Catchall meaning necessary resources were not available.
EX_SYNTAX	Syntax error in address.
EX_SOFTWARE	Internal software error, including bad arguments.
EX_OSERR	Temporary operating system error, such as cannot fork.
EX_NOHOST	Host name not recognized.
EX_TEMPFAIL	Message could not be sent immediately, but was queued.

If invoked as **newaliases, sendmail** will rebuild the alias database. If invoked as **mailq, sendmail** will print the contents of the mail queue.

Links to sendmail

Two additional commands are links to **sendmail**:

/usr/bin/mailq
> Prints the contents of the mail queue. This command is the same as running **sendmail** with the **-bp** flag.

/usr/bin/newaliases
> Builds a new copy of the alias database from the **/var/adm/sendmail/aliases** file. This command is the same as running **sendmail** with the **-bi** flag.

Mail Addresses

Mail addresses are based on the domain address (Internet) protocol. These addresses have the form:

user@host.domain

Note that the configuration file provided with **sendmail** specifies that blanks in addresses be converted to dots before being transmitted. This convention follows the Internet mail protocol described in RFC822, but does not match the Internet mail protocol described in RFC733 (NIC41952). You can change this setting by setting the **OB** flag in the **sendmail** configuration file (see the **sendmail.cf(4)** manpage).

A *domain* is a logical grouping of systems that are connected together by physical network links. No direct relationship exists between the actual physical interconnections and the way in which the systems are grouped in the domain. The *domain name* identifies a specific domain within a larger group of domains. The domain name has the format of a tree structure. Each node (or leaf) on the tree corresponds to a resource set, and each node can create and contain new domains below it. The actual domain name of a node is the path from the root of the tree to that node.

For example, if node **hera** is part of the domain **OSF**, which is in turn a subdomain of **ORG**, a message sent to user **geo** at that address, uses this format:

```
hera.OSF.ORG
```

The message router (usually **sendmail**) must determine how to send the message to its final destination. If the router is at **hera**, it delivers the message to user **geo**. If the router is at another system within the **OSF** domain, it corresponds with the name server for that domain to find out how to deliver the message. If the router is not a part of the **OSF** domain but is in a domain that is under the **ORG** domain, it corresponds with the name server for the **ORG** domain to find out how to deliver the message. The respective name server returns a network address to the router. That network address determines the actual path that the message takes to its destination.

The domain address is read from right to left, with each domain in the address separated from the next domain with a . (dot). This format does not imply any routing. Thus, although the example is specified as a **ORG** address, the message might actually travel by a different route if that were more convenient or efficient. At one site, the message associated with the sample address goes directly from the sender to node **hera** over a local area network. At another site, it might be sent over a UUCP network or a combination of other delivery methods.

Normally, the actual routing of a message is handled automatically. However, you can route the message manually through several specified hosts to get it to its final destination. An address using intermediate hosts, called a *route address*, has the following form:

   @hosta,@hostb:user@hostc

This address specifies that the message goes first to the remote system represented by *hosta*, then to the remote system represented by *hostb*, and finally to the remote system represented by *hostc*. This path is forced even if there is a more efficient route to *hostc*.

In some cases you may abbreviate the address rather than entering the entire domain name. In general, systems in the same domain do not need to use the full domain name. For example, a user on node **zeus.XYZ.COM** can send a message to **geo@hera.XYZ.COM** by entering only **geo@hera** because they are in the same local domain, **XYZ**.

Other mail address formats exist and the mail routing program (**sendmail**) converts most of these other formats to a format that the network routing system can use. However, if you use the domain address format, the routing program operates more efficiently.

For example, if **sendmail** receives an address in the following format:

   @host:user

it converts it to the corresponding domain address format:

   user@host

Similarly, if **sendmail** receives an address in the following format:

   host!user

the mail routing program routes the message directly to the **uucp** command. However, when sending mail via uucp, you must include a route address that indicates which uucp host(s) to send the message through to get to the final destination.

To route messages through the UUCP network, use one of the following domain address formats. Your choice depends on the way in which the systems at your site are connected:

1.   *@system_name.domain_name:uucp-route!user-ID*

     For example, the address:

     @zeus:hera!amy

     sends a message to user **amy** on uucp host **hera** by way of system **zeus**. The address:

     @apollo.802:merlin!lgh

     sends a message to user **lgh** on uucp host **merlin** via system **apollo** under the local domain **802**.

2.   *uucp-route:!user-ID@system_name.domain_name*

     In this case, the address:

     merlin!arthur!amy@hera.802

     sends a message to user **amy** on system **hera** under domain **802** via the uucp link **merlin** through **arthur**.

3.   *system_name.domain_name:uucp-route*
     :!user-ID@system_name.domain_name

     In this example, the address:

     @apollo.802:merlin!arthur!amy@hera.802

     sends a message to user **amy** on system **hera** under domain **802** that first goes through **apollo**, the gateway node for domain **802**, and then through the uucp link **merlin** through **arthur**. (Including **802** in this example is optional because the two domain names are identical.)

4.   *hosta!hostb!hostc!user*

     This example is a purely uucp route address:

     zeus!hera!kronos!amy

     sends a message to **amy** on **kronos** via the uucp link **zeus** through **hera**.

5.   *@hosta*.UUCP: *@hostb*.UUCP:*user@hostc*

This example, like the previous one, is a purely **uucp** route address:

@zeus.UUCP:@hera.UUCP:amy@kronos.UUCP

sends a message to **amy** on **kronos** via the uucp link **zeus** through **hera**.

Files

/usr/sbin/sendmail
>   Specifies the command path

Except for **/etc/sendmail.cf**, the following pathnames are all specified in **/var/adm/sendmail.cf.** Thus, these values are only approximations.

/var/adm/sendmail/aliases   raw data for alias names
/var/adm/sendmail/aliases.pag
/var/adm/sendmail/aliases.dir data base of alias names
/var/adm/sendmail/sendmail.cf configuration file
/var/adm/sendmail/sendmail.fc frozen configuration
/usr/share/lib/sendmail.hf   help file
/var/adm/sendmail/sendmail.st collected statistics
/var/adm/sendmail/mqueue/* temp files

Related Information

binmail(1), mail(1), rmail(1), syslog(3), aliases(4), rc(8);
DARPA Internet Request For Comments RFC819, RFC821, RFC822;
Sendmail - An Internetwork Mail Router (SMM:16);
Sendmail Installation and Operation Guide (SMM:7)

showmount

Purpose   Shows remote NFS compatible mounts on a host

Synopsis   **showmount** [**-ade**] [*host*]

Flags

-a   Lists all mount points in the form:
        host:dirpath

-d   Lists directory paths of mount points instead of hosts.

-e   Shows the *host's* exports list.

Description

The **showmount** command shows status information about the NFS server on *host*.
By default it prints the names of all hosts that have NFS file systems mounted on
the host. See *NFS: Network File System Protocol Specification, RFC1094,
Appendix A* for a detailed desciption of the protocol.

Cautions

The **mountd** daemon running on the server only has an idea of the actual mounts,
since the NFS server is stateless. **showmount** will only display the information as
accurately as the **mount** daemon reports it.

Files

/usr/bin/showmount
        Specifies the command path

Related Information

Commands: **mount(1)**

Daemons: **mountd(8)**

shutacct

Purpose   Turns process accounting off

See **acct(8)**

shutdown

Purpose   Ends system operation

Synopsis   **shutdown** [**-f -h -k -n -r**] *time* [*warning-message* ...]

Flags

    -f   Causes a fast shutdown, bypassing the messages to other users and bringing the system down as quickly as possible.

    -h   Causes the system to shutdown and halt.

    -k   Causes shutdown messages to be sent to users, warning them of an impending shutdown. The system does not actually shut down.

    -n   Causes a shutdown without syncing the disks.

    -r   Causes the system to shutdown and automatically reboot.

Description

The **shutdown** command provides an automated shutdown procedure. You must be **root** to use this command.

The *time* argument specifies when *shutdown* will bring the system down. You can use the word **now** (indicating an immediate shutdown) or specify a future time in one of two formats: +*number* or *yymmddhhmm* (where the year, month, and day may be defaulted to the current system values). The first form brings the system down in *number* minutes. The second form brings the system down at the absolute time specified. The hours and minutes in the second time format may be separated by a colon (:) for backward compatibility.

Any other arguments comprise the warning message that is broadcast to users currently logged into the system. Prior to shutdown, warning messages are displayed at the terminals of all users on the system. Messages are sent at intervals which get closer together as shutdown approaches. Five minutes before shutdown (or immediately, if shutdown is in less than five minutes) logins are disabled by creating the **nologin** file and copying the warning message there. If this file exists when a user attempts to log in, the **login** program prints its contents and exits. The **nologin** file is removed just before **shutdown** exits.

At shutdown time a message is written in the system log, containing the time of shutdown, who ran shutdown and the reason. A terminate signal is then sent to **init** to bring the system down to the single-user state. Alternatively, if you invoke **shutdown** with the **-r**, **-h**, or **-k** flag, the command executes the **reboot** command or the **halt** command, or avoids shutting the system down.

If you invoke the command with the **-f** flag, **shutdown** shuts down the system quickly (in the manner of the **fastboot** or the **fasthalt** program); the system halts or reboots without checking the file systems. For example, the **shutdown -f** *time* command brings the system to single user and creates the **/fastboot** file; when the system reboots to multiuser, it does not invoke **fsck. The shutdown -f -r** *time* command causes the system to shut down, create the **/fastboot** file, then immediately reboot. The **shutdown -f -h** *time* command causes the system to halt and create the **/fastboot** file.

The **-n** flag prevents the normal syncing of disks before stopping the system. The **-n** and **-f** flags together on the command line are incompatable.

The time of the shutdown and the warning message are placed in the **nologin** file and can be used to inform the users about when the system will be back up and why it is going down.

Files

/usr/sbin/shutdown
> Specifies the command path

Related Information

Commands: **login(1)**, **wall(1)**, **fastboot(8)**, **fasthalt(8)**, **halt(8)**, **reboot(8)**

slattach

Purpose   Attaches a serial line to a network interface

Synopsis   **slattach** *ttyname* [*baudrate*]

The **slattach** command assigns a tty line to a network interface.

Description

The **slattach** command assigns a tty line to a network interface to define the network source and destination addresses. The *ttyname* argument is the name of any valid tty device in **/dev**. The optional *baudrate* argument is used to set the speed of the connection. The default speed is 9600 baud.

Only a person with superuser authority can attach a network interface.

To detach the interface, use the **ifconfig** *interface_id* **down** command after terminating the **slattach** process. *interface_id* is the name that is shown by the **netstat** command.

Examples

To attach a tty device to a network interface, enter:

/usr/sbin/slattach /dev/tty01 4800

This command attached **tty01** to a network interface to be used by the Serial Line Internet Protocol (SLIP). The connection speed is **4800** baud.

Notes

The **slattach** command requires the Serial Line Internet Protocol (SLIP), which the kernel must support.

Files

/usr/sbin/slattach
Specifies the command path

Related Information

Commands: **netstat(1)**, **ifconfig(8)**

Specifications: SLIP is described in RFC1055.

startup

Purpose   Turns on the accounting functions

See **acct(8)**

strace

Purpose   Displays STREAMS event trace messages

Synopsis   **strace** [*mod_ID sub_ID priority_level*]
Description

Without arguments, the **strace** command gets STREAMS event trace messages from all drivers and modules via the STREAMS log driver (**log**). It then writes these messages to standard output.

You can limit the messages **strace** receives by specifying arguments to the command.

The **strace** command runs until terminated by the user.

Arguments

The following three arguments must be specified together.

mod_ID   Specifies the STREAMS module identification number.

sub_ID   Specifies a sub-identification number (often corresponding to a minor device).

priority_level Specifies a tracing priority level. The **strace** command gets messages of a level equal to or less than *priority_level*. (The value of *priority_level* must be a nonnegative integer.)

This set of three arguments specifies that **strace** receive trace messages from the specified module/driver and sub-ID (minor device), having a tracing priority level less than or equal to *priority_level*.

You can specify **all** as the value for any of these arguments. The value **all** indicates that there are no restrictions for that argument.

Note also that you can specify multiple sets of these three arguments on the same command line. However, specifying several sets of arguments may slow STREAMS performance. (See the section "Communicating with the STREAMS Log Driver".)

Trace Message Format

Each STREAMS event trace message is of the following format:

sequence_num   std_time   ticks_time   priority_level   notify_codes   mod_ID   sub_ID   mesg_text

where:

sequence_num
        Event trace sequence number.

std_time   The time the message was sent, in the format *hh*:*mm*:*ss*.

ticks_time   The time the message was sent, measured in machine ticks since the last boot.

priority_level Tracing priority level.

notify_codes Can be any of the following indicators:

     E   Indicates that the message has also been saved in the error log.

     F   Indicates that the message signaled a fatal error.

mod_ID   Module identification number of the trace message source.

sub_ID   Sub-identification number of the trace message source.

mesg_text Trace message text.

Communicating with the STREAMS Log Driver

Only one **strace** process can access the STREAMS log driver at a time. This restriction is intended to maximize performance. When you issue the **strace** command, the log driver compares the sets of arguments from the command line with actual trace messages, returning the messages that satisfy the criteria to **strace**.

Running **strace** with several sets of arguments can negatively affect STREAMS performance, particularly for those modules/drivers sending the messages returned to the **strace** command.

Also be aware that the **strace** command may not be able to handle a large number of messages. If the STREAMS log driver returns messages to **strace** too quickly, some of the messages may be lost.

Examples

1. To display all trace messages received from the driver/module identified by
    mod_ID **28**, enter:

    strace 28 all all

2. To display those trace messages from the driver/module identified by
    mod_ID **28** and the minor devices identified by the *sub_ID*s **2**, **3**, and **4**,
    enter:

    strace 28 2 all 28 3 all 28 4 all

    Notice that the messages displayed can be of any tracing priority level
    (indicated by the **all** value of the *priority_level* argument).

3. To display those trace messages from the same driver/module and sub-ID,
    but limited to certain priority levels, you could enter:

    strace 28 2 0 28 3 0 28 4 1

    This command specifies that messages from driver/module **28** and sub-IDs
    2 and **3** must have a tracing priority of **0** and those from sub-ID **4** must have
    a tracing priority equal to or less than **1**.

Files

/usr/sbin/strace
>   Specifies the command path.

Related Information

The **log** STREAMS driver.

swapon

Purpose   Specifies additional device for paging and swapping

Synopsis   /usr/sbin/swapon [-a] [-v] [-p] [-l *lowsize*] [-h *highsize*] *filename*

Flags

-a   Activates all swapon devices in the /etc/fstab file

-v   Generates verbose output

-p   The specified swapping file is preferred

-l   The low water mark

-h   The high water mark

Description

The **swapon** command is used to specify additional paging files. Calls to **swapon** normally occur in the system multiuser state initialization. When specified, the **-v** option generates verbose output. The **-p** option is used to specify a preferred paging file. A preferred paging file will be chosen by the operating system to be paged to before a non-preferred file. The **-l** option is used to specify the low water mark. Normally, the **-a** option is used, causing all devices marked as "sw" (swap devices) in the /etc/fstab file to be made available. The **-h** option is used to specify the high water mark. The operating system will not expand the paging file to be larger that then high water mark. If the paging file grows larger that the low water mark, and then shrinks below the low water mark, the operation system will not make the file smaller than the low water mark. The default value for the low water mark is 20Mbytes, the default value for the high water mark is unlimited.

Examples

1. To add the */paging/swapon* file to the paging list, enter:

    swapon /paging/swapon

2. To add the */paging/swapon2* file to the paging list and specify a low water mark of 16Mbytes and a high water mark of 64Mbytes, enter:

    swapon -l 16M -h 64M /paging/swapon2

Files

/usr/sbin/swapon
> Specifies the command path

Notes

There is no way to stop paging and swapping on a device. It is therefore not possible to make use of devices which may be dismounted during system operation.

Related Information

Calls: **swapon(2)**

sync

Purpose   Updates the inode table and writes buffered files to the disk

Synopsis   sync

Description

The **sync** command runs the **sync** system primitive. **sync** writes all unwritten system buffers to disk. This includes modified inodes and delayed block I/O.

Commands that bring the system down, such as the **shutdown** command, issue their own **sync** calls. Use the **sync** command if the system must be stopped under unusual circumstances, to ensure file system integrity.

Note that the writing of unwritten buffers, although scheduled, is not necessarily complete upon return from **sync**. In some cirumstances it may be appropriate to issue consecutive **sync** commands.

Files

/usr/sbin/sync
Specifies the command path

Related Information

Calls: **sync(2)**

sysconfig

Purpose   Modifies the system configuration

Synopsis   **sysconfig** [**-v**] [**-s**] {**-c** I **-u** I **-q**} *name*

Description

The **sysconfig** command is used to modify the subsystem configuration. The **sysconfig** command opens a communications socket to the configuration manager daemon process, **cfgmgr**. It sends the specified command request to the **cfgmgr** and receives output back from the **cfgmgr** by way of the socket.

Flags

-c   Configures the named subsystem into the currently running system. This option requests the **cfgmgr** daemon to load and configure the subsystem *name* into the kernel.

-u   Unconfigures the named subsystem from the currently running system. This option requests the **cfgmgr** daemon to deconfigure and unload the subsystem *name* from the kernel.

-q   Queries information about the named subsystem. This option requests the **cfgmgr** daemon to query information about the configured subsystem *name*.

-v   Requests verbose output from the **cfgmgr**.

-s   Requests that output from the **cfgmgr** be suppressed.

The subsystem *name* parameter is the name of the subsystem as specified in the **/etc/sysconfigtab** configuration database. To list the current subsystem names in the database, use the **/sbin/sysconfigdb** command.

sysconfig(8)

Files

/sbin/sysconfig
> Specifies the command path

/sbin/cfgmgr
> Specifies the configuration daemon command path

/etc/sysconfigtab
> Specifies the configuration database

Related Information

Commands: **cfgmgr(8), sysconfigdb(8)**

Files: **sysconfigtab(4)**

sysconfigdb

Purpose   Maintains the system configuration database

Synopsis   **sysconfigdb** [**-c** *database*] [**-f** *file*] [**-on** | **-off**] [**-a**] [**-d**] [**-l**] [**-u**] [**-p**] *name*

Flags

-a   Adds the named subsystem configuration entry from the named file to the configuration database.

-c *database*

Overrides the default subsystem configuration database with the specified *database*. The default system configuration database is **/etc/sysconfigtab**.

-d   Deletes the named subsystem configuration entry from the configuration database.

-f *file*   Specifies the file containing the named subsystem configuration entry used with the **-a** and **-u** options.

-l   Lists the named subsystem entry from the configuration database.

-p   Lists all subsystem entries in the configuration database.

-u   Updates the named subsystem configuration entry from the named file to the configuration database.

-on   Specifies that the named subsystem should be set to be automatically configured during subsequent system startup.

-off   Specifies that the named subsystem should not be set to be automatically configured during subsequent system startup.

Description

The **sysconfigdb** command is used to maintain the subsystem configuration database.

Files

/sbin/sysconfigdb
Specifies the command path

/etc/sysconfigtab
Specifies the configuration database

Related Information

Commands: **cfgmfr(8)**

Files: **sysconfigtab(4)**, **stanza(4)**

syslogd

Purpose   Logs system messages

Synopsis   **/usr/sbin/syslogd** [**-f** *config_file*] [**-m** *mark_interval*] [**-d**]

The **syslogd** daemon reads and logs messages into a set of files described by the configuration file **/etc/syslog.conf**.

Flags

-d   Turns on debugging.

-f *config_file*
            Specifies an alternate configuration file.

-m *mark_interval*
            Selects the number of minutes between mark messages.

Description

Each message is one line. A message can contain a priority code, marked by a number in angle braces at the beginning of the line. Priorities are defined in <**sys/syslog.h**>. **syslogd** reads from the domain socket **/dev/log** , from an Internet domain socket specified in **/etc/services**, and from the special device **/dev/klog** (to read kernel messages).

syslogd configures when it starts up and whenever it receives a hangup signal. Lines in the configuration file have a **selector** to determine the message priorities to which the line applies and an **action**. The **action** field is separated from the selector by one or more tabs.

Selectors are semicolon separated lists of priority specifiers. Each priority has a **facility** describing the part of the system that generated the message, a dot, and a **level** indicating the severity of the message. Symbolic names may be used. An * (asterisk) selects all facilities. All messages of the specified level or higher (greater severity) are selected. More than one facility may be selected using commas to separate them. For example:

*.emerg;mail,daemon.crit

The preceding command line selects all facilities at the **emerg** level and the **mail** and **daemon** facilities at the **crit** level.

Known facilities and levels recognized by **syslogd** are those listed in **syslog** without the leading **LOG_**. The additional facility **mark** has a message at priority

LOG_INFO sent to it every 20 minutes (this may be changed with the **-m** flag). The **mark** facility is not enabled by a facility field containing an * (asterisk). The level **none** may be used to disable a particular facility. For example:

*.debug;mail.none

Sends all messages except mail messages to the selected file.

The second part of each line describes where the message is to be logged if this line is selected. There are four forms:

- A filename (beginning with a leading / (slash)). The file will be opened in append mode.

- A hostname preceeded by an **@** (at sign). Selected messages are forwarded to the **syslogd** on the named host.

- A comma separated list of users. Selected messages are written to those users if they are logged in.

- An * (asterisk). Selected messages are written to all users who are logged in.

Blank lines and lines beginning with # (number sign) are ignored.

For example:

```
kern,mark.debug          /dev/console
*.notice;mail.info       /var/adm/syslog/mail
*.crit                   /var/adm/syslog/critical
kern.err                 @ucbarpa
*.emerg                  *
*.alert                  eric,kridle
*.alert;auth.warning     ralph
```

The preceding configuration file: logs all kernel messages and 20 minute marks onto the system console, all notice (or higher) level messages and all mail system messages except debug messages into the file **/var/adm/syslog/mail**, and all critical messages are logged into the **/var/adm/syslog/critical** file; kernel messages of error severity or higher are forwarded to **ucbarpa**. All users will be informed of any emergency messages, the users **eric** and **kridle** will be informed of any alert messages, and the user **ralph** will be informed of any alert message, or any warning message (or higher) from the authorization system.

Destinations for logged messages can be specified with full pathnames (beginning with a leading / [slash]). The **syslogd** daemon then opens the specified file(s) in append mode. If the pathname to a **syslogd** log file specified in **syslog.conf** is **/var/adm/syslog.dated**/*file*, **syslogd** inserts a *date* directory, and thus produces a day-by-day account of the messages received, directly above *file* in the directory structure. Typically, you will want to divert messages separately, according to facility, into files such as kern.log, mail.log, lpr.log, and debug.log.

If some pathname other than **/var/adm/syslog.dated/***file* is specified as the pathname to the logfile, **syslogd** does not create the daily *date* directory. For example, if you specify **/var/adm/syslog/mail.log** (without the **.dated** suffix after **syslog**), **syslogd** simply logs messages to the **mail.log** file and allows this file to grow indefinitely.

The **syslogd** daemon acts as a central routing facility for messages whose formats are determined by the programs that produce them. In other words, the message format for error messages and status information is not

The **syslogd** daemon creates the file **/etc/syslog.pid**, if possible, containing a single line with its process ID. This can be used to kill or reconfigure **syslogd.**

To bring **syslogd** down, it should be sent a terminate signal (for example: **kill 'cat /etc/syslog.pid`**).

If no **syslog.conf** configuration file is present, **syslogd** uses the following built-in defaults:

*.ERR	**/dev/console**
*.PANIC	*****

According to these defaults, all error messages are logged on the console and all panic messages (from the kernel) are sent to all logged-in users. No files are written. It is recommended, however, that administrators not use the built-in defaults, and create a **syslog.conf** file with the appropriate specifications.

Files

/usr/sbin/syslogd
> Specifies the command path

/etc/syslog.conf
> Configuration file.

/etc/syslog.pid
> Process ID.

/dev/log The name of the domain datagram log socket.

/dev/klog
> Kernel log device.

Related Information

"Error Logging" in the *OSF/1 System Administrator's Guide*.

talkd

Purpose   The remote communications server for the talk(1) command

Synopsis   **talkd**

talkd notifies users when a **talkd** client wants to initiate a conversation.

Description

The **talkd** server notifies a user or *callee* when a client or *caller* wants to initiate a conversation. The **talkd** daemon sets up the conversation if the callee accepts the invitation. The caller initiates a conversation by executing the **talk** command and specifying the callee. The callee accepts the invitation by executing the **talk** command specifying the caller.

The **talkd** daemon listens at a socket for a **LOOK_UP** request from a local or remote **talk** client. On receiving a **LOOK_UP** request, **talkd** scans its internal invitation table for an entry that pairs the client (the local or remote **talk** process) with a caller.

If an entry exists in the **talkd** daemon's international invitation table, the **talkd** daemon assumes that the client process is the callee. The **talkd** daemon returns the appropriate rendezvous address to the **talk** process for the callee. The callee process then establishes a stream connection with the caller process.

If an entry does not exist in the invitation table, the **talkd** daemon assumes that the client process is the caller. The **talkd** daemon then receives the client process's **ANNOUNCE** request. When **talkd** receives the **ANNOUNCE** request, **talkd** broadcasts an invitation on the console of the remote host where the callee is logged in, unless the caller specifies a particular tty. At approximately 1-minute intervals, **talkd** rebroadcasts the invitation until either the invitation is answered by the callee or the call is cancelled by the caller.

Debugging messages are sent to **syslogd(8)**. For further information on the files used by this daemon, see the **syslogd** command.

Files

/usr/sbin/talkd
Specifies the command path

/etc/services
Defines Internet socket assignments

/var/adm/utmp
Contains data about users who are currently logged in

Notes

The OSF/1 version of **talkd** uses the **talk** 4.3BSD protocol. This command is sometimes referred to as **ntalkd**. It is not compatible with 4.2BSD versions of **talk**.

Related Information

Commands: **inetd(8), syslogd(8), talk(1)**

telnetd

Purpose   The DARPA TELNET protocol server

Synopsis   /usr/sbin/telnetd [-debug [*port*]] [-l] [-D options] [-D report] [-D exercise] [-D netdata] [-D ptydata]

Description

The **telnetd** daemon is a server that supports the DARPA (Defense Advanced Research Projects Agency) standard TELNET virtual terminal protocol. **telnetd** is invoked by the Internet server (see **inetd**(8)) normally for requests to connect to the TELNET port as indicated by the /etc/services file (see **services**(5)). The **-debug** may be used, to start up **telnetd** manually, instead of through **inetd**(8). If started up this way, *port* may be specified to run **telnetd** on an alternate TCP port number.

The **-D options** may be used for debugging purposes. This allows **telnet** to print out debugging information to the connection, allowing the user to see what **telnetd** is doing. There are several modifiers: **options** prints information about the negotiation of TELNET options, **report** prints the **options** information, plus some additional information about what processing is going on , **netdata** displays the data stream received by **telnetd**, **ptydata** displays data written to the pty, and **exercise** has not been implemented yet.

The **telnetd** daemon operates by allocating a pseudoterminal device (see **pty**(4)) for a client, then creating a login process that has the slave side of the pseudoterminal as **stdin**, **stdout**, and **stderr**. **telnetd** manipulates the master side of the pseudo-terminal, implementing the TELNET protocol and passing characters between the remote client and the login process.

When a TELNET session is started up, **telnetd** sends TELNET options to the client side, indicating a willingness to do remote echo of characters, to suppress go ahead, to do remote flow control, and to receive terminal type information, terminal speed information, and window size information from the remote client. If the remote client is willing, the remote terminal type is propagated in the environment of the created login process. The pseudoterminal allocated to the client is configured to operate in cooked mode, and with **XTABS** and **CRMOD** enabled (see **tty**(4)).

The **telnetd** daemon is willing to do: echo, binary, suppress go ahead, and timing mark. **Telnetd** is willing to have the remote client do: line mode, binary, terminal type, terminal speed, window size, toggle flow control, environment, X display location, and suppress go ahead.

The **telnetd** daemon never sends TELNET *go ahead* commands.

Note that binary mode has no common interpretation except between similar operating systems (Unix compatible systems in this case).

Note also that the terminal type name received from the remote client is converted to lowercase.

Cautions

Some **Telnet** commands are only partially implemented.

Because of bugs in the original 4.2BSD **telnet(1)**, **telnetd** performs some dubious protocal exchanges to try to discover if the remote client is, in fact, a 4.2BSD **telnet (1)**.

Files

/usr/sbin/telnetd
Specifies the command path

Related Information

telnet (1)

tftpd

Purpose   The DARPA Trivial File Transfer Protocol server

Synopsis   **tftpd** [*directory* ...]

Description

The **tftpd** daemon is a server that supports the DARPA (Defense Advanced Research Projects Agency) Trivial File Transfer Protocol. The TFTP server operates at the port indicated in the **tftp** service description; see **services(4).** The server is normally started by **inetd(8).**

The use of **tftp** does not require an account or password on the remote system. Due to the lack of authentication information, **tftpd** will allow only publicly readable files to be accessed. Files may be written only if they already exist and are publicly writable. Note that this extends the concept of ''public'' to include all users on all hosts that can be reached through the network; this may not be appropriate on all systems, and its implication should be considered before enabling **tftp** service. The server should have the user ID with the lowest possible privilege.

Access to files may be restricted by invoking **tftpd** with a list of directories and including pathnames as server program arguments in **/etc/inetd.conf**. In this case, access is restricted to files whose names are prefixed by the one of the given directories.

Files

/usr/sbin/tftpd
Specifies the command path

Related Information

Commands: **tftp(1)**

Daemons: **inetd(8)**

timed

Purpose   Controls the time server daemon at system startup

Synopsis   **/usr/sbin/timed** [**-tM**] [**-n** *network*] [**-i** *network*]

The **timed** daemon is the time server daemon.

Flags

-**i** *network*
> Specifies networks to be excluded from clock synchronization.

-M   Specifies that a machine can become the time server if the master time server becomes inoperative.

-**n** *network*
> Specifies networks to be included in clock syncronization.

-t   Enables tracing of messages received in **/usr/adm/timed.log**.

Description

The **timed** daemon is normally invoked at boot time by an entry in the **inittab** file. The **timed** daemon synchronizes the host's clock with those of other machines on the local area network that are also running the **timed** daemon. The **timed** daemon slows the clocks of some machines and speeds up the clocks on other machines to create an average network time. The average network time is computed from measurements of clock differences using the ICMP (Internet Control Message Protocol) timestamp request message.

The service provided by **timed** is based on a master/slave (client/server) scheme. When **timed** is started on a machine, it asks the master **timed** daemon for the network time and sets the host's clock to that time. After that, the host accepts synchronization messages periodically sent by the master and calls the **adjtime** system call to perform the needed corrections on the host's clock.

The **timed** daemon also communicates with **date** in order to set the date globally, and with **timedc**, the **timed** control program.

If the machine running the master ceases to function, a machine that is running the **timed** daemon with the **-M** flag becomes the new master **timed** daemon.

timed(8)

Files

/usr/sbin/timed
Specifies the command path

/var/adm/timed.log
Contains messages traced for the **timed** command

/var/adm/timed.masterlog
Contains the log file for master **timed**

Related Information

Commands: **date(1)**, **timedc(8)**

Calls: **adjtime(3)**, **gettimeofday(3)**

timedc

Purpose   Controls the timed daemon

Synopsis   **timedc** [*command* [*argument* ...]]

The **timedc**, or **timed** control program, controls the operation of the **timed(8)** daemon.

Description

The **timedc** program can be used to

-     Measure the differences between machines' clocks.

-     Find the location of the master time server.

-     Enable or disable tracing of messages received by the **timed** daemon.

-     Debug.

Without any arguments, **timedc** prompts for commands from the standard input. If arguments are supplied, **timedc** interprets the first argument as a command and the remaining arguments as arguments to the command. The standard input may be redirected, causing **timedc** to read commands from a file.

Subcommands

Subcommands may be abbreviated. Recognized commands are

? [*command* ...] / help [*command* ...]
Prints a short description of each command specified in the argument list, or, if no arguments are given, prints a list of the recognized commands.

clockdiff *host* ...
Computes the differences between the clock of the host machine and the clocks of the machines given as arguments.

trace { on | off }
Enables or disables the tracing of incoming messages to **timed** in the file **/var/adm/timed.log**.

quit   Exits from **timedc**.

msite   Reports the hostname of the master **timed** server in use.

timedc(8)

Files

/usr/sbin/timedc
> Specifies the command path

/var/adm/timed.log
> Tracing file for **timed**

/var/adm/timed.masterlog
> Log file for master **timed**

Related Information

Commands: **date(1)**, **timed(8)**

Calls: **adjtime(3)**

trpt

Purpose   Transliterates protocol trace

Synopsis   **trpt** [-**afjst**] [-**p** *address*] *system core*

The **trpt** command, used for debugging sockets, queries the buffer of Transmission Control Protocol (TCP) trace records.

Flags

-a   Print the values of the source and destination addresses for each packet recorded, in addition to the normal output.

-f   Follows the trace as it occurs, waiting briefly for additional records each time the end of the log is reached.

-j   Lists the protocol control block addresses for which trace records exist.

-p *address*
                Shows only trace records associated with the protocol control block specified in hexadecimal by the *address* variable.

                You must include a space between the **-p** flag and the *address* variable when you specify this flag.

-s   Prints a detailed description of the packet-sequencing information, in addition to the normal output.

-t   Prints the values for all timers at each point in the trace, in addition to the normal output.

Description

The TCP trace record buffer is created when a socket is marked for debugging with the **setsockopt(2)** subroutine. The **trpt** command queries the buffer and then prints a description of the trace records.

When you specify no options, the **trpt** command prints all the trace records found in the system and groups them according to their TCP/IP connection Protocol Control Block (PCB).

trpt(8)

If you are debugging a system or core file other than the default, the *system* and *core* arguments can be used to replace the defaults.

Before you can use the **trpt** command, you must do the following:

1. Isolate the problem and mark for debugging the socket or sockets involved in the connection.

2. Find the address of the protocol control blocks associated with these sockets by using the **netstat -aA** command.

3. Then, you can run the **trpt** command, using the **-p** flag to supply the associated protocol control block addresses. You can specify multiple **-p** *address* flags with a single **trpt** command.

The **-f** flag can be used to follow the trace log once it is located. The **-j** flag can be used to check for the presence of trace records for the socket in question.

If the system image does not contain the proper symbols to find the trace buffer, the **trpt** command cannot succeed.

Files

/usr/sbin/trpt Specifies the command path

Related Information

Commands: **netstat(1)**

Calls: **setsockopt(2)**

tunefs

Purpose   Tune up an existing UFS file system

Synopsis   **/usr/sbin/tunefs** *options special* | *file_system*

Description

The **tunefs** command changes the dynamic parameters of a UFS file system which affect the layout policies. The parameters which are to be changed are indicated by the flags given below:

-a *maxcontig*   This specifies the maximum number of contiguous blocks that will be laid out before forcing a rotational delay (see the **-d** flag). The default value is one, since most device drivers require an interrupt per disk transfer. Device drivers that can chain several buffers together in a single transfer should set this to the maximum chain length.

-d *rotdelay*   This specifies the expected time (in milliseconds) to service a transfer completion interrupt and initiate a new transfer on the same disk. It is used to decide how much rotational spacing to place between successive blocks in a file.

-e *maxbpg*   This indicates the maximum number of blocks any single file can allocate out of a cylinder group before it is forced to begin allocating blocks from another cylinder group. Typically this value is set to about one quarter of the total blocks in a cylinder group. The intent is to prevent any single file from using up all the blocks in a single cylinder group, thus degrading access times for all files subsequently allocated in that cylinder group. The effect of this limit is to cause big files to do long seeks more frequently than if they were allowed to allocate all the blocks in a cylinder group before seeking elsewhere. For file systems with exclusively large files, this parameter should be set higher.

-m *minfree*   This value specifies the percentage of space held back from normal users; the minimum free space threshold. The default value used is 10%. This value can be set to zero, however up to a factor of three in throughput will be lost over the performance obtained at a 10% threshold. Note that if the value is raised above the current usage level, users will be unable to allocate files until enough files have been deleted to get under the higher threshold.

tunefs(8)

-o *optimization preference*

The file system can either try to minimize the time spent allocating blocks, or it can attempt minimize the space fragmentation on the disk. If the value of minfree (see above) is less than 10%, then the file system should optimize for space to avoid running out of full sized blocks. For values of minfree greater than or equal to 10%, fragmentation is unlikely to be problematical, and the file system can be optimized for time.

Bugs

This program should work on mounted and active file systems. Because the superblock is not kept in the buffer cache, the changes will only take effect if the program is run on unmounted file systems.

The system must be rebooted after the **root** file system is tuned. You must be **root** to use this command.

Files

/usr/sbin/tunefs

Specifies the command path

Related Information

Commands: **newfs(8)**

turnacct

Purpose   Provides an interface to the **accton** command to turn process accounting on or off, or to create a new **/var/adm/pacct**n process accounting file.

See **acct(8)**

umount

Purpose   Unmounts file systems

See **mount(8)**

update

Purpose   Periodically updates the superblock

Synopsis   **update**

Description

The **update** command executes a **sync** system call every 30 seconds. This ensures that the file system is up to date in the event of a system crash. This command is provided as a script in **/sbin**.

The **cron** program also provides the functionality of the **update** command. The **update** shell script typically provides the following functionality:

```
#!/bin/sh
while true
do
     sync
     sleep 30
done &
exit 0
```

Files

/usrsbin/update
        Specifies the command path

Related Information

Commands: **cron(8)**, **init(8)**, **sync(8)**

Call: **sync(2)**

uucheck

Purpose   Check for files and directories required by uucp

Synopsis   **uucheck** [**-v**] [**-x***debug_level*]

The **uucheck** command verifies the presence of the files and directories required by the **uucp** program.

Flags

    -v   Displays a detailed explanation of how the **uucp** program interprets the permissions file.

    -x *debug_level*

        Displays debugging information. The valid range for *debug_level* is 0 to 9. The higher the number, the more detailed the final report.

Description

In addition to checking for the presence of files required by the **uucp** program, the **uucheck** command also checks for some errors in the **/usr/lbin/uucp/Permissions** file.

The **uucheck** command does not check for correct file and directory modes or for errors in the **/usr/lbin/uucp/Permissions** file, such as duplicate login or machine names.

When the **uucp** program is installed, **uucheck** verifies that the directories, programs, and support files required to operate the networking facility are present. The command is executed automatically, as one of the first steps in the installation process, before the required **uucp** directories,
 programs, and files are actually installed.

Issue the **uucheck** command from the command line after installing **uucp**, configuring **uucp** for your site, or making changes in part of the **uucp** program, such as the **/usr/lbin/uucp/Permissions** file.

Note that the **uucheck** command can only be issued from the command line if you have superuser authority.

Examples

1. To find out how the **uucp** program interprets the **/usr/lbin/uucp/Permissions** file, enter:

    uucheck -v

    The **-v** flag instructs the **uucheck** command to verify that the **uucp** files exist and displays a detailed explanation of how the **uucp** programs interpret the permissions file.

2. To set the debug level to 8, enter:

    uucheck -x8

Files

/usr/lbin/uucp/uucheck
>   Specifies the command path

/usr/lbin/uucp/Devices
>   Information about available devices

/usr/lbin/uucp/Maxuuscheds
>   Limits scheduled jobs

/usr/lbin/uucp/Maxuuxqts
>   Limits remote command executions

/usr/lbin/uucp/Permissions
>   Describes access permissions for remote systems

/usr/lbin/uucp/Systems
>   Describes accessible remote systems

/var/spool/uucp/*
>   Spooling directory

/var/spool/uucppublic/*
>   Public directory

/etc/locks/LCK/*nn*
>   Prevents multiple use of device

Related Information

Commands: **uucico(8)**, **uusched(8)**, **uucp(1)**, **uustat(1)**, **uuto(1)**, and **uux(1)**

uucico

Purpose   Transfers uucp command, data, and execute files to remote systems

Synopsis   **uucico** [-r*role_number*][-x*debug_level*] -s*system_name*

The **uucico** daemon transfers files queued by the **uucp** and **uux** commands between systems.

Flags

-r*role_number*
> The *role_number*s are **1** for server mode and **0** (zero) for client mode. The default is **0** (zero). If **uucico** is started manually, set this flag to **1**.

-s*system_name*
> The name of the remote system. Use only when starting **uucico** manually. The *system_name* is supplied internally when **uucico** is started automatically.
>
> Note that system names must contain only ASCII characters.

-x*debug_level* Displays debugging information on the screen of the local terminal. The valid range for *debug_level* is 0 to 9. The higher the number, the more detailed the final report. This flag is useful in correcting problems with the **expect_send** sequence in the **Systems** file.

Description

The **uucico** daemon transports **uucp Command (C.*)**, **Data (D.*)**, and **Execute (E.*)** files created by the **uucp** and **uux** commands to a specified remote system. Both the local and remote systems run the **uucico** daemon, and the two daemons communicate with each other to complete transfer requests.

The **uucico** daemon performs the following actions:

-     Scans the spooling directory (**/var/spool/uucp**/*system_name*) on the local system for transfer requests.

-     Selects the device used for the communications connection after checking the **/usr/lbin/uucp/Devices** file and the lock files in the **/etc/locks** directory.

-     Places a call to the specified remote system using information in the **Systems**, **Dialers**, and **Dialcodes** files located in the **/usr/lbin/uucp** directory.

- Performs the required login sequence specified in the **Systems** file.

- Checks permissions listed in the **/usr/lbin/uucp/Permissions** file.

- Checks scheduling limits in the **Maxuuscheds** and **Maxuuxqts** files located in the **/usr/lbin/uucp** directory.

- Runs all transfer requests from both the local and the remote system, placing the transferred files in the public directories (**/var/spool/uucppublic/***).

- Logs transfer requests and completions in files in the **/var/spool/uucp/.Log/uucico** directory.

- Notifies specified users of transfer requests.

Usually the **uucico** daemon is called by the **uucp** and **uux** commands when needed, and is started periodically by the **uucp** scheduling daemon, **uusched**, which is started by the **cron** daemon.

The **uucico** daemon can be started from the command line for debugging. The **uucp** commands **uutry**, **Uutry**, **Nutry**, and **uukick** also start **uucico** with debugging turned on.

In the case of a **uux** command request for the execution of a command on a remote system, the **uucico** daemon transfers the files, and the **uuxqt** daemon executes the command on the remote system.

Examples

1. To start the **uucico** daemon from the command line as a background process and contact the remote system **hera** , enter:

    /usr/lbin/uucp/uucico -r1 -shera &

2. To debug **uucico** connections, start the **uucico** daemon with the **-x** flag, and enter:

    /usr/lbin/uucp/uucico -r1 -svenus -x9

Files

/usr/lbin/uucp/uucico
Specifies the command path

/usr/lbin/uucp
The **uucp** configuration files

/etc/locks
Contains lock files that prevent multiple uses of devices and multiple calls to systems

/usr/lbin/uucp
Contains all the configuration files for uucp

/usr/lbin/uucp/Devices
Contains information about available devices

/usr/lbin/uucp/Dialcodes
Contains dial-code abbreviations

/usr/lbin/uucp/Dialers
Specifies initial handshaking on a link

/usr/lbin/uucp/Maxuuscheds
Limits scheduled jobs

/usr/lbin/uucp/Maxuuxqts
Limits remote command executions

/usr/lbin/uucp/Permissions
Describes access permissions for remote systems

/usr/lbin/uucp/Systems
Describes accessible remote systems

/var/spool/uucp/.Admin/errors
Lists **uucico** daemon errors that uucp cannot correct

/var/spool/uucp/.Log/uucico
Contains **uucico** daemon log files

/var/spool/uucp/.Status/_system_name_
Lists the last time a remote system was contacted and the minimum time until the next retry

/var/spool/uucp/_system_name_
Contains **C.***, **D.***, and **E.*** files to be transferred by the **uucico** daemon

/var/spool/uucp/_system_name_**/C.***
Command files

/var/spool/uucp/_system_name_/**D.***
> Data files

/var/spool/uucp/_system_name_/**E.***
> Execute files

/var/spool/uucppublic/*
> Contains files after transfer by the **uucico** daemon

Related Information

Commands: **cron(8), uucp(1), uukick, uustat(1), uutry, uuto(1), uux(8)**

uucleanup

Purpose   Deletes selected old files from the uucp spool directory

Synopsis   **uucleanup** program [-C*days*] [-D*days*] [-m*string*] [-o*days*] [-s*system*] [-T*days*] [-W*days*] [-X*days*]

The **uucleanup** program removes outdated files from **/var/spool/uucp**.

Flags

Unless a *days* argument is specified with one of the following flags, **uucleanup** uses the default *days* value listed.

-C*days*   Removes any **C.***(Command) files as old as or older than the number of days specified by *days*, and sends appropriate information to the requester. The default *days* is 7 days. The **-C** and **-W** flags cannot be combined.

-D*days*   Removes any **D.***(Data) files as old as or older than the number of days specified in *days*. Also attempts to deliver any remaining mail messages. The default *days* is 7 days.

-m*string* Includes a specified line of text in the warning message generated by the **-W** flag. The default line is:

```
See your local administrator to locate the problem.
```

The **-m** flag can be used only with the **-W** flag.

-o*days*   Removes files in addition to those specified by the **-C**, **-D**, and **-X** flags that are as old as or older than the number of days specified in *days*. The default *days* is 2 days.

-s*system* Executes **uucleanup** only on the spool directory specified by *system*. The default is to clean up all uucp spool directories.

Note that system names can contain only ASCII characters.

-T*days*   Removes **TM.*** (Temporary) files as old as or older than the number of days specified by the *days* argument. Also attempts to deliver any remaining mail messages. The default *days* is 7 days.

-W*days*   Sends a mail message to the requester warning that **C*.** files as old as or older than the number of days specified in *days* are still in the spool directory. The message includes the job ID and, in the case of mail, the mail message. The administrator may use the **-m** flag to include a message line telling who to call to check the problem. The default *days* is 1 day.

-X*days*   Removes any **X.***(Execute) files as old as or older than the number of days specified in *days*. The default *days* is 2 days.

Note that unless one of the *days* arguments is set to a specific number of days, the **uucleanup** command uses the default *days* values.

Description

The **uucleanup** program scans the spool directory (**/var/spool/uucp**) for old files and takes appropriate action to remove them in a useful way. The **uucleanup** command performs the following tasks:

- Informs the requester of send/receive requests for systems that cannot be reached.

- Warns users about requests that wait more than a specified number of days (the default is 1 day).

- Returns mail that cannot be delivered to the sender.

- Removes all other files older than a specified number of days from the spool directory.

The **uucleanup** program is not usually invoked from the command line, but is executed by the shell procedure **uudemon.cleanup** located in **/usr/lbin/uucp**, which in turn is started by the **cron** script located in **/var/adm/cron/crontabs/uucp**. Only someone with superuser privileges can issue the **uucleanup** command from the command line.

To enable automatic cleanup, edit the file **/var/admn/cron/crontabs/uucp**. Remove the # (number sign) from the beginning of the **uudemon.cleanup** line.

Examples

1.   To locate files, enter:

uucleanup -W2

This form of the command locates **C.*** (Command) files 2 or more days old and warns the requesters that the files have not been sent.

2.   To send a message with a warning, enter:

uucleanup -W -mContact the System Administrator

This form of the command locates **C.*** (Command) files 1 or more days old (the default), warns requesters their files have not been sent, and gives them the message:

```
Contact the System Administrator about these files.
```

3.   To clean up command files, enter:

uucleanup -C8

This form of the command removes all **C.*** (Command) files 8 or more days old and sends an appropriate message to the requesters.

4.   To clean up data and execute files, enter:

uucleanup -D -X3

This form of the command removes all **D.*** (Data) files 7 or more days old (the default) and all **X.*** (Execute) files older than 3 days, and attempts to deliver all undelivered mail.

5.   To clean up other files, enter:

uucleanup -o

This form of the command removes uucp request files other than **C.***, **D.***, and **X.*** files if the files are 2 or more days old (the default).

6.   To clean up all files at once, enter:

uucleanup -C -D -X -o

This form of the command removes all **C.***, **D.***, and **X.*** files, and all other files older than the default times.

7.   To clean up files for system **hera**, enter:

uucleanup -shera -C

This form of the command removes all **C.*** files 7 or more days old (the default) from system **hera**.

Files

/usr/lbin/uucp/uucleanup
>   Specifies the command path

usr/sbin/cron
>   File that starts **uudemon.cleanup**

/usr/lbin/uucp
>   Contains all the configuration files for uucp, and the **uudemon.cleanup** shell procedure

/var/adm/cron/crontabs/uucp
>   Schedules uucp jobs for the **cron** daemon, including the **uudemon.cleanup** shell procedure

/var/spool/uucp/*
>   Contains files removed by the **uucleanup** command

Related Information

Commands: **cron(8)**, **uucp(1)**, **uustat(1)**, **uux(8)**

uucpd

Purpose   Manages communications between the uucp program and TCP/IP

Synopsis   **uucpd**

Description

The **uucpd** daemon cannot be started directly from the command line; instead, this daemon enables uucp connections via TCP/IP.

The **uucpd** daemon is started at system initialization or by the **inetd** daemon. The daemon runs as a background process on all the networked systems before the uucp program can use the TCP/IP system to communicate.

Files

/usr/lbin/uucp/uucpd
        Specifies the command path

/usr/lbin/uucp
        Directory containing the uucp configuration files

/etc/services
        Defines Internet socket assignments used by TCP/IP

/etc/hosts
        Contains the hostname table used by TCP/IP

/usr/lbin/uucp/Devices
        Contains information about available devices

/usr/lbin/uucp/Permissions
        Contains access permission codes for remote systems

/usr/lbin/uucp/Systems
        Lists accessible remote systems

Related Information

Commands: **inetd(8)**

uusched

Purpose   Schedules work for the file transport program

Synopsis   **uusched** [-**u**_DebugLevel_] [-**x**_DebugLevel_]

Flags

-**u**_DebugLevel_

Passes as the -**x**_DebugLevel_ flag to the **uucico** daemon. The _DebugLevel_ variable is a number from 0 to 9, with a default of 5. Higher numbers give more detailed debugging information, which is displayed on the screen of the local system

-**x**_DebugLevel_

Outputs debugging messages from the **uusched** daemon. The _DebugLevel_ variable is a number from 0 to 9, with a default of 5. Higher numbers give more detailed debugging information, which is displayed on the screen of the local system

Description

The **uusched** daemon schedules work for the **uucp** file transport program, **uucico**. It schedules the transfer of files that are queued in the **/var/spool/uucp/**_SystemName_ directory. The scheduling daemon first randomizes the work and then starts the **uucico** daemon, which transfers the files. The **uusched** daemon is usually started by the **uudemon.hour** command, a shell procedure, which is run periodically by the **cron** daemon. The **uusched** daemon can also be started from the command line for debugging purposes.

Example

To start the **uusched** daemon from the command line, enter:

/usr/lbin/uucp/uusched &

uusched(8)

Files

/usr/lbin/uucp/uusched
Specifies the command path

Related Information

Daemons: **cron, uucico(8)**
Commands: **uucp, uudemon.hour, uustat(1), uux(1)**

vgchange

Purpose   Sets the availability of a volume group to yes or no

Synopsis   **vgchange -a** *Availability* [**-l**] [**-p**] [**-s**] *VolumeGroupName*

Flags

-a *Availability*

Sets the availability of the volume group. The *Availability* parameter is represented by one of the following:

y   Makes a volume group available.

n   Makes a volume group temporarily unavailable.

-l   Disables the open of the logical volumes that belongs to the volume group.

-p   Activates the volume group only if all of the physical volumes that belong to it are available.

-s   Disables the synchronization of the stale physical extents within the volume group specified with the *VolumeGroupName* parameter. This flag only makes sense when **-a y** is specified.

Description

The **vgchange** command activates or deactivates one or more volume groups. The change depends on the value specified by the **-a** flag; namely, **y** or **n**.

The **vgchange -a n** command deactivates the *VolumeGroupName* and its associated logical volumes. You must close the logical volumes prior to invoking the **vgchange -a n** command. For example, if the logical volume contains a file system, you must unmount the filesystem.

The **vgchange -a y** command activates the *VolumeGroupName*, and all associated physical and logical volumes. When a volume group is activated, it is available for use, its logical volumes are available, and its physical extents are synchronized (if they are stale). However, if you included the **-s** flag on the command line, synchronization does not occur. If the program can not access a physical volume, it lists the volume's status as missing. If too many physical volumes in the volume group are missing, the program notifies you that the group does not have a quorum and cannot be activated. The **-p** flag allows you to activate the volume group only if all of the physical volumes belonging to the volume group are available. If the

-l flag is set, later attempts to open the logical volumes will fail. To make an open of these logical volumes succeed, the command **lvchange -a y** must be executed.

Examples

1.   To activate the volume group vg03, enter:

   vgchange -a y /dev/vg03

2.   To deactivate the volume group vg03, enter:

   vgchange -a n /dev/vg03

3.   To activate volume group vg03 without synchronizing extents that are not current, enter:

   vgchange -a y-s /dev/vg03

Files

   /usr/sbin/vgchange
      Specifies the command path

Related Information

   Commands: **vgcreate(8)**, **umount(8)**, **vgdisplay(8)**, **vgextend(8)**, **vgreduce(8)**

vgcreate

Purpose   Creates a volume group

Synopsis   **vgcreate** [**-x** *Extensibility*] [**-e** *MaxPhysicalExtents*] [**-l** *MaxLogicalVolumes*] [**-p** *MaxPhysicalVolumes*] [**-s** *PhysicalExtentSize*] [**-v** *VGDA*] *VolumeGroupName PhysicalVolumePath ...*

Flags

> **-x** *Extensibility*
>> Sets the allocation permission for adding physical extents on the physical volumes specified by the *PhysicalVolumePath* parameter. The *Extensibility* parameter is represented by one of the following:
>>
>> **y**   Allows the allocation of additional physical extents on the physical volume.
>>
>> **n**   Prohibits the allocation of additional physical extents on the physical volume. The logical volumes that reside on the physical volume can still be accessed, after the volume group has been activated with the **vgchange -a y** command.
>
> The default for *Extensibility* is **y**.
>
> **-e** *MaxPhysicalExtents*
>> Sets the maximum number of physical extents that can be allocated from any of the physical volumes in the volume group.
>>
>> The default for *MaxPhysicalExtents* is **1016**
>
> **-l** *MaxLogicalVolumes*
>> Sets the maximum number of logical volumes that the volume group is allowed to contain.
>>
>> The default for *MaxLogicalVolumes* is **255**.
>
> **-p** *MaxPhysicalVolumes*
>> Sets the maximum number of physical volumes that the volume group is allowed to contain.
>>
>> The default for *MaxPhysicalVolumes* is **32**.

-s *PhysicalExtentSize*

> Sets the number of megabytes in each physical extent, where *PhysicalExtentSize* is expressed in units of megabytes from 1 through 256. *PhysicalExtentSize* must be equal to a power of 2 (for example, 1, 2, 4, 8).

> The default for *PhysicalExtentSize* is **1** megabyte.

-v *VGDA* This option allows you to specify if a VGDA (Volume Group Descriptor Area) of the volume group has to be stored on the physical volume(s).

> A VGDA is always stored on the first physical volume specified. This flag impacts only the second, third, and so on, physical volumes specified. *VGDA* is represented by one of the following:

> **y**   Allows the creation of a VGDA on the physical volume.

> **n**   Prohibits the creation of a VGDA on the physical volume.

> The default for *VGDA* is **y**.

Description

The **vgcreate** command creates a new volume group. *VolumeGroupName* is a symbolic name for the volume group and must be used by all references to it. *VolumeGroupName* is the path to a directory-entry under **/dev** which must contain a character special file named **group**. Except for the **group** entry, the directory *VolumeGroupName* should not contain any other entries.

The **vgcreate** command leaves the volume group in an active state.

Before assigning a physical volume to a volume group, the physical volume has to be created with the **pvcreate** command.

If **vgcreate** fails to install the first specified physical volume into the volume group, the volume group is not created. If, for any reason, one of the remaining specified physical volumes cannot be installed into the volume group, an error message is printed, but the installation continues to the end of the list of physical volumes.

Examples

1. To create a volume group named /dev/my_vg that contains three physical volumes, with extent size set to 2 megabytes, enter:

    vgcreate -s 2 /dev/my_vg /dev/hdisk3 /dev/hdisk5 /dev/hdisk6

    If the directory /dev/my_vg exists with the character special file **group**, the volume group will be created.

2.   To create a volume group named /dev/user_vg that can contain a maximum
      of three logical volumes, with extent size set to 8 megabytes, enter:

      vgcreate -l 3 -s 8 /dev/user_vg /dev/hdisk3

      A new volume group, /dev/user_vg is created with extent size equal to 8
      megabytes.

Files

/usr/sbin/vgcreate
      Specifies the command path

Related Information

Commands: **pvcreate(8), vgchange(8), vgdisplay(8), vgextend(8), vgreduce(8)**

vgdisplay

Purpose   Displays information about volume groups

Synopsis   **vgdisplay** [**-v**] [*VolumeGroupName* ...]

Flags

-v   Lists additional information for each logical volume and for each physical volume on the volume group:

Logical volumes:
Lists information about logical volumes belonging to *VolumeGroupName*.

LV Name:
Name of the logical volume within the volume group.

LV Status:
State of the logical volume. Open/stale indicates the logical volume is open but contains extents that are not current. Open/syncd indicates the logical volume is open and synchronized. Closed indicates the logical volume has not been opened.

Total LE:
Number of logical extents in the logical volume.

Used PE:
Number of physical extents used by the logical volume.

Used PV:
Number of physical volumes used by the logical volume.

Physical volumes:
Lists information about physical volumes belonging to *VolumeGroupName*.

PV Name:
Name of the physical volume within the group.

PV status:
State of the physical volume.

Total PE:

Total number of physical extents on the physical volume.

Free PE:

Number of free physical extents on the physical volume.

Description

The **vgdisplay** command displays information about volume groups. If you use *VolumeGroupName,* only the information for that volume group is displayed. If you do not use *VolumeGroupName* a list of the names of all defined volume groups is displayed. If the **-v** (verbose) flag is not specified, only the following information is displayed:

VG Name:

Name of the volume group.

VG Status:

State of the volume group.

If the volume group is activated with the **vgchange -a y** command, the state is on. If the volume group is deactivated with the **vgchange -a n** command, the state is off.

Max LV:

Maximum number of logical volumes allowed in the volume group.

Cur LV: Current number of logical volumes within the volume group.

Open LV:

Number of logical volumes within the volume group that are currently open.

Max PV:

Maximum number of physical volumes allowed in the volume group.

Cur PV: Current number of physical volumes within the volume group.

Active PV:

Number of physical volumes that are currently active.

PE Size: Size of each physical extent.

Max PE per PV:
Maximum number (limit) of physical extents that can be allocated from any of the physical volumes in the volume group.

Total PE:
Total number of physical extents within the volume group: this is the sum of the number of physical extents belonging to each available physical volume in the volume group.

Alloc PE:
Number of physical extents currently allocated to logical volumes.

Free PE:
Number of physical extents not allocated.

VGDA: Number of volume group descriptor areas within the volume group.

Examples

1. To display information about all the volume groups within the system, enter:

    vgdisplay

2. To display all of the information about volume group vg02, enter:

    vgdisplay -v /dev/vg02

    The characteristics and status of both the logical and physical extents of volume group vg02 are displayed.

Files

/usr/sbin/vgdisplay
Specifies the command path

Related Information

Commands: **lvdisplay(8)**, **pvdisplay(8)**, **vgchange(8)**, **vgcreate(8)**

vgextend

Purpose   Extend a volume group by adding physical volumes to it

Synopsis   **vgextend** [**-x** *Extensibility*] [**-v** *VGDA*] *VolumeGroupName PhysicalVolumePath* ...

Flags

-**x** *Extensibility*

Sets the allocation permission for additional physical extents on the physical volume specified by the *PhysicalVolumePath* parameter. The *Extensibility* parameter is represented by one of the following:

y   Allows the allocation of additional physical extents on the physical volume.

n   Prohibits the allocation of additional physical extents on the physical volume. The logical volumes that reside on the physical volume can still be accessed.

The default for *Extensibility* is **y**.

-**v** *VGDA* This option allows you to specify if a VGDA (Volume Group Descriptor Area) of the volume group must be stored on the physical volume. *VGDA* is represented by one of the following:

y   Allows the creation of a VGDA on the physical volume.

n   Prohibits the creation of a VGDA on the physical volume.

The default for *VGDA* is **y**.

Description

The **vgextend** assigns physical volumes to the *VolumeGroupName*. The volume group must be active.

You extend the volume group by adding one or more physical volumes represented by the *PhysicalVolumePath* parameter(s).

After the physical volumes have been successfully added to the volume group, they can be used.

Before assigning a physical volume to a volume group, you must create the physical volume with the **pvcreate** command.

If, for any reason, one of the remaining specified physical volumes cannot be installed into the volume group, an error message is printed. However, the installation continues to the end of the list of physical volumes.

Examples

1. To add physical volumes hdisk03 and hdisk08 to volume group vg03, enter:

    vgextend /dev/vg03 /dev/hdisk03 /dev/hdisk08

    The physical volumes hdisk03 and hdisk08 now belong to volume group vg03.

Files

/usr/sbin/vgextend
> Specifies the command path

Related Information

Commands: **pvchange(8)**, **pvcreate(8)**, **vgchange(8)**, **vgcreate(8)**, **vgdisplay(8)**

vgreduce

Purpose   Reduce a volume group by removing one or more physical volumes from it

Synopsis   **vgreduce** *VolumeGroupName PhysicalVolumePath ...*

Description

The **vgreduce** command removes the physical volume(s) specified with the *PhysicalVolumePath* parameter from *VolumeGroupName*.

All but one physical volume can be removed. The last physical volume must remain in the volume group so that the logical volume driver can continue to operate. The last physical volume in the volume group will be removed by the **vgremove** command.

All logical volumes residing on the physical volume(s) represented by the *PhysicalVolumePath* parameter must be removed by executing the **lvremove** command before executing the **vgreduce** command.

Examples

1.   To remove physical volume hdisk1 from volume group vg01, enter:

vgreduce /dev/vg01 /dev/hdisk1

The physical volume hdisk1 no longer belongs to volume group vg01.

Files

/usr/sbin/vgreduce
      Specifies the command path

Related Information

Commands: **lvremove(8)**, **vgchange(8)**, **vgcreate(8)**, **vgdisplay(8)**, **vgextend(8)**

vgremove

Purpose   Removes the definition of one or more volume groups from the system

Synopsis   **vgremove** *VolumeGroupName ...*

Description

The **vgremove** command removes from the system the last physical volume of the volume group and the definition of the volume group(s) specified with the *VolumeGroupName* parameter. Since all system knowledge of the volume group and its contents are removed, you can no longer access that volume group.

All logical volumes residing on the last physical volume must be removed by executing the **lvremove** command before executing the **vgremove** command.

The **vgremove** command is the (effective) inverse of the **vgcreate** command called with one physical volume.

Before removing a volume group, you must do two things:

1.   Remove all but one of the logical volumes belonging to the group with the **lvremove** command.

2.   Remove the physical volumes belonging to the volume group with the **vgreduce** command.

Examples

1.   To remove volume group vg02 from the system, enter:

vgremove/dev/vg02

The definition of vg02 is removed from the system and the volume group cannot be accessed.

Files

/usr/sbin/vgremove
Specifies the command path

Related Information

Commands: **lvremove(8)**, **vgchange(8)**, **vgreduce(8)**

vgsync

Purpose   Synchronizes logical volume mirrors that are stale in one or more volume groups

Synopsis   **vgsync** *VolumeGroupName* ...

Description

The **vgsync** command synchronizes the physical extents. The synchronization occurs on the physical extents that are stale mirrors of the original logical extent of the logical volume(s) belonging to the volume group(s) specified by the *VolumeGroupName* parameter. The synchronization process can be time consuming, depending on the hardware characteristics and the amount of data. Unless disabled, the mirrors within a volume group are synchronized automatically when the volume group is activated by the **vgchange -a y** command.

Examples

1.   To synchronize the mirrors on volume group vg04, enter:

   vgsync/dev/vg04

Files

/usr/sbin/vgsync
       Specifies the command path

Related Information

Commands: **lvsync(8)**, **vgchange(8)**

vipw

Purpose   Edits the /etc/passwd file

Synopsis   **vipw**

Description

You use the **vipw** command to edit the **/etc/passwd** file with the editor defined in the **EDITOR** environment variable. If the variable is not set, the default editor is **vi** (hence the name, **vipw**).

The **vipw** command performs basic consistency checks on the edited file and invokes the **mkpasswd** command to create a hashed version in the **/etc/ptmp** temporary file.

The command must not be used on systems that use extended security attributes since it cannot set or change them. You must be **root** to run this co mand.   Only **root** and security administrators should have execute access to this command. The command should have **setuid** for **root** to have write access to the **/etc/passwd** file.

Since this command cannot effectively change all the attributes of users, it should not be used in a secure environment.

Files Accessed:

Permissions   File

rw	**/etc/passwd**
rw	**/etc/passwd.pag**
rw	**/etc/passwd.dir**
rw	**/etc/ptmp**
rw	**/etc/ptmp.pag**
rw	**/etc/ptmp.dir**
x	**/bin/mkpasswd**

Example

To edit the **/etc/passwd** file, enter:

vipw

When the file appears, you can edit it using the editor defined in the **EDITOR** environment variable, or if that variable is not set, the **vi** editor.

Files

/usr/sbin/vipw
> Specifies the command path

Related Information

Commands: **adduser(8)**, **mkpasswd(8)**, **passwd(1)**

wtmpfix

Purpose   Examines standard input or *File* records in the **wtmp** format for corrupted date and timestamp entries.

See **fwtmp(8)**

Chapter 2

File Formats

This chapter contains reference pages documenting OSF/1 system administration and network management file formats. The reference pages are arranged in alphabetical order (U.S. English).

/usr/spool/uucp/.Admin

Purpose   Contains administrative files used by the uucp program

Synopsis   **/usr/spool/uucp/.Admin**

Description

The **/usr/spool/uucp/.Admin** directory contains administrative files used by the **uucp** program to facilitate remote communications among systems. The **.Admin** directory contains the following files:

audit   Contains debug messages from the **uucico** daemon

Foreign   Logs contact attempts from unknown remote systems

errors   Records **uucico** daemon errors

xferstats   Records the status of file transfers

Related Information

Daemons: **cron(8)**, **uucico(8)**

Commands: **uudemon.cleanup**

Command (C.*)

Purpose   Contains file transfer directions for the uucico daemon

Synopsis   **/usr/spool/uucp/***LocalSystemName***/C.***SystemNamexxxx# ##*

Description

Command (C.*) files contain the directions that the uucp **uucico** daemon follows when transferring files. The full pathname of a command file is a form of the following:

/usr/spool/uucp/*SystemName***/C.***SystemNameNxxxx*

/C.*SystemName* indicates the name of the remote system. *N* represents the grade of the work, and *xxxx* is the 4-digit hexadecimal transfer-sequence number; for example, **C.merlinCE01F**.

The grade of the work specifies when the file is to be transmitted during a particular connection. The grade notation has the following characteristics:

- It is a single number (0 to 9) or letter (A to Z, a to z).

- Lower sequence characters cause the file to be transmitted earlier in the connection than do higher sequence characters.

- The number 0 (zero) is the highest grade, signifying the earliest transmittal; z is the lowest grade, signifying the latest transmittal.

- The default grade is *N*.

A command file consists of a single line that includes the following kinds of information in the following order:

1.   An **S** (send) or **R** (receive) notation.

   Note that a send command file is created by the **uucp** or **uuto** commands; a receive command file is created by the **uux** command.

2.   The full pathname of the source file being transferred. A receive command file does not include this entry.

3.   The full pathname of the destination file, or a pathname preceded by ˜ *user* (tilde *user*), where *user* is a login name on the specified system. Here, the tilde is shorthand for the name of the user's home directory.

4.   The sender's login name.

5.   A list of the options, if any, included with the **uucp**, **uuto**, or **uux** command.

6.   The name of the data file associated with the command file in the spooling directory. This field must contain an entry. If one of the data-transfer commands (such as the **uucp** command with the default **-c** flag) does not create a data file, the **uucp** program instead creates a placeholder with the name **D.0** for send files, or **dummy** for receive files.

7.   The source file permissions code, specified as a 3-digit octal number (for example, 777).

8.   The login name of the user on the remote system who is to be notified when the transfer is complete.

Examples

Examples of Two Send Command Files

1.   The send command file **/usr/spool/uucp/venus/C.heraN1133**, created with the **uucp** command, contains the following fields:

```
S /u/user1/f1 /usr/spool/uucppublic/f2 user1
      -dC D.herale3655 777 lgh
```

where:

S denotes that the **uucp** command is sending the file.

The full pathname of the source file is **/u/user1/f1**.

The full pathname of the destination is **/usr/spool/uucppublic/f2**, where **/usr/spool/uucppublic** is the name of the uucp public spooling directory on the remote computer and **f2** is the new name of the file.

Note that when the user's login ID is **uucp**, the destination name may be abbreviated as ˜ **uucp/f2**. Here, the ˜ (tilde) is a shorthand way of designating the public directory.

The person sending the file is **user1**.

The sender entered the **uucp** command with the **-C** flag, specifying that the **uucp** command program should transfer the file to the local spooling directory and create a data file for it. (The **-d** flag, which specifies that the command should create any intermediate directories needed to copy the source file to the destination, is the default.)

The name of the Data (**D.***) file is **D.herale3655**, which the **uucp** command assigns.

The octal permissions code is 777.

On system **hera, lgh** is the login name of the user who is to be notified of the file arrival.

2.   The **/usr/spool/uucp/hera/C.zeusN3130** send command file, produced by the **uuto** command, is as follows:

```
S /u/user1/out ~/receive/msg/zeus user1
      -dcn D.0 777[4~ msg
```

The **S** denotes that the **/u/user1/out** source file was sent to the **receive/msg** subdirectory in the public spooling directory on system **zeus** by user **user1**.

Note that the **uuto** command creates the **receive/msg** directory if it does not already exist.

The **uuto** command used the default flags **-d** (create directories), **-c** (transfer directly, no spooling directory or data file), and **-n** (notify recipient). The **D.0** notation is a placeholder, **777** is the permissions code, and **msg** is the recipient.

Example of a Receive Command File

The format of a receive command file is somewhat different from that of a send command file. When files required to run a specified command on a remote system are not present on that system, the **uux** command creates a receive command file.

For example, the following command

uux - "diff /u/user1/out hera!/u/user1/out2 > ~uucp/DF"

produces the **/usr/spool/uucp/zeus/C.heraR1e94** receive command file.

Note that the command in this example invokes the **uux** command to run a **diff** command on the local system, comparing file **/u/user1/out** with file **/u/user1/out2**, which is stored on remote system **hera**. The output of the comparison is placed in file **DF** in the public directory on the local system.

The actual receive command file looks like this:

```
R /u/user1/out2 D.hera1e954fd user1 - dummy 0666 user1
```

The **R** denotes a receive file. The **uucico** daemon, called by the **uux** command, gets the **/u/user1/out2** file from system **hera**, and places it in a data file called **D.hera1e954fd** for the transfer. Once the files are transferred, the **uuxqt** daemon executes the command on the specified system. User **user1** issued the **uux** command with the - (dash) flag, which makes the standard input to the **uux** command the standard input to the actual command string. No data file was created in the local spooling directory, so the **uucp** program uses **dummy** as a placeholder. The permissions code is **666** (the **uucp** program prefixes the 3-digit

Command(C.*)(4)

octal code with a **0** [zero]), and user **user1** is to be notified when the command finishes executing.

Files

/usr/lib/uucp/Permissions file
Describes access permissions for remote systems

/usr/lib/uucp/Systems file
Describes accessible remote systems

/usr/spool/uucp/_SystemName_ directory
Contains uucp command, data, and execute files

/usr/spool/uucp/_SystemName_**/D.*** files
Contains data to be transferred

/usr/spool/uucppublic/* directories
Contains transferred files

Related Information

Daemons: **cron(8)**, **uucico(8)**, **uusched(8)**, **uuxqt**

Commands: **uucp(1)**, **uudemon.cleanup**, **uupick(1)**, **uuto(1)**, **uux(1)**

/usr/spool/uucp/.Corrupt

Purpose   Contains copies of files that could not be processed

Synopsis   **/usr/spool/uucp/.Corrupt**

Description

The **/usr/spool/uucp/.Corrupt** directory contains copies of files that could not be processed by the **uucp** program. For example, if a file is not in the correct form for transfer, the **uucp** program places a copy of that file in the **.Corrupt** directory for later handling by the system manager. This directory is rarely used. The files in the **.Corrupt** directory are removed periodically by the **uudemon.cleanup** command, a shell procedure.

Related Information

Daemons: **uucico(8)**, **uuxqt**

Commands: **uudemon.cleanup**

Data (D.*)

Purpose   Contains data to be sent to remote systems

Synopsis   */usr/spool/uucp/LocalSystemName/**D.***SystemNamexxxx# ##*

Description

Data (**D.***) files contain the data to be sent to remote systems by the **uucp uucico** daemon. The full pathname of a data file is a form of the following:

/usr/spool/uucp/*SystemName/***D.***SystemNamexxxx# ##*

where the *SystemName* directory and the *SystemName* portion of the filename indicate the name of the remote system. The *xxxx###* notation is the hexadecimal sequence number of the **Command** (**C.***) file associated with that data file; for example, **D.venus471afd8**.

After a set period of time (specified by the **uusched** daemon), the **uucico** daemon transfers the data file to the designated system. It places the original data file in a subdirectory of the **uucp** spooling directory named **/usr/spool/uucp/***SystemName*, where the *SystemName* directory is named for the computer that is transmitting the file, and creates a **Temporary** (**TM.***) file to hold the original data file.

After receiving the entire file, the **uucp** program takes one of the three following actions:

1.   If the file was sent with the **uucp** command and there were no transfer problems, the program immediately renames the **TM.*** file with the appropriate data filename, such as **D.venus471afd8**, and sends it to the specified destination.

2.   If the file was sent with the **uuto** command, the **uucp** program also renames the temporary data file with the appropriate **D.*** filename. It then places the data file in the public directory **/usr/spool/uucppublic**, where the user receives the data file and handles it with one of the **uupick** command options.

3.   If there were transfer problems (such as a failed login or an unavailable device), the temporary data file remains in the spooling subdirectory. The **uudemon.cleanup** command, a shell script, removes these files automatically at specified intervals, or they can be removed manually.

Files

/usr/lib/uucp/Systems file
> Describes accessible remote systems

/usr/spool/uucp/_SystemName_ directory
> Contains **uucp** command, data, and execute files

/usr/spool/uucp/_SystemName_**/C.*** files
> Contain instructions for file transfers

/usr/spool/uucp/_SystemName_**/TM.*** files
> Store data files temporarily after they have been transferred to a remote system

/usr/spool/uucppublic/* directories
> Contain files that the **uucp** program has transferred

Related Information

Daemons: **uucico(8)**, **uusched(8)**, **uuxqt**

Commands: **uucp(1)**, **uudemon.cleanup**, **uupick(1)**, **uuto(1)**, **uux(1)**

Dialcodes

Purpose   Contains the initial digits of telephone numbers used to establish remote connections over a telephone line

Synopsis   **/usr/lib/uucp/Dialcodes**

Description

The **/usr/lib/uucp/Dialcodes** file contains the initial digits of telephone numbers used by the **uucp** program to establish remote connections over a telephone line. The **Dialcodes** file simplifies entries in the **/usr/lib/uucp/Systems** file for sites where a number of device telephone numbers have the same prefix. If users at your site communicate regularly by way of telephone lines and modems to multiple systems all located at the same remote site, or to multiple systems located at different remote sites, use dial-code abbreviations in the **/usr/lib/uucp/Systems** file rather than entering the complete telephone number of each remote modem in that file. The **Dialcodes** file contains dial-code abbreviations and partial telephone numbers that complete the telephone entries in the **/usr/lib/uucp/Systems** file. Entries in the **Dialcodes** file contain an alphabetic prefix attached to a partial telephone number that may include the following information, in the order listed:

1.   Codes for an outside line.

2.   Long-distance access codes.

        1 + the area code (if the modem is out of the local area).

3.   The 3-digit exchange number. The relevant alphabetic prefix (representing the partial telephone number), together with the remaining four digits of that number, is then entered in the *Phone* field in the **/usr/lib/uucp/Systems** file.

Following is the form of an entry in a **Dialcodes** file:

DialCodeAbbreviation DialingSequence

The *DialCodeAbbreviation* part of the entry is an alphabetic prefix containing up to eight letters, established when setting up the dial-code listing.

The *DialingSequence* comprises all the digits in the number that precede the actual 4-digit telephone number.

Note that if your site uses only a relatively small number of telephone connections to remote systems, include the complete telephone numbers of the remote modems in the **/usr/lib/uucp/Systems** file rather than using dial-code abbreviations.

Enter each prefix *only once* in the **Dialcodes** file. When you have set up a dial-code abbreviation, use that prefix in all relevant entries in the **/usr/lib/uucp/Systems** file.

Only someone with superuser authority can edit the **Dialcodes** file, which is owned by the **uucp** program login ID.

Examples

The **Dialcodes** file on system **venus** contains the following dial-code prefix for use with a number in the **/usr/lib/uucp/Systems** file:

```
local  9=555
```

The **Systems** file on system **venus** contains the following entry for system **zeus**, including a telephone number and a dial-code prefix:

```
zeus Any ACU 1200 local1212 in:--in: nuucp word: thunder
```

When the uucp program on system **venus** dials system **zeus**, it uses the expanded telephone number =5551212.

Files

/usr/lib/uucp directory
> Contains all the configuration files for the **uucp** program, including the **Dialcoddes file /usr/lib/uucp/Devices** file Contains information about available devices

/usr/lib/uucp/Dialers file
> Specifies initial handshaking on a connection

/usr/lib/uucp/Systems file
> Describes accessible remote systems

Related Information

Commands: **cu(1)**, **tip(1)**, **uucp(1)**, **uuto(1)**, **uux(1)**

Dialers

Purpose   Lists modems used for uucp remote communications links

Synopsis   **/usr/lib/uucp/Dialers**

Description

The **/usr/lib/uucp/Dialers** file lists the modems used by the **uucp** program and specifies the initial handshaking necessary to establish remote communications links. Handshaking is a series of *expect-send* sequences that specify the initial communications that occur on a link before it is ready to send or receive data. Using the handshaking, the local and remote systems confirm that they are compatible and configured to transfer data.

The **Dialers** file contains an entry for each autodialer that is included in the **/usr/lib/uucp/Devices** file. It also contains entries specifying no handshaking for direct hardware links (the direct entry) and TCP/IP links (the TCP entry). The first field of the **Dialers** file, which specifies the dialer, is matched to the fifth field of the **Devices** file, the *Dialer-Token Pairs* field, to determine handshaking when making a connection.

Note that only someone with superuser authority can edit the **Dialers** file, which is owned by the **uucp** program login ID.

Fields in the Dialers File

Every modem is listed on a line by itself in the **Dialers** file. Each line consists of three groups of information: the *Dialer Name* field, the *Dial Tone and Wait Characters* field, and the *Handshaking* field.

Dialer Name Field

The first field in the **Dialers** file, the *Dialer Name* field, specifies the type of autodialer (modem) used in the connection. It matches the fifth field in the **/usr/lib/uucp/Devices** file, the *Dialer-Token Pairs* field. When a particular device is used to make a connection, **uucp** uses the *Dialer-Token Pairs* field in the **Devices** file to find the handshaking entry in the **Dialers** file. If your system has direct hardware connections to one or more remote systems, include an entry with a *Dialer Name* of **direct**.

Similarly, if your system uses TCP/IP to connect to one or more other systems, include an entry with a *Dialer Name* of **TCP**. These entries correspond to the word **direct** or the word **TCP** in the *Dialer-Token Pairs* field of entries in the **/usr/lib/uucp/Devices** file. Omit the *Dial Tone and Wait Characters* field and the *Handshaking* field, since no handshaking is needed on these connections.

Dial Tone and Wait Characters Field

The second field, the *Dial Tone and Wait Characters* field, consists of two sets of two characters, for a total of four entries. These characters comprise a translation string. In the actual telephone number of the remote modem, the first character in each string is mapped to the second character in that set.

Entry	Action
=,-,	Translates the telephone number. Any = (equal sign) represents *wait for dial tone* and any - (dash) represents *pause*.
""	Waits for nothing; continues with the rest of the string. This field generally translates the = and - characters into whatever the dialer uses for *wait for dial tone* and *pause*. For **direct** and **TCP** entries, omit this field.

Handshaking Field

The handshaking, or dialer negotiations, is an *expect-send* sequence of ASCII strings. It is given in the *Handshaking* field, which comprises the remainder of the entry. This string is generally used to pass telephone numbers to a modem, or to make a connection to another system on the same data switch as the local system. The string tells the **cu** or **ct** programs or the **uucico** daemon the sequence of characters to use to dial out on a particular type of modem. If the connection succeeds, the line in the **Dialers** file is interpreted to perform the dialer negotiations.

The handshaking characters include entries such as \d to specify a delay, \p for a pause, \r for a carriage return, and \c for a newline. To determine the appropriate entries in the handshaking string, refer to the documentation that accompanied the modems that you are including in the **Dialers** file, and to the list of expect-send sequences given in the **/usr/lib/uucp/Systems** file format. For **direct** and **TCP** entries, omit this field.

Examples

Setting Up Entries in the Dialers File

1. The following example lists several entries in a typical **Dialers** file:

```
hayes =,-, "" \dAT\r\c OK \pATDT\T\r\c CONNECT
penril =W-P "" \d > s\p9\c )-W\p\r\ds\p9\c-) y
ventel =&-% "" \r\p \r\p-\r\p-$ <K\D%%\r>\c ONLINE!
vadiac =K-K "" \005\p *-\005\p-* D\p BER? \E\D\e \r\c LINE
direct
TCP
```

Note that in the **Dialers** file, each entry must be entirely on one line.

Notice that the next to last entry in the preceding example consists only of the word **direct**. This entry indicates that hardwired connections do not require any handshaking. Similarly, the last entry, **TCP**, indicates that TCP/IP connections require no handshaking.

2. The following example interprets the first line in the preceding **Dialers** file. This is a standard entry that may be included in your **Dialers** file with modifications for use at your site.

```
hayes =,-, "" \dAT\r\c OK \pATDT\T\r\c CONNECT
```

The first two sequences (=,- and "") comprise the *Dial Tone and Wait Characters* field. The remaining strings comprise the *Handshaking* field. Following is an explanation of how each entry affects the action of the dialer.

Entry	Action
=,-,	Translates the telephone number. Any = (equal sign) represents *wait for dial tone* and any - (dash) represents *pause*.
""	Waits for nothing; continues with the rest of the string.
\dAT	Delays, then sends **AT** (the Hayes Attention prefix).
\r\c	Sends a carriage return (**r**) followed by a newline (**c**).
OK	Waits for **OK** from the remote modem, signaling that the first part of the string was executed.
\pATDT	Pauses (**p**), then sends **ATDT**. **AT** is again the Hayes Attention prefix, **D** represents a dialing signal, and **T** represents a dial tone.

\T	Sends the telephone number, which is specified in the **/usr/lib/uucp/Systems** file, with dial-code translation from the **/usr/lib/uucp/Dialcodes** file.
\r\c	Sends a carriage return and a newline following the number.
CONNECT	Waits for **CONNECT** from the remote modem, signaling that the modems are connected at the baud rate specified in the **/usr/lib/uucp/Devices** file.

Note that if you need to modify this example for use at your site and are unsure about the appropriate entries in the handshaking string, refer to the documentation that accompanied the modems that you are including in the **Dialers** file.

Setting Up the Direct Entry

If your uucp configuration includes hardwired connections, the **Dialers** file must contain the **direct** entry. Enter:

direct

This entry indicates that hardwired connections do not require any handshaking. It corresponds to the word **direct** in the *Dialer-Token Pairs* field of the entries for hardwired devices in the **/usr/lib/uucp/Devices** file.

Setting Up the TCP/IP Entry

If your uucp configuration includes TCP/IP connections, the **Dialers** file must contain the **TCP** entry. Enter:

TCP

This entry indicates that TCP/IP connections do not require any handshaking. It corresponds to the word **TCP** in the *Dialer-Token Pairs* field of the entries for TCP/IP connections in the **/usr/lib/uucp/Devices** file.

Setting Up Entries for Both Local and Remote Systems

The following example illustrates the entries needed in the **Dialers** file to correspond to entries in the **/usr/lib/uucp/Devices** file for both local and remote systems so that the two systems can communicate using the **uucp** program.

These files are set up to connect systems **venus** and **merlin** over a telephone line using modems. System **venus** is considered the local system, and system **merlin** is considered the remote system. On both systems, the **tty1** device is hooked to a **hayes** modem at **1200** baud.

The **/usr/lib/uucp/Devices** file on system **venus** must contain the following entry for the connection to remote system **merlin**. Enter:

ACU tty1 - 1200 hayes

The **Dialers** file on system **venus** contains the following entry for its modem:

hayes =,-, "" \dAT\r\c OK \pATDT\T\r\c CONNECT

The **/usr/lib/uucp/Devices** file on system **merlin** must contain the following entry for the connection to system **venus**. Enter:

ACU tty1 - 1200 hayes

The **Dialers** file on system **merlin** must contain the following entry for its modem. Enter:

hayes =,-, "" \dAT\r\c OK \pATDT\T\r\c CONNECT

Troubleshooting Connection Problems

When establishing a connection between a local and a remote system using a telephone line and modem, the **uucp** program consults the **Dialers** file. (The **uucp** program also checks the **/usr/lib/uucp/Systems** file to make sure it contains a listing for the specified remote computer.) If users report a faulty connection, use the **uucico** command to debug the connection problem. For example, if users are experiencing difficulties connecting to remote system **venus**, enter:

/usr/lib/uucp/uucico -r1 -svenus -x9

where **-r1** specifies the server mode, **-svenus** is the name of the remote system to which you are trying to connect, and **-x9** is the debug level that produces the most detailed debugging information.

Expect-send debugging output produced by the **uucico** command can come either from information in the **Dialers** file or from information in the **/usr/lib/uucp/Systems** file. If the relevant line in the **Dialers** file is not set up correctly for the specified modem, the **uucp** program will probably display the following error message: DIALER SCRIPT FAILED

If the dialer script fails, verify the following:

1. Make sure that both the local and the remote modems are turned on, that they are both set up correctly, and that the telephone number of the remote modem is correct.

2. Check the **Dialers** file and make sure the information is correctly specified for the local modem. If possible, check the **Dialers** file on the remote system also.

3. Check the documentation that came with your modem to make sure you have used the correct expect-send sequence characters in the **Dialers** file.

Files

/usr/lib/uucp directory
> Contains all the configuration files for the **uucp** program, including the **Dialers** file

usr/lib/uucp/Devices file
> Contains information about available devices

/usr/lib/uucp/Dialcodes file
> Contains dial-code abbreviations

usr/lib/uucp/Systems file
> Describes accessible remote systems

Related Information

Daemons: **uucico(8)**

Commands: **ct(1)**, **cu(1)**, **uutry(1)**

Directories

Purpose   Contains queued requests for file transfers and command executions on remote systems

Synopsis   **/usr/spool/uucp/**SystemName

Description

The **/usr/spool/uucp/**SystemName directories are the **uucp** program spooling directories on the local system. The **uucp** program creates a SystemName directory for each system listed in the **/usr/adm/uucp/Systems** file, including the local system.

Each SystemName directory contains queued requests issued by local users for file transfers to remote systems and for command executions on remote systems.

The **uucp** program uses several types of administrative files to transfer data between systems. These files are stored in the SystemName directories. They are

Command (C.*) files
> Contain directions for the **uucico** daemon concerning file transfers.

Data (D.*) files
> Contain data to be sent to remote systems by the **uucico** daemon.

Execute (X.*) files
> Contain instructions for running commands on remote systems.

Temporary (TM.*) files
> Contain data files after their transfer to the remote system until the **uucp** program can deliver them to their final destinations (usually the **/usr/spool/uucppublic** directory).

Related Information

Daemons: **uucico(8)**, **uusched(8)**, **uuxqt**

Commands: **uucp(1)**, **uux(1)**

Execute (X.*)

Purpose   Contains instructions for running commands that require the resources of a remote system

Synopsis   **/usr/spool/uucp/**SystemName/**X.**RemoteSystemNxxxx

Description

The **uucp Execute (X.*)** files contain instructions for running commands that require the resources of a remote system. They are created by the **uux** command. The full pathname of a **uux** command execute file is a form of the following:

/usr/spool/uucp/SystemName/**X.**RemoteSystemNxxxx

where the SystemName directory is named for the local computer and the RemoteSystem directory is named for the remote system. The N character represents the grade of the work, and the xxxx notation is the 4-digit hexadecimal transfer-sequence number; for example, **X.zeusN2121**.

Note that the grade of the work specifies when the file is to be transmitted during a particular connection. The grade notation is a single number (0 to 9) or letter (A to Z, a to z). Lower sequence characters cause the file to be transmitted earlier in the connection than do higher sequence characters. The number 0 (zero) is the highest grade, signifying the earliest transmittal; z is the lowest grade, signifying the latest transmittal. The default grade is N.

Standard Entries in an Execute File

An execute file consists of several lines, each with an identification character and one or more entries:

Line	Format and Description
User Line	**U** UserName SystemName
	Specifies the login name of the user issuing the **uux** command and the name of the system from which the command was issued.
Error Status Line	**N** or **Z**
	Indicates the error status.
	The **N** character means that a failure message is *not* sent to the user issuing the **uux** command if the specified command does not execute successfully on the remote system.

Execute(X.*)(4)

The **Z** character means that a failure message is sent to the user issuing the **uux** command if the specified command does not execute successfully on the remote system.

Requester's Name   **R** *UserName*

Specifies the login ID of the user requesting the remote command execution.

Required File Line

   F *FileName*

Contains the names of the files required to execute the specified command on the remote system. The *FileName* parameter can be either the complete pathname of the file, including the unique transmission name assigned by the **uucp** program, or simply the transmission name without any path information.

The Required File Line can contain zero or more filenames. The **uuxqt** daemon checks for the existence of all listed files before running the specified command.

Standard Input Line

   I *FileName*

Specifies the standard input to be used.

The standard input is either specified by a < (less than) symbol in the command string, or is inherited from the standard input of the **uux** command if that command was issued with the - (dash) flag. If standard input is specified, it also is listed in an **F** (Required File) line. If standard input is not specified, the **uucp** program uses the **/dev/null** device file.

Standard Output Line

   O *FileName SystemName*

Specifies the names of the file and system that are to receive standard output from the execution of the command. Standard output is specified by a > (greater than) symbol within the command string. (The **>>** sequence is not valid in **uux** commands.) As was the case with standard input, if standard output is not specified, the **uucp** program uses the **/dev/null** device file.

Command Line   **C** *CommandString*

This is the command string that the user requests to be run on the specified system. The **uucp** program checks the **/usr/lib/uucp/Permissions** file on the designated computer to see whether the login ID can run the command on that system.

All required files go to the execute file directory, usually **/usr/spool/uucp/.Xqtdir**. After execution, the standard output is sent to the requested location

Examples

1. User **amy** on local system **zeus** entered the following command:

   uux - "diff /u/amy/out hera!/u/amy/out2 > ˜uucp/DF"

   The command in this example invokes the **uux** command to run a **diff** command on the local system, comparing file **/u/amy/out** with file **/u/amy/out2**, which is stored on remote system **hera**. The output of the comparison is placed in the **DF** file in the public directory on the local system.

   This command produced the **/usr/spool/uucp/hera/X.zeusN212F** execute file, which contains the following information:

   ```
   U amy zeus
   # return status on failure
   Z
   # return address for status or input return
   R amy
   F /usr/spool/uucp/hera/D.herale954fd out2
   O ˜uucp/DF zeus
   C diff /u/amy/out out2
   ```

   The user line identifies user **amy** on system **zeus**. The error status line indicates that **amy** will receive a failure status message if the **diff** command fails to execute. The requester is **amy**, and the file required to execute the command is the following data file:

   ```
   /usr/spool/uucp/hera/D.herale954fd out2
   ```

   The output of the command is to be written to the public directory on system **zeus** with the filename **DF**. (Remember that ˜**uucp** is the shorthand way of specifying the public directory.) The final line is the command string that user **amy** entered with the **uux** command.

2.   Following is another example of an execute file:

```
U uucp hera
# don't return status on failure
N
# return address for status or input return
R uucp
F D.hera5eb7f7b
I D.hera5eb7f7b
C rmail amy
```

This indicates that user **uucp** on system **hera** is sending mail to user **amy**, who is also working on system **hera**.

Files

/usr/lib/uucp/Permissions file
> Describes access permissions for remote systems

/usr/lib/uucp/Systems file
> Describes accessible remote systems

/usr/spool/uucp/*SystemName* directory
> Contains uucp command, data, and execute files

/usr/spool/uucp/*SystemName***/C.*** files
> Contain instructions for transfers

/usr/spool/uucp/.Xqtdir directory
> Contains lists of commands that remote systems are permitted to execute

/usr/spool/uucppublic/* directories
> Contain files that have been transferred

Related Information

Daemons: **uuxqt**

Commands: **diff(1)**, **uux(1)**

Foreign

Purpose   Logs contact attempts from unknown systems

Synopsis   **/usr/lib/uucp/.Admin/Foreign**

Description

The **/usr/lib/uucp/.Admin/Foreign** file lists access attempts by unknown systems. The **/usr/lib/uucp/remote.unknown** shell script appends an entry to the **Foreign** file each time a remote computer that is not listed in the local **/usr/lib/uucp/Systems** file attempts to communicate with that local system.

Someone with superuser authority can customize entries in the **Foreign** file to fit the needs of a specific site by modifying the **remote.unknown** shell script.

Examples

The following is a sample entry in the **Foreign** file:

```
Wed Sep 20 20:38:22 CDT 1989: call from the system merlin
```

System **merlin**, which is not listed in the **/usr/lib/uucp/Systems** file, attempted to log in on September 20 at 10:38p.m., but the **uucp** program did not allow the unknown system to log in.

Files

/usr/lib/uucp/Permissions file
    Describes access permissions for remote systems

/usr/lib/uucp/Systems file
    Describes accessible remote systems

/usr/lib/uucp/remote.unknown file
    Records contacts from unknown systems in the **Foreign** file

/usr/lib/uucp/.Admin directory
    Contains the **Foreign** file and other uucp administrative files

Related Information

Daemons: **cron(8)**, **uucico(8)**, **uuxqt**

Commands: **uucp(1)**, **uudemon.cleanup**, **uux(1)**

/usr/spool/uucp/.Log

Purpose   Contains the uucp program log files

Synopsis   **/usr/spool/uucp/.Log**

Description

The **/usr/spool/uucp/.Log** directories contain **uucp** program log files. The **uucp** program normally places status information about each transaction in the appropriate log file each time you use the networking utilities facility. All transactions of the **uucico** and **uuxqt** daemons are logged in files named for the remote system concerned. The files are stored in a subdirectory of the **/usr/spool/uucp/.Log** directory named for the daemon involved. Thus, the log files are named with a form of the following:

/usr/spool/uucp/.Log/*DaemonName/SystemName*

The **uucp** and **uuto** commands call the **uucico** daemon. The **uucico** daemon activities for a particular remote system are logged in the *SystemName* file in the **/usr/spool/uucp/.Log/uucico** directory on the local system.

The **uux** command calls the **uuxqt** daemon. The **uuxqt** daemon activities for a particular remote system are logged in the *SystemName* file in the **/usr/spool/uucp/.Log/uuxqt** directory on the local system.

When more than one **uucp** process is running, however, the system cannot access the standard log file, so it places the status information in a file with a **.Log** prefix that covers just the single transaction.

The **uucp** program can automatically append the temporary log files to a primary log file. This is called *compacting the log files*, and is handled by the **uudemon.cleanup** command, a shell procedure, which combines the log files of the activities of the **uucico** and **uuxqt** daemons on a system and stores them in the **/usr/spool/uucp/.Old** directory.

The default is for the **uudemon.cleanup** command to save log files that are 2 days old. This default can be changed by modifying the appropriate line in the shell script. If storage space is a problem on a particular system, reduce the number of days that the files are kept in the individual log files.

The **uulog** command can be used to view the **uucp** program log files.

Related Information

Daemons: **cron, uucico(8), uusched(8), uuxqt**

Commands: **uucp(1), uudemon.cleanup, uulog, uuto(1), uux(1)**

/usr/spool/uucp/.Old

Purpose Contains the combined uucp program log files

Synopsis **/usr/spool/uucp/.Old**

Description

The **/usr/spool/uucp/.Old** directory contains the combined **uucp** program log files. The **uucp** program creates log files of the activities of the **uucico** and **uuxqt** daemons in the **/usr/spool/uucp/.Log** directory. The log files are compacted by the **/usr/lib/uucp/uudemon.cleanup** command, a shell procedure, which combines the files and stores them in the **.Old** directory.

By default, the **uudemon.cleanup** command removes log files after 2 weeks. The length of time log files are kept can be changed to suit the needs of an individual system. The log files can be viewed using the **uulog** command.

Related Information

Daemons: **cron(8)**, **uucico(8)**, **uuxqt**

Commands: **uucp(1)**, **uudemon.cleanup**, **uulog**, **uux**

/usr/spool/uucp/.Status

Purpose   Contains information about the status of the uucp program contacts with remote systems

Synopsis   **/usr/spool/uucp/.Status**

Description

The **/usr/spool/uucp/.Status** directory contains information about the status of the **uucp** program contacts with remote systems.

For each remote system contacted, the **uucp** program creates a file in the **.Status** directory called *SystemName*, where the *SystemName* file is named for the remote system being contacted. In the **.Status**/*SystemName* file, the **uucp** program stores the following information:

- Time of the last call in seconds.

- Status of the last call.

- Number of retries.

- Retry time, in seconds, of the next call.

The times given in the **.Status**/*SystemName* file are expressed as seconds elapsed since midnight of January 1, 1970 (the output of a **time** system call). Thus, the retry time is in the form of the number of seconds that must have expired since midnight of January 1, 1970 before the system can retry. To make this entry in the **.Status**/*SystemName* file, **uucp** performs a **time** system call, adds 600 seconds, and places the resulting number of seconds in the file. If the last call was unsuccessful, the **uucico** daemon will wait until the time specified by the retry time before attempting to contact the system again. The retry time in the **.Status**/*SystemName* file can be overridden using the **-r** flag of the **uutry** or **Uutry** command.

Related Information

Daemons: **uucico(8)**

Commands: **uutry**, **Uutry**

System Calls: **time**

Temporary (TM.*)

Purpose   Stores data files during transfers to remote systems

Synopsis   **/usr/spool/uucp**/*SystemName*/**TM.***xxPID***.000**

Description

The **uucp Temporary** (**TM.***) files store data files during transfers to remote systems. After a **Data** (**D.***) file is transferred to a remote system by the **uucico** daemon, the **uucp** program places it in a subdirectory of the **uucp** spooling directory named **/usr/spool/uucp**/*SystemName*, where the *SystemName* directory is named for the computer that is transmitting the file. The **uucp** program creates a temporary data file to hold the original data file.

The full pathname of the temporary data file is in the following format

/usr/spool/uucp/*SystemName*/**TM.***xxPID***.000**

where the *SystemName* directory is named for the computer that is sending the file, and **TM.***xxPID***.000** is the name of the file; for example, **TM.00451.000**. The *PID* variable is the process ID of the job.

Files

/usr/lib/uucp/Systems file
>   Describes accessible remote systems

/usr/spool/uucp/*SystemName* directory
>   Contains **uucp** command, data, and execute files

/usr/spool/uucppublic/* directories
>   Contain files that **uucp** has transferred

/usr/spool/uucp/*SystemName*/**D.*** files
>   Contain data to be transferred.

Related Information

Daemons: **uucico(8)**

Commands: **uucp(1)**, **uudemon.cleanup**, **uupick(1)**, **uuto(1)**, **uux(1)**

/usr/spool/uucp/.Workspace

Purpose   Holds temporary files used internally by file transport programs

Synopsis   **/usr/spool/uucp/.Workspace**

Description

The **/usr/spool/uucp/.Workspace** directory holds temporary files of various kinds used internally by uucp file transport programs.

Related Information

Daemons: **uucico(8)**, **uuxqt**

/usr/spool/uucp/.Xqtdir

Purpose   Contains temporary files used by the uuxqt daemon to execute remote command requests

Synopsis   **/usr/spool/uucp/.Xqtdir**

Description

The **/usr/spool/uucp/.Xqtdir** directory contains temporary files used by the uucp **uuxqt** daemon to execute remote command requests.

Related Information

Daemons: **uuxqt**

Commands: **uux(1)**

acct.h

Purpose   Account include files

Synopsis   **#include <sys/acct.h>**

           #include <utmp.h>

Description

The **/usr/include/sys/acct.h** header file defines a type **acct** structure for accounting information used by various accounting files. The information in the **acct.h** structure is used in records in accounting files having various fixed formats.

The various accounting files provide the means to monitor system use and performance and to pass charges to system users. These accounting files also serve as the permanent record of billing information for each process, CPU real time, allocated resources, and services. The **acct** command is used to produce desired accounting files.

The **/usr/include/utmp.h** header file defines the record format for data written to the **/var/adm/wtmp** accounting login/logout database file whenever any user logs in or out. The type **utmp** structure defined in the **/usr/include/utmp.h** header file has the following members.

char ut_user[32]   The user login name listed in the **/etc/passwd** file.

char ut_id[14]   The user identification from the **/etc/inittab** ID file.

char ut_line[32]   The device name (console or tty43, for example).

short ut_type   This is a flag that defines the type of entry. The type of entry flag symbolic names are as follows.

      EMPTY No valid entry.

      RUN_LVL
            Run level changed by the **init** program.

      BOOT_TIME
            Boot time entry, generated by the **init** program.

      OLD_TIME
            Used by the **date** program when the system time is changed.

      NEW_TIME
            Used by the **date** program when the system time is changed.

INIT_PROCESS
Process spawned by the **init** program.

LOGIN_PROCESS
A *getty* process waiting for login.

USER_PROCESS
A user process.

DEAD_PROCESS
Terminated process.

ACCOUNTING
Private flag for accounting programs.

pid_t ut_pid   Process ID number.

short ut_exit.e_termination
Process termination status of a process whose **ut_type** member value is **DEAD PROCESS**.

short ut_exit.e_exit
Process exit status of a process whose **ut_type** member value is **DEAD PROCESS**.

time_t ut_time   Time that entry was made.

char ut_host[64]   Host machine name.

The **/usr/include/sys/acct.h** header file defines the record format for the data written to the process accounting database file when a process completes. The type **acct** structure defined in the **acct.h** header file contains the following members.

char ac_flag   An accounting flag for the process for which the accounting record is written. The accounting flag symbolic names are as follows:

AFORK   The process has been created using a **fork( )** system call, but an **exec( )** system call has not yet concluded. The **exec( )** system call resets the **AFORK** flag.

ASU   Superuser privileges have been invoked.

ACOMPAT   Compatibility mode used.

ACORE   Dumped core.

AXSIG   Process killed by a signal.

char ac_stat   Exit status. A flag that indicates how the process terminated.

uid_t ac_uid   The user ID of the process for which the accounting record is written.

gid_t ac_gid   The group ID of the process for which the accounting record is written.

dev_t ac_tty   The terminal from which the process was started.

time_t ac_btime   Beginning time. The time at which the process began.

comp_t ac_utime   The amount of user time (in a compressed format) used by the process.

comp_t ac_stime   The amount of system time (in a compressed format) used by the process.

comp_t ac_etime   The amount of elapsed time (in a compressed format) since the command ran.

short ac_mem   The average amount of memory used by the process.

comp_t ac_io   The number of characters (in a compressed format) transferred by the process.

comp_t ac_rw   The number of blocks (in a compressed format) read or written by the process.

char ac_comm[8]   The name of the command that was used to start the process. A child process created by a **fork**( ) system call receives up to 8 bytes from the parent process. An **exec**( ) system call changes the name in this field.

Compressed data, which is a condensed floating-point representation, may be expanded to normal floating point by using the **expacct**( ) routine.

The type **tacct** structure, which is not a part of the **/usr/include/utmp.h** or the **/usr/include/sys/acct.h** header file definitions, is defined in a private **tacct.h** header file. The type **tacct** structure members define a format for storage of all information available from both the **/var/adm/wtmp** login/logoff and **/var/adm/pacct** process accounting databases, whose members are used by various accounting commands to produce an output file to be used in an accounting report (see the **acctmerg** command). Members of the type **tacct** structure whose data types are specified as an array of two *double* elements have both prime-time and non-prime time values. The type **tacct** structure has the following members.

uid_t ta_uid   User ID.

char ta_name[NSZ]

A field for the login name having the same number of characters **NSZ** as the **ut_user** member of the **utmp** structure.

double ta_cpu[2]   Cumulative CPU time in minutes.

double ta_kcore[2]

Cumulative Kcore minutes.

acct.h(4)

double ta_io[2]	Cumulative number of characters transferred in blocks of 512 bytes.
double ta_rw[2]	Cumultive number of blocks read and written.
double ta_con[2]	Cumulative connect time in minutes.
double ta_du	Cumulative disk usage time in minutes.
long ta_qsys	Queueing system (printer) fee in number of pages.
double ta_fee	Special services fee.
long ta_pc	A count of the number of processes.

unsigned short ta_sc
A count of the number of login sessions.

unsigned short ta_dc
A count of the number of disk samples.

Files

/usr/include/sys/acct.h, /usr/include/utmp.h
Accounting header files that define formats for writing accounting files.

/var/adm/wtmp
The active login/logoff database file.

/var/adm/pacct
The active process accounting database file.

Related Information

Commands:
acct/*, **acctcms**, **acctcom**, **acctcon**, **acctdisk**, **acctmerg**, **acctprc**, **runacct**, **sa**

Calls: **acct( )**, **fork( )**, **exec( )**, **expacct( )**

aliases

Purpose   Contains alias definitions for the sendmail program

Synopsis   **aliases**

Description

By default, this file contains the required aliases for the **mail** program. Do not change these defaults because they are needed by the system. This file describes user ID aliases used by the **sendmail** command. It is formatted as a series of lines in the form:

name: *name_1*, *name_2*, *name_3*,..

The *name* is the name that needs an alias, and the *name_n* are the aliases for that name. Lines beginning with white space are continuation lines. Lines beginning with a # (number sign) are comments.

You can only define an alias on local names. Loops cannot occur, since no message is sent to any person more than once. For example, if *name_1* defines an alias that is *name_2* and *name_2* defines an alias that is *name_1*, **sendmail** does not send the same message back and forth. Local and valid recipients who have a **.forward** file in their home directory have messages forwarded to the list of users defined in that file.

This is only the raw data file; the actual information that defines the aliases is placed into a binary format in the files **/var/adm/sendmail/aliases.dir** and **/var/adm/sendmail/aliases.pag** using the **newaliases** command. For the change to take effect, the **newaliases** command must be executed each time the **aliases** file is changed.

Files

/var/adm/sendmail/aliases file
>   Contains system-wide aliases

/var/adm/sendmail/aliases directory
>   Contains the binary files created by the **newaliases** command

Related Information

Commands: **sendmail(8)**, **newaliases(1)**

audit

Purpose   Contains debug messages from the uucico daemon

Synopsis   **/usr/spool/uucp/.Admin/audit**

Description

The **/usr/spool/uucp/.Admin/audit** file contains debug messages from the **uucico** daemon when that daemon is invoked as a result of a call from another system. If the **uucico** daemon is invoked from the local system, the debug messages are sent to the **/usr/spool/uucp/.Admin/errors** file or to standard output.

Files

/usr/spool/uucp/.Admin directory
Contains the **audit** file and other uucp administrative files

Related Information

Daemons: **cron**(8), **uucico**(8)

Commands: **uudemon.cleanup**

errors

Purpose   Contains a record of uucico daemon errors

Synopsis   **/usr/spool/uucp/.Admin/errors**

Description

The **/usr/spool/uucp/.Admin/errors** file contains a record of **uucico** daemon errors that the **uucp** program cannot correct. For example, if the **uucico** daemon is unable to access a directory that is needed for a file transfer, the **uucp** program records this in the **errors** file. If debugging is enabled for the **uucico** daemon, the **uucp** program sends the error messages to standard output instead of to the **errors** file.

Examples

Following is the text of an error that might appear in the **errors** file:

```
ASSERT ERROR (uucico) pid: 303 (7/18-8:25:09)\
SYSTAT OPEN FAIL /usr/spool/uucp/.Status/ (21)\
[SCCSID: @(#)systat.c   7.2 87/07/08 16:43:37,\
FILE: systat.c, LINE:100]
```

This error occurred on July 18 at 8:25:09 a.m. [**(7/18-8:25:09)**] when the **uucico** daemon, running as process 303 [**(uucico) pid: 303**], could not open the **/usr/spool/uucp/.Status** directory [**SYSTAT OPEN FAIL /usr/spool/uucp/.Status/**]. To prevent this error from occurring again, you should make sure the permissions for the **.Status** directory are correct. It should be owned by the **uucp** login ID and group **uucp**, with permissions of 777 (read, write, and execute for owner, group, and all others).

Files

/usr/spool/uucp/.Admin directory
          Contains the **errors** file and other uucp administrative files

/usr/spool/uucp/.Status/*SystemName* file
          Lists the last time a remote system was contacted and the minimum time until the next retry

errors(4)

Related Information

Daemons: **uucico(8)**

Commands: **uudemon.cleanup**

exports

Purpose   Defines remote mount points for NFS mount requests

Synopsis   /etc/exports

Description

The **exports** file specifies remote mount points for the NFS mount protocol per the NFS server specification (see *Network File System Protocol Specification, RFC1094*).

Each line in the file specifies one remote mount point. The first field is the mount point directory path, followed optionally by export options and specific hosts separated by white space. Only the first entry for a given local file system may specify the export options, since these are handled on a per local file system basis. If no specific hosts are specified, the mount point is exported to all hosts.

The export options are as follows: **-root=**<*uid*> specifies how to map root's UID (default -2). The **-r** option is a synonym for **-root** in an effort to be backward compatible with older export file formats.

The **-ro** option specifies that the file system should be exported read-only (default read/write). The **-o** option is a synonym for **-ro** in an effort to be backward compatible with older export file formats.

For example, when you enter:

/usr -root=0 milan kuan_yin.cis.berkeley.edu
/usr/local 555.555.55.55
/u -root=5
/u2 -ro

given that **/usr**, **/u** and **/u2** are local file system mount points, specifies the following:

/usr is exported to hosts **milan** and **kuan_yin.cis.berkeley.edu** with root mapped to **uid=0**.
/usr/local is exported to host **555.555.55.55** with root mapped to root. (For security reasons, this example uses the fictitious IP address **555.555.55.55**.)
/u is exported to all hosts with root mapped to uid 5.
/u2 is exported to all hosts Read-only with root mapped to -2.

exports(4)

Note that **/usr/local -root=5** would have been incorrect, since **/usr** and **/usr/local** reside in the same local file system and export options are tied to local mount points.

Related Information

Daemons: **mountd (8), nfsd (8)**

Commands: **showmount (8)**

fstab

Purpose   Static information about filesystems

Synopsis   **#include <fstab.h>**

Description

The **/etc/fstab** file contains descriptive information about the known file systems. **/etc/fstab** is only read by programs and not written; by convention, you create and maintain this file. Each filesystem is described on a separate line; fields on each line are separated by tabs or spaces. The order of records in **/etc/fstab** is important because **fsck, mount,** and **umount** sequentially iterate through **/etc/fstab** during their work.

The first field, (*fs_spec*), describes the block special device or remote filesystem to be mounted. For filesystems of type **ufs**, the special file name is the block special file name, and not the character special file name. If a program needs the character special file name, the program must create it by appending the letter ''r'' after the last ''/'' (slash) in the special file name.

The second field, (*fs_file*), describes the mount point for the filesystem. For swap partitions, this field should be specified as ''none''.

The third field, (*fs_vfstype*), describes the type of the filesystem. The system currently supports four types of filesystems:

ufs   a local UNIX filesystem

nfs   a Network File System

swap   a disk partition to be used for swapping

s5fs   a System V file system

The fourth field, (*fs_mntops*), describes the mount options associated with the filesystem. It is formatted as a comma separated list of options and contains at least the type of mount (see *fs_type* below) plus any additional options appropriate to the filesystem type.

If the options ''userquota'' and/or ''groupquota'' are specified, the filesystem is automatically processed by the **quotacheck** command, and disk quotas are enabled with the **quotaon** command. By default, filesystem quotas are maintained in files named *quota.user* and *quota.group* which are located at the root of the associated filesystem. These defaults may be overridden by putting an equal sign and an alternative absolute pathname following the quota option. Thus, if the user quota file for **/tmp** is stored in **/var/quotas/tmp.user** this location can be specified as:

userquota=/var/quotas/tmp.user

The type of the mount is extracted from the *fs_mntops* field and stored separately in the *fs_type* field. It is not deleted from the *fs_mntops* field. If *fs_type* is "rw" or "ro" then the filesystem whose name is given in the *fs_file* field is normally mounted read-write or read-only on the specified special file. If *fs_type* is "sw" then the special file is made available as a piece of swap space by the **swapon** command at the end of the system reboot procedure. The fields other than *fs_spec* and *fs_type* are unused. If *fs_type* is specified as "xx" the entry is ignored. This is useful to show disk partitions which are currently unused.

The fifth field, (*fs_freq*), is used for these filesystems by the **dump** command to determine which filesystems need to be dumped. If the fifth field is not present, a value of zero is returned and **dump** assumes that the filesystem does not need to be dumped.

The sixth field, (*fs_passno*), is used by the **fsck** program to determine the order in which filesystem checks are done at reboot time. The root filesystem should be specified with a *fs_passno* of 1, and other filesystems should have a *fs_passno* of 2. Filesystems within a drive will be checked sequentially, but filesystems on different drives will be checked at the same time to utilize parallelism available in the hardware. If the sixth field is not present or zero, a value of zero is returned and **fsck** will assume that the filesystem does not need to be checked.

```
#define FSTAB_RW      "rw"   /* read-write device */
#define FSTAB_RO      "ro"   /* read-only device */
#define FSTAB_SW      "sw"   /* swap device */
#define FSTAB_XX      "xx"   /* ignore totally */

struct fstab {
      char *fs_spec;  /* block special device name */
      char *fs_file;  /* filesystem path prefix */
      char *fs_vfstype;/* type of filesystem */
      char *fs_mntops;/* comma separated mount options */
      char *fs_type;  /* rw, ro, sw, or xx */
      int  fs_freq;   /* dump frequency, in days */
      int  fs_passno; /* pass number on parallel dump */
};
```

The proper way to read records from **/etc/fstab** is to use the routines getfsent(), getfsspec(), getfstype(), and getfsfile().

Files

        /etc/fstab   Specifies the pathname of the file

Related Information

        Commands: **fsck(8), mount(8), umount(8)**

ftpusers

Purpose   The ftpd security file

Synopsis   **/etc/ftpusers**

Description

The **ftpd** security file rejects remote logins to local user accounts specified in **/etc/ftpusers**. Restricted accounts appear one to a line; white space is prohibited. Account names must match exactly the user account name in the **/etc/passwd** file. If the file does not exist, **ftpd** does not do security checks.

Examples

The following are sample entries in an **/etc/ftpusers** file:

```
root
guest
ftp
user1
UUCP
```

Related Information

Commands: **ftp(1)**

Daemons: **ftpd(8)**

gated.conf

Purpose   Contains configuration information for the gated daemon

Synopsis   /etc/gated.conf

Description

The **/etc/gated.conf** file contains configuration information that is read by the **gated** daemon at initialization time. This file contains stanzas that control tracing options, select routing protocols, manage routing information, and manage independent system routing.

Stanzas can appear in any order in the **gated.conf** file. The following sections describe the format of each stanza.

Controlling Trace Output

The option that controls trace output is read during the initialization of the **gated** daemon and whenever the **gated** daemon receives a **SIGHUP** signal. This option is overridden at initialization time if trace flags are specified to the **gated** daemon on the command line.

The **traceflags** stanza is in the following format; it tells the **gated** daemon what level of trace output you want.

traceflags *Flag* [*Flag Flag* . . .]

The valid flags for tracing are as follows:

internal   Logs all internal errors and interior routing errors

external   Logs all external errors due to Exterior Gateway Protocol (EGP), exterior routing errors, and EGP state changes

route   Logs all routing changes

egp   Traces all EGP packets sent and received

update   Logs all routing updates sent

rip   Traces all Routing Information Protocol (RIP) packets received

hello   Traces all HELLO packets received

timestamp
          Prints a timestamp to the log file every 10 minutes

general   Combines the **internal**, **external**, **route**, and **egp** flags

all   Enables all of the listed trace flags

If more than one **traceflags** stanza is used, the trace flags specified in all stanzas are enabled.

Selecting Routing Protocols

This section explains the configuration options for routing protocols. These options provide the **gated** daemon with instructions on how to manage routing for each protocol.

All references to point-to-point interfaces in the **gated** configuration file must use the address specified by the *Destination* parameter.

Using the gated Daemon with the RIP Protocol

The following stanza tells the **gated** daemon how to perform the RIP routing protocol.

RIP *Argument*

Only one of the following RIP *Arguments* is allowed after the **RIP** keyword. Since only the first argument is recognized if more than one is specified, choose the argument that describes the type of RIP routing you need. A list of the arguments to the **RIP** stanza follows:

yes   Performs the RIP protocol, processing all incoming RIP packets and supplying RIP information every 30 seconds only if there are two or more network interfaces.

no   Specifies that the RIP protocol not be performed.

supplier   Performs the RIP protocol, processing all incoming RIP packets and forcing the supply of RIP information every 30 seconds no matter how many network interfaces are present.

pointopoint

Performs the RIP protocol, processing all incoming RIP packets and forcing the supply of RIP information every 30 seconds no matter how many network interfaces are present. When this argument is specified, RIP information is not sent out in a broadcast packet. The RIP information is sent directly to the gateways listed in the **sourceripgateways** stanza.

quiet   Processes all incoming RIP packets, but does not supply any RIP information no matter how many network interfaces are present.

gateway *HopCount*

Processes all incoming RIP packets, supplying RIP information every 30 seconds and announcing the default route (network 0.0.0.0) with a metric specified by the *HopCount* variable. The metric should be specified in a value that represents a RIP hop count.

With this option set, all other default routes coming from other RIP gateways are ignored. The default route is only announced when actively peering with at least one EGP neighbor and therefore should only be used when EGP is used.

If no **RIP** stanza is specified, RIP routing is not performed.

Using the gated Daemon with the HELLO Protocol

The following stanza configures the Defense Communications Network Local Network Protocol (HELLO) routing protocol for the **gated** daemon:

HELLO *Argument*

The *Argument* variable parallels the RIP arguments, with some minor differences.

As with RIP, only one of the following HELLO *Arguments* is allowed after the **HELLO** keyword. Since only the first argument is recognized if more than one is specified, choose the argument that describes the type of RIP routing you need.

A list of the arguments to the **HELLO** stanza follows:

yes   Performs the HELLO protocol, processing all incoming HELLO packets and supplying HELLO information every 15 seconds only if there are two or more network interfaces.

no   Specifies that this gateway does not perform the HELLO protocol.

supplier   Performs the HELLO protocol, processing all incoming HELLO packets and forcing a supply of HELLO information every 15 seconds no matter how many network interfaces are present.

pointopoint

Performs the HELLO protocol, processing all incoming HELLO packets and forcing a supply of HELLO information every 15 seconds no matter how many network interfaces are present.

When this argument is specified, HELLO information is not sent out in a broadcast packet. The HELLO information is sent directly to the gateways listed in the **sourcehellogateways** stanza.

gated.conf(4)

quiet   Processes all incoming HELLO packets, but does not supply any HELLO information regardless of the number of network interfaces present.

gateway *MilliSeconds*

Processes all incoming HELLO packets, supplying HELLO information every 15 seconds and announcing the default route (network 0.0.0.0) with a time delay specified by the *MilliSeconds* variable. The time delay should be a numeric value specified in milliseconds.

The default route is only announced when actively peering with at least one EGP neighbor. Therefore, this stanza should only be used when running EGP.

If no **HELLO** stanza is specified, HELLO routing is not performed.

Using the gated Daemon with the EGP Protocol

The following stanzas specify the information necessary for the **gated** daemon to use EGP.

EGP yes | no

This stanza allows the processing of EGP by the **gated** daemon to be turned on or off. The arguments are interpreted as follows:

yes   Performs all EGP operations.

no   Specifies that no EGP processing should be performed.

Note that EGP processing takes place by default. If no **EGP** stanza is specified, all EGP operations take place.

autonomous system *Number*

When the **gated** daemon performs the EGP protocol, this stanza must be used to specify the independent (autonomous) system number. If this number is not specified, the **gated** daemon exits immediately with an error message.

egpmaxacquire *Number*

When the **gated** daemon performs the EGP protocol, this stanza specifies the number of EGP peers with whom the **gated** daemon performs EGP. The *Number* variable must be a value greater than zero and less than or equal to the number of EGP neighbors specified, or the **gated** daemon exits immediately. If this stanza is omitted, all EGP neighbors are acquired.

When the **gated** daemon performs the EGP protocol, this stanza specifies with whom the **gated** daemon is to perform EGP. The gateway specified by the *Gateway* variable can be eitherf a host address in Internet dotted-decimal notation or a symbolic name from the **/etc/hosts** file.

Each EGP neighbor should have its own **egpneighbor** stanza and is acquired in the order listed in the **gated.conf** file.

The arguments to the **egpmaxaquire***Number* stanza have the following definitions:

metricin *Delay*

egpmetricout *EGPMetric*

ASin *AutonomousSystem*

ASout *AutonomousSystem*

nogendefault

acceptdefault

defaultout *EGPMetric*

validate

intf *Interface*

sourcenet *Network*

metricin *Delay*

> Specifies the internal time delay to be used as a metric for all of the routes learned from this neighbor. The *Delay* variable should be specified as a time delay from 0 to 30,000. If this keyword and the **validate** keyword are not used, the internal metric used is the EGP distance multiplied by 100.

egpmetricout *EGPMetric*

> Sets the EGP distance used for all networks advertised to this neighbor. The *EGPMetric* variable should be specified as an EGP distance in the range of 0 to 255. If this keyword is not specified, the internal time delay for each route is converted to an EGP distance divided by 100, with distances greater than 255 being set to 255.

ASin *AutonomousSystem*

> Verifies the autonomous system number of this neighbor. If the *AutonomousSystem* number specified in neighbor acquisition packets does not verify, an error message is generated refusing the connection. If this keyword is not specified, no verification of autonomous system numbers is done.

ASout *AutonomousSystem*

> Specifies the autonomous system number in EGP packets sent to this neighbor. If an **ASout** stanza is not specified, the *AutonomousSystem* number specified in the **autonomoussystem** stanza is used. This stanza is reserved for a special situation that occurs between the ARPANET network and National Science Foundation (NSF) networks, and is not normally used.

nogendefault
> Specifies that this neighbor should not be considered for the internal generation of a default when the **RIP gateway** or the **HELLO gateway** argument is used. If not specified, the internal default is generated when actively peering with this neighbor.

acceptdefault
> Indicates that the default route (network 0.0.0.0) should be considered valid when received from this neighbor. If this keyword is not specified, on reception of the default route, the **gated** daemon displays a warning message and ignores the route.

defaultout *EGPMetric*
> Specifies that the internally generated default may be passed to this EGP neighbor at the specified distance. The distance should be specified as an EGP distance from 0 to 255. A default route learned from another gateway is not propagated to an EGP neighbor.
>
> Without this keyword, no default route is passed through EGP. The **acceptdefault** keyword should not be specified when the **defaultout** keyword is used. The EGP metric specified in the **egpmetricout** keyword does not apply when the **defaultout** keyword is used. The default route always uses the metric specified by the **defaultout** keyword.

validate Specifies that all networks received from this EGP neighbor must be defined in a **validAS** stanza that also specifies the autonomous system of this neighbor. Networks without a **validAS** stanza are ignored after a warning message is printed.

intf *Interface*
> Defines the interface used to send EGP packets to this neighbor. This keyword is only used when there is no common net or subnet with this EGP neighbor. This keyword is present for testing purposes and does not imply correct operation when peering with an EGP neighbor that does not share a common net or subnet.

sourcenet *Network*
> Specifies the source network to be used in EGP poll packets sent to this neighbor. If this keyword is not specified, the network (not subnet) of the interface used to communicate with this neighbor is used. This keyword is present for testing purposes and does not imply correct operation when used.

Managing Routing Information

The following configuration file stanzas determine how the **gated** daemon handles both incoming and outgoing routing information.

Specifying RIP or HELLO Gateways to Which the gated Daemon Listens

When the following stanzas are specified, the **gated** daemon only listens to RIP or HELLO information, respectively, from these RIP or HELLO gateways:

trustedripgateways *Gateway* [*Gateway Gateway ... *]
trustedhellogateways *Gateway* [*Gateway Gateway . . .*]

The *Gateway* variable may be either an Internet address in dotted-decimal notation, which avoids confusion, or a symbolic name from the **/etc/hosts** file. Note that the propagation of routing information is not restricted by this stanza.

Specifying Gateways for the gated Daemon to Send RIP or HELLO Information

With the following stanzas, the **gated** daemon sends RIP or HELLO information directly to the gateways specified:

sourceripgateways *Gateway* [*Gateway Gateway . . .*]
sourcehellogateways *Gateway* [*Gateway Gateway . . .*]

If the **pointopoint** argument is specified in the **RIP** or **HELLO** stanzas defined earlier, the **gated** daemon sends only RIP or HELLO information to the specified gateways and does *not* send out any information using the broadcast address.

If the **pointopoint** argument is not specified in those stanzas and the **gated** daemon is supplying RIP or HELLO information, the **gated** daemon sends information to the specified gateways and also broadcasts information using a broadcast address.

Turning Routing Protocols On and Off by Interface

The following stanzas turn routing protocols on and off by interface:

noripoutinterface *InterfaceAddress* [*InterfaceAddressInterfaceAddress . . .*]
nohellooutinterface *InterfaceAddress* [*InterfaceAddressInterfaceAddress . . .*]
noripfrominterface *InterfaceAddress* [*InterfaceAddressInterfaceAddress . . .*]
nohellofrominterface *InterfaceAddress* [*InterfaceAddressInterfaceAddress . . .*]

A **noripfrominterface** or **nohellofrominterface** stanza means that no RIP or HELLO information is accepted coming into the listed interfaces from another gateway.

A **noripoutinterface** or **nohellooutinterface** stanza means that no RIP or HELLO knowledge is sent out of the listed interfaces. The *InterfaceAddress* variable should be an Internet address in dotted-decimal notation.

Stopping the gated Daemon from Timing Out Interfaces

The following stanza stops the **gated** daemon from timing out the interfaces whose addresses are listed in Internet dotted-decimal notation by the *InterfaceAddress* arguments. These interfaces are always considered up and working.

passiveinterfaces *InterfaceAddress* [*InterfaceAddressInterfaceAddress* . . .]

This stanza is used because the **gated** daemon times out an interface when no RIP, HELLO, or EGP packets are being received on that particular interface, in order to dynamically determine if an interface is functioning properly.

Packet Switch Node (PSN) interfaces send a RIP or HELLO packet to themselves to determine if the interface is properly functioning, since the delay between EGP packets may be longer than the interface time-out. Interfaces that have timed out automatically have their routes reinstalled when routing information is again received over the interface.

If the **gated** daemon is not a RIP or HELLO supplier, no interfaces are aged and the **passiveinterfaces** stanza automatically applies to all interfaces.

Specifying an Interface Metric

The following stanza allows the specification of an interface metric for the listed interface:

interfacemetric *InterfaceAddress Metric*

On systems that support interface metrics, this stanza overrides the kernel's metric. On systems that do not support an interface metric, this feature allows one to be specified.

The interface metric is added to the true metric of each route that comes in with routing information from the listed interface. The interface metric is also added to the true metric of any information sent out through the listed interface. The metric of directly attached interfaces is also set to the interface metric, and routing information broadcast about directly attached networks is based on the interface metric specified.

The **interfacemetric** stanza is required for each interface on which an interface metric is desired.

Providing Hooks for Fallback Routing

The following stanza provides hooks for fallback routing in the **gated** daemon.

reconstmetric *InterfaceAddress Metric*

If this stanza is used, the metrics of the routes contained in any RIP information coming into the listed interface are set to the metric specified by the *Metric* variable. Metric reconstitution should be used carefully, since it could be a major contributor in the formation of routing loops. Any route that has a metric of infinity is not reconstituted and is left as infinity.

Note that the **reconstmetric** stanza should be used with extreme caution.

The following stanza also provides hooks for fallback routing for the **gated** daemon:

fixedmetric *InterfaceAddress Protocol* **rip** | **hello** *Metric*

If this stanza is used, all routing information sent out by the specified interface has a metric specified by the *Metric* variable. For RIP, specify the metric as a RIP hop count from 0 to infinity. For HELLO, specify the metric as a HELLO delay in milliseconds from 0 to infinity. Any route that has a metric of infinity is left as infinity.

Note that fixed metrics should be used with extreme caution.

Specifying Information to Be Ignored

The following stanza indicates that any information regarding the *Network* variable that comes in by means of the specified protocols and from the specified interfaces is ignored:

donotlisten *Network* **intf** *Address* [*Address* . . .] **proto rip** | **hello**
donotlistenhost *Host* **intf** *Address* [*Address* . . .] **proto rip** | **hello**

The **donotlisten** stanza contains the following information: the keyword **donotlisten**, followed by a network number specified by the *Network* variable, which should be in dotted-decimal notation, followed by the **intf** keyword. Next is a list of interfaces in dotted-decimal notation, then the **proto** keyword, followed by the **rip** or **hello** keyword.

The **all** keyword can be used after the **intf** keyword to specify all interfaces on the system. For example:

```
donotlisten 10.0.0.0 intf 128.84.253.200 proto rip
```

means that any RIP information about network **10.0.0.0** coming in by interface **128.84.253.200** will be ignored. One stanza is required for each network on which this restriction is desired. In addition:

```
donotlisten 26.0.0.0 intf all proto rip hello
```

means that any RIP and HELLO information about network **26.0.0.0** coming in through any interface is ignored.

The **donotlistenhost** stanza is defined in the same way, except that a host address is provided instead of a network address. Restrictions on routing updates are applied to the specified host route learned through the specified routing or protocols.

Specifying Network or Host Information to Which the gated Daemon Listens

The following stanzas indicate that the **gated** daemon should listen to specified protocols and gateways:

listen *Network* **gateway** *Address* [*Address* . . .] **proto rip** I **hello**
listenhost *Host* **gateway** *Address* [*Address* . . .] **proto rip** I **hello**

The **listen** and **listenhost** stanzas specify to listen only to information about a network or host on the specified protocol or protocols and from the listed gateways.

These stanzas read as follows: the **listen** or **listenhost** keyword is followed by a network or host address, respectively, in dotted-decimal notation. Next is the **gateway** keyword with a list of gateways in dotted-decimal notation, and then the **proto** keyword followed by the **rip** or **hello** keyword. For example:

listen 128.84.0.0 gateway 128.84.253.3 proto hello

indicates that any HELLO information about network **128.84** that comes in through gateway **128.84.253.3** is accepted. Any other information about network **128.84** from any other gateway is rejected. One stanza is needed for each net to be restricted.

Also, the stanza:

listenhost 26.0.0.15 gateway 128.84.253.3 proto rip

means that any information about host **26.0.0.15** must come through RIP from gateway **128.84.253.3**. All other information regarding this host is ignored.

Restricting Announcements of Networks and Hosts

The following stanzas allow restriction of the networks and hosts that are announced and the protocols that announce them:

announce *Network InterfaceAddress* [*Address* . . .] *Protocol Type* [*EGPMetric*]
announcehost *Host InterfaceAddress Protocol Type* [*EGPMetric*]
noannounce *Network InterfaceAddress* [*Address* . . .] *Protocol Type* [*EGPMetric*]
noannouncehost *Host InterfaceAddress Protocol Type* [*EGPMetric*]

The **announce{host}** and **noannounce{host}** stanzas cannot be used together on the same interface. With the **announce{host}** stanza, the **gated** daemon only announces the networks or hosts that have an associated **announce** or **announcehost** stanza with the appropriate protocol.

With the **noannounce{host}** stanza, the **gated** daemon announces everything, except those networks or hosts that have an associated **noannounce** or **noannouncehost** stanza. These stanzas provide a choice of announcing only what is on the announce list or everything, except those networks on the **noannounce** list on an individual basis.

The arguments are the same as in the **donotlisten** stanza, except that **egp** may be specified in the *Proto* field. The *Type* can be **rip, hello, egp,** or any combination of the three. When **egp** is specified in the *Proto* field, an EGP metric must be specified. This is the metric at which the **gated** daemon announces the listed network through EGP.

Note that these are not static route entries. These restrictions only apply if the network or host is learned through one of the routing protocols. If a restricted network suddenly becomes unreachable and goes away, announcement of this network stops until it is learned again.

Only one **announce{host}** or **noannounce{host}** stanza may be specified for each network or host. A network or host cannot, for instance, be announced through HELLO for one interface and through RIP for another.

Some example **announce** stanzas might include:

```
announce 128.84 intf all proto rip hello egp egpmetric 0
announce 10.0.0.0 intf all proto rip
announce 0.0.0.0 intf 128.84.253.200 proto rip
announce 35.0.0.0 intf all proto rip egp egpmetric 3
```

With only these four **announce** stanzas in the configuration file, the **gated** process only announces these four networks. Network **.84.0.0** is announced through RIP and HELLO to all interfaces and through EGP with a metric of 0 (zero). Network **.0.0.0** is announced through RIP to all interfaces.

Network **0.0.0.0** (default) is announced by RIP through interface **128.84.253.200** only. Network **35.0.0.0** is announced through RIP to all interfaces and announced through EGP with a metric of 3. These are the only networks that are broadcast by this gateway.

Once the first **announce** stanza is specified, only the networks with **announce** stanzas are broadcast, including local subnetworks. Once an **announce{host}** or **noannounce{host}** stanza has an **all** keyword specified after an **intf** keyword, that stanza is applied globally and the option of having individual interface restrictions is lost.

If no routing announcement restrictions are desired, **announce** stanzas should not be used. All information learned is then propagated out. That announcement has no affect on the information to which the **gated** daemon listens.

Any network that does not have an **announce** stanza is still added to the kernel routing tables, but it is not announced through any of the routing protocols. To stop networks from being added to the kernel, the **donotlisten** stanza may be used.

As another example:

```
announce 128.84 intf 128.59.2.1 proto rip
noannounce 128.84 intf 128.59.1.1 proto rip
```

indicates that on interface **128.59.2.1**, only information about network **128.84.0.0** is announced through RIP, but on interface **128.59.1.1**, all information is announced, except **128.84.0.0** through RIP.

The stanzas:

```
noannounce 128.84 intf all proto rip hello egp egpmetric 0
noannounce 10.0.0.0 intf all proto hello
```

mean that except for the two specified networks, all networks are propagated. Specifically, network **128.84.0.0** is not announced on any interface through any protocols. Knowledge of network **128.84.0.0** is not sent anywhere. Network **10.0.0.0** is not announced through HELLO to any interface.

The second stanza also implies that network **10.0.0.0** is announced to every interface through RIP. This network is also broadcast through EGP with the metric specified in the **defaultegpmetric** stanza.

Defining a Default EGP Metric

The following stanza defines a default EGP metric to use when there are no routing restrictions:

defaultegpmetric *Number*

Without routing restrictions, the **gated** daemon announces all networks learned through HELLO or RIP through EGP with this specified default EGP metric. If this stanza is not used, the default EGP metric is set to 255, which causes any EGP advertised route of this nature to be ignored.

When there are no routing restrictions, any network with a direct interface is announced through EGP with a metric of 0 (zero). Note that this does not include subnetworks, but only the nonsubnetworked network.

Defining a Default Gateway

The following stanza defines a default gateway, which is installed in the kernel routing tables during initialization and reinstalled whenever information about the default route is lost:

defaultgateway *Gateway* [*Metric*] *Protocol* [**active** | **passive**]

This route is installed with a time delay equivalent to a RIP metric of 15, unless another metric is specified with the *Metric* variable.

If the **RIP gateway** or **HELLO gateway** is in use, this default route is deleted.

An **active** default route is overridden by any other default route learned through another routing protocol. A **passive** default route is only overridden by a default route with a lower metric. In addition, an **active** default route is not propagated in routing updates, while a **passive** default route is propagated.

The gateway specified by the *Gateway* variable should be an address in Internet dotted-decimal notation. The *Metric* variable is optional and should be a time delay from 0 to 30,000. If a *Metric* is not specified, a time delay equivalent to a RIP metric of 15 is used.

The *Protocol* variable should be either **rip**, **egp**, or **hello**. The *Protocol* variable initializes the protocol by which the route was learned. In this case the *Protocol* variable is unused but remains for consistency.

Installing a Static Route

The following stanzas install static routes:

net *NetworkAddress* **gateway** *Address* **metric** *HopCount* **rip** | **egp** | **hello**
host *HostAddress* **gateway** *Address* **metric***HopCount* **rip** | **egp** | **hello**

The **net** and **host** stanzas install a static route to the network specified by the *NetworkAddress* variable or the host specified by the *HostAddress* variable. The route is through a gateway specified by the *Address* variable at a metric specified by the *HopCount* variable learned through RIP, HELLO, or EGP. Again, dotted-decimal notation should be used for the addresses. These routes are installed in the kernel's routing table and are never affected by any other gateway's RIP or HELLO announcements. The protocol by which they were learned is important if the route is to be announced through EGP.

If the protocol is RIP or HELLO and there are no routing restrictions, then this route is announced by EGP with a metric of **defaultegpmetric**. If the protocol keyword is **egp** and there are no routing restrictions, then this route is announced by EGP with a metric specified by the *HopCount* variable.

Restricting EGP Announcements

The following stanza provides a *soft restriction* to the **gated** daemon:

egpnetsreachable *Network* [*Network Network* . . .]

It cannot be used when the **announce** or **noannounce** stanzas are used. With no restrictions, the **gated** daemon announces all routes learned from RIP and HELLO through EGP. The **egpnetsreachable** stanza restricts EGP announcement to those networks listed in the stanza.

The metric used for routes learned through HELLO and RIP is the value given in the **defaultegpmetric** stanza. If this stanza does not specify a value, the value is set to 255. With the **egpnetsreachable** stanza, unique EGP metrics cannot be set for each network. The **defaultegpmetric** is used for all networks, except those that are directly connected, which use a metric of 0 (zero).

Specifying Invalid Networks

The following stanza appends to the **gated** daemon's list of martian networks, which are those that are known to be invalid and should be ignored:

martiannets *Network* [*Network Network* . . .]

When the **gated** daemon receives information about one of these networks through any means, it immediately ignores it. If **external** tracing is enabled, a message is printed to the trace log. Multiple occurrences of the **martiannets** stanza accumulate.

The initial list of martian networks provided by the **gated** daemon contains the following networks: 127.0.0.0, 128.0.0.0, 191.253.0.0, 192.0.0.0, 223.255.255.0, and 224.0.0.0.

Managing Autonomous System Routing

In the internal routing tables, the **gated** daemon maintains the autonomous system number from which each route was learned. Independent (autonomous) systems are used only when an exterior routing protocol is in use, in this case EGP.

Routes are tagged with the autonomous system number of the EGP peer from which they were learned. Routes learned through the interior routing protocols, RIP and HELLO, are tagged with the autonomous system number specified in the **autonomoussystem** stanza of the **gated.conf** file.

The **gated** server does not normally propagate routes learned from exterior routing protocols to interior routing protocols, since some gateways do not have adequate validation of routing information they receive. Some of the following stanzas allow exterior routes to be propagated through interior protocols. Therefore, it is imperative that utmost care be taken when allowing the propagation of exterior routes.

The following stanzas provide limited control over routing based on autonomous system numbers.

Validating Networks from an Independent (Autonomous) System

The following stanza is used for validation of networks from a certain independent system:

validAS *Network* **AS** *System* **metric** *Number*

When an EGP update is received from a neighbor that has the **validate** keyword specified in the associated **egpneighbor** stanza, a search is made for a **validAS** stanza that defines the network and the autonomous system number of the EGP neighbor.

If the appropriate **validAS** stanza is located, the network is considered for addition to the routing table with the specified metric. If a **validAS** stanza is not located, a warning message is printed and the network is ignored.

A network may be specified in several **validAS** stanzas as being associated with several different autonomous systems.

Controlling Exchange of Routing Information Between Autonomous Systems

The following stanzas control routing information exchange:

announcetoAS   *AutonomousSystem1*   **ASlist**   *AutonomousSystem2*
[*AutonomousSystem3* . . .]
noannouncetoAS   *AutonomousSystem1*   **ASlist**   *AutonomousSystem2*
[*AutonomousSystem3* . . .]

The **announcetoAS** and **noannouncetoAS** stanzas control the exchange of routing information between different autonomous (independent) systems. Normally, the **gated** daemon does not propagate routing information between independent systems.

The exception to this is that routes learned from the **gated** daemon's own independent system through RIP and HELLO are propagated through EGP. These stanzas allow information learned through EGP from one autonomous system to be propagated through EGP to another autonomous system or through RIP and HELLO to the **gated** daemon's own autonomous system.

If the **announcetoAS** stanza is specified, information learned through EGP from autonomous systems *AS1*, *AS2*, *AS3*, and so on, is propagated to autonomous system *AS0*. If the **gated** daemon's own autonomous system, as specified in the **autonomoussystem** stanza, is specified as *AS0*, this information is propagated through RIP and HELLO. Routing information from autonomous systems not specified in the **ASlist** are not propagated to autonomous system *AS0*.

gated.conf(4)

If the **noannouncetoAS** stanza is specified, information learned through EGP from all autonomous systems, except *AS1*, *AS2*, *AS3*, and so on, is propagated to autonomous system *AS0*. If the **gated** daemon's own autonomous system is specified as *AS0*, this information is not propagated through RIP and HELLO.

Only one **announcetoAS** or **noannounceAS** stanza may be specified for each target autonomous system.

Examples

An example **gated.conf** file for a **gated** server that performs only EGP routing might contain the following entries. The following three lines specify which protocol will be running. RIP and HELLO do not run. EGP does run.

```
RIP     no
HELLO   no
EGP     yes
#
```

The **traceflags** stanza tells what level of trace output is desired:

internal   Logs all internal error and interior routing errors.

external   Logs all external errors due to EGP, exterior routing errors, and EGP state changes.

route   Logs all routing changes.

egp   Traces all EGP packets sent and received.

update   Logs all routing updates.

The autonomous system stanza specifies the autonomous system number. This must be specified if running EGP.

traceflags   internal external route egp update
autonomoussystem   178

The following **egpneighbor** stanza specifies with whom you are going to perform EGP. This line says that your EGP neighbor is the host **192.100.9.1**. The **defaultegpmetric** stanza specifies that when there are no routing restrictions, the default EGP metric is **132**.

```
egpneighbor         192.100.9.1
defaultegpmetric    132
#
```

The next line indicates that for network **192.200.9** the gateway is **192.101.9.3** with a hop count of 50 when using RIP protocol. This is a static route.

The **egpnetsreachable** stanza restricts EGP announcements to those networks listed:

```
net 192.200.9 gateway 192.101.9.3 metric 50 rip
egpnetsreachable 192.200.9 192.101.9
```

The following lists the static routes, showing the host address, gateway address, hop count, and protocol used:

```
# Static routes
host 129.140.46.1      gateway 192.100.9.1    metric 5 rip
host 192.102.9.2       gateway 192.100.9.1    metric 5 rip
host 192.104.9.2       gateway 192.100.9.1    metric 5 rip
host 149.140.3.12      gateway 192.100.9.1    metric 5 rip
host 129.140.3.12      gateway 192.100.9.1    metric 5 rip
host 129.140.3.13      gateway 192.100.9.1    metric 5 rip
host 129.140.3.14      gateway 192.100.9.1    metric 5 rip
host 192.3.3.54        gateway 192.101.9.3    metric 5 rip
```

Related Information

Daemons: **gated(8)**

gateways

Purpose   Specifies Internet routing information to the routed daemon

Synopsis   /etc/gateways

Description

The **/etc/gateways** file identifies gateways for the **routed** daemon. Ordinarily, the **routed** daemon queries the network and builds routing tables. The **routed** daemon builds the tables from routing information transmitted by other hosts directly connected to the network. However, there may be gateways that this command cannot identify through its queries. These unidentified gateways are known as distant gateways. Such gateways should be identified in the **/etc/gateways** file, which the **routed** daemon reads when it starts.

The general format of an file entry in the **/etc/gateways** is

Destination
Name1
gateway
Name2
metric
Value
Type

The following is a brief description of each element in an **/etc/gateways** file entry:

Destination
        A keyword that indicates whether the route is to a network or to a specific host. The two possible keywords are **net** and **host**.

Name1   The name associated with *Destination*. *Name1* can be either a symbolic name (as used in the **/etc/hosts** or **/etc/networks** file) or an Internet address specified in dotted-decimal format.

gateway   An indicator that the following string identifies the gateway host.

Name2   The name or address of the gateway host to which messages should be forwarded.

metric   An indicator that the next string represents the hop count to the destination host or network.

Value   The hop count, or number of gateways, from the local network to the destination network.

Type   A keyword that indicates whether the gateway should be treated as active, passive, or external. The three possible keywords are as follows:

active   An active gateway is treated like a network interface. That is, it is expected to exchange RIP (Routing Information Protocol) routing information. Information about it is maintained in the internal routing tables as long as it is active and is included in any routing information that is transmitted through RIP. If it does not respond for a period of time, the route associated with it is deleted from the internal routing tables.

passive   A passive gateway is not expected to exchange RIP routing information. Information about it is maintained in the routing tables indefinitely and is included in any routing information that is transmitted through RIP.

external   An external gateway is identified to inform the **routed** daemon that another routing process will install such a route and that alternative routes to that destination should not be installed. Information about external gateways is not maintained in the internal routing tables and is not transmitted through RIP.

Note that these routes must be to networks.

Examples

1.   To specify a route to a network through a gateway host with an entry in the **gateways** file, enter:

net net2 gateway host4 metric 4 passive

This example specifies a route to a network, **net2**, through the **gateway host4**. The hop count **metric** to **net2** is **4**, and the gateway is treated as **passive**.

2.   To specify a route to a host through a gateway host with an entry in the **gateways** file, enter:

host host2 gateway host4 metric 4 passive

This example specifies a route to a host, **host2**, through the **gateway host4**. The hop count **metric** to **host2** is **4**, and the gateway is treated as **passive**.

3. To specify a route to a host through an active Internet gateway with an entry in the **gateways** file, enter:

    host host10 gateway 192.100.11.5 metric 9 active

    This example specifies a route to a specific host, **host10**, through the gateway **192.100.11.5**. The hop count **metric** to **host10** is 9 and the gateway is treated as **active**.

4. To specify a route to a host through a passive Internet gateway with an entry in the **gateways** file, enter:

    host host10 gateway 192.100.11.5 metric 9 passive

    This example specifies a route to a specific host, **host10**, through the gateway **192.100.11.5**. The hop **metric** count to **host10** is **9** and the gateway is treated as **passive**. To specify a route to a network through an external gateway, enter a line in the following format:

    net net5 gateway host7 metric 11 external

    This example specifies a route to a network, **net5**, through the gateway **host7**. The hop count **metric** to **net5** is **11** and the gateway is treated as **external** (that is, it is not advertised through RIP, but is advertised through an unspecified routing protocol).

Related Information

Daemons: **routed(8)**

hosts

Purpose   The host name data base

Description

The **hosts** file contains information regarding the known hosts on the network. For each host a single line should be present with the following information:

official host name   Internet address   aliases

Items are separated by any number of blanks and/or tab characters. The # (number sign) indicates the beginning of a comment; characters up to the end of the line are not interpreted by routines which search the file.

When using the name server **named(8)**, this file provides a backup when the name server is not running. For the name server, it is suggested that only a few addresses be included in this file. These include address for the local interfaces that **ifconfig(8)** needs at boot time and a few machines on the local network.

This file may be created from the official host data base maintained at the Network Information Control Center (NIC), though local changes may be required to bring it up to date regarding unofficial aliases and/or unknown hosts. As the data base maintained at NIC is incomplete, use of the name server is recommend for sites on the DARPA Internet.

Network addresses are specified in the conventional "." notation using the **inet_addr()** routine from the Internet address manipulation library, **inet(3N)**. Host names may contain any printable character other than a field delimiter, newline, or comment character.

Files

/etc/hosts

Related Information

gethostbyname(3N), ifconfig(8), named(8)
Name Server Operations Guide for BIND

hosts.equiv

Purpose   A file containing the names of remote systems and users that can execute commands on the local system

Synopsis   **/etc/hosts.equiv**

Description

The **/etc/hosts.equiv** file and the **.rhosts** file in a user's home directory contain the names of remote hosts and users that are equivalent to the local host or user. An equivalent host or user is allowed to access a local nonsuperuser account with the **rsh** command or **rcp** command, or to log in to such an account without having to supply a password.

The **/etc/hosts.equiv** file specifies equivalence for an entire system, while a user's **.rhosts** file specifies equivalence between that user and remote users. The **.rhosts** file must be owned by the user in whose home directory the file is located, or by the superuser. It cannot be a symbolic link.

Each line, or entry, in **hosts.equiv** or **.rhosts** may consist of the following:

- A blank line.

- A comment (begins with a #).

- A hostname (a string of any printable characters except newline, #, or white space).

- A hostname followed by white space and then a username.

To be allowed access, a user's remote hostname and username must match an entry in **hosts.equiv** or **.rhosts**. **hosts.equiv** is searched first; if a match is found, the search ends. If a match is not found, **.rhosts** is searched if it exists in the user's home directory.

A hostname or username can match an entry in **hosts.equiv** or **.rhosts** in one of the following ways:

- The official hostname (not an alias) of the remote host matches a hostname in **hosts.equiv** or **.rhosts**.

- The remote username matches a username in **hosts.equiv** or **.rhosts**.

- If the remote username does not match a username in **hosts.equiv** or **.rhosts**, the remote username matches the local username.

To explicitly exclude particular hostnames or usernames, make an entry like the following in **hosts.equiv** or **.rhosts**:

name

where *name* is a hostname or username. If the remote hostname matches *name*, access is denied, regardless of the username. If the remote username matches *name*, access is denied. If access is denied this way by **hosts.equiv**, access may be allowed with **.rhosts**.

Cautions

For security purposes, the files **/etc/hosts.equiv** and **.rhosts** should exist and be readable and writable only by the owner, even if they are empty.

Examples

The following are sample entries in an **/etc/hosts.equiv** file:

```
# Allows access to host1 and host2:
host1
host2
# Allows access to user johnson on host1:
host1 johnson
# Allows access to host3, and user romero on host3:
host3 romero
```

Files

/etc/hosts.equiv
    Contains the list of equivalent hosts

Related Information

Commands: **rcp(1)**, **rlogin(1)**, **rsh(1)**

Daemons: **lpd, rlogind(8), rshd(8)**

inetd.conf

Purpose   The default configuration file for the inetd daemon

Synopsis   **/etc/inetd.conf**

Description

If the **inetd** daemon is started without specifying an alternate configuration file, the **inetd** daemon reads this file for information on how to handle Internet service requests. The **inetd** daemon reads its configuration file only when the **inetd** daemon starts or when the **inetd** daemon receives a **SIGHUP** signal. Each line in the **inetd** configuration file defines how to handle one Internet service request.

Each line is of the form:

*ServiceName SocketType ProtocolName Wait/NoWait UserName
ServerPath ServerArgs*

These fields must be separated by spaces or tabs. Continuation lines are terminated with a \ (backslash). Comments are denoted with a # (number sign). The fields have the following meanings:

ServiceName   Contains the name of an Internet service defined in the **/etc/services** file. For services provided internally by the **inetd** daemon, this name must be the official name of the service. That is, the name must be identical to the first entry on the line that describes the service in the **/etc/services** file.

SocketType   Contains the name for the type of socket used for the service. You can use either the **stream** value for a stream socket or the **dgram** value for a datagram socket.

ProtocolName   Contains the name of an Internet protocol defined in the **/etc/protocols** file. For example, use the **tcp** value for a service that uses the TCP/IP protocol and the **udp** value for a service that uses the UDP protocol.

Wait/NoWait   Contains either the **wait** or the **nowait** instruction for datagram sockets and the **nowait** instruction for stream sockets. The *Wait/NoWait* field determines whether or not the **inetd** daemon waits for a datagram server to release the socket before continuing to listen at the socket.

UserName   Specifies the username that the **inetd** daemon should use to start the server. This variable allows a server to be given less permission than root.

ServerPath   Specifies the full pathname of the server that the **inetd** daemon should execute to provide the service. For services that the **inetd** daemon provides internally, this field should be internal.

ServerArgs   Specifies the command line arguments that the **inetd** daemon should use to execute the server. These arguments begin with the name of the server used. For services that the **inetd** daemon provides internally, this field should be empty.

Examples

The following are example entries in the **/etc/inetd.conf** file for an **inetd** daemon that

- Uses the **ftpd** daemon for servicing **ftp** requests
- Uses the **talkd** daemon for **ntalk** requests
- Provides time requests internally

```
ftp   stream tcp nowait root /usr/sbin/ftpd ftpd
ntalk dgram  udp wait   root /usr/sbin/talkd talkd
time  stream tcp nowait root internal
time  dgram  udp wait   root internal
```

Related Information

Daemons: **inetd(8)**
Files: **protocols(4)**, **services(4)**, **inetd.sec**

inittab

Purpose   Controls the initialization process

Description

The **inittab** file supplies the **init** program with instructions for creating and running initialization processes. The **init** command reads the **inittab** file each time **init** is invoked. The file typically contains instructions for the default initialization, the creation and control of processes at each run level, and the line process, **getty** which controls the activation of terminal lines.

The **inittab** file is composed of lines, each with four fields; each field is separated by a colon. There is no limit to the number of lines in the **inittab** file. The fields are:

```
Identifier:Runlevel:Action:Command
```

`Indentifier`
This is a fourteen character field used to uniquely identify an object.

`Runlevel`
This is a twenty character field which defines the run levels in which the object is to be processed. `Runlevel` corresponds to a configuration of processes in a system. Each process spawned by the **init** command is assigned one or more run levels in which it is allowed to exist. The run levels are represented by the characters **0**, **2**, **3**, **S**, and **s**. The `Runlevel` field can define multiple run levels for a process by selecting more than one run level in any combination of `Runlevel` characters.

`Action` This is a twenty character field that tells **init** how to treat the specified process. **init** recognizes the following actions:

respawn. If the process does not exist or dies, **init** starts it. If the process currently exists, **init** does nothing and continues scanning the **inittab** file

wait. When **init** enters a run level that matches the run level of the entry, it starts the process and waits for its termination. As long as **init** continues in this run level, it does not act on subsequent reads of the entry in the **inittab** file.

once. When **init** enters a run level that matches the line's run level, it starts the process and does not wait for its termination. When the process stops, **init** does not restart it. If **init** enters a new run level where the process is still running from a previous runlevel change, **init** does not restart the process.

boot. When **init** first executes and reads the **inittab** file, it processes this entry. **init** starts the process and does not wait for its termination. When the process stops, **init** does not restart it. The run level specified in this line entry should be the default run level, or it must match the run level at which **init** operates at boot time.

bootwait. When **init** first executes and reads the **inittab** file, it processes this line entry. **init** starts the process, waits for its termination and, when it dies, does not restart the process.

powerfail. When **init** receives the **SIGPWR** power fail signal, it execute the process associated with this line.

powerwait. When **init** receives the the **SIGPWR** power fail signal, it executes the process associated with this line and waits until the process terminates before continuing any processing of the **inittab** file.

off. If the process associated with this line is currently running, **init** sends the warning signal **SIGTERM** and waits 20 seconds before sending the kill signal **SIGKILL**. If the process is nonexistent, **init** ignores the line.

initdefault. A line with this action is processed when **init** is originally invoked. **init** uses this line to determine which run level to enter originally. It does this by taking the highest run level specified in the run level field and using that as its initial state. If the run level field is empty, this is interpreted as 0s23, so **init** will enter run level **3**. If **init** does not find an **initdefault** line in the **inittab** file, it requests an initial runlevel from the operator.

sysinit Entries of this type are executed before **init** tries to access the console. It is expected that this line will be only used to initialize devices on which **init** might try to request a run level.

Command

This is a 1024 character field which holds the **sh** command to be executed. The entry in the command field is prefixed with exec. Any legal **sh** syntax can appear in the command field. Comments can be inserted with the #comment syntax. The line continuation character may be placed at the end of a line.

inittab(4)

Files

/etc/inittab
Specifies the pathname of the file

/etc/getty
Specifies the command that initializes and controls terminal lines

Related Information

Commands: **init(8)**

Call: **kill(2)**

/usr/spool/mqueue

Purpose   Contains the log file and temporary files associated with the messages in the mail queue

Synopsis   **/usr/spool/mqueue**

Description

The **/usr/spool/mqueue** directory contains temporary files associated with the messages in the mail queue and may contain the **log** file. Temporary files have names that include the mail queue ID (*MQID*) of the message for which the file was created:

df*MQID*   Data file

lf*MQID*   Lock file

nf*MQID*   Backup file

qf*MQID*   Queue control file

tf*MQID*   Temporary control file

xf*MQID*   Transcript file for session

Related Information

Commands: **sendmail(8)**

Daemons: **/etc/syslogd**

named.boot

Purpose   named configuration file

Synopsis   **/etc/named.boot**

Description

This file is the default configuration (or boot) file for the **named** server.

The **named** daemon reads the start-up file when the **named** daemon starts and when receiving signal SIGHUP.

The records in the **named.boot** file tell the **named** daemon what type of server it is, which domains (or zones of authority) it has authority over, and where to get the data for initially setting up its database.

The name server first needs to know the root name server, which is the authority server for the network. The root name server is established in the **named.boot** file by specifying the root server filename (**named.ca**) as the cache for this name server.

The general format of each line in this file is as follows:

Type Domain Source

Type   Determines the type of information required for the database. The *Type* field can have one of the following values:

    domain   Indicates that the following *Domain* entry is the name of the default domain. When the **named** daemon receives a query with a domain or hostname that does not end with a . (dot), the **named** daemon appends the default domain name to the queried name.

    primary   Indicates that the local **named** server is the primary name server for the domain specified in the *Domain* field and that the **named** daemon is to get the data describing the domain from the file specified in the *Source* field.

    secondary

        Indicates that the local **named** server is a secondary name server for the domain specified in the *Domain* field and that the **named** daemon is to get the data describing the domain from one or more remote primary name servers using the Internet address or addresses specified in the *Source* field. The **named** daemon tries each address in the order listed until it successfully receives the data from one of the name servers.

cache   Indicates that the local **named** server is a caching name server for the domain specified in the *Domain* field and that the **named** daemon is to get the data describing the domain from the file specified in the *Source* field.

Domain   Specifies the domain.

Source   Specifies a file containing information that describes the domain.

Note that the **named** daemon does not provide other hosts with the information contained in a cache file. Cache files are usually used for listing the name servers for domains higher than the local domain.

Comments in the boot file begin with a ; (semicolon) and end at the end of the line.

These data files can have any name. However, for convenience in maintaining the **named** database, they are generally given names in the following form: **/etc/named.***extension*. The general format of **named** data files is described in **/etc/named.***.

Examples

The following examples show the various ways to use the **named** start-up file.

1.   The **/etc/named.boot** file for **venus**, a primary name server, contains these entries:

```
; Boot file for primary name server
;
; type        domain                    source file or host
domain        abc.aus.osf.com
cache         .                         /etc/named.ca
primary       abc.aus.osf.com           /etc/named.abcdata
primary       xyz.aus.osf.com           /etc/named.xyzdata
primary       201.9.192.in-addr.arpa    /etc/named.abcrev
primary       100.114.128.in-addr.arpa  /etc/named.xyzrev
primary       0.0.127.in-addr.arpa      /etc/named.local
```

In this example, the primary name server is **venus** and the Internet address is **192.9.201.1**.

2.   The **/etc/named.boot** file for **kronos**, a secondary name server, contains these entries:

```
; Boot file for secondary name server
;
; type        domain                    source file or host
domain        abc.aus.osf.com
cache         .                         /etc/named.ca
secondary     abc.aus.osf.com           192.9.201.1 192.9.201.2
secondary     xyz.aus.osf.com           192.9.201.1 192.9.201.2
secondary     201.9.192.in-addr.arpa    192.9.201.1 192.9.201.2
secondary     100.114.128.in-addr.arpa 192.9.201.1 192.9.201.2
primary       0.0.127.in-addr.arpa      /etc/named.local
```

In this example the secondary name server is **kronos** and the Internet address is 192.9.201.2.

3.   The **/etc/named.boot** file for **hera**, a cache-only name server, contains these entries:

```
; Boot file for cache only server
;
; type        domain                    source file or host
domain        abc.aus.osf.com
cache         .                         /etc/named.ca
primary       0.0.127.in-addr.arpa      /etc/named.local
```

Files

/etc/named.boot
        Contains the configuration information for the **named** server.

Related Information

Command: **named**

File: **named.***

named.*

Purpose   Defines the data that the named daemon uses to initialize the BIND (Berkeley Internet Name Domain) name server file

Synopsis   **/etc/named.***

Description

The data files referenced in the **named.boot** file can have any names, but they are generally given names of the form **/etc/named.***. This naming convention is used for convenience in maintaining the **named** daemon's file.

The records in the **named** data files are called resource records. Except for comments (starting with a ; [semicolon] and continuing to the end of the line), the resource records in the data files generally follow the format of the resource records that the **named** daemon returns in response to queries from resolver routines.

The **named.boot** file is the default configuration (or boot) file for the **named** server. The **named** daemon reads the start-up file when the **named** daemon starts and when receiving the signal **SIGHUP**.

Examples

1. The following examples portray two domains on two different networks:

```
Domain
abc.aus.osf.com,
Internet address 192.9.201.n
```

(where n varies for each system on the network)

```
Domain
xyz.aus.osf.com,
Internet address 128.114.100.n
```

(where n varies for each system on the network)

In this sample configuration, both the primary and the secondary name servers are in the **abc.aus.osf.com** domain, and host **hera** is the gateway host.

named.*(4)

2. The following are sample entries in a **named.ca** file:

```
; root name servers.
          1         IN    NS    relay.osf.com.
relay.osf.com.   3600000    IN    A    129.114.1.2
```

3. The following two files are sample entries from the **named.data** files for hosts **venus** and **allen**. (The data files can have any name you choose, as long as that name is defined in the **named.boot** file. In this case, the names are **named.abcdata** and **named.xyzdata**.)

The **named** file for host **venus** is in the following file, called **named.abcdata**:

```
;OWNER          TTL        CLASS TYPE     RDATA
;local domain server is venus
@   IN   SOA   venus   bob.robert.abc.aus.osf.com. (
                           1.1      ;serial
                           3600     ;refresh
                           600      ;retry
                           3600000 ;expire
                           86400)  ;minimum
     IN   NS   venus
     IN   NS   kronos
     IN   MX   10        venus.abc.aus.osf.com.
; address for local loopback
localhost         IN    A        127.1
; address of machines in the same domain
venus             IN    A        192.9.201.1
venus             IN    A        128.114.100.1
venus             IN    MX       10   venus.aub.aus.osf.com.
veabc             IN    CNAME    venus
                  IN    WKS      192.9.201.1 udp (tftp
                                 nameserver domain)
                  IN    WKS      192.9.201.1 tcp (echo telnet
                                 smtp discard uucp-path systat
                                 daytime netstat chargen ftp
                                 time whois finger hostnames
                                 domain)
```

```
; delimiter for WKS
kronos              IN    A         192.9.201.2
krabc               IN    CNAME     kronos
hera                IN    A         192.9.201.5
                    IN    A         128.114.100.5
robert              IN    A         192.9.201.6
ernie               IN    A         192.9.201.7
                    IN    HINFO     HP-800 OS1
robert.abc.aus.osf.com.  IN    MX 10     venus.abc.aus.osf.com.
```

4. The **named** file for host **allen** is in the following file, called **named.xyzdata**:

```
;OWNER           TTL         CLASS TYPE       RDATA
;local domain server is venus
xyz.aus.osf.com.  IN    SOA   venus.abc.aus.osf.com.  bob.robe
rt.abc.aus.osf.com. (
                            1.1       ;serial
                            3600      ;refresh
                            600       ;retry
                            3600000  ;expire
                            86400)   ;minimum
xyz.aus.osf.com.  IN    NS    venus.abc.aus.osf.com.
                  IN    NS    kronos.abc.aus.osf.com.
                  IN    MX    10      venus.abc.aus.osf.com.
; address for local loopback
localhost         IN    A         127.1
; address of machines in the same domain
allen             IN    A         128.114.100.3
allen             IN    MX        10    venus.aub.aus.osf.com.
alxyz             IN    CNAME     allen
                  IN    WKS       128.114.100.3 udp (tftp
                                  nameserver domain)
                  IN    WKS       128.114.100.3 tcp (echo telnet
                                  smtp discard uucp-path systat
                                  daytime netstat chargen ftp
                                  time whois finger hostnames
                                  domain)
; delimiter for WKS
fred              IN    A         128.114.100.10
mike              IN    A         128.114.100.11
                  IN    HINFO     HP-800 OS1
```

5. The following is a sample **named.local** file that might appear on hosts in either of the sample domains:

```
@   IN   SOA   venus.abc.aus.osf.com. gail.zeus.abc.aus.osf.com.
(
                            1.1      ;serial
                            3600     ;refresh
                            600      ;retry
                            3600000  ;expire
                            86400)   ;minimum
        IN   NS    venus.abc.aus.osf.com.
1       IN   PTR   localhost.
```

6. The following two files are sample entries from the **named.rev** files for hosts **venus** and **allen**. For this example, the files are called **named.abcrev** and **named.xyzrev**.

The reverse file for host **venus** is in the following file, called **named.abcrev**:

```
@   IN   SOA   venus.abc.aus.osf.com. bob.robert.abc.aus.osf.com.
(
                            1.1      ;serial
                            3600     ;refresh
                            600      ;retry
                            3600000  ;expire
                            86400)   ;minimum
9.201.192.in-addr.arpa.    IN   NS    venus.abc.aus.osf.com.
                           IN   NS    kronos.abc.aus.osf.com.
                           IN   PTR   hera.abc.aus.osf.com.
;ABC.AUS.OSF.COM Hosts
1.201.9.192.in-addr.arpa.  IN   PTR   venus.abc.aus.osf.com.
2.201.9.192.in-addr.arpa.  IN   PTR   kronos.abc.aus.osf.com.
5.201.9.192.in-addr.arpa.  IN   PTR   hera.abc.aus.osf.com.
6.201.9.192.in-addr.arpa.  IN   PTR   robert.abc.aus.osf.com.
7.201.9.192.in-addr.arpa.  IN   PTR   ernie.abc.aus.osf.com.
```

The reverse file for host **allen** is in the following file, called **named.xyzrev**:

```
@  IN   SOA   venus.abc.aus.osf.com. bob.robert.abc.aus.osf.com.
(
                              1.1      ;serial
                              3600     ;refresh
                              600      ;retry
                              3600000  ;expire
                              86400)   ;minimum
100.114.128.in-addr.arpa.     IN       NS    venus.abc.aus.osf.com.
                              IN       NS    kronos.abc.aus.osf.com.
                              IN       PTR   hera.abc.aus.osf.com.
;XYZ.AUS.OSF.COM Hosts
3.100.114.128.in-addr.arpa.  IN       PTR    allen.abc.aus.osf.com.
10.100.114.128.in-addr.arpa. IN       PTR    fred.abc.aus.osf.com.
11.100.114.128.in-addr.arpa. IN       PTR    mike.abc.aus.osf.com.
;ABC.AUS.OSF.COM Hosts
1.100.114.128.in-addr.arpa. IN       PTR    venus.abc.aus.osf.com.
5.100.114.128.in-addr.arpa. IN       PTR    hera.abc.aus.osf.com.
```

Related Information

Daemon: **named(8)**

networks

Purpose   Contains the network name file

Synopsis   **/etc/networks**

Description

The **networks** file contains information about the known networks that comprise the DARPA (Defense Advanced Research Projects Agency) Internet. Each network is represented by a single line in the **networks** file. The format for the entries in the **networks** file is as follows:

Name Number Aliases

The fields contain the following:

Name   The official network name.

Number   The network number.

Aliases   The unofficial names used for the network.

Items on a line are separated by one or more spaces or tab characters. Comments begin with a # (number sign). Routines that search the **networks** file do not interpret characters from the beginning of a comment to the end of that line. Network numbers are specified in dotted-decimal notation. A network name can contain any printable character except a field delimiter, newline character, or comment character (#).

The **networks** file is normally created from the official network database maintained at the Network Information Center (NIC). The file may need to be modified locally to include unofficial aliases or unknown networks.

Files

/etc/networks
        Contains the network name database

Related Information

Daemons: **routed(8)**

Routines: **getnetent(3)**, **getnetbyname(3)**, **getnetbyaddr(3)** ;...

printcap

Purpose   printer capability data base

Synopsis   /etc/printcap

Description

The **printcap** file is a simplified version of the **/etc/termcap** database format, but is used to describe line printer characteristics. The host **lpd** line printer daemon accesses the **/etc/printcap** file every time a file is passed to the spooler for printing. The print spooling system uses the **printcap** file for dynamic addition and deletion of printers. Each entry in the **printcap** database is used to describe a single printer. This database may not be substituted as is possible with the **/etc/termcap** file because its substitution could cause printer accounting to be bypassed.

The default printer normally has the device reference **lp**, although environment variable **PRINTER** may be used to override this reference. Each spooling utility supports the option, **-P**_printer_, to allow explicit naming of a destination printer.

Printer Characteristic Parameters

Each printer served by the printer spooler has various characteristics that the **lpd** line printer daemon must know about to communicate with the printing device defined in the **/dev** directory. The following table lists the printer characteristic parameters. The **Name** column lists the 2-character nmemonic used to define the parameter. The parameter must be specified exactly as it appears in this column.

The **Type** column defines the type of data expressed by the entry as **str**, **num**, or **bool**. When the parameter you define is referenced as a string variable (**str**) in the **Type** column, it must be followed by an = (equal sign) together with the string; when you do not define the string parameter, it remains a **NULL** string and contains no data or it takes the value specified in the **Default** column. When the **Type** column defines a parameter type as **bool**, it may only be logically **true** (yes) or logically **false** (no).

When the parameter you define is a numerical variable, it must be followed with a **#** (pound sign) together with the numerical value you assign; when you do not define the numerical parameter it takes the value specified in the **Default** column of the table.

The **Description** column tells you the reason for the parameter. Refer to the **/etc/termcap** manpage for a description of a typical **printcap** file layout.

printcap(4)

Name	Type	Default	Description
af	str	NULL	name of accounting file
br	num	none	if **lp** is a **tty**, set the baud rate (**ioctl** call)
cf	str	NULL	**cifplot** data filter
df	str	NULL	**tex** data filter (DVI format)
fc	num	0	if **lp** is a tty, clear flag bits (**sgtty.h**)
ff	str	\f	string to send for a form feed
fo	bool	false	print a form feed when device is opened
fs	num	0	like **fc** but set bits
gf	str	NULL	graph data filter (plot format)
hl	bool	false	print the burst header page last
ic	bool	false	driver supports (non standard) **ioctl** to indent printout
if	str	NULL	name of text filter that does accounting
lf	str	**/dev/console**	error logging filename
lo	str	**lock**	name of lock file
lp	str	**/dev/lp**	device name to open for output
mx	num	1000	maximum file size (in BUFSIZ blocks), zero = unlimited
nd	str	NULL	next directory for list of queues (unimplemented)
nf	str	NULL	**ditroff** data filter (device independent troff)
of	str	NULL	name of output filtering program
pc	num	200	price per foot or page in hundredths of cents
pl	num	66	page length (in lines)
pw	num	132	page width (in characters)
px	num	0	page width in pixels (horizontal)
py	num	0	page length in pixels (vertical)
rf	str	NULL	filter for printing FORTRAN style text files
rg	str	NULL	restricted group; only members of group allowed access
rm	str	NULL	machine name for remote printer
rp	str	**lp**	remote printer name argument
rs	bool	false	restrict remote users to those with local accounts
rw	bool	false	open the printer device for reading and writing
sb	bool	false	short banner (one line only)
sc	bool	false	suppress multiple copies
sd	str	**/usr/spool/lpd**	spool directory
sf	bool	false	suppress form feeds
sh	bool	false	suppress printing of burst page header
st	str	**status**	status filename
tf	str	NULL	**troff** data filter (**cat** phototypesetter)
tr	str	NULL	trailer string to print when queue empties
vf	str	NULL	raster image filter
xc	num	0	if **lp** is a **tty**, clear local mode bits (**tty**)
xs	num	0	like **xc** but set bits

When the local line printer driver supports indentation, the **lpd** line printer daemon must understand how to invoke this capability.

Filter and Flags

The **lpd** line printer daemon creates a pipeline of **filters** to process files for various different printer device. The filters you select depend on the flags that are passed to the **lpr** command. The pipeline set up is:

-p	**pr | if**	regular text + **pr**
none	**if**	regular text
-c	**cf**	**cifplot**
-d	**df**	DVI (**tex**)
-g	**gf**	**plot**
-n	**nf**	**ditroff**
-f	**rf**	FORTRAN
-t	**tf**	**troff**
-v	**vf**	raster image

The **if** filter is invoked with arguments:

   if [**-c**] **-w***width* **-l***length* **-i***indent* **-n***login* **-h***host acct-file*

The **-c** flag is passed only when the **-l** flag (pass control-characters literally) is specified to the **lpr** command. The **-w***width* and **-l***length* parameters specify the page width and length (from the assigned or default values of **pw** and **pl** respectively in the **printcap** file) in characters. The **-n** and **-h** flags specify the login name and hostname of the owner of the job, respectively. The *acct-file* is passed from the **af** entry in the **printcap** file.

The **if** filter is opened for all individual jobs, which makes it suitable for accounting. When the **if** filter is not specified, the system uses the **of** filter as the default value. The **of** filter however, is opened only once and is only given the **-w***width* **and -l***length* **flags.**

All other filters are called as:

   filter -x*width* **-y***length* **-n***login* **-h** *host acct-file*

Where **-x***width* and **-y***length* are represented in pixels as specified by the **px** and **py** entries, respectively, in the **printcap** file.

All filters take standard input (**stdin**) as the source file and standard output (**stdout**) as the destination. The printer may log either to standard error (**stderr**) or use **syslogd**, and must not ignore the **SIGINT** signal.

printcap(4)

Error Logging

Error messages generated by the line printer programs (that is, the **lp*** programs) are logged by **syslogd** using the **lpr** facility. Messages printed on the **stderr** of one of the filters are sent to the corresponding **lf** file specified in the **printcap** file. The filters may, of course, also use **syslogd.**

Error messages sent to the console have a carriage return and a line feed appended to them, rather than just a line feed.

Related Information

Commands: **lpc(8), lpd(8), pac(8), lpr(1), lpq(1), lprm(1)**

Files: **/etc/termcap**

protocols

Purpose   Defines the Internet protocols used on the local host

Synopsis   **/etc/protocols**

Description

The **/etc/protocols** file contains information about the known protocols used in the DARPA (Defense Advanced Research Projects Agency) Internet. Each protocol is represented by a single line in the **protocols** file. Each entry is of the form:

Name Number Aliases

The fields contain the following information:

Name   Official Internet protocol name.

Number   Protocol number.

Aliases   Unofficial names used for the protocol.

Items on a line are separated by one or more spaces or tab characters. Comments begin with the # (number sign), and routines that search the **protocols** file do not interpret characters from the beginning of a comment to the end of the line. A protocol name can contain any printable character except a field delimiter, newline character, or comment character.

The lines in the file appear as follows:

```
#
# Internet (IP) protocols
#       @(#)protocols 5.1 (Berkeley) 4/17/90
#
ip        0    IP        # internet protocol, pseudo protocol number
icmp      1    ICMP      # internet control message protocol
ggp       3    GGP       # gateway-gateway protocol
tcp       6    TCP       # transmission control protocol
egp       8    EGP       # exterior gateway protocol
pup       12   PUP       # PARC universal packet protocol
udp       17   UDP       # user datagram protocol
hmp       20   HMP       # host monitoring protocol
xns-idp   22   XNS-IDP   # Xerox NS IDP
rdp       27   RDP       # "reliable datagram" protocol
```

protocols(4)

Related Information

Subroutines: **getprotoent(3),** **getprotobynumber(3),** **getprotobyname(3),** **setprotoent(3), endprotoent(3)**

remote.unknown

Purpose   Logs access attempts by unknown remote systems

Synopsis   **/usr/lib/uucp/remote.unknown**

Description

The **/usr/lib/uucp/remote.unknown** file contains a shell procedure. It is executed by the **uucp** program when a remote computer that is not listed in the local **/usr/lib/uucp/Systems** file attempts to communicate with that local system. The **uucp** program does not permit the unknown remote system to connect with the local system. Instead, the **remote.unknown** shell procedure appends an entry to the file **/usr/spool/uucp/.Admin/Foreign**.

Modify the **remote.unknown** file to fit the needs of your site. For example, to allow unknown systems to contact your system, remove the execute permissions for the **remote.unknown** file. You can also modify the shell script to send mail to the **uucp** administrator or to recognize certain systems and reject others.

Only someone with superuser authority can edit the **remote.unknown** file, which is owned by the **uucp** program login ID.

Files

/usr/lib/uucp directory
> Contains all the configuration files for uucp, including the **remote.unknown** file

/usr/lib/uucp/Systems(4) file
> Describes accessible remote systems

/usr/spool/uucp/.Admin(4)
> **Foreign(4)** file   Lists access attempts by unknown systems

resolv.conf

Purpose   resolver configuration file

Synopsis   **/etc/resolv.conf**

Description

The resolver is a set of routines in the C library (**resolver(3)**) that provide access to the Internet Domain Name System. The resolver configuration file contains information that is read by the resolver routines the first time they are invoked by a process. The file is designed to be human readable and contains a list of keywords with values that provide various types of resolver information.

On a normally configured system this file should not be necessary. The only name server to be queried will be on the local machine, the domain name is determined from the host name, and the domain search path is constructed from the domain name.

The file format is as follows:

nameserver *Address*

Internet address (in dot notation) of a name server that the resolver should query. Up to MAXNS (currently 3) name servers may be listed, one per keyword. If there are multiple servers, the resolver library queries them in the order listed. If no nameserver entries are present, the default is to use the name server on the local machine. (The algorithm used is to try a name server, and if the query times out, try the next, until out of name servers, then repeat trying all the name servers until a maximum number of retries are made).

domain *DomainName*

Local domain name. Most queries for names within this domain can use short names relative to the local domain. If no domain entry is present, the domain is determined from the local host name returned by gethostname(2); the domain part is taken to be everything after the first '.'. Finally, if the host name does not contain a domain part, the root domain is assumed.

search

Search list for host-name lookup. The search list is normally determined from the local domain name; by default, it begins with the local domain name, then successive parent domains that have at least two components in their names. This may be changed by listing the desired domain search path following the search keyword with spaces or tabs separating the names. Most resolver queries will be attempted using each component of the search path in turn until a match is found. Note that this process may be slow and will generate a lot of network traffic if the servers for the listed domains are not local, and that queries will time out if no server is available for one of the domains.

The search list is currently limited to six domains with a total of 256 characters.

The domain and search keywords are mutually exclusive. If more than one instance of these keywords is present, the last instance will override.

The keyword and value must appear on a single line, and the keyword (e.g. nameserver) must start the line. The value follows the keyword, separated by white space.

Cautions

Any white space entered after the domain name is not ignoried but is interpreted as part of the domain name.

Files

/etc/resolv.conf

Related Information

gethostbyname(3N), resolver(3), hostname(7), named(8)
Name Server Operations Guide for BIND

sendmail.cf

Purpose   Contains the **sendmail** configuration file data

Synopsis   **sendmail.cf**

Description

The **/var/adm/sendmail/sendmail.cf** file contains configuration information for the **sendmail** daemon. Use the **sendmail -bz** command after changing any information in the **sendmail.cf** file. The **sendmail -bz** command builds a configuration file that the **sendmail** daemon can read.

The **sendmail.cf** configuration file consists of a series of control lines, each of which begins with a single character that defines how the rest of the line is used. Lines beginning with a space or a tab are continuation lines. Blank lines and lines beginning with a # (number sign) are comments. The control line can be used for the following functions:

- Defining macros and classes for use within the configuration file

- Defining message precedence for mail delivery

- Defining administrative IDs to override the sender's address

- Defining message headings

- Defining the mail daemon to use

- Setting options used by the **sendmail** command

You can edit the **sendmail.cf** configuration file with any text editor.

The configuration file entries consist of lines, each of which begins with a single-character command and an operand. Continue entries onto multiple lines by placing white space at the beginning of each subsequent line. The # (number sign) indicates that the following line is a comment line.

Defining Macros and Classes (D Control Line and C Control Line)

Macros and classes in the **sendmail.cf** configuration file are interpreted by the **sendmail** daemon. A **macro** is a symbol that represents a value or string, for example, or an Internet address. A macro is defined by a **D** control line in the **sendmail.cf** file. Macros are not expanded until the **sendmail** daemon loads the rule sets when it starts up. The **sendmail.cf** file contains *system-defined macros* and *required macros* that you must define.

A **class** is a symbol that represents a set of one or more words, for example, or a filename. Classes are used in pattern matching when the **sendmail** daemon is parsing addresses. You can create a class using a list or you can create a class using a file.

The following letters introduce configuration-file control lines that define macros and classes to set up the **sendmail** daemon:

D*MacroValue*   Defines a macro and assigns a value to it. If a second **D***MacroValue* defines the same symbol, the second definition replaces the first definition. The symbol must be a single character selected from the ASCII set. Use uppercase letters for macros and classes that you define. Lowercase letters and special symbols are macros and classes defined by the daemon.

C*Class String*   Defines *Class* to be a class and assigns a word or group of words (*String*) to it. If a second **C***Class String* defines the same symbol, the *String* from the second definition is added to the *String* from the first definition. No words are deleted from the class definition. Class specifiers may be any of the uppercase letters from the ASCII character set. Lowercase letters and special characters are reserved for system use.

F*Class FileName* [*Format*]

   Defines symbol *Class* to be a class and assigns a word or group of words listed in a separate file to the symbol. You can specify an optional **scanf** format specifier. Class specifiers may be any of the uppercase letters from the ASCII character set. Lowercase letters and special characters are reserved for system use.

To use a macro or class in a control line, put a **$** (dollar sign) before its name. For example, if the name of the macro is **x**, use **$x** when using that macro in a control line. Without the preceding **$**, the daemon interprets **x** as only the letter x. The format for specifying conditional expressions is as follows:

```
$?Macro Text1 $| Text2 $.
```

In this format, the symbols have the following meaning:

$?	If.
Macro	The macro being tested.
Text1	The pattern to be used if $x is defined.
$|	Else. (This symbol is not required.)
Text2	The pattern to be used if $*Macro* is not defined.
$.	Specifies the end of the conditional expression.

Do not use any of the characters defined as tokens (by the required macro **o**) when defining a word in a class. The **sendmail** daemon may not be able to read the definition correctly.

Defining Message Precedence (P Control Line)

The **sendmail.cf** configuration file also contains lines to define mail-queue precedence for messages that contain a **Precedence:** field. Normally, you do not need to change the values in the default **sendmail.cf** configuration file.

The name defined and the numerical value assigned are based on the needs of the network. Higher numbers have higher priority; numbers less than 0 (zero) indicate that error messages will not be returned to the sender of these messages. The precedence value is 0 (zero) for any precedence name not defined in this file. For example, the configuration file may contain the following entries:

```
Pfirst-class=0
Pspecial-delivery=100
Pbulk=-60
Pjunk=-100
```

These entries set **special-delivery** as the highest priority message and **junk** as the lowest priority

Defining Administrative IDs (T Control Line)

Administrative IDs can override the sender address using the **-f** flag to the **sendmail** command. The **sendmail.cf** configuration file defines these IDs with the **T** control line. For example, the configuration file may contain the following entries:

```
Troot
Tdaemon
Tuucp
```

These entries define IDs **root, daemon,** and **uucp** as administrative IDs for the **sendmail** command.

These IDs could have been defined using only one **T** control line:

```
Troot daemon uucp network
```

Defining Message Headings (H Control Line)

The **sendmail** daemon expects mail to have the following parts in the following order:

1. An operating system **From:** line (defined by the five characters: **F, r, o, m,** and space)

2. Mail header lines that begin with a keyword followed by a colon, such as **From:** or **To:**

3. An empty line

4. The body of the message

The **sendmail** daemon detects the operating system **From:** line by checking the first five characters of the first line. After that, header lines are processed. When it detects a line that does not begin with a keyword followed by a colon, it ends header line processing. If an empty line occurs at that point, it is ignored.

Mailer flags or the mailer itself determine if an operating system **From:** line is generated. Other header lines are present (or not) depending on those defined in the **sendmail** configuration file, those specified by mailer flags, and those present in incoming mail.

Note that the **binmail** daemon generates a **From:** line on all local deliveries. The **sendmail** mailer flags do not allow you to alter this.

Lines in the configuration file that begin with a capital letter **H** define the format of the headers used in messages. The format of the **H** control line line is as follows:

H[?*MailerFlags*?]*FieldName*: *Content*

In this format, the variable parameters have the following meaning:

MailerFlags   This field is optional. If you supply it, surround it with ? (question marks). This field contains mailer flags that determine whether this **H** line is used. If the mailer being used requires the information specified by the mailer flag, then this **H** control line is included when formatting the heading. Otherwise, this **H** control line is ignored.

FieldName   This field contains the text that is displayed as the name of the field in the heading information. The actual text used is a matter of choice. Some typical field names include **From:**, **To:**, and **Rcvd From:**.

Content   This field defines the information that is displayed following the field name. It usually uses a **sendmail** macro to specify the information.

The following example lines are from a typical **sendmail.cf** file:

```
H?P?Return-Path: <$g>
```

This line defines a field called **Return-Path:** that displays the content of the **$g** macro (sender address relative to the receiver). The **?P?** portion indicates that this line is only used if the mailer uses the **P** flag (the mailer requires a **Return-Path** line).

```
HReceived: $?sfrom $s $.by $j ($v/$Z)
        id $i; $b
```

This line defines a field called **Received**. This field displays the following information:

$?sfrom $s $. If an **s** macro is defined (sender's hostname), displays the text **from** followed by the content of the **$s** macro.

by $j   Displays the text **by** followed by the content of the **$j** macro (official name for this site).

($v/$Z)   Displays the version of the **sendmail** daemon (**$v**) and the version of the **sendmail.cf** file (**$Z**) set off by parentheses and separated by a slash.

id $i;   Displays the text **id** followed by the content of the **$i** macro (mail-queue ID of the message) and a **;** (semicolon).

$b   Displays the current date.

Defining a Mailer (M Control Line)

A mailer is a daemon that delivers mail either locally or over some type of network to another system. Use control lines that begin with the letter **M** to define the characteristics of a mailer daemon that interfaces with **sendmail**.

Note that defining a mail daemon entry (mailer) in the **sendmail.cf** configuration file does not ensure that it will be used. You must also define rewrite rules to ensure the address format resolves to that mailer.

The format of a mailer definition control line is as follows:

```
M MailerName,
P=Path,
F=Flags,
S=Integers,E=EndOfLine,
A=String,
M=Limit
```

The following paragraphs and examples describe the parameters for the mailer definition.

Specifying a Mailer Name (M*MailerName*)

Each mailer must have an internal name. The name can be any string that you choose, except that the names **local** and **prog** are reserved for the mailers for local delivery and delivery to daemons. You must provide definitions for these two mailers in the **sendmail.cf** configuration file if they are not already there (the default configuration file contains these definitions). To define the mailer name, put the name immediately after the **M** in the mailer-definition control line:

M*MailerName*

For example, the following segment introduces the definition line for a mailer called **lan**:

```
Mlan
```

Defining the Path to the Mailer Daemon (P=*Path*)

Specify the location of the mailer daemon with the **P** field in the mailer definition. This field has the format:

P=*Path*

The *Path* defines the full pathname of the mailer daemon on the local system. If the mailer daemon is the **sendmail** daemon version of Simple Mail Transfer Protocol (SMTP) (daemon), use the string **[IPC]** as the path. For example, the following two mailer-definition fragments define a local mailer at **/usr/bin/mail** and another mailer that is the **sendmail** daemon implementation of SMTP:

```
Mlocal, P=/usr/bin/mail,
Mlan, P=[IPC],
```

Specifying Mailer Flags (F=*Flags*)

Mailer flags provide further information to the **sendmail** daemon about the mailer daemon being described. Specify mailer flags with the **F** field in the mailer-definition. This field has the format:

F=*Flags*

This field defines the meaning for the flags that the **sendmail** daemon recognizes. For example, the following mailer-definition fragment uses the **-rlsm** flags to indicate that the mailer requires a **-r** flag, delivers locally, needs quotation marks stripped from addresses, and can deliver to more than one user at a time:

```
Mlocal, P=/usr/bin/mail, F=rlsm,
```

Flags available for the **F=***Flags* field are as follows:

C   If this flag is set, this mailer inspects the address of any incoming mail that it processes for the presence of an @ (at sign). If it finds an @, it saves the @ and the remainder of the address to be used when rewriting addresses in header lines in the message (when mail is forwarded to any mailer).

           The receiving mailer adds the saved portion of the address to any address that does not contain an @, after the address has been processed by rule set 3 (this processing does not depend upon a mailer flag; it always occurs). Do not use this flag for general operation, since it does not interpret complex, route-based addresses properly.

D   The mailer defined in this mailer-definition control line needs a **Date:** or **Resent-Date:** header line.

e   The mailer defined in this mailer-definition control line is expensive to connect to. If the **C** configuration option is set, mail for this mailer is always placed in the queue.

E   This flag causes the mailer in the definition control line to allow lines beginning with the exact six characters >, **F, r, o, m**, and space to appear in the text of a message. Normally **From:** lines are treated as header lines. The **E** flag allows operating system **From:** lines (or any other text lines beginning with those six characters) to appear in the body of the message without being interpreted as the start of a new message.

f   The mailer in the mailer-definition control line needs a **-f** flag. The flag is inserted into the call for the mailer followed by the expansion of the **$g** macro (sender's address relative to the receiver).

F   The mailer in the mailer-definition control line needs a **From:** or **Resent-From:** header line.

h   Preserves uppercase letters in hostnames for the mailer in the mailer-definition control line.

I   The mailer in the mailer-definition control line uses Simple Mail Transfer Protocol (SMTP) to communicate with another SMTP server that is part of the **sendmail** daemon. When communicating with another **sendmail** daemon, the mailer can use features that are not part of the standard SMTP protocol. This option is not required, but causes the transmission to operate more efficiently than without the option.

l   The mailer in the mailer-definition control line is local; final delivery will be performed.

L   The **L** flag enforces SMTP line lengths.

m   The mailer in the mailer-definition control line can be sent to multiple users on the same host in one transaction. When a **$u** macro occurs in the *String* part of the mailer-definition, that field will be repeated as necessary for all qualifying users.

M   The mailer in the mailer-definition control line needs a **Message-ID:** or **Resent-Message-ID:** header line.

n   This flag causes the mailer in the mailer-definition control line to omit an operating system **From:** line at the front of the message.

p   This flag causes the mailer in the mailer-definition control line to use the return path in the Simple Mail Transfer Protocol (SMTP) **MAIL FROM:** command rather than the return address only. Although this type of return address is required for the transfer protocol, many hosts do not process return paths properly.

P   The mailer in the mailer-definition control line needs a **Return-Path:** header.

r   The mailer in the mailer definition control line needs an **r** flag. The flag is inserted into the call for the mailer followed by the expansion of the **$g** macro (sender's address relative to the receiver). Specify this flag to pass the name of the sender as a **-r** flag under certain circumstances.

s   This flag causes the mailer in the mailer-definition control line to strip quotation marks from the address before calling the mailer.

S   This flag prevents the mailer in the mailer-definition control line from resetting the user ID before calling the mailer. Use this flag in a secure environment where the **sendmail** daemon runs as root to help avoid forged addresses. This flag is suppressed if issued from an unsafe environment; for example, a user's **.mailrc** file. Use the **S** flag if the mailer must be called as root.

u   This flag preserves uppercase letters in usernames for the mailer in the mailer-definition control line.

U   The mailer in the mailer-definition control line needs OSF/1 format **From:** lines combined with UUCP format **remote from Host** lines at the end.

x   The mailer in the mailer-definition control line needs a **Full-Name:** header line.

X   The mailer in the mailer-definition control line uses a hidden dot algorithm that adds an extra . (dot) to the beginning of any line that begins with the dot character. The leading dot must then be removed at the other end of the transmission. This method ensures that lines in the message that contain a dot do not end the message prematurely.

You can also define mailer flags to match flags that you define in special header definitions in your **sendmail** configuration file.

Specifying the Rewrite Rule Set for the Mailer (**S**=*Integers*,**R**=*Integers*)

The **sendmail** daemon uses sets of rewrite rules to change the format of incoming addresses to a style that the receiving mailer daemon can understand. Specify the rewrite rule set to use on sender addresses for this mailer with the **S** field; specify the rewrite rule set to use on receiver addresses for this mailer with the **R** field. These fields have the following format:

S=*Integers*,**R**=*Integers*,

In this format, *Integers,* specifies a particular rule set number for processing the addresses for this mailer. These rules can perform operations such as appending the current domain to addresses that do not already have a domain. For example, if the following header were being processed by the local **sendmail** daemon, it would require further processing before being sent to another location:

```
From: geo
```

If the header were sent on a domain address network, it could be changed to

```
From: geo@zeus.aus
```

If the header were sent on a UUCP network, it could be changed to

```
From: zeus!geo
```

Defining a Different End-of-Line Character (E=*EndOfLine*)

The normal indication of the end of line is a string that contains only the newline character. To change this character, use the optional **E** field. The format of this field is

E=*EndOfLine***,**

In this format, *EndOfLine,* is the character string that specifies the end of the line. You can use normal \ (backslash) escape characters to specify the end-of-line character (**\r, \n, \f, \b**).

Passing Information to the Mailer (A=*String*)

Specify information to be passed to the mailer with the optional **A** field. This field has the following format:

A=*String*

In this format, *String* can be any string of words with embedded spaces allowed. Any or all of the words can be symbols, such as **$u** (receiving username) defined in **sendmail.cf**. If you do not include this field, or the field does not contain the **$u** symbol, the **sendmail** daemon uses the Simple Mail Transfer Protocol SMTP to send messages to the mailer. If the **P** field for this mailer (access pathname) is **[IPC]**, indicating a mailer accessed with interprocess communications, the following information is used in this field:

```
A=IPC $h [Port]
```

In this notation, *Port* is the optional port number for the connection.

Limiting Message Size (M=*Limit*)

Use the optional **M=***Limit* mailer flag to specify the maximum size in bytes of messages that the mailer daemon handles. For example, the following field specifies a maximum limit of 10,000 bytes:

```
M=10000
```

Example Mailer Specifications

A local delivery mailer is specified as follows:

```
Mlocal, P=/usr/bin/mail, F=lsDFMmn, S=10, R=20, A=mail $u
```

The mailer daemon is called **local** and is located in the /bin/bellmail file. The mailer takes the following flags:

l   Local delivery.

s   Strips quotations marks from addresses

DFM   Needs **Date:**, **From:**, and **Message-ID:** fields

m   Delivers to multiple users

n   Does not need an operating system **From:** line at the start of the message

Rule set 10 should be applied to sender addresses in the message, and rule set 20 should be applied to receiver addresses. Additional information sent to the mailer in the **A** field is the word **mail** and words containing the name of the receiving user. If a **-r** flag is inserted, it will be between the words **mail** and **$u**.

A mailer for local area network delivery is specified as follows:

```
Mlan, P=[IPC], F=meC, S=11, R=21, A=IPC $h, M=100000
```

The mailer daemon is called **lan** and is connected through the **sendmail** daemon internal SMTP mailer. It can handle multiple users at once (**m**), the connection is defined as expensive (**e**), and any domain from the sender address on incoming mail is saved for use by an outgoing mailer (**C**). Sender addresses should be processed by rule set **11** and receiver addresses by rule set **21**. There is a 100,000 byte limit on messages passed through this mailer (**M**).

Configuration Options

You can set configuration options for use by **sendmail** with a control line in the configuration file. The options that can be set are the same as those options that you can specify with the **-o** flag to the **sendmail** command. An option is named with a single character. The format of the set-option control line is:

O*OptionValue*

In this format, *Option* is a single character name for the option being set and *Value* is either a string, an integer, a time interval, or a Boolean option. Legal values for a boolean option are **t** or **T** for a true value, and **f** or **F** for a false value. If you do not specify a value for a boolean variable, it becomes a true value.

For example, the following entries from the default **sendmail.cf** file show the format of the set-option control line:

OL9   Sets the log-level option variable **-L** to a value of **9**. This entry occurs early in the **sendmail.cf** file to ensure that the log is maintained during the reading of the file.

OQ/usr/spool/mqueue

Sets the mail-queue directory option variable **Q** to a directory (**/usr/spool/mqueue**) that defines where the mail log is to be kept.

OA/var/adm/sendmail/aliases

Sets the option variable **A** to the full pathname of the aliases file (**/var/adm/sendmail/aliases**).

Setting Delivery Mode (Od*Value*)

The **sendmail** daemon can operate in several delivery modes. The default configuration file sets the delivery mode to **b**. However, you can change the delivery mode with the **Od***Value* option in the configuration file. These modes specify how quickly mail will be delivered. Legal values include the following:

i   Deliver interactively.

b   Deliver in background. (This is the default.)

q   Queue the message and deliver during queue run.

Time-Out Option (Or*Number* and OT*Number*)

The **sendmail** daemon can time out when reading standard input or when reading from a remote SMTP server. The default configuration file sets this value to 5 minutes. This value should be correct for most situations. However, if you need to change the time-out value, change the **r** option in the configuration file. The **r** option has the format:

Or*Number*

In this format, *Number* is the number of minutes that the **sendmail** daemon should wait until timing out.

After sitting in the queue for a few days, a message times out. The **sendmail** daemon notifies the sender of the message that it could not be sent. The time out is typically set to 3 days. Set this time out with the **T** option in the **sendmail.cf** configuration file:

OT*Number*

In this format, *Number* is the number of days the **sendmail** daemon leaves the message in the queue before timing out the message.

Operational Logging Level Option (OL*Number*)

The **OL** option specifies the log level to be used when the **sendmail** daemon is running.

The format of the line to change the operational logging level is

OL*Number*

Following is a list of valid levels (*Number*) and the activities that they represent (each number includes the activities of all numbers of lesser value and adds the activity that it represents):

0	No logging.
1	Major problems only.
2	Message collections and failed deliveries.
3	Successful deliveries.
4	Messages being deferred (due to a host being down, and so on).
5	Placing messages in the queue (normal event).
6	Unusual but benign incidents (trying to process a locked file, and so on).
9	Log internal queue ID to external message ID mappings. This can be useful for tracing a message as it travels among several hosts.
12	Several messages that are of interest when debugging.
16	Verbose information regarding the queue.

The default level is **OL9**.

Message Queue Options (O*Option*[*Value*])

Three options adjust the way the **sendmail** daemon handles the message queue. To use this control line in the **sendmail.cf** configuration file, use the format:

O*Option*[*Value*]

The following *Options* values are allowed:

c   Causes **sendmail** to queue messages for that mailer daemon without sending them if an outgoing mailer is marked as expensive to use. The queue can be run when costs are lower or when the queue is large enough to send the message efficiently.

Q*Directory*

      Sets the directory in which to queue messages. The directory will be created if it does not exist.

s   Enqueues before delivery, even when in immediate delivery mode.

Y   The **sendmail** daemon delivers each message in the mail queue from a separate process. This option is not required; it can increase system overhead in the OSF/1 environment.

Mail Statistics File Option (O*Option*[*Value*])

One option for the **O** control line changes the mail statistics file. Use the format:

O*Option*[*Value*]

The following option is allowed:

S*File*   Sets the mail statistics file to *File*. Statistics are only collected if the file exists. This file must be created by the user. The recommended path for this is **/var/adm/sendmail/sendmail.st**. Statistics can be printed out using **/usr/sbin/mailstats**.

Returned Mail Options (OP*Address*)

You can specify someone to receive copies of all returned mail.

P*Address*
           Identifies the person who is to receive a copy of all returned mail.

Alias Options (O*Option*[*Value*])

A*File*   Uses the named *File* as the alias file.

m   If the sender uses an alias, and that sender is a member of the group named by the alias, then also send to the sender.

Header Options (O*Option*[*Value*])

f   Saves **From:** lines at the front of messages. These lines are normally discarded. Causes all other headers to be regarded as part of the message body.

o   Indicates that this message can have old style headers. Without this option, the message has new style headers (commas instead of spaces between addresses). If this option is set, an adaptive algorithm correctly determines the header format in most cases.

Verbose Mode Option (Ov)

v   Runs in verbose mode.

sendmail.cf(4)

SMPT Helpfile Option (H*FileName***)**

H*FileName*
> Specifies the name of the SMTP help file.

ID Options (O*OptionNumber***)**

The following options allow you to set group and user IDs for specific mailers. Use the format:

O*OptionNumber*

The following options are available to set group and user IDs:

g*Number* Sets the default group ID to the value specified by *Number*. The **sendmail** daemon uses this ID when it calls mailers.

u*Number*
> Sets the default user ID to the value specified by *Number*. The **sendmail** daemon uses this ID when it calls mailers.

Character Interpretation Options (O*Option*[*Value*])**

The **sendmail** daemon interprets certain characters as having a special function. Use the format:

O*Option*[*Value*]

You can set the interpretations with the following options:

B*Character*
> Sets the blank substitution character to the character specified in the *c* parameter. The **sendmail** daemon replaces unquoted spaces in addresses with *Character*. The supplied configuration file uses the . (dot) for *Character*.

i
> Does not interpret a . (dot) on a line by itself as a message terminator. Removes the excess dot inserted by a remote mailer at the beginning of a line if mail is received through SMTP. In addition, if receiving mail through SMTP, any dot at the front of a line followed by another dot is removed. This is the opposite of the action performed by the **X** mailer flag.

Rewrite Rules Options (O*Option*[*Value*])

The following two options allow you to alter the **sendmail** daemon's use of rewrite rules. Use the format:

O*Option*[*Value*]

The following options are available to the **sendmail** daemon for rewrite rules:

-n   Validates the right-hand side of alias rewrite rules when the **sendmail** daemon performs the **newaliases** function.

-I   Indicate that **sendmail** should use the Internet domain name server if it can.

Error Processing Modes Option (Oe*Value*)

The following options set the error-processing mode. Use the format:

-Oe*Value* Oe*Value*

-e*Value*   Sets error processing to mode *Value*. Valid modes are:

-e   Mails the error message to the user's mailbox, but always exits with a 0 (zero) exit status (normal return).

-m   Mails the error message to the user's mailbox.

-p   Displays the error message on the terminal (default).

-q   Discards the error message and returns the exit status only.

Host Network Name Option (ON*NetworkName*)

Sets the name of your host network with an option in the **O** control line in the **sendmail.cf** file.

-N*NetworkName*

Sets the name of the host network to *NetworkName*. The **sendmail** daemon compares the argument of an SMTP **HELLO** command to *HostName.NetworkName* (value of *HostName* comes from the kernel). If these values do not match, it adds the *HostName.NetworkName* string to the **Received:** line in the message so that messages can be traced accurately.

sendmail.cf(4)

Macro Definition Option (O*MacroValue*)

You can use the **O** control line to define a macro. Use the following option to do so:

-M*Macro Value*
> Defines *Macro* to have *Value*. This option is normally used only from the **sendmail** daemon command line.

Configuration File Revision Level Option (DZ*Number*)

The configuration file revision level macro, **Z**, helps you track changes that you make to the **sendmail** configuration file. Each time that you make a change to the **sendmail** configuration file, you should also change the value of this macro. Choose any format for the number that you define. For example, if the **sendmail** configuration file is at level 3.1, the following entry appears in the **sendmail** configuration file:

```
DZ3.1
```

A text string can also be used for this macro:

```
DZversion_one
```

Files

> **/var/adm/sendmail.cf** file
> > The configuration file for the **sendmail** command

Related Information

> Commands: **sendmail(8)**

services

Purpose   Defines the sockets and protocols used for Internet services

Synopsis   **/etc/services**

Description

The **/etc/services** file associates Internet service names and aliases to the port number and protocol used by the service. Each service is listed in this file on a single line of the form:

ServiceName PortNumber/ProtocolName Aliases

The fields contain the following information:

ServiceName   The official Internet service name.

PortNumber/ProtocolName

The socket port number used for the service and the the transport protocol used for the service.

Aliases   A list of unofficial service names.

Items on a line are separated by spaces or tabs. Comments begin with a # (number sign) and continue to the end of the line.

Examples

Entries in the **/etc/services** file for the **inetd** internal services might look like this:

```
echo        7/tcp
echo        7/udp
discard     9/tcp      sink null
discard     9/udp      sink null
daytime     13/tcp
daytime     13/udp
chargen     19/tcp     ttytst source
chargen     19/tcp     ttytst source
ftp         21/tcp
time        37/tcp     timeserver
time        37/udp     timeserver
```

Related Information

Subroutines: **getservent**, **getservbyport**, **getservbyname**, **setservent**, **endservent**

Specification: RFC923.

stanza

Purpose   Stanza file format

Synopsis   **stanza**

Description

A stanza file format is used in conjunction with the stanza file library (libAF(3)).

The stanza file syntax rules are as follows:

Separate entries by one or more blank lines.

A colon (:) terminates a entry name.

A newline terminates a stanza name and value pair.

Separate a attribute name and attribute value with the equal sign (=) character.

Separate multiple attribute values with the comma (,) character.

Entry names and attribute names may contain any printable character other than whitespace, newline, or special characters unless appropriately quoted.

Entry attribute values may contain any printable character other than newline, or special characters unless appropriately quoted.

Trailing blanks or tabs are allowed at the beginning or end of the line.

A pound sign (#) at the beginning of a line indicates a comment.

Each stanza file entry in the file is usually of the form:

Entry_name:
    Attribute1_name = Attribute1_value
    Attribute2_name = Attribute2_value
    Attribute3_name = Attribute3_value1, Attribute3_value2

In this sample, *Entry_name* is the entry name and its attributes are: *Attribute1_name*, *Attribute2_name*, and *Attribute3_name*. Each attribute has its respective attribute values listed after the equal sign. Notice that the attribute name *Attribute3_name* has two distinct values associated with it: *Attribute3_value1* and *Attribute3_value2*.

stanza(4)

Several special quoting characters exist to allow attribute values contain special values and data representations. When using any quoting characters, encapsulate the attribute value with quotes; "quoted value", for example. To specify an octal value use the slash character; "\007", for example.

Related Information

Commands: **sysconfigdb(8)**

Calls: **libAF(3)**

Files: **sysconfigtab(4)**

sysconfigtab

Purpose   Subsystem definition data base

Synopsis   **sysconfigtab**

Description

The sysconfigtab file contains information about dynamically configurable subsystems. The file consists of stanza formatted entries describing each subsystem (see **stanza(4)**). Entries in a stanza file consist of a number of newline separated fields. The first line of each entry specifies the subsystem name and subsequent lines specify the various attribute names and values of the entry.

The configuration manager uses the following subsystem entry attributes when handling configuration requests:

Subsystem_Description
    A short literal string used as a description.

Subsystem_Type   Specifies the subsystem as static or dynamic.

Subsystem_Path   Specifies the file path name of the subsystem object module.

Subsystem_Flags   Specifies loader flags for the dynamic kernel subsystem.

Method_Name   The unique logical name of the configuration method associated with the subsystem.

Method_Type   Specifies the configuration method as static or dynamic.

Method_Path   Specifies the file path name of the configuration method object module.

Method_Flags   Specifies the loader flags for the configuration method.

    Other attributes are subsystem type specific.

Related Information

Commands: **sysconfig(8)**, **sysconfigdb(8)**

Files: **stanza(4)**

xferstats

Purpose   Contains information about the status of file transfer requests

Synopsis   **/usr/spool/uucp/.Admin/xferstats**

Description

The **/usr/spool/uucp/.Admin/xferstats** file contains information about the status of each uucp file transfer request. The **xferstats** file contains the following information:

- System name
- Name of the user requesting the transfer
- Date and time of the transfer
- Name of the device used in the transfer
- Size of the transferred file

Files

/usr/spool/uucp/.Admin directory
     Contains the **xferstats** file and other uucp administrative files

Related Information

Daemons: **cron(8)**, **uucico(8)**, **uuxqt**

Commands: **uucp(1)**, **uudemon.cleanup**, **uux(1)**

Index

A

abort printer spooling, 1-135
ac, 1-2
accept, 1-138
accounting
    active files, 1-269
    automatic, 1-4
    commands, 1-4
    complete disk usage, 1-29
    connect sessions, 1-2
    connect time, 1-33
    daily, 1-4, 1-268
    daily records, 1-4
    daily summary file, 1-40
    default summary, 1-278
    directory, 1-4
    disk, 1-4, 1-63
    disk samples, 1-35
    disk usage, 1-29, 1-33
    fee, 1-33, 1-35
    file formats, 2-31
    files, 2-31
    files, creating, 1-4
    files, printing, 1-4
    files, removing, 1-4
    initialization of, 1-4
    intermediate disk
        information, 1-64
    monthly, 1-4
    plotter, 1-198
    printer, 1-198
    printer queueing, 1-33
    printer records, 1-269
    process, 1-268, 2-31
    process accounting records,
        1-15
    processes, 1-33
    process statistics, 1-20
    record summaries, 1-275
    shell scripts, 1-4
    shutoff, 1-4
    startup, 1-4
    summary total records,
        1-269
    total connect session
          summaries, 1-24
    total disk usage, 1-29
    total file, 1-35
    total files, 1-33
    total process records, 1-269
    total records, 1-12, 1-269
    turnoff, 1-23
        reason, 1-4
    turnon, 1-23
    working files, 1-269
acct, 1-4
acctcms, 1-12
acctcom, 1-15
acctcon, 1-22

acctcon1, 1-22, 1-103, 1-269
acctcon2, 1-22, 1-104
acctdisk, 1-29, 1-64
acctdusg, 1-29
acct format, 1-12
acct.h, 2-30
acctmerg, 1-25, 1-33, 1-40, 1-268
accton, 1-39
acctprc, 1-39
acctprc1, 1-39
acctprc2, 1-39
acct_sum, 1-198
acctwtmp, 1-102
active, 1-268
adding, users, 1-45
address, device, 1-25
addresses, Internet-to-hardware
        translation, 1-47
addressing mail, 1-288
adduser command, 1-45
Admin, 2-2
administrative files, 2-2
aliases, 2-35
altering process scheduling
        priority, 1-238
arp, 1-47
ASCII total accounting records,
        1-33
assigning a tty line to a network
        interface, 1-296
attaching a serial line to a network
        interface, 1-296
audit, 2-36
automatic
        accounting, 1-4
        accounting, turnoff, 1-4
average, number of disk blocks,
        1-35

B

backup
        file, 1-67
        level, 1-67
        output file size, 1-70
        tape, 1-70
        write density, 1-70
bad tape blocks, 1-246
biff server, 1-57
binary record, 1-40
binary total accounting records,
        1-33
block, storage, 1-70
block mode device, 1-70
blocks
        disk, 1-34, 1-35, 1-64
        disk usage, 1-30
        free printer spool, 1-138
        I/O transferred, 1-19
        number used, 1-34, 1-279
block size, tape, 1-244

C

calling process, 1-124
cfgmgr command, 1-50
change date, connect session,
        1-104
changing, root directory of a
        command, 1-53
characters, number transferred,
        1-12
characters transferred, process

accounting, 1-19
charge, user fees, 2-34
chargefee, 1-4, 1-269
charges, printer, 1-198
checking file system quota
    consistency, 1-223
checking for uucp files and
    directories, 1-328
chroot command, 1-53, 1-54
ckpacct, 1-4
cleaning up the uucp spool
    directory, 1-334
clri command, 1-56
cms, 1-269
Command, 2-3
command
    accept, 1-138
    acctcon1, 1-22, 1-103, 1-269
    acctcon2, 1-22, 1-104
    acctdisk, 1-64
    acctdusg, 1-29
    acctmerg, 1-29, 1-268
    acctwtmp, 1-102
    chargefee, 1-269
    CPU time, 1-12
    dodisk, 1-29, 1-64
    enable printer spooling,
        1-136
    exec, 1-130
    fwtmp, 1-102
    init, 1-102
    inittab, 1-103
    last, 1-130
    lastcomm, 1-130
    listen, 1-138
    login, 1-102
    lp, 1-138
    lpc, 1-135
    lpd, 1-138

lpr, 1-138
lptest, 1-142
monacct, 1-268
pac, 1-198
percentage of total
    processed, 1-278
prdaily, 1-268
printer, 1-135
printer daemon restart,
    1-136
printer daemon start, 1-136
printer daemon status, 1-136
printer daemon stop, 1-136
printer down, 1-136
printer exit, 1-136
printer queue disable, 1-135
printer spool abort, 1-135
printer spool clean, 1-135
printer topq, 1-136
printer up, 1-136
printpw, 1-208
process, 1-130
runacct, 1-103, 1-268
sa, 1-275
shutdown, 1-128
summary, 1-12
superuser, 1-130
sysconfigdb, 1-307
terminal, 1-130
times used, 1-278
time to process, 1-279
wtmpfix, 1-102, 1-269
command name, process, 1-19
commands
    accounting, 1-4
    changing root directory,
        1-53
    interactive restore, 1-242
    remote, 2-19

running automatically, 1-60
shell-like, 1-242
complete dump, 1-242
complete restore, 1-244
completion time, process, 1-19
comsat, 1-57
config command, 1-58
connect session
   active ports, 1-23
   daily report, 1-25
   date, 1-104
   date and timestamp, 1-25
   date change, 1-23
   end time, 1-23
   entry type, 1-103
   fix record, 1-104
   line usage records, 1-23
   nonprime time, 1-25
   overall record, 1-23
   prime time, 1-25
   reason, 1-103
   records, 1-2, 1-24, 1-102,
      1-269
   starting time, 1-103
   start time, 1-23
   time, 1-34, 2-34
   total accounting records,
      1-25
   total accounting summaries,
      1-24
   total records, 1-2
   user ID, 1-25
connect time, 1-2
   accounting, 1-33
control, printer daemon, 1-139
controlling the time server daemon,
   1-317, 1-319

controlling timed, 1-319
core dump, saving, 1-281
correction, connect session records,
   1-102
Corrupt, 2-7
CPU
   command time, 1-12
   run time, 1-34
   time, 1-12
   time used, 1-278
   usage, 1-12
creating, special files, 1-160
creating accounting files, 1-4
cron, 1-64, 1-268
   crontabs file, 1-5
   daemon, 1-5
cron command, 1-60, 1-61
cron daemon, 1-19
crontabs
   file, 1-4
   specifying time, 1-31
current directory, 1-242

D

daemon
   cron, 1-19, 1-29, 1-64, 1-268
   gated, 1-106, 2-45
   printer, 1-138
      restart, 1-136
      start, 1-136
      status, 1-136
      stop, 1-136
   printer debugging, 1-138
   routed, 1-260
   spooling, 1-135, 1-136

time server, 1-317
daemons, uucpd, 1-338
daily accounting, 1-4, 1-268
daily accounting record, 1-40
daily report, connect session, 1-25
daily summary accounting, 1-40
daily summary file, 1-268
DARPA, 1-98, 1-205, 1-314, 1-316
Data, 2-8
database
    files, 1-270
    login/logout, 1-128
    printpw, 1-208
    user, 1-31
data blocks, transfer, 2-34
date
    connect session, 1-23, 1-104
    record change, 1-104
date and timestamp
    connect session, 1-25
        default, 1-23
    process accounting, 1-19
daytacct, 1-35, 1-268
debug
    mode, 1-244
    remote tape access, 1-254
debugging
    printer daemon, 1-138
    restore mode, 1-242
    ripple pattern, 1-142
default
    connect session date and
        timestamp, 1-23
    directory, 1-242
    file system, 1-67, 1-72
    printer reference, 2-83
    process accounting file,
        1-278
    storage medium, 1-67

tape device, 1-244
tape drive, 1-70
tape size, 1-70
tape storage device, 1-247
delete files, 1-242
deleting files, accounting, 1-4
deleting old uucp spool directory
    files, 1-334
device
    block mode, 1-70
    default storage, 1-67
    default tape, 1-244
    major and minor address,
        1-25
    name, 1-103, 2-31
    remote, 1-70
    tape archive, 1-244
df, 1-62
diagnostic messages
    runacct, 1-270
    wtmpfix, 1-104
diagnostics
    common errors, 1-248
    consistency checks, 1-248
    restore error, 1-247
    volume to mount, 1-247
Dialcodes, 2-10
Dialers, 2-12
Directories, 2-18
directories
    changing root, 1-53
    lost and found, 1-159
directory
    accounting, 1-4
    current, 1-242
    default, 1-242
    login, 1-30, 1-208
    owner, 1-242
    root, 1-244

spool, 1-138
tape restore, 1-246
usr/sbin, 1-19
usr/spool, 1-138
uucp, checking for, 1-328
disable printer queue, 1-135
disk
    accounting, 1-4, 1-63
    accounting, intermediate
        information, 1-64
    accounting records, 1-269
    accounting samples, 1-35
    blocks, 1-34
    blocks used, 1-30
    number of blocks, 1-64
    number of samples, 2-34
    printer spool free blocks,
        1-138
    read error, 1-67
    usage, 1-268
    usage accounting, 1-29, 1-33
    usage time, 2-34
diskusg, 1-63
displaying, Internet-to-hardware
    address translation, 1-47
dodisk, 1-29, 1-64
drive, default tape, 1-70
dump, 1-67
    complete, 1-242
    core, saving, 1-281
    file, 1-245
    file system, 1-67
    incremental, 1-67
    level, 1-67
    tape size, 1-70
dumpfs, 1-73

E

editing, password file, 1-354
editing user quotas, 1-74
edquota command, 1-74, 1-76
empty file system, 1-242
enable printer spooling, 1-136
end of dump, 1-67
end time, connect session, 1-23
entry
    connect session type, 1-103
    time made, 2-32
    type of, 2-31
environment variable
    printer, 2-83
    time, 1-20
Epoch, 1-25
epoch, 1-67
error
    disk read, 1-67
    opening file, 1-140
    remote tape access, 1-254
    restore, 1-247
    tape, recovery from, 1-245
    tape open, 1-67
    tape write, 1-67
errors, 2-37
etc/exports, 2-39
etc/ftpusers, 2-44
etc/hosts.equiv, 2-66
etc/named.*, 2-77
/etc/networks, 2-82
/etc/services, 2-109
exec, 1-19, 1-130
Execute, 2-19
execution time, process, 1-19
exit
    printer control program,
        1-136

process status, 1-103
exports, 2-39

F

factor, hog, 1-12, 1-19
fastboot command, 1-77
fasthalt command, 1-78
fee accounting, 1-33
fees, 1-35
    charging users, 1-4
file
    acct.h, 1-39, 2-30
    acctmerg, 1-40
    acct_sum, 1-198
    active, 1-268
    back up, 1-67
    backup tape size, 1-70
    chargefee, 1-35
    cms, 1-269
    contact attempts, 2-23
    crontabs, 1-5
        adm, 1-4
    crontabs time, 1-31
    daily summary, 1-40, 1-268
    data, 2-28
    database, 1-270
    daytacct, 1-35, 1-268
    dump, 1-245
    etc/fstab, 1-70
    etc/group, 1-70
    etc/passwd, 1-34
    fiscal, 1-268
    format, acct, 1-12
    fstab, 2-41
    gated daemon, 2-45

holidays, 1-12
hosts, 2-65
hosts.equiv, 1-138
hosts.lpd, 1-138
inetd configuration, 2-68
inittab, 2-70
lastdate, 1-270
line use, 1-23
lock, 1-268
log, 2-73
logacct, 1-23
minfree, 1-138
monacct, 1-35
monthly summary, 1-35
mount requests, 1-172
named.boot, 2-74
name server, 2-77
network names, 2-82
nite, 1-270
number to restore, 1-246
pacct, 1-130, 1-268, 1-277
pacct length, 1-4
passwd, 1-39, 1-63
password, 1-30, 2-31
pathname, 1-246
printcap, 1-135, 1-138, 1-199, 2-83
printer lock, 1-139, 1-140
printer service, 1-138
printpw, 1-208
process accounting, 1-19, 1-278, 2-32
reboots, 1-23
remote, 1-254
remote command requests, 2-30
remote systems, 2-66, 2-89
resolv.conf, 2-90
restore, pathname, 1-242

savacct, 1-277
security, 2-44
sitetacct, 1-269
stanza, 2-111
state file, 1-270
summary, 1-268, 1-277
sumtacct, 1-268
tacct, 1-35, 1-40, 1-269
temporary, 2-29, 2-30, 2-73
termcap, 2-83
total account format, 1-35
total accounting, 1-33, 1-35
transfer, 1-98, 2-18, 2-28,
        2-114
transport, 1-339
unprocessed, 2-7
utmp, 1-12, 1-39
utmp.h, 2-30
uucp, 2-2, 2-3, 2-7, 2-8, 2-
        19, 2-37, 2-114
uucp, checking for, 1-328
uucp log, 2-24
wtmp, 1-2, 1-24, 1-102, 1-
        128, 1-269
files
        accounting, 1-4, 2-31
        billing, 1-268
        buffered, 1-304
        cleanup, 1-242
        creating, pacct, 1-4
        daily ASCII, 1-268
        delete, 1-242
        list
                to delete, 1-242
                to restore, 1-242
        local, 1-242
        password, 1-354
        printing, 1-138
        read, 1-243

read to tape, 1-242
remote, 1-242
runacct active, 1-269
runacct temporary, 1-269
runacct working, 1-269
skeletal, 1-45
special, 1-160
storage, 1-67
uucp, 1-330
writing, to, 1-304
file system
        default, 1-67
        dump, 1-67
        empty, 1-242
        ownership, summarizing,
                1-222
        quota consistency, checking,
                1-223
        quotas, turning on and off,
                1-226
        quotes, summarizing, 1-240
file system names, 1-63
file transfer
        list, 2-18
        uucico, 2-3
fingerd, 1-79
FINGER protocol, 1-79
fiscal, 1-268
        subdirectory, 1-35
fix record, connect session, 1-104
flags
        modifier, 1-244
        restore function, 1-242
        restore modifier, 1-242
Foreign, 2-23
fork, 1-19
forking program, 1-279
format
        acct, 1-39

tacct records, 1-33
total accounting files, 1-35
utmp, 1-102
utmp record, 2-31
formats, accounting files, 2-31
fsck command, 1-81
fsdb, 1-89
fstab file, 2-41
ftpd, 1-98
FTP protocol, 1-106
ftpusers, 2-44
function flags, restore, 1-242
fwtmp, 1-102

G

gated, 1-106
gated.conf, 2-45
gated daemon, 1-106, 2-45
gateways, 2-62
generating, hashed password table,
        1-162
getty command, 1-110
group, process accounting statistic,
        1-20
group ID, 1-208

H

halt command, 1-112
halting the system, 1-78

hashed password table, 1-162
hog, factor, 1-12
hog factor, 1-19
        process accounting, 1-16
host, name, 1-103
hosts.equiv, 2-66
hosts.equiv file, 1-138
hosts file, 2-65
hosts.lpd file, 1-138

I

icheck command, 1-114
identification
        process number, 1-103
        user, 2-31
ifconfig, 1-116
incoming mail reports, 1-57
incremental dump, 1-67
incremental file system dump, 1-67
inetd, 1-120
        configuration file, 2-68
inetd.conf, 2-68
information, tape header, 1-242
init, 1-102
init command, 1-122, 1-123
initialization
        accounting, 1-4
        process, 1-122
inittab, 1-103, 2-70
inittab file, 2-70
inode, number, 1-242, 1-246
inode numbers, 1-243
inodes, 1-64

inode table, 1-304
interactive file restoration, 1-242
Internet Protocol, 1-98, 1-120, 1-173, 1-283
    local, 2-87
Internet-to-hardware address translation, 1-47
I/O, number of operations, 1-279
I/O blocks, 1-34

J

jobs, printer queue, 1-135

K

K-core, 1-34
    minutes, 2-33
    time, total, 1-12
kernel, 1-40
killall command, 1-124, 1-125
kloadsrv command, 1-126

L

last, 1-128, 1-130
lastcomm, 1-130
lastdate file, 1-270

lastlogin, 1-4
level, backup, 1-67
lib_admin command, 1-133, 1-134
libraries, 1-133
line usage, report, 1-25
list, files to read, 1-242
listen, 1-138
lock, 1-268
lock file, printer, 1-140
Log, 2-24
login, 1-4, 1-102, 1-128
    directory, 1-30
    name, 1-2, 1-35, 1-40
    number of sessions, 2-34
    records, 1-24, 1-102
    shell, 1-208
    user name, 1-34, 1-103, 2-31
login directory, 1-208
login/logout, records, 1-2
login name, 1-64
login names, 1-39
    printer, 1-199
logins, 1-35
logout, 1-4, 1-128
    records, 1-24
lost and found directory, 1-159
lpc, 1-135
lpd, 1-138
lptest, 1-142
lvchange command, 1-143, 1-144
lvcreate command, 1-145, 1-147
lvdisplay command, 1-148, 1-150
lvextend command, 1-151
lvreduce command, 1-153, 1-154
lvremove command, 1-155
lvsync command, 1-156

M

machine
    name, 2-32
    remote, 1-70
    restarting, 1-235
mail, 1-57, 1-157, 1-283, 2-73, 2-92
    addresses, 1-288
    from runacct, 1-268
mailstats, 1-157
managing, network routing tables,
    1-260
managing accounting volume,
    1-275
memory
    K-core, 1-34
    kiloblocks used, 1-279
    used by process, 1-15
merge, total accounting records,
    1-269
messages, runacct diagnostic,
    1-270
minfree, 1-138
mklost+found command, 1-159
mknod command, 1-160, 1-161
mkpasswd command, 1-162, 1-163
mkproto command, 1-165
mode
    debug, 1-244
    debuging, restore, 1-242
    set, 1-243
    single user, 1-23
    tape access, 1-242
modem, 2-12
modifier flags, 1-244
    restore, 1-242
monacct, 1-4, 1-35, 1-268

monthly accounting, 1-4
mount, 1-167, 1-292
    points, 2-39
    requests, 2-39
mountd, 1-172
mqueue, 2-73
multiuser mode, bringing the
    system to, 1-294
multivolume tape, 1-244

N

name
    connect session host, 1-103
    device, 1-103, 2-31
    login, 1-2, 1-35, 1-64
    machine, 2-32
    user, 1-35
named, 1-173
named.*, 2-77
named.boot file, 2-74
names
    file system, 1-63
    user login, 1-30
name server, 1-173, 1-190
ncheck command, 1-178
network, 1-201
    interface parameters, 1-116
network interface
    assigning a tty line to, 1-296
    attaching a serial line to,
    1-296
networks, 2-82
    managing routing tables,
    1-260

newfs command, 1-180
new users, 1-45
NFS, 1-172, 1-186, 1-188, 1-189,
        1-292
        export, 2-39
nfsd, 1-186
nfsiod, 1-188
nfsstat, 1-189
nite, 1-270
nonprime time, 1-12, 1-34, 2-33
        connect session records,
        1-25
notify, restored file, 1-246
nslookup, 1-190
nulladm, 1-4
number
        file to restore, 1-246
        inode, 1-242, 1-246
number of processes, 2-34
numbers, inode, 1-243

O

Old, 2-26
old-stype dump tape, 1-244
opening, file for printing, 1-140
operations, I/O, 1-279
owner, process accounting statistic,
        1-20

P

pac, 1-198
pacct, 1-19, 1-130, 1-277, 2-32
        creating new files, 1-4
        files, 1-4
pages, printed, 1-35
passwd, 1-39
password file, 1-63, 1-354
passwords, hashed table, 1-162
pathname
        file, 1-246
        file restoration, 1-242
ping, 1-201
plotter, accounting information,
        1-198
port characteristics, setting, 1-110
portmap, 1-205
ports, connect session, 1-23
prctmp, 1-4
prdaily, 1-268
prime time, 1-12, 1-34, 2-33
        connect session records,
        1-25
printcap, 1-135, 1-138, 1-199
printcap file, 2-83
printer
        abort command, 1-135
        accounting, 1-33
        accounting information,
        1-198
        charges, 1-198
        clean command, 1-135
        commands, 1-135
        control program, 1-135
        daemon status, 1-136
        disable command, 1-135
        disable spooling, 1-135
        down command, 1-136

enable daemon, 1-136
enable spooling, 1-136
environment variable, 2-83
exit command, 1-136
job queue, 1-136
lock file, 1-139, 1-140
login names, 1-199
page costs, 1-198
pages output, 1-35
pages printed, 1-199
pages queued, 2-34
queueing, 1-268
quit command, 1-136
remote service, 1-138
restart command, 1-136
restart daemon, 1-136
service file, 1-138
spool directory, 1-138
spooling, 2-83
spooling commands, 1-138
spooling queue, 1-136
start command, 1-136
start daemon, 1-136
status, 1-135
status command, 1-136
status file, 1-136
stop command, 1-136
stop daemon, 1-136
topq command, 1-136
up command, 1-136
printer daemon, 1-138
debugging, 1-138
printer queue disable, 1-135
printing
opening file, 1-140
queues, 1-138
printing accounting files, 1-4

printpw, 1-208
priority, process, altering, 1-238
procedures, shell, 1-4
process
accounting, 1-33, 1-268,
2-31
accounting database, 2-32
accounting file, 1-278
active accounting, 1-268
average statistics, 1-15
command name, 1-19
completion time, 1-19
CPU seconds, 1-19
execution time, 1-19
exit status, 1-103
hog factor, 1-16
ID, 1-103
memory blocks used, 1-279
memory size, 1-19
number of, 2-34
printer daemon control,
1-139
real time, 1-19
real time used, 1-278
scheduling priority, altering,
1-238
start time, 1-19
tape dump, 1-70
termination status, 1-103,
2-32
time required, 1-279
process accounting, 1-39
characters transferred, 1-19
date and timestamp, 1-19
file, 1-19
file size, 1-19
memory used, 1-15

tty, 1-20
process accounting procedures,
    1-39
process accounting record,
    summaries, 1-15
process accounting statistics, 1-20
processes
    calling, 1-124
    initialization, 1-122
    terminating, 1-124
processor, stopping, 1-112
program
    forking, 1-279
    lpc, 1-135
protocol, 1-79, 1-98, 1-120, 1-314,
    1-316, 1-321
    FTP, 1-106
protocols, 2-87
prtacct, 1-4
ps, 1-20
pvchange command, 1-211, 1-212
pvcreate command, 1-213, 1-215
pvdisplay command, 1-216, 1-218
pvmove command, 1-219, 1-220
pwck command, 1-221

Q

queue
    enable spooling, 1-136
    printer, 1-268
    printer pages, 2-34
    printer spooling, 1-135,
    1-136

queues, printing, 1-138
quit, 1-128
    printer control program,
    1-136
quota
    file system, checking, 1-223
    file system, turning on and
        off, 1-226
quotacheck command, 1-223,
    1-224
quotaoff command, 1-226, 1-227
quotaon command, 1-226, 1-227
quotas, file system, summarizing,
    1-240
quotas, user, 1-74
quot command, 1-222

R

rc0 command, 1-228
rc2 command, 1-230, 1-231
rc3 command, 1-232, 1-233
rcmd, 1-254
rdump, 1-67, 1-254
read
    characters transferred, 1-34
    files from tape, 1-242
read error, tape, 1-248
read files, 1-243
real, time, 1-12
real time, commands, 1-278
reason
    connect shut, 1-103
    connect start, 1-103

reboot, system, 1-23
reboot command, 1-235, 1-236
rebooting the system, 1-77
reboots, 1-128
record
    binary, 1-40
    daily accounting, 1-40
    overall, connect session,
        1-23
    summary, 1-275
    total accounting, 1-40
    utmp format, 2-31
records
    acct, 1-39
    connect session, 1-2, 1-24,
        1-102, 1-268, 1-269
    connect session total
        acounting, 1-25
    daily accounting, 1-4
    login, 1-24, 1-102
    login/logout, 1-2
    logout, 1-24
    managing, 1-275
    printer accounting, 1-199
    process accounting, 1-15,
        1-269
    site dependent, 1-269
    sort, 1-12
    summary, 1-269
    tacct format, 1-33
    total account
        ASCII, 1-33
        binary, 1-33
    total accounting, 1-12, 1-33,
        1-269
    total connect session, 1-24
    total printer accounting,
    1-269

recursive tape search, 1-244
remote
    access, read and write,
        1-254
    device, 1-70
    filename, 1-254
    files, 1-242
    machine, 1-70
    printer service, 1-138
    server, 1-242
        rdump, 1-254
        rrestore, 1-254
    tape, 1-242
    tape access debug, 1-254
remote execution, 1-250
remote login server, 1-252
remote shell server, 1-265
remote storage, 1-67
remote.unknown, 2-89
remove printer spooling files,
    1-135
removing accounting files, 1-4
renice command, 1-238, 1-239
report, line use, 1-25
repquota command, 1-240, 1-241
requests, list, 2-18
resolv.conf file, 2-90
restarting runacct, 1-270
restarting the machine, 1-235
restart printer deamon, 1-136
restoration, files, interactive, 1-242
restore, 1-242
    complete, 1-244
    diagnostics
        full tape, 1-247
        read error, 1-247
    file cleanup, 1-242
    file notify, 1-246
    from directory, 1-246

function flags, 1-242
incremental, 1-248
interactive commands, 1-242
internal checks, 1-244
modifier flags, 1-242
tape read errors, 1-248
restore erorr, abort, 1-246
rewind, tape, 1-70
rexec, 1-254
rexecd, 1-250
rlogind, 1-252
rmt, 1-254
rmt0h, 1-247
root directory, 1-244
root directory, changing, 1-53
route, 1-257
routed, 1-260
routed daemon, 1-260
routing, 2-62
tables, 1-257
routing, gateway, 1-106
rrestore, 1-242, 1-254
rshd, 1-265
runacct, 1-12, 1-24, 1-25, 1-35, 1-39, 1-103, 1-268
cleanup state, 1-269
cms state, 1-269
connect1 state, 1-269
connect2 state, 1-269
disk state, 1-269
fees state, 1-269
merge state, 1-269
mergetacct state, 1-269
process state, 1-269
process states, 1-268
queueacct state, 1-269
restarting, 1-270
setup state, 1-269

userexit state, 1-269
wtmpfix state, 1-269
run levels, 1-122
running, commands automatically, 1-60
run time, CPU, 1-34
runtime error, runacct, 1-268
rwhod, 1-273

S

sa, 1-275
samples, disk, 2-34
savacct, 1-277
savecore command, 1-281, 1-282
saving a core dump, 1-281
scheduling priority, process, altering, 1-238
security, 1-208
security file, 2-44
sendmail, 1-283
alias definitions, 2-35
sendmail.cf, 2-92
serial line, attaching to a network interface, 1-296
server
remote, 1-70, 1-242
rdump, 1-254
rrestore, 1-254
time, 1-317
time, controlling, 1-319
servers, 1-265, 1-273, 1-314, 1-316
routed, 1-260
talkd, 1-312

uucpd, 1-338
services, 2-109
session, number of logins, 2-34
set modes, 1-243
setting, port characteristics, 1-110
shared libraries, 1-133
shell
        command execution, 1-60
        daily accounting, 1-268
        login, 1-208
        procedure, 1-4
shell procedure
        ckpacct, 1-19
        runacct, 1-24
shell scripts, accounting, 1-4
showmount, 1-292
shutacct, 1-4
shutdown, 1-128
        reason, 1-103
shutdown command, 1-294
shutoff, accounting, 1-4
shutting down the system, 1-294
single user, 1-63
single user mode, 1-23
site, accounting records, 1-269
sitetacct, 1-269
skeletal files, 1-45
slattach, 1-296
sort, records, 1-12
special files, 1-160
spool, directory, 1-138
spool directory
        uucp, cleaning up, 1-334
        uucp, deleting old files from,
        1-334
spooling
        clean, 1-135
        disable, 1-135
        printer, 2-83

printer enable, 1-136
stanza file, 2-111
start
        connect session time, 1-103
        system, 1-104
start printer daemon, 1-136
start time
        connect session, 1-23
        process, 1-19
startup, 1-4
state file, 1-270
statistics, process accounting, 1-15
Status, 2-27
status
        printer, 1-135
        printer deamon, 1-136
        process termination, 2-32
stopping the processor, 1-112
stop printer daemon, 1-136
storage
        default device, 1-67
        files, 1-67
        medium, 1-67
        remote, 1-67
storage blocks, 1-70
storage used, 1-12
storage volume, 1-70
strace command, 1-299, 1-301
STREAMS event trace, 1-299
structure, tacct, 2-31
subdirectory, fiscal, 1-35
summaries, process accounting,
        1-15
summarizing file system
        ownership, 1-222
summarizing file system quotas,
        1-240
summary
        command, 1-12

default accounting, 1-278
file, monthly, 1-35
pacct, 1-277
records, 1-275
system resource use, 1-268
summary format, ASCII, 1-12
summary total accounting records,
        1-269
sumtacct, 1-268
superblock, updating, 1-326
swapon command, 1-302
switch, turnacct, 1-4
sync command, 1-304
sysconfig command, 1-305
sysconfigdb, 1-307
sysconfigtab database, 2-113
syslogd, 1-309
system
        files, default, 1-72
        multiuser mode, 1-294
        reboot, 1-23
        resource use summary,
                1-268
        shutting down, 1-294
system startup, 1-104, 1-122
system time, 1-278

T

tables
        hashed password, 1-162
        network routing, 1-260
tacct, 1-35, 1-40
        record format, 1-33

structure, 2-31
talkd, 1-312
tape
        backup, 1-70
        bad blocks, 1-246
        block size, 1-244
        default size, 1-70
        determining size, 1-244
        dump size, 1-70
        header information, 1-242
        multivolume, 1-244
        old-style dump, 1-244
        reading, 1-242
        recursive search, 1-244
        remote, 1-242
        remote access, 1-254
        remote read and write,
                1-254
        restore error recovery, 1-245
        restoring, 1-242
        rewind, 1-70
        volume number, 1-245
        volume to mount, 1-242
tape access mode, 1-242
tape open error, 1-67
tape restore error, abort, 1-246
tape write error, 1-67
telinit command, 1-123
telnetd, 1-314
Temporary, 2-28
terminal, tty reference, 1-23
terminal reference, 1-128
terminating, processes, 1-124
termination
        process, 1-103
        process status, 2-32
test
        pattern generator, 1-142

printer ripple pattern, 1-142
tftpd, 1-316
time
    connect session, 1-34, 2-34
    contabs files, 1-31
    CPU, 1-12, 1-34
    disk usage, 2-34
    entry, 2-32
    environment variable, 1-20,
        1-25
    K-core, 1-12
    K-core minutes, 2-33
    locale, connect session, 1-25
    locale dependent, 1-20
    nonprime, 1-12, 1-34, 2-33
    prime, 1-12, 1-34, 2-33
    real, 1-12
    time zone, 1-23
    to process a command,
        1-279
timed, 1-317
timedc, 1-319
time server daemon, 1-317
    controlling, 1-319
timestamp, standard, 1-67
time used, total CPU, 1-278
time zone, 1-23
total
    accounting records, 1-12
    K-core time, 1-12
    resource usage, 1-12
total account, file format, 1-35
total accounting
    ASCII records, 1-33
    binary records, 1-33
total accounting file, 1-35
total accounting format, 1-33

total accounting record, disk usage,
    1-29
total accounting records, 1-33,
    1-269
tower of Hanoi, 1-70
trace records, 1-321
transfer
    characters, number of, 1-12
    characters read, 1-34
    characters written, 1-34
    data blocks, 2-34
    I/O blocks, 1-34
    I/O operations, 1-279
translation, Internet-to-hardware
    addresses, 1-47
transporting uucp requests, 1-330
trpt, 1-321
tty, 1-23
    process accounting, 1-20
tty line, assigning to a network
    interface, 1-296
tunefs command, 1-323
tuning file systems, 1-323
turnacct, 1-4
    switch, 1-4
turning file system quotas on and
    off, 1-226
turnoff
    accounting, 1-4, 1-23
    automatic accounting, 1-4
turnon, accounting, 1-23
type of entry, 2-31

U

update command, 1-326, 1-327
updating, inode table, 1-304
usage
    CPU, 1-12
    disk, 1-268
    resource, total, 1-12
user, 1-128, 1-130
    adding, 1-45
    CPU time, 1-278
    database file, 1-31
    fee charge, 2-34
    ID, 1-34, 1-35, 1-39, 2-31
    login name, 1-34, 1-103,
        2-31
    login names, 1-30
    quotas, 1-74
    user ID, connect sessions,
        1-25
user ID, 1-63, 1-208
user name, 1-35, 1-40
usernames, 1-208
users
    fees, 1-4
    number logged in, 1-35
usr/spool, 1-138
/usr/spool/mqueue, 2-73
utmp, 1-39, 1-102
utmp.h, 2-30
uucheck, 1-328
uucico, 1-330
    errors, 2-37
    file transfer, 2-3
uucleanup, 1-334
uucp, 1-339
    administrative files, 2-2
    file, 2-30
    files, 2-3, 2-7, 2-24, 2-26, 2-
        29, 2-114

    log, 2-26
    modem list, 2-12
    program contacts, 2-27
    remote systems, 2-27, 2-28,
        2-89
    spool directory, cleaning up,
        1-334
    spool directory, deleting old
        files from, 1-334
    temporary, 2-30
uucpd, 1-338
uucp files and directories, checking
    for, 1-328
uucp requests, transporting, 1-330
uudemon.cleanup, 2-7
uusched, 1-339

V

vgchange command, 1-341, 1-342
vgcreate command, 1-343, 1-345
vgdisplay command, 1-346, 1-348
vgextend command, 1-349, 1-350
vgreduce command, 1-351
vgremove command, 1-352
vgsync command, 1-353
vipw command, 1-354, 1-355
volume, storage, 1-70
volume number, tape, 1-245

W

wall, 1-70
Workspace, 2-29
write, characters transferred, 1-34
write density, backup, 1-70
writing, buffered files, 1-304
wtmp, 1-24, 1-128
      file, 1-2
wtmpfix, 1-102, 1-269

X

xferstats, 2-114
Xqtdir, 2-30

Y

yellow pages, 1-208

Notes

Notes

Notes

Notes

Notes

Notes

Notes

OPEN SOFTWARE FOUNDATION™
INFORMATION REQUEST FORM

Please send to me the following:

( )   OSF™ Membership Information

( )   OSF/1™ License Materials

( )   OSF/1 Training Information

Contact Name   _____

Company Name   _____

Street Address   _____

Mail Stop   _____

City   _____ State _____ Zip _____

Phone   _____ FAX _____

Electronic Mail   _____

MAIL TO:

Open Software Foundation
11 Cambridge Center
Cambridge, MA 02142

Attn: OSF/1

For more information about OSF/1 call OSF Direct Channels at 617 621 7300.